SPECULUM

OF THE OTHER WOMAN

LUCE IRIGARAY

SPECULUM

OF THE OTHER WOMAN

TRANSLATED BY GILLIAN C. GILL

CORNELL UNIVERSITY PRESS

ITHACA, NEW YORK

The publisher gratefully acknowledges the assistance of the French Ministry of Culture in defraying part of the cost of translation.

Originally published in French under the title *Speculum de l'autre femme,* © 1974 by Les Editions de Minuit.

The quotations from "Femininity," from *New Introductory Lectures on Psycho-Analysis* by Sigmund Freud, translated and edited by James Strachey, in Volume XXII of *The Standard Edition of the Complete Psychological Works of Sigmund Freud,* ed. James Strachey, are used by permission of Sigmund Freud Copyrights Ltd, The Institute of Psycho-Analysis, The Hogarth Press Ltd, and W. W. Norton & Company, Inc. Copyright © 1965, 1964 by James Strachey. Copyright 1933 by Sigmund Freud. Copyright renewed 1961 by W. J. H. Sprott.

Translation copyright © 1985 by Cornell University Press.

First published 1985 by Cornell University Press.
Fourth printing, Cornell Paperbacks, 1989.

International Standard Book Number (cloth) 0-8014-1663-9
International Standard Book Number (paper) 0-8014-9330-7
Library of Congress Catalog Card Number 84-45151
Printed in the United States of America

*Librarians: Library of Congress cataloging information
appears on the last page of the book.*

*The paper in this book is acid-free and meets the guidelines
for permanence and durability of the Committee on Production
Guidelines for Book Longevity of the Council on Library Resources.*

Contents

Acknowledgments   9

THE BLIND SPOT OF AN OLD DREAM OF SYMMETRY   11

Woman, Science's Unknown   13
How Can They Immediately Be So Sure?, 13. The Anatomical Model,
14. A Science That Still Cannot Make Up Its Mind, 15. A Question of
Method, 16. What Is Involved in (Re)production, and How It Aids and
Abets the Phallic Order, 18. A Difference Not Taken into Account, 21.
The Labor "to Become a Woman," 24.

The Little Girl Is (Only) a Little Boy   25
An Inferior Little Man, 25. The Cards Turned Over, 26. The Dream
Interpreters Themselves, 27. Penis Masturbation: A Necessarily Phallic
Auto-eroticism, 28. The Change of "Object" or the Crisis of a
Devaluation, 31. The Law of the Self-same, 32.

Is Her End in Her Beginning?   34
An Unsuspected Love, 34. The Desire to Have a Child by the Mother,
34. The Father's Seduction: Law but Not Sex, 37. The "Reasons" Why a
Girl Hates Her Mother and a Boy Goes on Loving His, 40. An Economy
of Primal Desire That Cannot Be Represented, 42. One More Child, 44.

Another "Cause"—Castration   46
As Might Be Expected, 46. The Gaze, Always at Stake, 47. Anatomy Is
"Destiny," 48. What the Father's Discourse Covers Up, 49. The
Negative in Phallocentric Dialectic, 50. Is Working Out the Death Drives
Limited to Men Only? 53.

"Penis-Envy"   55
Waiting in Vain, 55. An Indirect Sublimation, 56. "Envy" or "Desire"
for the Penis? 57. Repression, or Inexorable Censorship? 58. Mimesis
Imposed, 59.

Contents

A Painful Way to Become a Woman   61
And the Father, Neutral and Benevolent, Washes His Hands of the
Matter, 61. A (Female) A-Sex? 62. Is the Oedipus Complex Universal or
Not? 63. Free Association on Onanism, 65.

A Very Black Sexuality?   66
Symptoms Almost Like Those of Melancholia, 66. A Setback She Cannot
Mourn, 67. That Open Wound That Draws Everything to Itself, 70.
That Necessary Remainder: Hysteria, 71.

The Penis = the Father's Child   73
The Primacy of Anal Erotism, 73. Those Party to a Certain Lease, 74.
Woman Is/and Also Mother, 76. Forbidden Games, 77. The Hymen of
Oedipus, Father and Son, 78.

The Deferred Action of Castration   81
Capitalism without Complexes, 81. The Metaphorical Veil of the Eternal
Feminine, 82. The Other Side of History, 83. The Submission of a Slave?
87. A Super-ego That Rather Despises the Female Sex, 88.

An Indispensable Wave of Passivity   90
A Redistribution of Partial Instincts, Especially Sadistic-anal Instincts, 90.
"There Is Only One Libido," 93. Idealization, What Is One's Own, 95.
The (Re)productive Organ, 96. Confirmation of Frigidity, 97.

Female Hom(m)osexuality   98
The "Constitutional Factor" Is Decisive, 98. Homosexual Choice Clearly
Expounded, 99. A Cure Fails for Lack of Transference(s), 100. Female
Sameness, 101.

An Impracticable Sexual Relationship   104
An Ideal Love, 104. Were It Not for Her Mother? 105. Or Her Mother-
in-law? 106. Squaring the Family Circle, 106. Generation Gap, or Being
Historically out of Phase? 109. Woman's Enigmatic Bisexuality, 110.

"Woman Is a Woman as a Result of a Certain Lack
of Characteristics"   112
An Ex-orbitant Narcissism, 113. The Vanity of a Commodity, 113. The
Shame That Demands Vicious Conformity, 115. Women Have Never
Invented Anything but Weaving, 115. A Very Envious Nature, 117.
Society Holds No Interest for Women, 119. A Fault in Sublimation, 123.
"La Femme de Trente Ans," 127.

SPECULUM

Any Theory of the "Subject" Has Always Been Appropriated
by the "Masculine"   133
Korē: Young Virgin, Pupil of the Eye   147

Contents

On the Index of Plato's Works: Woman   152
How to Conceive (of) a Girl   160
Une Mère de Glace   168
". . . and if, taking the eye of a man recently dead . . ."   180
La Mystérique   191
Paradox A Priori   203
The Eternal Irony of the Community   214
Volume-Fluidity   227

PLATO'S *Hystera*

The Stage Setup   243
Turned Upside-down and Back-to-front, 244. Special Status for the Side
Opposite, 245. A Fire in the Image of *a* Sun, 245. The Forgotten Path,
246. Paraphragm/Diaphragm, 248. The Magic Show, 250. A Waste of
Time? 252. A Specular Cave, 253.

The Dialogues   256
One Speaks, the Others Are Silent, 256. Like Ourselves, They Submit to
a Like Principle of Identity, 258. Provided They Have a Head, Turned in
the Right Direction, 260. What Is = What They See, and Vice Versa,
261. The *A-lētheia*, a Necessary Denegation among Men, 262. Even Her
Voice Is Taken Away from Echo, 263. A Double Topographic Error, Its
Consequences, 265.

The Avoidance of (Masculine) Hysteria   268
A Hypnotic Method, 268. That Buries and Forbids "Madness," 270. A
Remainder of Aphasia, 273. The Misprision of Difference, 274. The
Unreflected Dazzle of Seduction, 275.

The "Way Out" of the Cave   278
The "Passage," 278. A Difficult Delivery, 279. Then Whence and How
Does He Get Out? 281. A World Peopled by Ghosts, 282.

The Time Needed to Focus and Adjust the Vision   283
Impossible to Turn Back (or Over), 283. Were It Not, Right Now, for a
Sophistry Played with Doubles, 286. A Frozen Nature, 289. The
Auto . . . Taken in by the *A-lētheia*, 291. Bastard or Legitimate
Offspring? 293.

The Father's Vision: Engendering with No History of Problems   294
A Hymen of Glass/Ice, 294. The Unbegotten Begetter, 294. Exorcism of
the Dark Night, 296. Astrology as Thaumaturgy: A Semblance (of a)
Sun, 297. A Question of Property, 298.

Contents

A Form That Is Always the Same   303
The Passage Confusing Big and Little, and Vice Versa, 303. The
Standard Itself/Himself, 304. Better to Revolve upon Oneself—But This
Is Possible Only for God-the-Father, 304. The Mother, Happily, Does
Not Remember, 307. A Source-mirror of All That Is, 308. The Analysis
of That Projection Will Never Take (or Have Taken) Place, 310.

Completion of the *Paideia*   311
The Failings of an Organ That Is Still Too Sensible, 311. A Seminar in
Good Working Order, 312. An Immaculate Conception, 315. The
Deferred Action of an Ideal Jouissance, 316. The End of Childhood, 318.

Life in Philosophy   319
Always the Same (He), 319. An Autistic Completeness, 321. Love
Turned Away from Inferior Species and Genera/Gender, 322. The
Privilege of the Immortals, 324. The Science of Desire, 325. A *Korē*
Dilated to the Whole Field of the Gaze and Mirroring Herself, 327.

Divine Knowledge   330
The Back Reserved for God, 330. The Divine Mystery, 330. This Power
Cannot Be Imitated by Mortals, 334. How, Then, Can They Evaluate
Their Potency? 334. Except over Someone Like Themselves? 336. The
Father Knows the Front Side and Back Side of Everything, at Least in
Theory, 337. The Meaning of Death for a Philosopher, 339.

An Unarticulated/Inarticulate Go-Between: The Split between
Sensible and Intelligible   339
A Failure of Relations between the Father and Mother, 339. A One-way
Passage, 341. Compulsory Participation in the Attributes of the Type,
343. A Misprized Incest and an Unrealizable Incest, 343.

Return to the Name of the Father   346
The Impossible Regression toward the Mother, 346. A Competition the
Philosopher Will Decline to Enter, 347. Two Modes of Repetition:
Property and Proximity, 349. Better to Work the Earth on the Father's
Account Than to Return to It: Metaphor/Metonymy, 352. The Threat of
Castration, 353.

"Woman's" *Jouissance*   353
A Dead Cave Which Puts Representation Back into Play, 353. That
Marvelously Solitary Pleasure of God, 356. A Diagonal Helps to Temper
the Excessiveness of the One, 357. The Infinite of an Ideal Which Covers
the Slit (of a) Void, 361. Losing Sight of "the Other," 362. The
Vengeance of Children Freed from Their Chains, 364.

Acknowledgments

I thank Ellen Peel and Margaret Homans for their encouragement and support in the early stages of this translation project, and for their thoughtful suggestions on two sections of the translation. Suzanne Relyea also read parts of the manuscript, and I thank her in particular for her expert advice on the Descartes section. Christopher Lenney was an invaluable research assistant, locating and referencing the many cited passages for me. He also gave detailed suggestions on parts of the translation, for which I am very grateful. James Hulbert of the University of Rochester gave the manuscript a most careful, sympathetic, and informed reading. I owe him a debt of gratitude for his comments and specifically for his identification of several passages from Plato, Aristotle, Kant, and Hegel which were quoted without reference in the French text. Working with the editors at Cornell University Press, first Barbara Burnham and later Bernhard Kendler and Kay Scheuer, has been a pleasure and a learning experience for me. This translation would not have been done without a fellowship from the Translations Program of the National Endowment for the Humanities, an independent federal agency. My dealings with officials at the Endowment were uniformly cordial and helpful, and Susan A. Mango in particular gave me excellent counsel at a crucial stage in my proposal. Finally, let me thank my husband, Mike, for his encouragement, support, and practical assistance during this long project.

G. C. G.

Lexington, Massachusetts

Publisher's Note

In the original edition of this book the first and third sections, the long essays on Freud and Plato, were divided internally only by spaces, varying in length, and text ornaments, which marked the major breaks. Subdivisions were named only in the table of contents. For this translation (as for the Italian translation) it has been deemed preferable to have these subheadings appear in the text as well, as an aid to the reader. Certain other minor modifications of format have been made in accordance with the conventions of book-making in the English-speaking world. Greek words have been transliterated in the Latin alphabet.

THE BLIND SPOT
OF AN OLD DREAM
OF SYMMETRY

Woman, Science's Unknown

"Ladies and Gentlemen . . . Throughout history people have knocked their heads against the riddle of the nature of femininity—. . . Nor will *you* have escaped worrying over this problem—those of you who are men; to those of you who are women this will not apply—you are yourselves the problem."[1]

So it would be a case of you men speaking among yourselves about woman, who cannot be involved in hearing or producing a discourse that concerns the *riddle,* the logogriph she represents for you. The enigma that *is* woman will therefore constitute the *target,* the *object,* the *stake,* of a masculine discourse, of a debate among men, which would not consult her, would not concern her. Which, ultimately, she is not supposed to know anything about.

How Can They Immediately Be So Sure?

"When you meet a human being," he says, they say, first of all, "the first distinction you make is 'male or female?' and you are accustomed to

[1]Sigmund Freud, "Femininity," in *New Lectures on Psycho-analysis*. The choice of this text—a fictional lecture—can be justified by its late date in Freud's work. It groups, thus, a fair number of statements developed in other essays that I shall in fact be referring to. Except where otherwise stated, it is I who have italicized Freud's remarks in one way or another. I shall also have occasion to modify the translation somewhat, to complete it in certain cases where fragments of statements in the original have been omitted. But the most meticulous translation would not have changed much of the significance of this speech on "femininity."

(All quotations from Freud, unless otherwise noted, are from *The Standard Edition of the Complete Psychological Works of Sigmund Freud,* under the general editorship of James Strachey, 24 vols. [London: Hogarth Press, 1953–74], henceforth referred to as *SE*. The essay "Femininity" can be found in *SE* XXIII 112–35. The quotation above is from p. 113, and the italics are Strachey's. Henceforth page numbers will be given in the text. In LI's French text, page references are given only a few times in footnotes, but here the more comprehensive citation policy usual in English has been followed. The *Standard Edition* text is unaltered, except for the addition of LI's italics.—Tr.)

making the distinction with unhesitating certainty" (p. 113). How? This remains implicit and seems to require no remark among yourselves. Silence, then, on the subject of that extreme assurance which keeps you from being mistaken *at first sight* about the sex of the person you run across. The important point, it seems, is for you to be firmly convinced, without possible hesitation, that you cannot be in error, that there is no ambiguity possible. That culture (?) assures you, reassures you—or once did so—of an infallible discrimination.

The Anatomical Model

"Anatomical science shares your certainty at one point and not much further. The male sexual product, the spermatozoon, and its vehicle are male; the ovum and the organism that harbours it are female. In both sexes organs have been formed which serve exclusively for the sexual functions; they were probably developed from the same [innate] disposition into two different forms" (p. 113). Which disposition? It must surely be concluded that up to this point the element defined as both specific to each and common to both sexes involves nothing but a process of *reproduction and production.* And that it is as a function of the way they participate in this economy that one will with certainty label some male and others female. So-called scientific objectivity can be decisive in the matter only after inspection, under the microscope, of the difference between reproductive cells. Unless that objectivity equally recognizes the (anatomico-physiological) evidence of the *product* of copulation. Everything else, in fact, appears too murky for science to risk—as you risk—making a judgment, coming to a differentiated verdict.

For of course "the other organs, the bodily shapes and tissues, show the influence of the individual's sex, but this is inconstant and its amount variable" (p. 113). And should you happen carelessly to rely on such secondary sexual characteristics, science is honor-bound to put you on your guard. In fact, science "tells you something that runs counter to your expectations and is probably calculated to confuse your [and its?] feelings. It draws your attention to the fact that portions of the male sexual apparatus also appear in women's bodies, though in atrophied state and vice versa in the alternative case" (p. 114). Science thus forces you to see in this objective fact "the indications of *bisexuality* [Freud's italics], as though an individual is not a man or a woman but always both" (p. 114). You are then man and woman. Man, or woman? Yet— you may be assured, reassured—one character always prevails over the other. But all the same you are asked to make yourselves familiar with the idea that "the proportion in which masculine and feminine are mixed in an individual is subject to quite considerable fluctuations" (p. 114). It is fitting therefore to display some caution before claiming to belong to one sex or the other. Nonetheless, let us be serious and get back to scientific certainties, "only one kind of sexual *product*—ova or semen—is nevertheless present in one person." Apart, alas, from "the very rarest of cases" (p. 114).

All this, certainly, is very embarrassing and you are going to be led to conclude that "what constitutes masculinity or femininity is an *unknown* characteristic which anatomy cannot lay hold of" (p. 114). It is, thus, the expectation of the discovery of an unknown that arrests and obstructs the objectivity of scientific or at least anatomical discourse, as far as sex difference is concerned.

A Science That Still Cannot Make Up Its Mind

Can psychology lay hold of this unknown characteristic? Can it re-solve the problem of attributing some value to the unknown variable(s)? It seems that you have been accustomed to "*transfer* the notion of bisex-uality to mental life" and that you speak, hence, of the same person "behaving" in a more masculine or a more feminine way. But in doing so, your so-called psychological discourse has simply "given way to anatomy and convention" (p. 114). In other words, the distinction is not of a psychological nature. Moreoever, in general, you take the term "masculine" to connote "active," the term "feminine" to connote "pas-sive," and "it is true that a relation of the kind exists." For "the male sex cell is actively mobile and searches out the female one and the latter, the ovum, is immobile and waits passively" (p. 114). And I, Freud, am here to tell you that the "behaviour of the *elementary* sexual organisms is indeed a model for the conduct of sexual individuals during intercourse" (p. 114). My way of envisaging things, these "things," would therefore imply that the psychic is prescribed by the anatomical according to a *mimetic order,* with anatomical science imposing the truth of its model upon "psychological behaviour." In intercourse, man and woman *mime* the type of relationship between sperm and ovum. "The male pursues the female for the purpose of sexual union, seizes hold of her and pene-trates into her" (p. 114). But "by this you have precisely reduced the characteristic of masculinity to the factor of aggressiveness as far as psy-chology is concerned" (p. 114–15). As for the characteristic of feminini-ty, I, you, we . . . let's say nothing about it. On the other hand, *you* have in this demonstration, or testimony, lent "desire" to the sperm in its race toward the ovum.

But let us return to this somewhat unfavorable determination of the

15

psychic character of masculinity. It is now zoo-logy that invites you to be cautious in your univocal attribution of aggressivity to the male alone. Zoology reminds you, in fact, that "in some classes of animals, the females are the stronger and more aggressive" (p. 115). Remember, to take one example, the sexual behavior of the *spider!*

Moreover, zoology casts doubt on the idea that "rearing and caring for the young" are specifically female functions. "In quite *high* species we find that the sexes share the task of caring for the young between them or even that the male alone devotes himself to it" (p. 115). Is the necessary conclusion, then, that such animals are more able than you, than we, to distinguish beteeen the sexual function and the parental function? And notably that they at least notice the distinction between female and maternal, between female sexuality and mothering, a distinction that "culture" might perhaps have effaced?

A Question of Method

But the reminder, or exemplary appeal, of the zoo-logical in this matter will be ill attended to and perhaps worse understood. For it is nonetheless the mother "in the sphere of human sexual life" that will now serve as *paradigm* for the female in the debate about the relations between the masculine/feminine and the active/passive pairings. In fact, Freud goes on, "you soon see how inadequate it is to make masculine behaviour coincide with activity and femininity with passivity. *A mother is active in every sense* towards her child" (p. 115). The example of breast-feeding that is immediately adduced in evidence, is, of course, questionable; it is difficult to see how the verb "to breast-feed" can be simply reduced to an activity by the mother unless by virtue of purely grammatical criteria (as an active, transitive verb, etc.). And in any case, such criteria become immediately questionable when opposed to the verb "to suck," for then the mother finds herself the object of the infant's "activity." Unless of course breast-feeding—and we've been here before— is assimilated to the fabrication in concert (?) of a *product?* One might have assumed *milk* was the one single product that is incontestably attributed to the female—the mother—and, moreover, one that she makes alone.

Any consideration of pleasure in breast-feeding seems here to be excluded, misunderstood, under silent ban. That factor would certainly introduce a little shading to statements such as these last. But it really seems that at stake here is the *monopoly of productive "activity,"* the distribution of a *"phallic"* power. Obviously, the way this is announced in relation to breast-feeding is dubious, though not perhaps as dubious as the identification of the female with the maternal—an identification whose impact, impasse, and prescriptions are still hard to measure. Yet the Freudian discourse does not stop here, but goes on to pursue its strange gynecology, leaving behind in mid-air an image of a (woman) mother *actively* breast-feeding her child.

All this leaves our gentlemen perplexed in their discussion of the criteria of sexual difference. But the text goes on. . . . Apparently without a problem, a rupture. Yet on this occasion as on so many others, particularly when it is a question of woman, the text will have surreptitiously broken the thread of its reasoning, its logic. Striking off on another path that will no doubt intersect with the previous one, will in some way take up where it had left off, but in a zigzag fashion that defies all resumption of a linear discourse and all forms of rigor as measured in terms of the law of excluded middle. Here the unconscious is speaking. And how could it be otherwise? Above all when it speaks of sexual difference.

So you will now hear that "the further you go from the narrow sexual sphere"—constitutable then as a regional activity? compartmentalized? specialized? but in regard to what generality? totality? capital?—"the more obvious will the 'error of superimposition' become" (p. 115) (an error to which recourse has been and will be made almost continuously, even as an effort is made to dissuade you yourselves from having recourse to it). "For certain women, with whom only men capable of showing themselves passively docile can manage to get along [?], may display, in many domains, tremendous activity."[2] The important thing here is the way certain terms mediate the statement, suggesting that in the case of these women, it must be a question of activism exerting itself by gracious permission of the submissive docility of the male. A curious choice of example for bisexuality. . . . In any case, the essential activity would still be allotted to the male: that during intercourse. You will remember, in fact, that this is the pattern of behavior with certain animals: "in some classes of animals, the females are the stronger and more aggressive and the male is *active* only in *the single act of sexual union*" (p. 115). And yet, if you stand by the conviction that passivity is equivalent to femininity and activity with masculinity, "I advise you against it" and "it seems to serve no useful purpose and adds nothing to our knowledge" (p. 115). So what now?

<hr />

[2](Here the French translation of Freud differs significantly from the Strachey translation, and I have had to give an English version of the French version of the German. The *Standard Edition* text runs: "Women can display great activity in various directions, men are not able to live in company with their own kind unless they develop a large amount of passive adaptibility" [p. 115]—Tr.)

What Is Involved in (Re)production, and How It Aids and Abets the Phallic Order

Let us begin again, or rather let us continue to listen, without impatience. "One might consider characterizing femininity psychologically as giving preference to *passive aims*. This is not, of course, the same thing as passitivity; to achieve passive aims may call for a large amount of activity. It is perhaps the case that in a woman, on the basis of her share in the *sexual function,* a preference for passive behaviour and passive aims is carried over into her life to a greater or lesser extent, in proportion to the limits, restricted or far-reaching, within which her sexual life thus serves as a model" (pp. 115–116). Thus, now that it has been decreed that the active/passive opposition is not pertinent to the characterization of the male/female difference, an attempt is to be made to save what is at stake in that opposition by bringing in the difficult notion of "passive aims." Not that such a notion is lacking in interest and would not merit more extensive commentary, but what does it involve but a complication of the economy of active/passive relationships? By giving them authority to function within each of the two poles of masculine and feminine but in differentiated and in some way complementary times and tenses. The "roles" are being cast in such a way that, yet again and in all instances, passivity is required of woman at the moment of intercourse by reason of its usefulness in sexual functioning. A certain tendency to activity may, on the other hand, be recognized in woman insofar as that activity prepares for sexual functioning and is rigorously regulated in proportion to the so-called sexual life's involvement as model.

The reproductive function is not explicitly named, but passages before and after, as well as reference to other texts,[3] indicate clearly that when it comes to sexual function and its model-value, the reproductive function alone is being referred to. The point being that man is *the* procreator, that sexual *production-reproduction* is referable to his "activity" alone, to his "pro-ject" alone. Woman is nothing but the receptacle that passively receives his *product,* even if sometimes, by the display of her passively aimed instincts, she has pleaded, facilitated, even demanded that it be placed within her. Matrix—womb, earth, factory, bank—to which the seed capital is entrusted so that it may germinate, produce, grow fruitful, without woman being able to lay claim to either capital or interest since she has only submitted "passively" to reproduction. Herself held in receivership as a certified means of (re)production.[4]

---

[3]Cf. the *Three Essays on the Theory of Sexuality, SE,* vii.

[4]A very old point of contention, whose different transformations can be followed throughout the history of philosophy.

One may agree that it is difficult to decide between what is activity and what passivity in the economy of sexual reproduction. But this in no way prevents us from wishing to interpret correctly the appeal to a (supposedly) other economy which claims (*a*) to cure indecision or to suspend the undecidable that is set in play by such a question, (*b*) to resolve the question by attributing "activity" to man in the process of generation, in other words, to settle the question in terms of the active/passive opposition.

Moreover, this recourse to an "other" order intervenes at this point in Freud's argument in an unforeseeable and inexplicit fashion. As it were in parentheses, and in a curiously injunctive form: "But we must beware in this of underestimating the influence of social customs, which *similarly* force women into passive situations" (p. 116). Of which social customs must we beware of understanding the influence? What influence is capable of forcing women to remain in "passive situations"? What is meant by "similarly"? An enumeration of concurrent factors? But might one not envisage the possibility that the one might prescribe "the other," that is to say by legitimating, even by producing the discourse, the ideology, which determine it as a factor? The question would doubtless be unavoidable were it not that these "social customs" are left in an evocative imprecision so general, so devoid of commitment, as to lose all impact. The only pertinence is to be found, so it would seem, in the almost compulsory recall of a problem that butts in, insists, harps back, but whose data appear to escape the "lecturer." He admits that "all this is *far from being cleared up*." As obscure, as black, perhaps, as the *dark* continent of femininity?

He continues, nonetheless; "There is one particularly constant relation between femininity and instinctual life which we do not want to overlook. The suppression of women's aggressiveness which is prescribed for them constitutionally [whatever that means] and imposed upon them socially [by what mechanisms?] favours the development of powerful masochistic impulses" (p. 116). Somehow, there seems to be no permitted mode of female aggression. But, once again, the mobilization of arguments as heterogeneous as "constitution" and "social pressure" raises questions as to how the said pressure might have prescriptive power over the representation of the said constitution, how the former might have a vested interest in becoming the prop, the accomplice in such an estimation of "the female constitution." Must one see here proof that customs and indeed Freud's own text, which finds support in them, evaluate all aggressiveness by the yardstick of *masculine homosexuality?* Since competitiveness and rivalry in commerce, notably sexual commerce, can be practiced only by males? Whence these redoubled prohibitions on female aggression? And with the result that woman, on pain of infringing the laws of both social custom and constitution, develops strongly masochistic tendencies which succeed in eroticizing destructive tendencies that are directed "inward." For it is equally necessary to assign her a role in the function of the inside/outside pairing that turns up here in some way to intersect and sustain the active/passive opposition. As far as the "inside" goes—her own, of course—woman will thus tend to be destructive, since nothing authorizes her aggression or activity toward another "inside" or toward the outside. (One might bring up the "activity" of breast-feeding, but that has been left hanging in mid-air somewhere.) If activity or aggression there be in woman, it will hence be given the connotation of "masculine" or "destructive." "Thus masochism, *as people say,* is truly feminine" (p. 116). And as I, Freud, say again. "But if, as happens so often, you meet with masochism in men, what is left to you but to say that these men exhibit very plain feminine traits?" (p. 116). This seems sufficiently vexatious to break off the line of argument, move on to the next paragraph, and conclude that:

"And now you are already prepared to hear that psychology too is unable to solve the riddle of femininity". Who has managed to follow the links in the chain of this argument except he who gets some bonus of pleasure out of it? A pleasure which gives it a force that cannot easily be defrayed. For, in fact, once bisexuality has been admitted, why cut short its implications, notably with regard to masculine masochism? The riddle—the mysteria/hysteria?—might perhaps concern not only femininity, even in this lecture on the problem of femininity. Why, in that case, wish to reserve the mystery to women? As if, for the argument to be possible, "male sexuality" at the very least had to impose itself as clearly defined, definable, even practicable.

So psychology does not offer us the key to the mystery of femininity—that black box, strongbox, earth-abyss that remains outside the sphere of its investigations: *light* must no doubt come from elsewhere (p. 116). (One cannot give up so soon, when so much energy has been invested in a metaphoricity dominated by the photological.) But the illumination "cannot come till we have learnt how in general the differentiation of living organisms into two sexes came about. We know nothing about it . . ." (p. 116). So you can be assured that the explanation is not immediately available. But understand, however, that you are once more being referred to science in order to understand "the mystery of femininity."

Unless you interpret this statement as meaning that as far as the differentiation into two sexes is concerned, we can know something certain about only one of the terms of the difference. Ultimately this alone would be envisaged as the variable factor in a re-marking of sexuality— but which one?—through its own process. In other words, for light to be or be spoken in the matter of (so-called) female sexuality, we can assume that difference is always already in operation although no acknowledgment is made of it (perhaps because its character is only representable with difficulty?). Out of this difference will be lifted one of the two terms—but determined in relation to what?—and this one term will be constituted as "origin," as that by whose differentiation the other may be engendered and brought to light. *The same re-marking itself*—more or less—would thus produce the other, whose function in the differentiation would be neglected, forgotten. Or else carried back into mere extrapolation, into the infinity of some capital letter: Sexuality, Difference, Phallus, etc. Up to now, therefore, nothing can be clearly articulated but the history of the practice of "male sexuality" with regard to Sexuality.

A Difference Not Taken into Account

"Yet the existence of two sexes is a most striking characteristic of organic life which distinguishes it sharply from inanimate nature" (p. 116). Could this not be a difference thus clearly cut out in the service of argument? Once the heterogeneous is found to be reduced in sexual practice, would we not observe a proliferation of differences, a compulsion to differentiate, either to retain the pleasure, or calm the anguish of indifference, at least in the art or science of dialectic?

Whereas "we find enough to study in those human individuals who, through the possession of female genitals, are characterized as manifestly or predominantly feminine. In conformity with its peculiar nature, psycho-analysis does not try to describe what a woman is—that would be a task scarcely performable—but sets about enquiring how she comes into being, how a woman develops out of a child with a bisexual disposition" (p. 116). One can only agree in passing that it is impossible exhaustively to represent what woman might be, given that a certain economy of representation—inadequately perceived by psychoanalysis, at least in the "scientific discourse" that it speaks—functions through a tribute to woman that is never paid or even assessed. The whole problematic of Being has been elaborated thanks to that loan. It is thus, in all exactitude, unrealizable to *describe the being* of woman. As for how "a woman develops out of a child with a bisexual disposition," one might begin by being surprised, being suspicious, that it should be necessary to *become* a woman—and a "normal" woman to boot—and that this evolution should be "more difficult and more complicated" than becoming a man. This is again a question that arises out of an economy—and again an economy of representation—to which Freud has recourse without criticism, without sufficient questioning: this is an organized system whose meaning is regulated by paradigms and units of value that are in turn determined by male subjects. Therefore, the feminine must be deciphered as inter-dict: within the signs or between them, between the realized meanings, between the lines . . . and as a function of the (re)productive necessities of an intentionally phallic currency, which, for lack of the collaboration of a (potentially female) other, can immediately be assumed to need *its* other, a sort of inverted or negative alter ego— "black" too, like a photographic negative. Inverse, contrary, contradictory even, necessary if the male subject's process of specul(ariz)ation is to be raised and sublated. This is an intervention required of *those* effects of negation that result from or are set in motion through a censure of the feminine, though the feminine will be allowed and even obliged to return in such oppositions as: be/*become*, have/*not have* sex (organ), phallic/*nonphallic*, penis/*clitoris* or else penis/*vagina*, plus/*minus*, clearly representable/*dark continent*, logos/*silence* or idle chatter, desire for the mother/*desire to be the mother*, etc. All these are interpretive modalities of the female function rigorously postulated by the pursuit of a certain game for which she will always find herself signed up without having begun to play. Set between—at least—two, or two half, men. A hinge bending according to their exchanges. A reserve supply of *negativity* sustaining the articulation of their moves, or refusals to move, in a partly fictional progress toward the mastery of power. Of knowledge. In which she will have no part. Off-stage, off-side, beyond representation, beyond selfhood. A power in reserve for the dialectical operations to come. We shall come back to this.

But as far as "becoming woman" is concerned—and the task will consist mainly in recognizing and accepting her atrophied member—one might stress in passing that in the elaboration of analytic theory there will be little question of reducing bisexual tendencies in men. Doubtless a more delicate matter than in the case of the aforementioned female sexuality. For what male "organ" will be set forth in derision like the clitoris?—that penis too tiny for comparison to entail anything but total devaluation, complete decathexization. Of course, there are the breasts.

But they are to be classed among the *secondary,* or so-called secondary, characteristics. Which no doubt justifies the fact that there is so little questioning of the effects of breast atrophy in the male. Wrongly, of course. Let us recall all the perplexity about the criteria of sexual difference entailed by the question of breast-feeding. But it seems, all the same, that one might be able to interpret the fact of being deprived of a womb as the most intolerable deprivation of man, since his contribution to gestation—his function with regard to the origin of reproduction—is hence asserted as less than evident, as open to doubt. An indecision to be attenuated both by man's "active" role in intercourse and by the fact that he will mark the product of copulation with *his own name.* Thereby woman, whose intervention in the work of engendering the child can hardly be questioned, becomes the anonymous worker, the machine in the service of a master-proprietor who will put his trademark upon the finished product. It does not seem exaggerated, incidentally, to understand quite a few products, and notably cultural products, as a counterpart or a search for equivalents to woman's function in maternity. And the desire that men here displays to determine for himself what is constituted by "origin," and thereby eternally and ever to reproduce him (as) self, is a far from negligible indication of the same thing.

There is, therefore, for man no prohibition upon substitutes that permit the realization of bisexual tendencies, provided that these have been historically valorized. (This is not the case, you will recall, with masochism. Nor, one might add, with passive homosexuality, which is doubtless too close to the function required of woman in intercourse.) Whereas a repression of the so-called phallic desires is supposed to have held woman back from a potential participation in the elaboration of the symbolic. Such participation is still liable to provoke suspicion and irony on the part of psychoanalysts. Thus, for example: "In recent times we have begun to learn a little about this, thanks to the circumstance that several of our excellent [?] women colleagues in analysis have begun to work at the question." So, *their practice* has brought us some information that elucidates *our theory.* "The discussion of this has gained special attractiveness from the distinction between the sexes. For the ladies, whenever some comparison seemed to turn out unfavourable to their sex, were able to utter a suspicion that we, the male analysts, had been unable to overcome certain deeply-rooted prejudices against what was feminine, and that this was being paid for in the partiality of our researches. We, on the other hand, standing on the ground of bisexuality, had no difficulty in avoiding impoliteness [?]. We had only to say: 'This doesn't apply to *you* [Freud's italics]. You're the exception; on this point you're *more masculine than feminine*'" (pp. 116–117). So, in order to avoid all im-

23

politeness toward our excellent "female colleagues," who are capable of affording a few insights on fragmentary aspects of our theory, it was/is sufficient to treat them explicitly as *male colleagues,* thus preventing any parallelism that would necessarily be unfavorable to their sex. Sic. . . .

The Labor "to Become a Woman"

"We approach the investigation of the sexual development of women with two expectations. The first is that here once more the constitution will not adapt itself to its function without struggle" (p. 117). A statement that is in itself somewhat enigmatic since it has just been asserted that "woman's own constitution" demanded she repress all signs of aggressivity—a repression encouraged by "social custom" and certainly also by the "sexual function" that we recognize in or attribute to her. How, therefore, is this proposition to be understood? As a result of the section that follows? That is, the section explaining that certain precocious abilities observed in the little girl—an earlier control of her excretory functions, a greater, more lively intelligence, a better disposition toward the external world—will yield only with a struggle to the sexual function she will have to fulfill? This is a possible reading, though one hesitates to assert it. In any case, these leads in development recognized in the little girl are immediately explained away as "greater dependency," "pliancy," "a greater need to be shown affection," or again are said to be outweighed by the fact that she forms "stronger object-cathexes." Her precociousness in the controlled production of feces, of language, of social relationships—whose relation to the production and circulation of currency you will be familiar with—would thus be envisaged as merely the effect of her desire to function, herself, as "merchandise." Her childish superiority would be motivated simply by the desire to appear the most attractive of all negotiable assets.

Yet, and even if the preceding remarks concerning the advantages of the little girl do not seem confirmed "by exact observations," it remains true that "girls cannot be described as intellectually *backward*"! But, he goes on, "these sexual differences are not of great consequence: they can be outweighed by individual variations. For our immediate purpose they can be disregarded" (p. 117). Let us, then, forget the troublesome question that might be raised by the incidental precociousness of the little girl, and the problem of what may *become of it,* so that we can keep to the heart of the matter, to the capital, that is to say.

The second point to be noted in our study of sexuality consists in the fact that "the decisive turning points will already have been prepared for or completed before puberty" (p. 117). This second observation and claim are no more supported than the first. At any rate, at the point when the claim is made. One may, of course, consider the whole of the text—the whole of the Freudian corpus—as a demonstration of its relevance: the role of the castration complex in the "becoming (of) a woman" intervenes well before puberty. Yet it is not perhaps vain to express surprise that the game should be played out, or at any rate the rules agreed upon, before reproduction—whose implicit or explicit precedence in this theory of sexuality has already been hinted at—can be effectively possible, materially fulfilled. It must be concluded, once again, that this preeminence finds its rationality elsewhere or otherwise. In any case, the culturally, socially, economically valorized female characteristics are correlated with maternity and motherhood: with breast-feeding the child, restoring the man. According to a certain dominant ideology, the little girl can thus have *no value* before puberty. Moreover, by Freud's own assertion, at the age at which the castration complex would be stressed by the little girl, "the truly female vagina is still undiscovered" (p. 118). This is to say, then, that everything concerning woman's allotted role and the representations of that role proposed or lent to her would be decided even before the socially recognized specificity of her intervention in the sexual economy is practicable, and before she has had access to a particular "essential feminine pleasure." It is hardly surprising, then, that she seems as a result to be "lacking in," "deprived of," "envious of," "jealous of" . . . But of what?

The Little Girl Is (Only) a Little Boy

An Inferior Little Man

Individuals of both sexes seem to pass through the early phases of libidinal development *in the same manner*. Contrary to all expectations, the little girl, in the sadistic-anal phase, shows *no less aggressiveness than the little boy*. . . . The aggressive impulses of little girls are *no less abundant and violent* [than those of little boys]. . . . From the onset of the phallic phase, the *differences between the sexes are completely eclipsed by the agreements*. . . . THE LITTLE GIRL IS THEREFORE A LITTLE MAN. . . . The little girl uses, with the *same* intent [as the little boy] her *still smaller clitoris* . . . a penis *equivalent* . . . man *more* fortunate [than she] . . . as

25

she passes from her masculine phase to the feminine. . . . During this (preoedipal, "masculine") phase, *everything* that will later be found in the oedipal situation *already exists* and later is *merely transferred* to the person of the father [?!] . . . the *ultimate differentiation* of the sexes . . . the little girl when she discovers her *disadvantage* . . . the little girl who had up till then lived *like a little boy* . . . the *comparison with the boy* . . . *activity more resembling* that of the male . . . regressing toward the *old masculinity complex* . . . residual manifestations of the *primitive masculinity* . . . the libido suffers a *greater* repression . . . nature pays *less* attention to the girl's demands than is the case with masculinity . . . *more* developed narcissism . . . *more* jealous . . . women have *fewer* social interests *than* men and the faculty for sublimating instincts is *weaker* . . . as far as social concern goes, the *inferiority* of women [with respect to men] . . . When laying *side by side* the development of the little boy and little girl, we find that the latter must, to *become a normal woman,* [?] suffer a *more* painful and *more* complex evolution and surmount two difficultues that have no *equivalent* for boys.[5]

So we must admit that THE LITTLE GIRL IS THEREFORE A LITTLE MAN. A little man who will suffer a more painful and complicated evolution than the little boy in order to become a normal woman! A little man with a smaller penis. A disadvantaged little man. A little man whose libido will suffer a greater repression, and yet whose faculty for sublimating instincts will remain weaker. Whose needs are less catered to by nature and who will yet have a lesser share of culture. A more narcissistic little man because of the mediocrity of her genital organs (?). More modest because ashamed of that unfavorable comparison. More envious and jealous because less well endowed. Unattracted to the social interests shared by men. A little man who would have no other desire than to be, or remain, a man.

The Cards Turned Over

Thus Freud discovers—in a sort of blind reversal of repressions—certain variously disguised cards that are kept preserved or stored away and that lie beneath the hierarchy of values of the game, of all the games: the desire for the same, for the self-identical, the self (as) same, and again of the similar, the alter ego and, to put it in a nutshell, the desire for the auto . . . the homo . . . the male, dominates the representational economy. "Sexual difference" is a derivation of the problematics of sameness, it is, now and forever, determined within the project, the projection, the

[5]All these statements can be found in this essay on femininity.

26

sphere of representation, of the same. The "differentiation" into two sexes derives from the a priori assumption of the same, since the little man that the little girl is, must become a man minus certain attributes whose paradigm is morphological—attributes capable of determining, of assuring, the reproduction-specularization of the same. A man minus the possibility of (re)preśenting oneself as a man = a normal woman. In this proliferating desire of the same, death will be the only representative of an outside, of a heterogeneity, of an other: woman will assume the function of representing death (of sex/organ), castration, and man will be sure as far as possible of achieving mastery, subjugation, by triumph-ing over the anguish (of death) through intercourse, by sustaining sexual pleasure despite, or thanks to, the horror of closeness to that absence of sex/penis, that mortification of sex that is evoked by woman; the trial of intercourse will have, moreover, as teleological parameter the challenge of an indefinite regeneration, of a reproduction of the *same* that defies death, in the procreation of the *son,* this same of the procreating father. As testimony, for self and others, of his imperishable character, and warranty of a new generation of self-identity for the male seed.

The Dream Interpreters Themselves

Still incomplete is the enumeration, and, of course, the interpretation of the faces, the forms, the morphologies that can be taken on by that old dream of "the same" which has defied the most prescient diviners, since their *method* did not question the credits that the method itself had already invested in that dream. The interpreters of dreams themselves had no desire but to rediscover the same. Everywhere. And, indeed, it was not hard to find. But was not *interpretation* itself, by that fact, caught up in the dream of identity, equivalence, analogy, of homology, symmetry, com-parison, imitation, was it also not more or less *adequate,* that is to say more or less *good?* Since, after all, the most able of the interpreters were also the most gifted, the most inventive dreamers, those most inspired by what was liable to perpetuate, even to reactivate the desire of the same?

But when this same desire comes to speak, and theorize, and prescribe itself in the very name of, in the very place of, the relation between the sexes, of sexual difference, then it seems that the paroxysm of that dem-onstration, of that exhibition, is equivalent to announcing that the central postulate is in fact being called into question. Required by every figure in the ontology, the a priorism of the same was able to maintain itself only through an expatriation, an extrapolation, an expropriation of a quasi-theological nature. Under the direction of man, but not directly at-tributable to him. Referred back to some transcendence that was sup-

27

posed to make capital of the interest of the operation. But if man is explicitly presented as the yardstick of the same, if the underlying and hitherto masked desire of the same—that is, the autoeroticism more or less deferred or differentiated into the autological or homologous representations of a (masculine) "subject"—if that desire is interpreted overtly, then the representation project is confounded in its detours and in its idealist justifications. The pleasure man can take therein becomes apparent. At the same time as the question is inevitably raised: why should this pleasure be his alone?

Thus Freud would strike at least *two blows* at the scene of representation. One, as it were, directly, when he destroys a certain conception of the present, or of presence, when he stresses secondary revision, overdetermination, repetition compulsion, the death drive, etc., or when he indicates, in his practice, the impact of so-called unconscious mechanisms on the discourse of the "subject." The other blow, blinder and less direct, occurs when—himself a prisoner of a certain economy of the logos, of a certain logic, notably of "desire," whose link to classical philosophy he fails to see—he defines sexual differences as a function of the a priori of the same, having recourse, to support this demonstration, to the age-old processes: analogy, comparison, symmetry, dichotomic oppositions, and so on. When, as card-carrying member of an "ideology" that he never questions, he insists that the sexual pleasure known as masculine is the paradigm for all sexual pleasure, to which all representations of pleasure can but defer in reference, support, and submission. In order to remain effective, all this certainly needed at the very least to remain hidden! By exhibiting this "symptom," this crisis point in metaphysics where we find exposed that sexual "indifference" that had assured metaphysical coherence and "closure," Freud offers it up for our analysis. With his text offering itself to be understood, to be read, as doubtless the most relevant re-mark of an ancient dream of self . . . one that had never been interpreted.

Penis Masturbation: A Necessarily Phallic Auto-eroticism

So Freud thinks individuals of both sexes go through the first libidinal stages *in the same way*. With the little girl showing equal aggressiveness at the sadistic-anal stage (perhaps her "constitution" has not yet forbidden her to do so?). And, from the onset of the phallic phase, the little girl is a little man. How could it be otherwise? Since the access to the phallic stage means access to the pleasure afforded by the phallus, which (even in its hold over the signifier) is the sign of the male sex/organ? Freud is therefore right in saying that at the phallic stage the little girl is a little boy. But why does he describe this "stage" as a necessary step in "becoming a normal woman"? And even more, why, if stages there be, is there no question, for example, of a vulvar stage, a vaginal stage, a uterine stage, in a discussion of female sexuality?

At the phallic stage, then, the little girl is searching for a possible penis-equivalent that can give her "pleasurable sensations." She finds this in the clitoris, a penis even smaller than the small penis of the small boy. And *all* her masturbatory acts involve this organ that is comparable to a tiny penis. Whereas the "truly feminine vagina is still undiscovered by both sexes."[6] Just like the lips, any of the lips, and the vulva, though all of these are so perfectly accessible that the little girl cannot fail to have discovered their sensitivity. Whether through her mother's ministrations or through the rubbing of diapers or underpants, or when her hand searches for the "little penis". The pleasure gained from touching, caressing, parting the lips and vulva simply does not exist for Freud, He is unaware of it or prefers not to know about it. At this stage or any other. Just as he will never refer to the pleasure associated with the sensitivity of the posterior wall of the vagina, the breasts, or the neck of the womb. All organs, no doubt, that lack masculine parameters?

In any case, he claims that "we are *entitled* to our view that in the phallic phase of girls the clitoris is the leading erotogenic zone" and that whereas "a few isolated reports"[7] refer to early vaginal sensations as well, it is first of all not easy to distinguish these from sensations in the anus or vestibulum—which do not seem important enough to bother about—and, second, such vaginal sensations cannot *in any case* play a great part. These are assertions whose trenchant and peremptory tone might well suggest negation and exorcism. Why does Freud, against all rhyme and reason, want little girls' masturbation to involve only the clitoris? Why, in the phallic phase, is the clitoris alone recognized as erotogenic for a girl? Why, when discussing the little girl, give the name "phallic" to this moment when her discovery of erotogenic sensitivity is, or is supposed to be, so incomplete and impoverished? Why amputate certain parts of the female genitals, and not necessarily those with the least erotic potential? Why retain only those that have, or are supposed to

[6]The "fundamentally male" character of little girls' sexuality and the exclusive role therein of the clitoris are further developed by Freud in the *Three Essays on Sexuality,* notably in the section called "The Transformations of Puberty."

[7]Here reference should be made to the debate on woman's sexual development between Karen Horney, Melanie Klein, and Ernest Jones. (Cf. the following articles, all published in the *International Journal of Psycho-Analysis:* Karen Horney, "On the Generation of the Castration Complex in Women," *IJPA,* 5 [1924]; "The Flight from Womanhood," *IJPA,* 7 [1926]: Ernest Jones, "The Early Development of Female Sexuality," *IJPA,* 8 [1927]; Melanie Klein, "Early Stages in the Oedipus Conflict," *IJPA,* 9 [1928].—Tr.)

have, their guarantor, their raison d'être, in the male sex/organ? Or, again, retain those that correspond to the representation man may have of sexual desire?

So, at the phallic stage, the little boy indulges in masturbation. There-fore the little girl does too, using her supposed penis-equivalent, the clitoris. They both do the same thing, more or less successfully. "But it is not, of course, going to remain so. With the *change to* femininity [?], the clitoris should wholly or in part hand over its sensitivity and, at the same time, its importance, to the vagina. This would be one of the two tasks which a woman has to perform in the course of her development whereas the more fortunate man has only to continue at the time of his sexual maturity the activity that he had previously carried out at the period of the efflorescence of his sexuality" (p. 118). Which means, if you like, that the little girl will practice her small-scale masturbation for as long as the little boy is allowed his, for as long as he has not incurred the fear of being castrated should he persevere with masturbation. That is the point at which the "change to femininity" has to occur, with the vagina becoming the indispensable instrument of male pleasure. The interpretation has validity. For, after all, if it is hard to understand— except for the sake of the argument—why the little girl would be onanistically interested only in the clitoris, it is even harder to see why the clitoris should have to yield its "sensitivity" and hence its "impor-tance" to the vagina. After all, the two organs are in no way interchange-able, but rather contribute, along with others, and with specific sen-sitivities, to woman's sexual pleasure.[8] One could conclude from all this that the little girl will not masturbate "herself," but rather a penis-equivalent[9] (just as the woman will not have access to a female pleasure functionally differentiated in accordance with her sex organs), and her vagina will, in due time, take over the function that the little boy's hand has been forbidden to perform. And the change in erotogenic zone is decided for her by the various transformations undergone by male mas-turbation. The man, on the other hand, more fortunate, has only to elaborate in maturity what he planned out during the first efflorescence of his sexuality.

[8]The role of kindling that Freud assigns to the clitoris in adult female sexuality ("just as pine shavings can be kindled to set a log of *harder* wood on fire," *Three Essays on Sexuality, SE* VII:221) still seems modeled on a male representation of female desire. One conforming to his desire, no doubt?

[9]Freud's phraseology is as ambiguous as this: "the little girl's recognition of the anatom-ical distinction between the sexes forces her away from masculinity and *masculine masturba-tion.*" "Some Psychical Consequences of the Anatomical Distinctions between the Sexes," *SE,* XIX:256).

The Blind Spot of an Old Dream of Symmetry

The Change of "Object" or the Crisis of a Devaluation

The second difficulty met by the little girl as she becomes a woman is apparently what Freud calls a *change of object*. "A boy's mother is the first object of his love, and she remains so too during the formation of his Oedipus complex and, in essence, ALL THROUGH HIS LIFE. For a girl too her first object must be her mother (and the figures of wet-nurses and foster-mothers that merge into her). The first object-cathexes occur in attachment to the satisfaction of major and simple vital needs, and the circumstances of the care of children are *the same* for both sexes. But in the Oedipus situation the girl's father has become her love-object, and we expect that in the *normal* course of development she will find her way from this paternal object to her final choice of an object. In the course of time, therefore, a girl has to change her erotogenic zone and her object— both of which a boy retains" ("Femininity," pp. 118–119). So the issue—put to "us men," as always—is: "how this happens, how does a girl pass from her masculine phase to the feminine one to which she is *biologically destined*" (p. 119).

It seems pointless to reiterate that such statements are perplexing because they are so imperious, normative, moralizing ("*we expect* in the *normal* course of development . . . a girl *has to* change . . . she is biologically *destined*"). Let us simply hazard a few questions, so impertinent and vain in the face of a fate thus inexorably decreed as to invite instant repression.

(*A*) If man remains fixated on his first love object, his mother, throughout his life, what will be his wife's role in his sexual economy? Will there ever be any kind of relationship between the sexes? Or, again, will desire ever break away from mere repetitive automatism?[10] (*B*) If, in order to correspond to man's desire, woman must play the part of or identify with his mother, he will be in some sense the *brother* of his children, since he has the same (type of) love object: the maternal. In which case, how does this involve or resolve the *question of the Oedipus complex*—which is the pivot of sexual differentiation structure for Freud?[11] (*C*) Why does the work of sexual change devolve upon wom-

---

[10]Would this explain why the problem of origins is so insistent? The most subtle detour taken by life in its course toward death, as Freud explains it in *Beyond the Pleasure Principle,* would be to repeat the link to the original place of conception by progressively sublating it from the materiality of its beginning. To erase birth by an infinite love of the Other('s) ideality.

[11]In other words, the Oedipus complex would not serve to articulate the difference between the sexes, but to ensure the passage of the (socio-symbolic) law of the father. He holds onto his first love forever. But language comes between him and this impossible

an?[12] And what is the ultimate purpose of all that work—that she become like *her mother-in-law?*[13] (Don't laugh too quickly.) (*D*) A woman finds herself therefore required to give up her first love object in order to conform to the man's. To have only one desire—that of being *as much as possible like man's eternal object of desire,* and meanwhile of correlating her own pleasure with her success in this operation. There will be only *one* tropism, then, and *one* object of desire or pleasure at stake, not a relation, an interplay, between *two* desires. Which explains, incidentally, why Freud can speak of *the* object of desire. (*E*) Why does Freud apply the term *masculine* to the phase in which the little girl loves and desires her mother? Doesn't he thereby miss the singularity of the relationship of the female child to her mother and to maternity, just as, though in a quite other way, he scotomizes elsewhere the originality of a desire among women?[14] Doesn't he reduce all these specific modalities of libido to the desire the man feels for the woman-mother or that the man (include here the little girl at the "masculine phase," since the little girl = the little boy, etc.) feels for the phallus (represented here by the phallic mother)? Or perhaps that the man feels for the man? More exactly, that the phallus feels for the phallus. (*F*) In the development toward the "female phase," Freud cites woman's "biological destiny," an expression to which we shall rarely find him resorting in the discussion of male sexuality, and which refers, once again, to woman's maternal "destiny."[15] Now, is there any more obvious device or more explicit way of banishing the auto-erotic, homosexual, or indeed fetishistic character of the relationship of man to woman than to stress the production of a child? Is the appeal to biological naturalism brought in to cover up the fantasy system governing the sexual economy of the couple? Or is the implication rather that maternal omnipotence is reduced by "destiny"? These two imaginary symptomatics are in no way mutually exclusive, of course.

The Law of the Self-same

"It would be a solution of ideal simplicity if we could suppose that from a particular age onwards the elementary influence of the mutual

---

"object"—impossible because idealized—which sanctifies the function of the logos as such: all of which impedes sexual relations.

[12]And what are we to make of the increase in value which the phallus—or Phallus—enjoys because the work on this genesis of "becoming a woman" is effaced?

[13]Need one point out, in this context, that it is the *wife's* mother who is detested, despised, and caricatured? She is the character who most threatens the nostalgia a man feels for his own mother.

[14]The problem of female homosexuality will be developed in the eleventh and twelfth sections of this essay.

[15]"Biological destiny" will be cited to justify woman's castration also. Freud writes "'Anatomy is destiny,' to vary a saying of Napoleon's'" ("Dissolution of the Oedipus Complex," *SE,* xix:178).

attraction between the sexes made itself felt and impels the small woman toward men, while the *same law* allows the boy to continue with his mother" (p. 119). How simply ideal, indeed, if the same law could sanction relations as different as the little girl's to men and the little boy's to his mother. . . . But how can such a law be formulated? When it is obviously not the law, at a given age, of the "mutual attraction between the sexes." Except, perhaps, for the little girl who, as the terminology goes, has "become a woman." Who, in order to become one, has supposedly resolved the question of her primal relationship—as well as the question of her original desire and of the origin of her desire—and has put down or put away her auto-erotic, homosexual pleasure, sublimated her partial drives, etc. Man, meanwhile, would remain polarized by his relation to origin. Both on the scene of representation—where the age-old urgency of this fundamental question is as well known as the ever repeated attempt to "unveil" it—and in his sexual practice where his most violent and recurrent desire is to deflower the woman-his mother (the relation between two scenes is obvious, yet its interpretation relies upon some detour through the ideal. We shall come back to this). Virginity, represented by the hymen, would thus be the thing which in its very figuration of the *impossible,* in its virtual role of *negation,* permits incest (she isn't my mother because she isn't a mother yet).[16]

But of course the paths marked out for the two sexes are not the *same,* and cannot obey the *same* law, whatever Freud would like. At best they may obey Law itself, the law of the same, which requires that the little girl abandon her relation to the origin and her primal fantasy so that henceforth she can be inscribed into those of men which will become the "origin" of her desire. In other words, woman's only relation to origin is one dictated by man's. She is crazy, disoriented, lost, if she fails to join in this *first* male desire. This is shown, specifically, in the way she is forced to renounce the marks of her ancestry and inscribe herself on man's pedigree. She leaves her family, her "house," her name—though admittedly it too is only a patronymic—her family tree, in favor of her husband's. And it would certainly be very interesting to raise the question of the "phallus" and its power in these terms: it would not be the privileged signifier of the penis or even of power and sexual pleasure were it not to be interpreted as *an appropriation of the relation to origin and of the desire for and as origin.* The tropism, as well as the rivalry, is in fact between the man and (his) mother. And woman is well and truly castrated from the viewpoint of this economy.

[16]This would be another possible interpretation of the "Taboo of Virginity" (*SE,* XI), whereby the hymen is the veil masking the mystery of the appropriation of the mother. All this can, of course, lead to a proliferation of fetishes that defer the testing of potency-impotence.

But sexual difference is reduced also. And even if Freud goes on to admit his disappointment at finding that children do not, univocally, follow the path of sexual preference that their parents have—which leads him to doubt "the power of which poets talk so much and with such enthusiasm but which *cannot be further dissected* analytically"!—one may object that the inclination the little boy feels for his mother and the little girl feels for men, and even for her father, does not boil down to the attraction felt by one sex for what Freud calls its "opposite." For, although this inclination—and here we continue to follow Freud's theory—leaves the little boy to his first love, it requires the little girl to turn away from hers. Whence the subsequent lengthy discussion in which Freud feels impelled to show how, why . . . the little girl will, as far as her mother is concerned, pass from love to hate.

Is Her End in Her Beginning?

An Unsuspected Love

"For you must know that the number of women who remain till a late age tenderly dependent on a paternal object, or indeed on their real father, is very great" (p. 119). Now, when investigating this intense and long-term fixation, one is led to "some *surprising* facts," namely the importance, the persistence, the consequences . . . of the phase of the girl's fixation to her mother, facts that *we did not know about*. We Freud, that is. This "phase" may last beyond the fourth year and "*almost everything that we find later in her relation to her father was already present in this earlier attachment* and has been *transferred* subsequently onto her father." So are we to assume that the love and the desire for the father repeat and re-present those felt for the mother, *less something* that would allow them to be transferred and displaced? The origin of love and of desire would remain, implicitly, linked to the mother. The primary set of metaphors for desire would indeed appear to be correlated, according to Freud, with what he calls the "maternal object." Not with the father as such, since the father merely suffers the displacement of the libido. Nor with the relation *between* father and mother, a man and a woman, and thus with sexual difference.

The Desire to Have a Child by the Mother

If, now, one investigates the libidinal feelings of the little girl toward her mother, one finds that "they are of very many different kinds" and persist through the three 'phases' of infantile sexuality"—taking on the characteristics of each and expressing themselves by oral, sadistic-anal, and phallic wishes. "These wishes represent active as well as passive impulses; if we relate them to the *differentiation of the sexes* [?] which is to appear later—*though we should avoid doing so as much as possible*—we may call them masculine and feminine. . . . It is not always easy to point to a formulation of these early sexual wishes; what is most clearly expressed is a wish to get the mother with child and the corresponding wish to bear her child—both belonging to the phallic period and sufficiently surprising, but established beyond doubt by analytic observation" (pp. 119–120).

The first of these two wishes can be interpreted as the fact that, in the phallic phase, the little girl is a little boy and therefore wishes to get her mother with child by means of her little penis (though all of this would have you confuse, in one and the same phallism, erection, penetrating the mother, and impregnating her). As for the wish to bear the mother's child, it is even harder to reconcile this within the imaginary configuration of this "phase" as Freud describes it, for it would lead us to suppose that the little girl is not simply a little boy, that bisexuality is already at work in her libidinal economy, and that as a girl she can desire a child from her phallic mother at the same time that, as the bearer of a small penis, she wishes to test its potency by getting her mother with child. This proves, in any case, that she already experiences a tropism that is both *centripetal* and *centrifugal,* and that *her sexual organ of reference is not simply the clitoris.*

Incidentally, we may regret that here Freud gives no hint as to the sex of the child to be conceived by mother and daughter, though he does so on other occasions: "Her happiness is great if later on this wish for a baby finds fulfilment in reality, and quite especially so if the baby is a *little boy* who brings the longed for penis with him" (p. 128). One might advance the hypothesis that the child who is desired in the relationship with the mother must be a girl if the little girl herself is in any degree valued for her femaleness. The wish for that girl child conceived with the mother would signify for the little girl a desire to *repeat and represent* her own birth and the separation of her "body" from the mother's. Engendering a girl's body, bringing a third woman's body into play, would allow her to identify both herself and her mother as sexuate women's bodies. As *two* women, defining each other as both like and unlike, thanks to a third "body" that both by common consent wish to be "female."[17] This

---

[17] A "different" version of the third-man argument. (The third-man argument is set out in Plato, *Parmenides,* 132a–133a, esp. 132a–b, and in Aristotle, *Metaphysics,* 990b; 1039a; 1079a.—Tr.).

would attenuate the lack of differentiation between the daughter and the mother or the maternal function which is inevitable when the desire for origin is not referred back to a relation between a man and a *woman*—a relation that in turn implies a positive representation of femininity (not just maternity) in which the little girl can inscribe herself as a woman in the making. In other words, this fantasy of the woman-daughter conceived between mother and daughter would mean that the little girl, and her mother also, perhaps, want to be able to represent themselves as women's bodies that are both desired and desiring—though not necessarily "phallic." But all this would require the repetition-displacement of the maternal function as it has been cathected by man.

If the child the little girl wishes for is a boy, one may suppose she wants to produce-represent herself as a boy, or else that, with her mother—like her mother?—she also wants to take over the father's role in procreation: with two women being sufficient to give life—and give life to a representative of the father. And his power would thus be dominated, in the imaginary.

Before leaving this fantasy of the child conceived with the mother, one may wonder why Freud introduces it only at the phallic stage, and not at the oral and anal stages also. Whereas elsewhere he insists that in the childish imaginary the production of a child is equated with the production of feces. "People get babies by eating some particular thing (as they do in fairy tales) and babies are born through the bowel like a discharge of faeces" (*Three Essays on Sexuality*, p. 196). You drink your mother's milk and you give her a baby or she gives you one.

Another variant of the pre-oedipal relation to the mother is "the fear of being murdered or poisoned, which may later form the core of a paranoiac illness" ("Femininity," p. 120). Here again we may note that the metaphors used are particularly concerned with the "body"—which is "murdered," "poisoned"—and we would like Freud to be more explicit as to how the body and the sex/organ connected, most particularly in the primeval relation of the child to its mother but also throughout Freud's theory, where it seems that a certain sexualism obliterates the materiality of the "sexuate body."[18] It would seem that the idea—or Idea—of sex or at any rate of sexual function shapes Freudian "discourse" to some extent. And this must obviously entail both modifying the economy of the

[18]Are we to assume that this materiality is reserved to the stages of partial drives? And that the "immortal" nature of the semen—a determinant in "sexual function" for Freud—implies an idealization of genital sexuality?

Idea and trapping sex in a logos, a logic, that is still derived from the Eidos, in its various guises. And it is certainly no accident if this point emerges in the context of paranoia, or the fear of being murdered, poisoned by the mother. The system structuring paranoia—and theory too perhaps—seems indeed like a play to achieve mastery through an organized set of signifiers that surround, besiege, cleave, out circle, and outflank the dangerous, the embracing, the aggressive mother/body. A set that has passed and passes, now and forever, in and by language. Oral. Language which, like and yet quite unlike the mother's breast or her milk, is able to nourish but also to kill, rape, or poison the sexuate body of the child.

The little girl's wish to get her mother with child or to have a child by her, as well as the fear of being killed, poisoned, during the pre-oedipal relation to the mother, are *"surprising"* discoveries which constitute the *"attractiveness"* of analytic practice and research.

The Father's Seduction: Law but Not Sex

Let us add this other revelation, which "caused me [Freud] many distressing hours." "In the period in which the main interest was directed to discovering infantile sexual traumas, almost all my women patients told me that they had been seduced by their father. I was driven to recognize in the end that these reports were untrue and so came to understand that hysterical symptoms are derived from phantasies and not from real occurrences" (p. 120).

Imagine that a certain Mr X, of mature years, as the saying goes, was addressing you in this way: how would you interpret expressions such as "which caused me many *distressing* hours," "almost all *my* female patients told *me* that they had been seduced by their *father*," "I was driven to recognise that these reports were *untrue*," "and *so* came to understand that hysterical symptoms are derived from *phantasies* and not from *real* occurrences." And let us leave the interpretation up to every analyst, even one improvised for the occasion. In fact, it would be better if he were improvised, for otherwise, whatever the analyst's gender or sex, we would run the risk of him or her having already been seduced by the *father* of psychoanalysis.

The seduction is, of course, covered up both in theory and practice by a normative statement, a *law*, which denies it. Thus: "It was only later that I was able to recognise in this phantasy of being seduced by the father the *expression of the typical Oedipus complex* in women." It would apparently be too risky to admit that the father might be a seducer, and even that he might want to have a daughter *in order to* seduce. Or that he might want to become an analyst in order—by means of hypnosis, suggestion, transfer, and interpretations that deal with the sexual economy and with forbidden, proscribed sexual representations—to achieve a lasting seduction of the hysterical woman.[19] The whole thing must be tidied up and whitewashed by the law. But, of course, if, under cover of the law, seduction can now be practiced at leisure, it seems equally urgent to question the *seduction function of law itself*. And its role in producing fantasies. When it suspends the realization of a seduced desire, law organizes and arranges the world of fantasy at least as much as it forbids, interprets, and symbolizes it.

Thus, it is neither simply true, nor indeed false, to claim that the little girl fantasizes being seduced by her father, since it is equally valid to assume that the father *seduces his daughter* but that, because (in most cases, though not in all) he refuses to recognize and live out his desire, *he lays down a law that prohibits him from doing so*. That said, it is his desire which, come what may, prescribes the force, the shape, the modes, etc., of the law he lays down or passes on, a law that reduces to the state of "fantasy" the little girl's seduced and rejected desire—a desire still faltering, barely articulate, silent perhaps, or expressed in signs or body language, a desire that must be seduced to the discourse and law of the father. *In place of the desire for the sexuate body of the father*—a desire labeled a "seduction fantasy" that must be verbalized and submitted to interpretation— we find a law proposed and imposed, that is, a discourse that institutionalizes and is already institutionalized. In some measure as a defense. (Think of those "distressing hours". . . . .)

Henceforth, how could the daughter recognize herself in her desire, particularly her desire for her father, how could she fail to suspend it in appetites both tied to and adrift from signifiers? At once overpowering in their authority and insignificant, pathetic, as substitutes for a desire that is defiled and denied. All this does not mean that the father *necessarily* makes love to his daughter—now and again it is advisable to say things very clearly—but it would be good to take issue with the cloak of the law in which he wraps his desire, his penis. And if for him the law guarantees an increment of pleasure, and power, it would be good to uncover what

[19]Which can be compared to the lasting effects of suggestion and subordination that result from deflowering. Cf. "The Taboo of Virginity," *SE*, xi.

this implies about his desire—*he seems to get more sexual satisfaction from making laws than love*—and about the eternally abortive, reductive, diversionary effects that this extra satisfaction for the father and the paternal function has upon the little girl, the future hysteric. Her sexuate desire is, in fact, labeled a fantasy, with non-fantasy being henceforward equated with a desire for a discourse of the father's sexual negation, exorcism, and even impotence. Her duty would be to sustain with her desire the enticing delusion of a legislative discourse, of a legal text that would state, among other things, that the father has no desire for her.

For more mundane realities, she will be referred back to the seducing mother. Indeed, as far as seduction by the mother is concerned, Freud tells us, "phantasy touches the ground of reality." "For it was really the mother who by her activities over the child's bodily hygiene inevitably stimulated, and perhaps even aroused for the first time, pleasurable sensations in her genitals" (p. 120).[20]

So here is our little girl, really and truly seduced by her mother (but no more than is necessary in the interests of good hygiene) and jilted by her father in the name of the law. Becoming a woman really does not seem to be an easy business. At least on the stage that has been set by the fantasies, phobias, and taboos a man (Freud in this instance) has about woman's sexuality.[21]

"I have no doubt you are ready to suspect that this portrayal of the abundance and strength of a little girl's sexual relations with her mother is very much overdrawn" (p. 121). Unless, on the contrary, we (women) were amazed by your need for us to be surprised by such obvious things, by your insistence on proving, demonstrating something that goes without saying. It is not so much the fact of the little girl's many rich ties to her mother that surprises us as the fact that these ties must "disappear" and that "the attachment to the mother ends in hate." This hate would be

---

[20]Should one see as a specific result of these early maternal seductions the fact that women are supposed to be constantly anxious about being clean and neatly dressed? Or should one rather interpret this negation of woman's anal possession as a submission to man's desire? The pages Rousseau devotes to female cleanliness, for example, would be relevant here.

[21]In a sort of vicious circle, since these fantasies proliferate all the more as a function of the status assigned to female sexuality in this way.

characterized by its strength and also by its tenacity: "it may last all through life." One must also stress that "as a rule one part of it is overcome while another part persists" and that in certain women the hate may be "carefully overcompensated."

All this raises the question of the implicit *parallelism* here between the daughter's hostility toward the mother and the son's love for her *all through life*. What does this obligation in reverse mean? Why must a girl's affection for her mother necessarily change into hatred if she is to turn toward her father? Desiring the father implies hating the mother. Desiring a representative of the "opposite" sex entails, at least for the little girl, rejecting a representative of one's own sex and, indeed, as we shall see, the representation of one's own sex. Which will mean no possible cathexis of the relation *between* the sexes? If one loves, desires one sex, one necessarily denigrates, detests the other. What is more, with only one sex being desirable, it becomes a matter of demonstrating how the little girl comes to devalue her own sex by devaluing her mother's.

Someone will bring up at this point the complaints, grievances, re-criminations, and accusations that women hysterics have made against their mothers to the father of psychoanalysis. But none of the transferen-tial and countertransferential determinants of those complaints will be interpreted.

The "Reasons" Why a Girl Hates Her Mother and a Boy Goes on Loving His

"The reproach against the mother which goes back furthest is that she gave the child too little milk—which is construed against her as lack of love" (p. 122). This reproach is often justified in our society, Freud goes on, but it is nonetheless so constant and persistent that we are led to doubt its foundation in reality. We should rather understand it as nostal-gia for the earliest nourishment, for which the child is "altogether in-satiable" as it never "gets over the pain of losing its mother's breast." And the children of primitive peoples, suckled until the age of two, would express the same reproaches. The hypothesis is not unreasonable. One could equally, however, see the child's manifest resistance to wean-ing as a symptom of the trauma occasioned by the *final break in material contact with the inside of the mother's body:* rupture of the fetal membranes, cutting of the umbilical cord, denial of the breast. A series of breaks with all that might be represented as the material causes of the child's body. Could its "insatiable hunger" perhaps be the need to reabsorb its material cause? This would imply the inadmissible urge to devour the mother, to destroy this original nature-body from which one must eternally separate and be separated but to which one must eternally return and refer back.

40

But if she is eaten, she will no longer be there to serve your needs-desires or to guarantee a certain representation of the place of origin and the original bond. So this "hunger" is indeed insatiable, and no food will ever satisfy it. In fact it is not a matter of its being satisfied. Food can make you ill, can poison you if it should run short—as Freud tells us— but all the more if it falls short in its function of repeating-representing closeness to the mother, until such a time as the desire for origin can find an(other) economy.

For example, making babies. But the feces-babies that are the first you can "make" are still a result of absorbing the mother-material. And even though they mean a triumph for the child's digestion,[22] they also mark the digestion's *partial* nature, and in any case they will *break away from* the child as soon as they are produced: another break in material contact which the child will try to master. But the child will never have simple possession of these "children of the mother." Society will take them away as soon as the child has made them, in the name of cleanliness.

This, then, is no solution. Therefore, if you are a boy, you will want, as soon as you reach the phallic stage, to return to the origin, turn back toward the origin. That is, possess the mother, get inside the mother who is the place of origin, in order to reestablish continuity with it and to see and know what happens there. And moreover to reproduce yourself there. If you are born a girl, the question is quite other. No return to, toward, inside the place of origin is possible unless you have a penis. The girl will herself be the place where origin is repeated, re-produced and reproduced, though this does not mean that she thereby repeats "her" original topos, "her" origin. On the contrary, she must break any contact with it, or with her, and, making one last turn, by a kind of vault— up one *more* branch of the family tree—she must get to the place where origin can be repeated *by being counted*.

And yet this extra turn, this extra twist—performed on the spot and one space along because it marks a calculation—*can never be turned* to woman's account as the *other side of the representational coin,* an "other side" of the representation of origin. Woman cannot turn it into her project of return or turning back. It (id) is counted and reproduced in figures, but woman is not able to take a(c)count of it, or to supply any symbol for it. At least within the economy of representation that still prevails and that Freud is too prone to neglect. Freud is still party to a certain logos and therefore to a certain economy of "presence," a certain representation of "presence," and he will be able to picture the little girl

---

[22]Cf. in this regard "the triumph accomplished in the duodenum" in Hegel, *Encyclopedia of the Philosophical Sciences, in Outline,* Part 2, "Philosophy of Nature," sec. 371.

becoming a woman only in terms of *lack, absence, default,* etc. To take an example or paradigm, Freud can discuss the little girl's relation to the place of origin only as a vacancy, a taking leave of the mother: as rejection, or hatred of the mother. That is to say, as a fault in the re-presentation of origin. In lieu of the girl's own relation to the place of origin, Freud substitutes the penis, or rather he imposes the penis as the only possible and desirable replacement. The penis—or better still the phallus! *Emblem of man's appropriative relation to the origin.* She, on the other hand, obviously does not and cannot have a privileged relation to whatever the penis replaces, she can in fact desire nothing unless she neither loves nor detests her mother, but has used the mother, who is supposedly her place of origin and original bond, in order to vault *one more step* up in the counting, or discounting, of the enumeration of origin.

An Economy of Primal Desire That Cannot Be Represented

So, to return to the issue of weaning, it would seem pertinent to say that the little girl is weaned with far greater trauma than the little boy as she will have nothing—at least as things stand at present—to make up for, substitute for, or defer this final break in physical contact with her mother: she cannot turn back toward her mother, or lay claim to seeing or knowing what is to be seen and known of that place of origin; she will not represent "her" relation to "her" origin; she will never go back inside the mother; she will never give the mother a drink of sperm from her penis, in a substitution-reversal of the lost breast and milk;[23] she will never reproduce her (like) self inside the/her mother, etc. She is left with a *void,* a *lack* of all representation, re-presentation, and even strictly speaking of all mimesis of her desire for origin.[24] That desire will henceforth pass through the discourse-desire-law of man's desire. "You will be my woman-mother, my wife, if you would, and (like) my mother, if you could,"[25] is a statement equivalent to: "You will be for me the possibility of repeating-representing-appropriating the/my relation to

---

[23]"But the interest in that part of the body has, in addition to its anal-erotic root, an oral one which is perhaps more powerful still: for when sucking has come to an end, the penis also becomes heir to the mother's nipple" ("Anxiety and Instinctual Life," *New Introductory Lectures on Psychoanalysis, SE,* XXII:101).

[24]How else are we to interpret the fact that playing with dolls is "bad," i.e. masculine, whenever the little girl simply enjoys miming her relations with her mother rather than seeing the doll as the child she desires by the father? Or again the fact that woman's supreme desire is supposedly to bear a male child? These questions and others remarking the ban placed on this "bad" mimesis will be developed further on in this essay.

[25]"Even a marriage is not made secure until the wife has succeeded in making her husband her child as well and in acting as a mother to him" ("Femininity," pp. 133–34).

the origin." Now this operation—and we can quote Freud's own words against him here—in no way constitutes a *displacement* of the origin-desire of the little girl, of the woman. It is more in the nature of an exile, an extradition, an exmatriation, from this/her economy of desire. And she is actually held responsible for it: does she not hate her mother? What really occurs, of course, is that the representation, the signifier of one stage in woman's libidinal economy (and not the least important stage since it is the one in which she was perhaps marked off from her first stage by her re-mark) is proscribed.[26] But let us say that *in the beginning was the end of her story,*[27] and that from now on she will have one dictated to her: by the man-father.

Woman would thus find no possible way to represent or tell *the story of the economy of her libido.* Just as man would find no possible meaning in "female libido." The libido is masculine, or at any rate neuter. "Nevertheless the juxtaposition 'female libido' is without justification" (p. 133). Which must obviously be translated as saying: within a given economy of meaning (*vouloir-dire*)—whose relation to the desire for sameness and to the repetition-representation-reproduction of sameness is well known—the words "female libido" cannot mean anything, since the possibility that they might mean anything would inevitably lead us to question the project and projections of that meaning itself. The "unjustifiable," intolerable nature of those words "female libido," would be one symptom of something outside that threatened the signs, the sense, the syntax, the systems of representation of a meaning and a praxis designed to the precise specifications of the (masculine) "subject" of the story.

Now, if the expression "female libido" has no justification, this means also and at the same time that the strength of woman's sexual impulses will be reduced. As Freud goes out of his way to demonstrate, laying most of the blame upon nature. (See "Femininity," p. 133.) Thus, the a priori and the desire for sameness can be maintained only if *a single* desire is in control.

[26]This proscription could certainly be interpreted in Lacanian terms as the "foreclosure" (*forclusion*) of a key signifier for woman's libidinal economy. But thereby "foreclosure" itself would need to be questioned about its privileged relation to the name of the father, which has acted to lay down the law that proscribes woman from having any relation to a representation indispensable to "symbolization."

[27]In fact Freud admits as much when he says that he has dealt only with the "prehistory" of female sexuality or recognizes that everything concerning the girl's pre-Oedipus had succumbed to so inexorable a repression that one would need to go back "as it were" through all the marks of that history to find, at the back, the vestiges of a more ancient civilization. Cf. "Female Sexuality", *SE,* XXI:222–23.

As a result, psychoanalysts often complain ironically about women being unanalyzable.[28] Which is quite true if one adheres to Freud's theories and to the closure of representation that here imprisons him. "Female libido" (and indeed, strictly speaking, the sexual difference of which woman's "castration" would nowadays be the most flagrant remark) is in effect excluded. The phallus, quite to the contrary, functions all too often in psychoanalysis as the guarantee of sense, the sense of sense(s), the "figure," the "form," the ultimate signifier through which the ancient metaphors of onto-theology would be set straight. Off with the masks. The suspicion is unavoidable that the Same is being postulated again in this "new" signifying economy, organized under the control of the said Phallus.

One More Child

"When the next baby appears in the nursery," another reproach is leveled at the mother by the little girl—or, indeed, the little boy. "If possible the connection with oral frustration is preserved: the mother could not or would not give the child any more milk because she needed the nourishment for the new arrival. In cases in which the two children are so close in age that lactation is prejudiced by the second pregnancy, this reproach acquires a real basis, and it is a remarkable fact that a child, even with an age difference of only 11 months, is not too young to take notice of what is happening. But what the child grudges the unwanted intruder and rival is not only the suckling but all the other signs of maternal care. It feels that it has been dethroned, despoiled, prejudiced in its rights; it casts a jealous hatred upon the new baby and develops a grievance against the faithless mother which often finds expression in a disagreeable change in its behaviour. It becomes 'naughty', perhaps, irritable and disobedient and goes back on the advances it has made towards controlling its excretions. All this has been very long familiar and is accepted as self-evident; but we rarely form a correct idea of the strength of these jealous impulses, of the tenacity with which they persist and of the magnitude of their influence on later development. Especially as this jealousy is constantly receiving fresh nourishment in the later years of childhood and the whole shock is repeated with the birth of each new brother or sister. Nor does it make much difference if the child happens to remain the mother's preferred favourite. A child's demands

[28]Statements that can be compared with Kant's on this subject. The relation of Freud and the theoretical discourse of psychoanalysis on the one hand and Kant on the other hand poses a certain number of problems. Such as: what suspense may have been left uninterpreted on both sides with regard to the "transcendental imagination"? So that they end up forced to bend before a "practice" commanded by "morals."

for love are immoderate, they make exclusive claims and tolerate no sharing" (p. 123).

It surely seems unlikely that the child's reactions are *the same* whether or not it remains the mother's favorite, whether the new-born is of the *same sex* as the older sibling, or of a *different sex,* whether a girl follows a boy or a boy is born after a girl. Moreover, must the refusal to master one's excretory functions be interpreted simply as a regression? Could it not also be an attempt to imitate the mother, to have a baby? In view of the child's ignorance of female genitals at this stage, it could mimic a birth only through defecation, and this symptom would therefore be the child's way of abreacting, revolting against, all that is not being explained. A way of using its body to express a lack of representations for conception, pregnancy, and giving birth.

That said, one must certainly agree that the birth of a younger sibling greatly disturbs a child. And, in objection to Freud's insistence on stressing oral frustration as explanation, one might claim that oral frustration is only a reactivation, and no doubt a more discernible re-mark, of another disturbance, another "crisis." A new, a "second"—and "third," etc.—birth would completely disrupt the child's comprehension of where it stands in relation to its own birth and conception. The child's desire for a relation to an origin, *one* origin, would thereby be seriously thwarted. And here the child would find himself or herself once more faced with the question of *counting back to the very beginning,* a question he or she will always have to take into a(c)count. And it is really in terms of numbering that one will have to, would have to, consider the conceptualization and the practice of castration, if one reckons to stand by it and keep it effective. Every time an exclusive, unitary relation to the origin or the fantasy of a primeval simplicity has to be enumerated, castration is involved. As, for example, when there is a repetition—not pure and simple, but with "plus one" resulting from the operation—of a conception, of a birth, that is to say, in the enumeration of the tribe. Even if the child is still wholly or partially ignorant of the sexual difference at work in fertilization, one more birth, like any "plus one," calls up or recalls the functioning of castration. And the child's regressive behavior on this occasion is certainly to be understood as a sign of its (castration) anxiety, but also perhaps as an aggressive riposte to fantasies about the omnipotence of the mother, or sometimes of the parents, who have wished to gull the child into believing in a monopoly on origin. In this perspective, not only the child but also the mother, or the father, or the parents as a familial institution "make exclusive claims and tolerate no sharing." Each child shall have the right (only the right?) to a *unique* relation with her, with him, or with them. Yet, one, and one, and one . . . as many

45

ones as you like—even as many one + one + one + one +. . . .—can never add up to, never give a count of, the relation at stake between children of the same mother, of the same father, of the same parents. And in fact psychoanalysts know now that the problems young—and not so young—children have with counting can be traced back to the difficulty they had in finding their place when the family tribe was being counted. Quite apart from their math phobia. . . .

Another "Cause"—Castration

As Might Be Expected

The little girl's hostility toward her mother finds other justifications. Such as: the impossibility of satisfying the child's sexual desires; the mother inciting the child to masturbate and then forbidding it to do so; the fact that the bond to the mother is supposedly destined to disappear as a result of its primitive character, since early object cathexes are always highly ambivalent; "it is the special nature of the mother-child relation that leads, with equal inevitability, to the destruction of the child's love; for even the mildest upbringing cannot avoid using compulsion and introducing restrictions, and any such intervention in the child's liberty must provoke as a reaction an inclination to rebelliousness and aggressiveness." But "all these factors . . . are, after all, also in operation in the relation of the *boy* [Freud's italics] to his mother and are yet unable to alienate him from the maternal object." So some specific factor must intervene in the mother-daughter relation and in the development of that relation which would explain "the termination of the attachment of girls to their mother" (p. 124).

"I *believe* we have found this specific factor, and indeed *where we expected to find it,* even though in a surprising form. *Where we expected to find it,* I say, for it lies in the castration complex. After all, the *anatomical* distinction [between the sexes] *must* express itself in *psychical* consequences. *It was, however, a surprise to learn from analyses that girls hold their mother responsible* for their lack of a penis and do not forgive her for their being thus put at a disadvantage" (p. 124).

One might cite or even recite Freud at length, the Freud of "female sexuality" at least, on the basis of these "I believes," these "where we expected to find its," these "castration complexes"; and also relate them to his failure to be "surprised" at the "psychical consequences" of an "anatomical distinction," or to his rather univocal appeal to anatomy to explain a psychical economy—which would supposedly know no other mimesis than that of "nature" according to this interpretation?—and to all those expressions of surprise which, perhaps, mask the upsurge of an *unheimlich* that is much more uncanny, blinding. . . .

The Gaze, Always at Stake

So the little girl does not forgive her mother for not giving her a penis. At the "*sight* of the genitals of the other sex," girls "*notice the* [sexual?] *difference* and, it must be admitted, its significance too. They feel seriously *wronged*, often declare that they want to '*have something like it too*' . . . and fall victim to '*envy for the penis*', which will leave ineradicable traces on their development and the formation of their character" (p. 125).

The dramatization is quite good, and one can imagine, or dream up, recognition scenes along these lines in the consulting room of psychoanalyst Freud. By rights, though, the question should still be raised of the respective relationships between the gaze and sexual difference, since, he tells us, you have to see it to believe it. And therefore, one must lose sight of something to see it anew? Admittedly. But all the same. . . . Unless all the potency, and the difference (?) were displaced into the gaze(s)? So Freud will see, without being seen? Without being seen seeing? Without even being questioned about the potency of his gaze? Which leads to envy of the omnipotence of gazing, knowing? About sex/about the penis. To envy and jealousy of the eye-penis, of the phallic gaze? He will be able to see that I don't have one, will realize it in the twinkling of an eye. I shall not see if he has one. More than me? But he will inform me of it. Displaced castration? *The gaze is at stake from the outset.* Don't forget, in fact, what "castration," or the knowledge of castration, owes to the gaze, at least for Freud, The gaze has always been involved.

Now the little girl, the woman, supposedly has *nothing* you can see. She exposes, exhibits the possibility of *a nothing to see.* Or at any rate she shows nothing that is penis-shaped or could substitute for a penis. This is the odd, the uncanny thing, as far as the eye can see, this nothing around which lingers in horror, now and forever, an overcathexis of the eye, of appropriation by the gaze, and of the *phallomorphic* sexual metaphors, its reassuring accomplices.[29]

---

[29]Cf. the relationship Freud establishes between castration anxiety, the fear of losing one's sight, and the fear of one's father's death (in "The Uncanny," *SE*, xvii:219–52). Or

This nothing, which actually cannot well be mastered in the twinkling of an eye, might equally well have acted as an inducement to perform castration upon an age-old oculocentrism. It might have been interpreted as the intervention of a difference, of a deferent, as a challenge to an imaginary whose functions are often improperly regulated in terms of sight. Or yet again as the "symptom," the "signifier," of the possibility of an *other* libidinal economy, of a heterogeneity unknown in the practice of and discourse about the (designated) libido. Now the "castration complex" in becoming a woman will merely close off, repress? or censure? such possible interpretations. Woman's castration is defined as her having nothing you can see, as her *having* nothing. In her having nothing penile, in seeing that she has No Thing. Nothing *like* man. That is to say, *no sex/organ* that can be seen in a *form* capable of founding its reality, reproducing its truth. *Nothing to be seen is equivalent to having no thing. No being* and *no truth.*[30] The contract, the collusion, between *one* sex/organ and the victory won by visual dominance therefore leaves woman with her sexual void, with an "actual castration" carried out in actual fact. She has the option of a "neutral" libido or of sustaining herself by "penis-envy."

Anatomy Is "Destiny"

This "neuter" is hard for Freud to account for in his theory of the difference of the sexes, as we can see from his repeated admissions that the subject of woman's sexuality is still very "obscure." As for what he will have to say about it, what has become "apparent" to him about it, female sexuality can be graphed along the axes of visibility of (so-called) masculine sexuality. For such a demonstration to hold up, the little girl must immediately become a little boy. In the beginning . . . the little girl was (only) a little boy. In other words THERE NEVER IS (OR WILL BE) A LITTLE GIRL. All that remains is to assign her sexual function to this

---

again this: "It often happens that neurotic men declare that they feel there is something uncanny about the female genital organs. This *unheimlich* place, however, is the entrance to the former *Heim* (home) of all human beings, to the place where each one of us lived once upon a time and in the beginning. . . . In this case, too, then, the *unheimlich* is what was once *heimisch,* familiar; the prefix 'un' is the token of repression" ("The Uncanny," p. 245). For the moment let us concentrate on the strange disquiet felt about the female genitals. The woman-mother would be *unheimlich* not only by reason of a repression of a primitive relationship to the maternal but also because her sex/organs are strange, yet close; while "heimisch" as a mother, woman would remain "un" as a woman. Since woman's sexuality is no doubt the most basic form of the *unheimlich.*

[30]This echoes Leibniz's question in *Principles of Nature and of Grace Founded on Reason:* "Why is there something rather than nothing?" Or again: "That which is truly not *one* entity, is not truly one *entity* either": Leibniz, letter to Arnauld, April 30, 1687. (Leibniz, *Philosophical Writings,* ed. G. H. R. Parkinson, trans. Mary Morris and G. H. R. Parkinson [London: Dent, 1934 and 1973], pp. 199 and 67.)

"little boy" with no penis, or at least no penis of any recognized value. Inevitably, the trial of "castration" must be undergone. This "little boy," who was, in all innocence and ignorance of sexual difference, *phallic,* notices how ridiculous "his" sex organ looks. "He" *sees* the disadvantage for which "he" is *anatomically destined:* "he" has only a tiny little sex organ, no sex organ at all, really, an almost invisible sex organ. The almost imperceptible clitoris. The humiliation of being so badly equipped, of cutting such a poor figure, in *comparison* with the penis, with *the* sex organ can only lead to a desire to "have something like it too," and Freud claims that this desire will form the basis for "normal womanhood." In the course of the girl's discovery of her castration, her dominant feelings are of envy, jealousy, and hatred toward the mother— or in fact any woman—who has no penis and could not give one. She desires to be a man or at any rate "like" a man since she cannot actually become one.[31] The little girl does not submit to the "facts" easily, she keeps waiting for "it to grow," and "believes in that possibility for improbably long years." Which means that no attempt will be made by the little girl—nor by the mother? nor by the woman?—to find symbols for the state of "this nothing to be seen," to defend its goals, or to lay claim to its rewards. *Here again no economy would be possible whereby sexual reality can be represented by/for woman.* She remains forsaken and abandoned in her lack, default, absence, envy, etc. and is led to submit, to follow the dictates issued univocally by the sexual desire, discourse, and law of man. Of the father, in the first instance.

What the Father's Discourse Covers Up

So, borrowing Freud's own terms, let us question him for example, about his relationship to the parental function. That is, to the exercise of the law—notably the psychoanalytic law—of castration. Why this fear, horror, phobia . . . felt when there is nothing to be seen, why does having nothing that can be seen threaten *his* libidinal economy? And remember in this regard that in the castration scenario Freud has just outlined, it is the boy who looks and is horrified first, and that the little girl merely doubles and confirms by reduplication what he is supposed to have seen. Or not seen. "In [boys] the castration complex arises after they have learnt *from the sight of the female genitals* that the organ which they value so highly need not necessarily accompany the body. At this the boy calls to mind the threats he brought on himself by his doings

[31]In other words, the "fact of castration" will leave woman with only one option—the semblance, the mummery of femininity, which will always already have been to "act like" the value recognized by/for the male. The fact that certain men want to "act like" women thus raises the question whether they thereby take back for themselves that "femininity" which was assigned to woman as an inferior copy of their relation to the origin.

with that organ, he begins to give credence to them and falls under the influence of *fear of castration,* [Freud's italics] which will be the most powerful motive force in his subsequent development" (p. 125). After which, Freud goes on: "The castration complex of girls is *also* started by the *sight* of the genitals of the other sex. Etc."

Here again the little girl will have to act *like* the little boy, feel the same urge to see, look in the same way, and her resentment at not having a penis must follow and corroborate the horrified astonishment the little boy feels when faced with the strangeness of the nonidentical, the nonidentifiable. The "reality" of the girl's castration could be summed up as follows: you men can see nothing, can know nothing of this; can neither discover nor recognize yourselves in this. All that remains, therefore, is for me, for her (or them), to accept this fact. As a biological fact! The girl thus "enters" into the castration complex in the same way as the boy, like a boy. She "comes out" of it feminized by a decision, which she is duty bound to ratify, that there cannot be a nothing to be seen. The idea that a "nothing to be seen," a something not subject to the rule of visibility or of specula(riza)tion, might yet have some reality, would indeed be intolerable to man. It would serve to threaten the theory and practice of the representation by which he aims to sublimate, or avoid the ban on, masturbation. Auto-erotism has been permitted, authorized, encouraged insofar as it is deferred, exhibitited in sublated ways. All this is endangered (caught in the act, one might say) by a *nothing*—that is, a nothing the same, identical, identifiable. By a fault, a flaw, a lack, an absence, outside the system of representations and autorepresentations. Which are man's. By a *hole* in men's signifying economy. A nothing that might cause the ultimate destruction, the splintering, the break in their systems of "presence," of "re-presentation" and "representation." A nothing threatening the process of production, reproduction, mastery, and profitability, of meaning, dominated by the phallus—that *master signifier* whose law of functioning erases, rejects, denies the surging up, the resurgence, the recall of a *heterogeneity* capable of reworking the principle of its authority. That authority is minted in concepts, representations and formalizations of language which prescribe, even today, the prevailing theory and practice of "castration." And what weak instruments these are, products of the very system they pretend to challenge. Such collusion with phallocentrism serves only to confirm its power.

The Negative in Phallocentric Dialectic
Thus the matter before us leads us to ask ourselves, and to ask them:

(1) Does the little girl, the woman, really have "penis-envy" in the sense Freud gives to that expression; that is, of wanting "to have some-

thing like it too"? This assumption, in fact, governs everything said now and later about female sexuality. For this "envy" programs all of woman's instinctual economy, even, though she does not realize it, *before* the discovery of her castration, at the point when, supposedly, she only was, and wanted to be, a boy.

(2) What is the relationship of that "envy" to man's "desire"? In other words, is it possible that the phobia aroused in man, and notably in Freud, by the uncanny strangeness of the "nothing to be seen" cannot tolerate *her* not having this "envy"? *Her* having other desires, of a different nature from *his* representation of the sexual and from *his* representations of sexual desire. From his projected, reflected *auto-representations* shall we say? If woman had desires other than "penis-envy," this would call into question the unity, the uniqueness, the simplicity of the mirror charged with sending man's image back to him—albeit inverted. Call into question its flatness. The specularization, and speculation, of the purpose of (*his*) desire could no longer be two-dimensional. Or again: the "penis-envy" attributed to woman soothes the anguish man feels, Freud feels, about the coherence of his narcissistic construction and reassures him against what he calls castration anxiety. For if his desire can be signified only as "penis-envy," it is a good thing that he has it (one). And that what he has should represent the only goods acceptable for sexual trading.

(3) Why does the term "envy" occur to Freud? Why does Freud choose it? Envy, jealousy, greed are all correlated to lack, default, absence. All these terms describe female sexuality as merely the *other side* or even the *wrong side* of a male sexualism. It could be admitted that the little girl accords a special status to the penis as the instrument of her sexual pleasure and that she displays a centrifugal-centripetal tropism for it. But "penis-envy," in the Freudian and indeed psychoanalytic sense, means nothing less than that the little girl, the woman, must despise *her own* pleasure in order to procure a—doubtless ambiguous—remedy for man's castration anxiety. The possibility of losing his penis, of having it cut off, would find a real basis in the *biological* fact of woman's castration. The fear of not having it, of losing it, would be re-presented in the anatomical amputation of woman, in her resentment at lacking a sex organ and in her correlative "envious" urge to gain possession of it. The castration anxiety of not having it, or losing it, would thus be supported by the representation of the female sex, whereas *the desire to have it* would confirm man in the assurance that he has it, still, while reminding him at the same time—in one of the essential rules of the game—that he risks having her take it away from him. The fact remains that "penis-envy"

must above all be interpreted as a symptomatic index—laid down as a law of the economy of woman's sexuality—of the pregnancy of the desire for the same, whose guarantee, and transcendental signifier or signified, will be the phallus. The Phallus. If it were not so, why not *also* analyze the "envy" for the vagina? Or the uterus? Or the vulva? Etc. The "desire" felt by each pole of sexual difference "to have something like it too"? The resentment at being faulty, lacking, with respect to a heterogene, to an other? The "disadvantage" mother nature puts you to by providing only *one* sex organ? All of this would require, entail, demand an other sex, a different sex—a sex that shared in the same while remaining different[32]—for sexual pleasure to be possible. But finally, in Freud, sexual pleasure boils down to being plus or minus one sex organ: the penis. And sexual "otherness" comes down to "not having it." Thus, woman's lack of penis and her envy of the penis *ensure the function of the negative,* serve as representatives of the negative, in what could be called a *phallocentric*—or phallotropic—dialectic.[33] And if "sexual function" demands that the little boy should turn away from his—real—mother whom convention forbids he should get with child, if what is indicated by the "castration complex" forces him to "sublimate" his instincts toward his mother, let us say that, as far as he is concerned, man will *lose nothing* thereby, and that the loss will amount only to a risk, a fear, a "fantasy" of loss. And that the *nothing* of sex, the *not* of sex, will be borne by woman.

But, ipso facto, "castration" cannot be what makes the relation between the sexes practicable or assures the possibility for both repetition and "displacement" of the relation *between two sexes.* It must serve as a reminder of the negative which is attributed to woman, to the female sex—in *reality* too, for more verisimilitude—an attribution that would guarantee its "sublation"[34] in the sublimation of the penis. With sex and sexualness being sublated into representations, ideas, laws, dominated by the Phallus. The relationship to the negative, for man, will always have been imaginary—imagined, imaginable—, hence the impetus it gives to fictive, mythic, or ideal productions that are only afterward defined as laws assuring the permanence and circularity of this system. The legislation re-establishes, then, the castration complex, notably of woman,

[32]Of course this will initially imply bisexuality, but here it would evoke instead the "brilliance" of the mirror which explodes into sexual pleasure, like and unlike according to each sex.

[33]This might be understood as a tautology, unless the word "a" is re-marked. In other words, if dialectic has *the* one, *the* same as the horizon of its process, then it is necessarily phallocentric.

[34]Translation of *Aufhebung.*

which will serve, along with other edicts, to transform into a historical program the fables relating to men's sexual practices.

(4) As for woman, one may wonder why she submits so readily to this make-believe, why she "mimics" so perfectly as to forget she is acting out man's contraphobic projects, projections, and productions of her desire. Specifically, why does she accept that her desire only amounts to "penis-envy"? What fault, deficiency, theft, rape, rejection, repression, censorship, of representations of her sexuality bring about such a subjection to man's desire-discourse-law about her sex? Such an atrophy of her libido? Which will never be admissible, envisionable, except insofar as it props up male desire. For the "penis-envy" alleged against woman is—let us repeat—a remedy for man's fear of losing one. If *she* envies it, then *he* must have it. If *she* envies what *he* has, then it must be valuable. The only thing valuable enough to be envied? The very standard of all value. Woman's fetishization of the male organ must indeed be an indispensable support of its price on the sexual market.

Is Working Out the Death Drives Limited to Men Only?
So let us speculate that things happen this way because, in psychoanalytic parlance, *the death drives can be worked out only by man*,[35] never, under any circumstances, by woman. She merely "services" the work of the death instincts. Of man.

Thus, by suppressing her drives, by pacifying and making them passive, she will function as pledge and reward for the "total reduction of tension." By the "free flow of energy" in coitus, she will function as a promise of the libido's evanescence, just as in her role as "wife" she will be assigned to maintain coital homeostasis, "constancy." To guarantee that the drives are "bound" in/by marriage. She will also be the place referred to as "maternal" where the automatism of repetition, the re-establishment of an earlier economy, the infinite regression of pleasure, can occur. Back to the sleep of Lethe, to lethargy. Except that she is charged at the same time with preserving, regenerating, and rejuvenating the organism, notably through sexual reproduction. She is wholly devoted to giving life, then, source and re-source of life. To being still the restoring, nourishing mother who prolongs the work of death by sustaining it; death makes a detour through the revitalizing female-maternal.

---

[35]For the following section, the reader should refer to *Beyond the Pleasure Principle*, "Instincts and their Vicissitudes," *SE*, xiv, and "The Economic Problem of Masochism," *SE*, xix.

You will have realized that the "sexual function" also requires aggressiveness from the male, and that this authorizes an economy of death drives whereby the "subject" disengages and protects himself by diverting his energies to the "object." And, by maintaining the subject-object polarity in sexual activity, woman will provide man with an outlet for that "primary masochism" which is dangerous and even life-threatening for the "psychic" as well as the "organic" self. Now, Freud states that this "primary" or "erogenous" masochism will be reserved to woman and that both her "constitution" and "social rules" will forbid her any sadistic way to work out these masochistic death drives. She can only "turn them around" or "turn them inward." The sadism of the anal-sadistic stage is also transformed, at a secondary level, into masochism: activity is turned into passivity, sadism is "turned back" from the "object" onto the "subject." Secondary masochism added to primary masochism—this is apparently the "destiny" of the death drives in woman, and they survive only because of their unalterably sexuate nature, through the erotization of this "masochism."

But further, in order to trans-form his death drives and the whole instinctual dualism, in order to use his life to ward off death for as long as it takes to choose a death, man will have to work on building up his ego. On raising his own tomb, if you like. This new detour along the road to death, through/for the construction of narcissistic monuments, involves pulling the libido back from the object onto the self and desexualizing it so it can carry out more sublimated activities. Now, if this ego is to be valuable, some "mirror"[36] is needed to reassure it and re-insure it of its value. Woman will be the foundation for this specular duplication, giving man back "his" image and repeating it as the "same." If an *other* image, an *other* mirror were to intervene, this inevitably would entail the risk of mortal crisis. Woman will therefore be this sameness—or at least its mirror image—and, in her role of mother, she will facilitate the repetition of the same, in contempt for her difference. Her own sexual difference. Moreover, through her "penis-envy," she will supply anything that might be lacking in this specula(riza)tion. Calling back, now and forever, that *remainder* that melts into the depths of the mirror, that sexual energy necessary to carry out the work. The work of death.

So "woman" can function as place—evanescent beyond, point of discharge—as well as time—eternal return, temporal detour—for the sub-

---

[36]A certain flat mirror would thus serve to desexualize drives and thereby work out funeral monuments for the "subject's" ego.

limation and, if possible, mastery of the work of death. She will also be the representative-representation (*Vorstellung-Repräsentanz*), in other words, of the death drives that cannot (or theoretically could not) be perceived without horror, that the eye (of) consciousness refuses to recognize. In a protective misprision that cannot be put aside without the failure of a certain gaze: which is the whole point of castration. Up to this point, *the main concepts of psychoanalysis, its theory, will have taken no account of woman's desire,* not even of "her" castration. For their ways are too narrowly derived from the history and the historicization of (so-called) male sexuality. From that process by which consciousness comes into being and woman remains the place for the inscription of repressions. All of which demands that, without knowing it, she should provide a basis for such fantasies as the amputation of her sex organ, and that the "anatomy" of her body should put up the security for reality. She provides irrefutable, because natural, proof that this is not a matter of the silent action of the death drives. She will therefore be despoiled, without recourse, of all valid, valuable images of her sex/organs, her body. She is condemned to "psychosis," or at best "hysteria," for lack—censorship? foreclusion? repression?—of a valid signifier for her "first" desire and for her sex/organs.

This doesn't mean that the question of castration isn't raised for woman but rather that it refers back in reality to the father's castration, including the father of psychoanalysis—to his fear, his refusal, his rejection, of an *other* sex. For if to castrate woman is to inscribe her in the law of the *same* desire, of *the desire for the same,* what exactly is "castration"? And what is the relationship of the agent of castration to the concept and its practice?

"Penis-Envy"

Waiting in Vain

The little girl, therefore, having seen the genital organs of the other sex, scorns all the pleasure that her own had afforded her and now has only one wish—to have a penis herself one day. And she does not "submit easily to the fact of being without a penis." On the contrary, "she believes . . . for improbably long years" in the possibility of possessing the male organ." And analysis can show that, at a period when knowledge of reality has long since rejected the fulfilment of the wish as unattainable, it persists in the unconscious and retains a considerable cathexis of energy." In fact "the wish to get the longed-for penis eventually may contribute to the motives that drive a mature woman to analysis."

Of course, let us not neglect the fact that the woman, the hysteric, is particularly liable to submission, to suggestion, to fabrication even, where the discourse-desire of the other is concerned. And that what she comes to say while in analysis will not be very different from what she is expected to say there. And if she didn't say it there, why should she bother to come? To this scene that is organized, also, by/for her "penis-envy." And what could an analyst make of a desire of hers that would not correspond to *his* wish? For the penis. He would be, Freud confides in us, quite helpless. Therefore, she will express and express again her greed for the male organ and perhaps she will get, from the analytic treatment of this "envy," "a capacity to carry on an intellectual profession," "a sublimated modification of this repressed wish."

An Indirect Sublimation

You must understand that the analytic scene will not solve "penis-envy" for woman, it will not free her from her condition as sexual proletarian, it will not help in interpreting the credit surplus given to this "sex/organ" of the man (father), but it will allow her—perhaps—to enter into the system of a discourse whose "sense," whose "meaning" is based exclusively on a phallic standard. "Penis-envy" would represent, would be the only effective representative of woman's desire to enter into symbolic exchange as a "subject" and raise woman from her status as a mere "commodity."[37] So, she will have to undergo treatment for this "envy" in order to achieve sublimation. Which means, here, paying the price of repression of the appetite for sexual potency so as to gain access to a discourse that denies woman any right on the exchange market. Woman can realize the "capacity to carry on an intellectual profession," once again, only by indirect means. The casting couch, or the analyst's couch!

For there is no way out of this "envy." For her in particular. "One cannot very well deny the importance of envy for the penis. You may take it as an instance of male injustice if I assert that envy and jealousy play an even greater part in the mental life of women than of men . . . but I am inclined to attribute their greater amount in women to this latter influence [i.e. of penis-envy]" (p. 125). Which in no way lays to rest the

---

[37]And as the analytic scene has not raised the question of woman's social and economic condition, the language of the hysteric will become a "commodity" that serves the (theoretical) exchanges between psychoanalysts.

question of "injustice" that was raised. Social injustice, obviously. For, once again, woman as such has no means of participating in so-called "spiritual" life (?), since she takes no part in working it out, in its "symbolization," its exchanges. This accounts for her grievance at being excluded as "subject" from a phallocentric scene upon which she can appear only if she accepts derision, guilt, and the loss of what they call, or he calls, her "femininity." In any case, only if she disavows, represses? or, rather perpetuates, the repression of what she herself might put forward as exchange values. Intellectuality only at the price of her female condition.

"Envy" or "Desire" for the Penis?

"Some analysts, however, have shown an inclination to depreciate the importance of this first instalment of penis-envy in the phallic phase. They are of the opinion that what we find of this attitude in women is in the main a secondary structure which has come about on the occasion of later conflicts by regression to this early infantile impulse. This, however, is a general question of *depth* psychology. In many *pathological*—or even *unusual*—instinctual attitudes (for instance, in all the *sexual perversions*) the question arises of how much of their strength is to be attributed to early infantile fixations and how much to the influence of later experiences and developments" (pp. 125–26). "In all cases," with regard to the matter in hand—which we find to be equated with a "pathological" attitude, or at least to something "unusual" like a "sexual perversion," even though this "envy" is stated to be indispensable in the making of a "normal woman"—"the infantile factor sets the pattern, but does not always determine the issue, though it often does. Precisely in the case of penis-envy I should argue decidedly in favour of the preponderance of the infantile factor" (p. 126).

How has Freud read, or understood, these psychoanalysts (male or female) who depreciate the importance of penis-envy? For it seems that they don't all consider it as coming "first."[38] Yet it is as a function of this archaism, of something that comes before another, that Freud answers them. What is at stake in this need to establish priority? Particularly since the "envy" that Freud now, for the purposes of argument, is claiming to be primary was earlier defined as coming after the girl's castration com-

---

[38]In actual fact, these men and women analysts discuss the little girl's early "desire" for the penis, which would suggest that she "discovers" her genitals long before Freud thinks. Cf. the articles of Horney, Klein and Jones on female sexuality cited in note 7.

plex. The little girl could not have felt this "envy" earlier on because, according to Freud himself, the difference between the sexes did not exist then, since the little girl was simply a little boy. She had a clitoris-penis. Therefore she could not have an "envy" for one in the sense Freud gives to the term until after the intervention of the castration complex.

Therefore let us turn the question around again. Is the primitive, or most primitive, character of "penis-envy" not an essential factor in establishing the *primacy of the male organ?* In making the phallus necessarily the archetype for sex? The primal sex? And making the penis the best representational equivalent of the Idea of sex? There can only be one desire: the desire to ensure dominion by greed, by appetite for appropriation. If anything were to contradict this desire—the little girl's pleasures, for example—the whole economy of sexual affects, and affectations, would have to be reinterpreted. And it is difficult to predict where a shift in the attribution of sexual powers might lead. But the misprisions needed to maintain the established order lead one to suspect that such an operation might take us far.

Arguments that premise the early onset of penis-envy to justify a belief in it are still heard within the field of analytic prolematics. Thus, woman's avidity for his sex organ supposedly means for man, among other things, a projection of his "primitive" oral instincts, of his wish to devour the mother's breast. And in this reminder of primary appetites, one might detect also the fear of having destroyed woman's sex, of having castrated her out of insatiable hunger, biting in an attempt to seize, incorporate, or eliminate something that is becoming elusive. Whence the guilt, the horror at the sight of the reality of these fantasies, which thereby become all-powerful, perhaps. And hence the terrible anxiety that *she,* the maternal-substitute, in retaliation or also moved by hunger, might do the same thing to his penis-breast.

Repression, or Inexorable Censorship

Be this as it may, when she sees the penis, when she compares—as if this were possible—her sex organ to the little boy's, the little girl is supposed to give up all her previous libidinal workings; her oral, sadistic-anal, and phallic instincts, her desire to bear the mother's child or give her a child, and her infantile masturbation. That whole economy would in some way be blotted out, forgotten, repressed—but by whom or what? how? from what motives of pleasure or displeasure?—or "converted" so that "penis-envy" might thus be validated as the basis of female sexuality from now on.

"We know how children react to their first impressions of the absence of a penis. They disavow the fact and believe that they *do* [Freud's italics] see a penis all the same. They gloss over the contradiction between observation and pre-conception by telling themselves that the penis *is still small and will grow bigger presently;* and they then slowly come to the emotionally significant conclusion that after all the penis *had at least been there before and been taken away afterwards.* The lack of a penis is regarded as a result of castration, and so now the child is faced with the task of coming to terms with castration in relation *to himself.*"[39] Why are these feelings, these representations, these defenses, attributed *also* to the little girl? She is supposed to experience her lack of penis as an "accomplished fact" that is presumably a punishment for her earlier (phallic-viril-clitoral) masturbations.[40] She believes that "it had at least been there before." She would refuse the facts, telling herself that "the penis is still small and will grow bigger presently," hoping against hope that her(?) wish will some day come true. Etc. All of which is a postulate of the phallic imperialism that will also lead the little girl to "turn away from her mother" and despise herself and all women since all lack a penis. "We know, too, to what a degree *depreciation* of women, *horror* of women, and a *disposition to homosexuality* are derived from the final conviction that women have no penis."[41] Or again: "two reactions . . . permanently determine the boy's relation to women: horror of the mutilated creature or triumphant contempt for her."[42] Or: "One thing that is left over in men from the influence of the Oedipus complex is a certain amount of disparagement in their attitude toward women, whom they regard as being castrated."[43]

Mimesis Imposed

Why make the little girl, the woman, fear, envy, hope, hate, reject, etc. in more or less the *same terms* as the little boy, the man? And why does she comply so readily? Because she is suggestible? Hysterical? But now we begin to be aware of the vicious circle. How could she be otherwise, even in those perversities which she stoops to in order to "please" and to live up to the "femininity" expected of her? How could she be anything but suggestible and hysterical when her sexual instincts have been castrated, her sexual feelings, representatives, and representa-

---

[39]"The Infantile Genital Organisation," *SE*, XIX:143–44.
[40]"The Dissolution of the Oedipus Complex," *SE*, XIX:177–79.
[41]"The Infantile Genital Organisation," p. 144.
[42]"Some Psychical Consequences of the Anatomical Distinction between the Sexes," *SE*, XIX:252.
[43]"Female Sexuality," *SE*, XXI:229.

tions forbidden? When the father forces her to accept that, while he alone can satisfy her and give her access to pleasure, he prefers the added sexual enjoyment to be derived from laying down the law, and therefore penalizes her for her (or his own?) "seduction fantasies"?

And anyway why would she not be "hysterical"? Since hysteria holds in reserve, in suspension/suffering, something in common with the mime that is a sine qua non of sexual pleasure. The problem is that the ludic mimicry, the fiction, the "make believe," the "let's pretend"—which, as we know, made the hysteric subject to all kinds of disbelief, oppression, and ridicule—are stopped short, impeded, *controlled by a master-signifier,* the Phallus, and by its representative(s). Emblem(s) not so much of interplay between the sexes as of power that masters and appropriates the relationship to the origin (of desire, "for example"). After that, the hysteria scenario, that privileged dramatization of feminine sexuality, is condemned as so many "bad" copies or gross caricatures of a "good," and valuable and valid, relationship to origin. Hysteria is stigmatized as a place where fantasies, ghosts, and shadows fester and must be unmasked, interpreted, brought back to the reality of a repetition, a reproduction, a representation that is congruent to, consistent with, the original. And, of course, someone will at this point cite the "initial trauma," the supposed origin of the "illness," but the game is all over by this time. And the question would rather be—to risk repetition—that woman's symbolization of her beginning, of the specificity of her relationship to the origin, has always already been erased, or is it repressed? by the economy that man seeks to put in place in order to resolve the problem of his primary cause. A problem to be solved by putting the Phallus at the beginning, and at the end. As the signifier of sexual potency and precedence, in the face of which there can only be "lack," "atrophy," "envy," "acting as if one had it," "pretending to be it or to have it," etc. But as the Phallus is never stated as *terminus, origin, and cause of desire,* there will be no possibility of interplay between two different modes of relationship to the origin, the primary, the desire for origin. With each modality comprising measure and folly. On the one hand the "serious role"—truth?—played out in a genealogy, a genetics, and on the other hand, copies, fantasies, reflections, semblances, specular anamorphoses, that will transform the part, the parts, even before they are produced, or reproduced. Now, under these conditions, one might have a relationship between the sexes, an enactment of sexual difference—which obviously precludes the predominance of one sex. But. . . . Between the "obsessive" on this side, who wants and demands and repeats, and turns around and around in his original desire, which he claims to master in order, finally, to establish his omnipotence, and the

60

"hysteric" on the other side, who drifts aimlessly, wanting nothing, no longer knowing her own mind or desire, acting "as if" or "as you like it," her body the only reminder of what has been . . . the game seems to have got off to a bad start. At best a mournful pleasure seems in store. Sadly repetitive, painstaking, or infinitely fragmenting things, rambling on with pauses only for explosions. Pleasure (?) full of histories but no possible historiography.

A Painful Way to Become a Woman

And the Father, Neutral and Benevolent, Washes His
Hands of the Matter

"The discovery that she is castrated is a turning point in a girl's growth. Three possible lines of development start from it: one leads to sexual inhibition or to neurosis, the second to change of character in the sense of a masculinity complex, the third, finally, to normal femininity" (p. 126).

"That is all I had to say to you about femininity. It is certainly incomplete and fragmentary and does not always sound friendly" (p. 135).

However, let us take a closer look. "The essential content of the first is as follows: the girl has hitherto lived *in a masculine way,* has been able to get pleasure by the excitation of her *clitoris* and has brought this activity into relation with her sexual desires *directed towards* her mother, which are often *active* ones" (p. 126). Reminder, then, of the little girl = little boy, clitoris = little penis equation. As for the fact that masturbation is simply an "active" process, one might demur. For the moment, however, let us take up the question of the "direction toward the mother" which Freud stresses. Why "toward the mother," rather than toward parental intercourse, which might affect the child and lead it to react and abreact through masturbation? And anyway, wouldn't masturbation be one method the boy or girl could use in trying to direct themselves away from the mother, to differentiate their (auto-)erotism from the instincts involved in the libidinal relationship to the mother? Which would mean that the mother, in fantasy and reality, would be the one to forbid onanism, as she is unwilling to allow this separation from her?

Be that as it may, it is striking to note the degree to which Freud holds the mother responsible for both the awakening and the suppression of sexual life. Notably in the case of the little girl. We have already seen that it was the mother who seductively aroused the first sexual feelings. "The

61

fact that the mother thus unavoidably initiates the child into the phallic phase is, I think, the reason why, in phantasies of *later* years, the father regularly appears as the sexual seducer."[44] The father, as we have already seen, cannot be the seducer. But again "her resentment at being prevented from free sexual activity plays a big part in her detachment from her mother. The same motive comes into operation again after puberty, when her mother takes up her duty of guarding her daughter's chastity."[45] In the same way, "a girl may later construe the fact of castration as a punishment for her masturbatory activity, and she will attribute the carrying out of this punishment to her father, but neither of these ideas can have been a *primary* one."[46] The father does not seduce or capture or repress his daughter's sexuality. He would only *secondarily* be the one to represent the castrating agent for her. In fact, if the girl turns toward her father, this is because she turns away from her mother in disillusion, and transfers, transports to her father her disappointed maternal cathexes. Very strange, this economy regulating the father-daughter relations! And it is odd that, in the whole adventure of female sexuality as described by Freud, the father makes his appearance only at the end and in such a dim, secondary, even "passive" role. With no desires, no instincts, no dealings, of any kind, in regard to his daughter. Neutral and benevolent. But why?

A (Female) A-sex?

Now, still with reference to the first of the three possible lines of development, "owing to the influence of penis-envy, [the little girl] loses her enjoyment in her phallic sexuality" (p. 126). In her sexuality, that is? For what sexuality, apart from the phallic, is she being offered? Were some other sexuality presented, or represented, the question of penis-envy—to pick one particularly symptomatic question—would certainly be less insistent. But in this deficiency, this latency of any happier solution, any other possible choice, "her self-love is mortified by the comparison with the boy's far superior equipment." Now we know about the enclitic relationship between narcissistic cathexes and sexual instincts.[47] Therefore "she renounces her masturbatory satisfaction from her clitoris, repudiates her love for her mother and at the same time not infrequently *represses a good part of her sexual trends in general*." It's not unreasonable. Under beneficium inventorii, she pays out only as much as the pressure of repression allows her. "No doubt her turning away from

---

[44]Ibid., p. 238.
[45]Ibid., p. 233.
[46]Ibid.
[47]Cf. for example the essay "Instincts and Their Vicissitudes," *SE*, xiv.

her mother does not occur all at once, for to begin with the girl regards her *castration* as an individual *misfortune,* and only gradually extends it to other females and finally to her mother as well. Her love was directed to her *phallic* mother [Freud's italics]; with the discovery that her mother is castrated it becomes possible to drop her as an object, so that the motives for hostility, which have long been accumulating, gain the upper hand. This means, therefore, that as a result of the discovery of women's lack of a penis they are *debased in value* for girls JUST AS they are for boys and later perhaps for men" ("Femininity," pp. 126–127).

So the little girl who has lost her narcissism and given up not only her so-called object cathexes but even her appetite for auto-erotism, is forced into a virtually total repression of her sexual instincts. A repression? A censorship? Prescribed by whom? By what? In whose interest? The only interest she could have would be that of trying to seduce the law-giving father. Which is forever relegated to the status of duly reproved "fantasies" and will in any case fail to resolve the question of how to displace the feelings cathected upon the mother. For whereas the little boy's first love object was his mother and "she remains so until she is replaced by someone who resembles her or is derived from her";[48] whereas throughout his life man remains fixated to his "primary object," his mother, or wife-mother; and whereas he can go on loving and desiring with the same sex organ the same "object," his "primary" object, everything is quite different for the little girl since she cannot escape the upsurge of sexual *heterogeneity*. When Freud solves this problem by insisting that the girl has always been a boy, and that her femininity is characterized by "penis-envy," he is obviously defending his male point of view and his wish to perpetuate sexual homogeneity: a non-sex-organ, a castrated sex/organ, or "penis-envy," does not constitute a sexual heterogene but rather represents a type of negativity that sustains and confirms the homogeneity of masculine desire.

Is the Oedipus Complex Universal or Not?

As for the mother-daughter relationship, Freud will admit in his old age—and curiously also *at the end* of the text, of this text written at the end of his life—"that the *duration* [Freud's italics] of this attachment had also been greatly underestimated," "that a number of women remain arrested in their original attachment to their mother and never achieve a true change-over towards men," that "the pre-Oedipus phase in women gains an importance which we have not attributed to it hitherto," and *"we must retract the universality of the thesis that the Oedipus complex is the*

---

[48]"Female Sexuality," p. 228.

nucleus of all neuroses." Notably because he suspects that "this phase of attachment to the mother is especially intimately related to the aetiology of *hysteria*." But "everything in the sphere of this first attachment to the mother seemed to me so difficult to grasp in analysis—so grey with age and shadowy and almost impossible to revivify—that it was as if it had succumbed to an especially inexorable repression." "Our insight into this early, pre-Oedipus, phase in girls comes to as a *surprise,* like the *discovery,* in another field [but is it really another?] of the *Minoan-My-ceanaean civilization behind the civilization of Greece."*[49] It is as if, finally, so late on,—perhaps because he was close to *his* death—and with the wish for "scientific honesty" that is never to be doubted in him, Freud had an inkling that woman's sexuality was indeed foreign to all that history. To history in general? That it remained covered up—repressed?—by the shape of this Greek civilization and that it would take an archaeologist, such as Freud was also, to excavate deeper into the earth, to where the cultural vestiges lie concealed, and to rediscover there a more archaic arche behind that beginning represented by Greece, and the concept of origin which Greece set in place.

Whatever we make of these belated insights,[50] Freud continues, elsewhere, to interpret and to prescribe female development in terms of that history and, notably, its conceptual economy. As, and in the same way as, it is certainly within that history that woman had to "repress a good part of her sexual trends," submit everything related to her primary relationships to a "especially inexorable repression," "almost impossible to revivify," which leaves that first bond to the mother so "grey with age," "so difficult to grasp in analysis." This prepetuates woman's "hysteria," even her "paranoia,"[51] which cannot be "sublimated" or "sublated" by working out a theory since theory will always already have excluded her appearance as a sexuate female subject. So woman's hysteria and paranoia cannot be interpreted without recourse to a historic

[49]Need I stress that this can all be understood: it is not only in a signifying economy of the alphabetic kind that women's sexuality will be deciphered. Any more than the mechanisms of the unconscious will be interpeted in such a way. This last point is in fact made very clearly by Freud. All the quotations in this paragraph are from "Female Sexuality," pp. 225–27.

[50]The insights in this analytic work on woman were in fact imposed upon him by certain female colleagues, whose names "since its subject is woman, I will venture on this occasion to mention" ("Femininity," p. 130) and whose *empirical* contributions he appreciated insofar as they advance his *theory*. These women analysts "have been able to perceive these facts more easily and clearly because they were helped in dealing with those under their treatment by the transference to a suitable mother-substitute," whereas women analyzed by Freud "were able to cling to the very attachment to the father in which they had taken refuge from the early phase that was in question" ("Female Sexuality," pp. 227 and 226.)

[51]"Female Sexuality," p. 227.

process whose re-mark by the libidinal dramatization acted out in the "family" is ever and always a result of, and an agent of, that "History."[52]

Free Association on Onanism

There follows what could be termed an aside—or a more or less rationalized free association—on masturbation. This parenthetic quality could be shown with the following punctuation: "As a result of the discovery of women's lack of a penis they are debased in value for girls just as they are for boys and later perhaps for men.

[You all know the immense aetiological importance attributed by our neurotic patients to their masturbation. They make it responsible for all their troubles, and we have the greatest difficulty in persuading them that they are mistaken. In fact, however, we ought to admit to them that they are right, for masturbation is the executive agent of infantile sexuality, from the faulty development of which they are indeed suffering. . . . I wish I might have an opportunity some time of explaining to you at length how important all the factual details of early masturbation become for the individual's subsequent neurosis or character: whether or not it was discovered, how the parents struggled against it or permitted it, or whether he succeeded in suppressing it himself. . . . But I am on the whole glad that I need not do this. It would be a hard and *tedious* task and at the end of it you would put me in an *embarrassing situation* by quite certainly asking me to give you some practical advice as to how a parent or educator should deal with the masturbation of small children. From the development of girls, which is what my present lecture is concerned with, I can give you an example of a child herself trying to get free from masturbating. She does not always succeed in this. If envy for the penis has provoked a powerful impulse against clitoridal masturbation but this nevertheless refuses to give way, a violent struggle for liberation ensues in which the girl, as it were, herself takes over the role of her deposed mother and gives expression to her entire dissatisfaction with her inferior clitoris in her efforts against obtaining satisfaction from it. Many years later, when her masturbatory activity has long since been suppressed, an interest still persists which we must interpret as a defence against a temptation that is still dreaded. . . . Disposing of early infantile masturbation is truly no easy or indifferent business.]" [Pp. 127–28]

Which can be understood as saying: if woman is castrated, devalued as a result of her "lack of phallus," what libidinal cathexis is the male

---

[52]The form of the "family romance," both in its impact upon psychoanalytic theory and practice and in its "literary" enactment, now as ever abets this same history.

neurotic left with (the case of the female neurotic is more complex, as we have seen and shall see) except an onanism that is more or less deferred, differentiated, possibly even "sublimated," into all sorts of auto. . . . or homo. . . ?

A Very Black Sexuality?

Symptoms Almost Like Those of Melancholia

For the little girl it is quite different. Unlike the little boy—"who exhibits, therefore, two psychologically distinct ties: a straightforward [?] sexual object-cathexis towards his mother and an identification with his father which takes him as his model"[53]—the little girl takes her mother as her first object of love and also as her privileged identificatory reference point for her "ego" as well as for her sex. In point of fact, if all the implications of Freud's discourse were followed through, after the little girl discovers her own castration and that of her mother—her "object," the narcissistic representative of all her instincts—she would have no recourse other than melancholia.

And if you reread "Mourning and Melancholia" in this perspective,[54] you will be struck by the way the libidinal economy of the little girl, after she finds out that both she and her mother are castrated, crosschecks with the symptoms of melancholia:

—*profoundly painful dejection,* which can be diagnosed by the absence of any libidinal activity and by the loss of interest in masturbation that occurs when the previously cathected organ and object are devalued.

—*abrogation of interest in the outside world,* which, in the case of the little girl, takes the form of a faltering effort to master the external world. The latter is perpetuated in women's "weaker social interests" ("Femininity," p. 134) and their "few contributions to the discoveries and inventions in the history of civilization" (p. 132).

—*loss of the capacity for love,* which leads the little girl to "turn away from her mother" and indeed from all women, herself included. Her desire for her father would in no way imply "love": "the wish with which the girl turns to her father is no doubt originally the wish for the penis which her

[53]"Group Psychology and the Analysis of the Ego," ch. 7, "Identification," *SE,* XVIII:105.
[54]*SE,* XIV:243–58. (Page references to "Mourning and Melancholia"—referred to as MM—will be given in the text—Tr.)

mother has refused her and which she now expects from her father" (p. 128). So there is nothing here but envy, jealousy, greed. . . .

—*inhibition of all activity:* "Passivity now has the upper hand" (p. 128). "The transition to the father-object is accomplished with the help of the passive trends in so far as they have escaped the catastrophe," for "when the small girl represses her previous masculinity a considerable portion of her sexual trends in general is permanently injured too."[55] "It is our impression that more constraint has been applied to the libido when it is pressed into the service of the feminine function" (p. 131), and "the comparatively lesser strength of the sadistic contribution to her sexual instinct, which we may no doubt connect with *the stunted growth* of her penis, makes it easier in her case for the direct sexual trends to be transformed into aim-inhibited trends of an affectionate kind."[56]

—*fall in self-esteem,* which, for the little girl, signals the end of the "phallic phase" and the entry into the Oedipus complex. "After the girl has discovered that her genitals are unsatisfactory," "her self-love is mortified by the comparison with the boy's far superior equipment." She is a "mutilated creature" who, after she "becomes aware of the wound to her narcissism . . . develops, like a scar, a sense of inferiority." "She acknowledges the fact of her castration and with it, too, the superiority of the male and her own inferiority."[57]

A Setback She Cannot Mourn

This disturbance of the little girl's self-esteem after she discovers she is castrated is something Freud places great stress on. According to him, it will trigger all the other psychic modifications, especially when the little girl learns that her "misfortune" is shared by her mother, by all women. Now this is the same symptom that he uses to distinguish "melancholia" from "mourning." One may already note, as a consequence, that the little girl's separation from her mother, and from her sex, cannot be worked through by mourning.

All the more because—another difference from mourning—in melancholia "the object has not perhaps actually died, but has become lost as an object of love" and more especially because "one cannot see clearly what it is that has been lost, and it is all the more reasonable to suppose that the patient cannot consciously perceive what he has lost either. This, indeed, might be so even when the patient is aware of the loss which has given rise to his melancholia, but only in the sense that he knows *whom*

[55]"Female Sexuality," p. 239.
[56]"Dissolution of the Oedipus Complex," *SE,* XIX:179.
[57]These phrases can be found in "Femininity," in "Female Sexuality," and in "Some Psychical Consequences of the Anatomical Distinctions between the Sexes."

he has lost but not *what* [Freud's italics] he has lost in him. This would suggest that melancholia is in some way related to an object-loss which is withdrawn from consciousness" (MM, p. 245). The little girl, obviously, does not know *what* she is losing in discovering her "castration" or in the "catastrophe" of her relationship first with her mother and subsequently with other women. She has then no *consciousness* of her sexual impulses, of her libidinal economy and, more particularly, of her original desire and her desire for origin. In more ways than one, it is really a question for her of a "loss" that radically escapes any representation. Whence the impossibility of "mourning" it. "The efforts to detach the libido are made in this same system, but in it nothing hinders these processes from proceeding in the normal way through the Pcs to consciousness. This way is blocked for the work of melancholia, owing perhaps to a number of causes or a combination of them" (MM, p. 257). Thus "in melancholia . . . countless separate struggles are carried on over the object in which *love* and *hate* contend with each other; the one seeks to detach the libido from the object, the other to maintain this position of the libido against the assault. The location of these separate struggles cannot be assigned to any system but the *Ucs,* the region of memory-traces of *things* (as contrasted with *word*-cathexes)" (Freud's italics; pp. 256–57). Now the girl's relationship with her mother is not lacking in ambivalence and becomes even more complicated when the little girl realizes that the phallic mother to whom—according to Freud—she addressed her love, is in fact castrated. This devaluation of the mother accompanies or follows on the devaluation of the little girl's own sex organ. Thus in her case the relationship to the (lost) object is not simple, but complicated by conflict and ambivalence that remain unconscious. It should be added that no language, no system of representations, will replace, or assist, this "unconsciousness" in which is grounded the girl's conflictual relationship to her mother and to her sex/organ. Which may result in their being "remembered" in the form of "somatic affections" that are characteristic of melancholia? And also, of course, of hysteria. . . .

But *the "loss" suffered by the little girl also affects the "ego."* As in melancholia. The little boy is narcissized, ego-ized by his penis—since the penis is valued on the sexual market and is overrated culturally because it can be seen, specularized, and fetishized—but this is not true for the little girl's sex organ(s). What is more, mother, whom the little girl is identifying with and using to build her ego, suffers from the same misfortune. Thus, in the ordeal of castration as "accomplished fact," the little girl's ego suffers, helplessly, a defeat, a wound, whose effects are to be made out in the broad outlines of melancholia. For example, in the patient's "dissatisfaction with the self on moral grounds," his plaints with regard to his "bodily infirmity, ugliness, weakness, social inferiority." But all the same, and here one should refer to Freud's writings on female sexuality, "they are far from evincing towards those around them the attitude of humility and submission that would alone befit such worthless people. On the contrary, they make the greatest nuisance of themselves and always seem as though they feel slighted and had been treated with great injustice," presenting "a mental constellation of revolt" (MM, p. 248).

The whole symptomology of melancholia could be explained thus: "An object-choice, an attachment of the libido to a particular person, had at one time existed; then, owing to a real slight or disappointment coming from this loved person, the object-relationship was shattered. The result was not the normal one of a withdrawal of the libido from this object and a displacement of it to a new one, but something different, for whose coming-about various conditions seem to be necessary. The object-cathexis proved to have little power of resistance and was brought to an end. But the free libido was not displaced on to another object; it was withdrawn into the ego. There, however, it was not employed in any unspecified way, but served to establish an *identification* [Freud's italics] of the ego with the abandoned object. Thus the *shadow* of the object fell upon the ego, and the latter could henceforth be judged by a special agency, as though it were an object, *the forsaken object.* In this way an object-loss was transformed into an *ego-loss,* and the conflict between the ego and the loved person into a cleavage between the critical faculty of the ego and the ego as altered by identification [with the castrated mother, woman, little girl]. One or two things may be directly inferred with regard to the preconditions and effects of such a process as this. On the one hand, a strong fixation to the love-object must have been present; on the other hand, in contradiction to this, the object-cathexis must have had little power of resistance. . . . The *narcissistic identification with the object then becomes a substitute for the erotic cathexis.* . . . We have elsewhere shown that identification is a preliminary stage of object-choice, that it is the first way—and one that is expressed in ambivalent fashion—in which the ego picks out an object. The ego wants to incorporate this object into itself, and in accordance with the oral or cannibalistic phase of libidinal development in which it is, it wants to do so by devouring it." This would account for "the refusal of nourishment met with in severe forms of melancholia" (MM, pp. 249–50).

69

Consider, in this regard, that anorexia is so specifically a female symptom that it can be correlated with the girl's inability to accept her sexual "destiny" and can be seen as a sort of desperate rejection of the sexual blossoming to which she is fated. More generally, one may cite here the lack of sexual appetite attributed to women, often correctly, and also the "oral" use she makes of her sex. One of the characteristic traits of melancholia is in fact "this regression from object-cathexis to the still narcissistic oral phase of the libido" (MM, p. 250).

That Open Wound That Draws Everything to Itself

As for the factors that produce the state of melancholy, they "include all those situations of being *slighted, neglected or disappointed* which can import opposed feelings of love and hate into the relationship or reinforce an already existing ambivalence" (MM, p. 251). "As regards one particular striking feature of melancholia that we have mentioned (MM, p. 248), the prominence of the fear of becoming poor, it seems plausible to suppose that it is derived from anal erotism which has been torn out of its context and altered in a regressive sense" (MM, p. 252). "The complex of melancholia behaves like an *open wound,* drawing to itself cathetic energy—which in the transference neuroses we have called anti-cathexes—from all directions, and emptying the ego until it is totally impoverished" (MM, p. 253). All these quotations from "Mourning and Melancholia" have to be set against the statements about the "normal" development of women, and particularly about the ways her "castration complex" affects the little girl.

Let us add that the *moral sanction* that is of critical importance in the process of malancholia also takes *specific forms in that state.* It is not exerted against "objectionable impulses that remained outside the ego" as in obsessional neuroses; "in melancholia the object to which the superego's wrath applies has been taken into the ego by identification:"[58] the object of wrath being the castrated mother, or woman-object. The super-ego would represent the "paternal" figure, "providence," "fate," which as—unconscious?—agents and critical sanctions of that operation, make stern judgments about woman's sexual "destiny." According to Freud's ideas on the girl's pre-Oedipus, this moral sanction could also be traced back to the little boy that the little girl once was, a little boy who valued "his" sex/organ and "his" masculine pleasures and who mercilessly condemns "his" formation or transformation into a girl. This

[58] *The Ego and the Id*, ch. 5, "The Dependent Relationships of the Ego," *SE*, XIX:51.

might help account for female masochism and the way woman's sadistic and hostile instincts are turned back upon herself. . . .

That Necessary Remainder: Hysteria

In fact the little girl will not choose melancholia as her privileged form of withdrawal. She probably does not have a capacity for narcissism great enough to allow her to fall back on melancholia, and that capacity is too depleted to build up such a complex defense against anxiety and the "catastrophe" brought upon her by the "accomplished fact" of castration. The economy of female narcissism and the fragility of the girl's or the woman's ego make it impossible for the melancholic syndrome to establish a firm and dominant foundation. This is not to say that the sexuality of this "*dark* continent" will not show a good number of the symptoms of melancholia. But they will be scattered about rather than organized in a coherent and permanent manner. The nonsymbolization of her desire for origin, of her relationship to her mother, and of her libido acts as a constant appeal to polymorphic regressions (be they melancholic, maniacal, schizophrenic, paranoiac . . .). She functions as a *hole*—that is where we would place it at its point of greatest efficiency, even in its implications of phobia, for man too—in the elaboration of imaginary and symbolic processes. But this fault, this deficiency, this "hole," inevitably affords woman too few figurations, images, or representations by which to represent herself. It is not that she lacks some "master signifier" or that none is imposed upon her, but rather that access to a signifying economy, to the coining of signifiers, is difficult or even impossible for her because she remains an outsider, herself (a) subject to their norms. She borrows signifiers but cannot make her mark, or re-mark upon them. Which all surely keeps her deficient, empty, lacking, in a way that could be labeled "psychotic": a *latent* but not actual psychosis, for want of a practical signifying system.

Or it could be that woman's relationship to auto-erotism is too weakened for her to be allowed simply to fall back on certain "psychotic" positions, Or, could it even be that her "libido" is too powerful to get satisfaction that way?—let's keep in mind the little girl's "precociousness," her "incredible phallic activity" established by "some assured observations" of Jeanne Lampl de Groot.

So her instincts are, in a way, in abeyance, in limbo, in vacuo: not cathected, really, in the construction of a psychosis, nor in auto-erotism, nor in the development of narcissism, nor in the desire of love for her first object, nor in the appropriation, the possession (even if affected by the detour of sublimation) of her own sexuality, of her sex organs, etc. *Hysteria is all she has left.* Is it hysterical psychosis? Or neurosis? As a result of suspension, within a suspension, of the economy of her primal instincts, she will do "as" she is asked. But this "as" or "as if" is not ludic, not under her control, though sometimes it seems that way and is, in some measure, a foretaste of what the "play" between the sexes might be. But here the game is controlled—as we have already seen—by the Phallus's mastery of the sexual economy. And woman will play it with the ground rule that the phallus is to be equated with the appropriation of the desire (for) origin. Yet the play we are envisaging would exclude any relationship of mastery to origin: any master signifier for the desire of origin or the origin of desire. And hysterical miming will be the little girl's or the woman's effort to save her sexuality from total repression and destruction. She will keep up that effort with an "activity" that is, basically, quite as amazing as her "phallic activity." Since the suffering of her body and her demand for sexual unsatisfaction (?) are reminders of all that is latent in her sexual instincts. One can argue, of course, that this effort and this suffering, this slavery, are the price woman pays *for refusing to face death.* At work, for example, in representation, symbolization, sublimation. But in history, as defined so far, there can be no question of that death for her. She is always specularized and specula(riza)ble. Coming to terms with death in that way is quite alien to her. The choice she faces would be between censoring her instincts completely—which would lead to death—or treating them as, converting them into, hysteria. Actually, there is no real alternative. The two operations entail each other.

The little girl will thus "turn" into a woman, "turn" to "normal" femininity. Which will be recognized as such when the "repression" following upon the discovery of her castration "is not too great." "Turning" into a woman, the "inception" of femininity, assume that the little girl "renounces her phallic activity," that "passivity has the upper hand," and that "the girl's turning to her father is accomplished." "The wish with which the girl turns to her father is no doubt *originally the wish for the penis* that her mother has refused her and that she now expects from her father." Not a trace, in this "development," of a desire for female pleasure. The girl's only objective in the formation of femininity, the only "sufficient reason" that could decide her to become a (so-called) woman, would be that thereby she appropriated in her turn the instrument of sexual pleasure, and possessed—whether by imitation, replica, or duplication—the sex organ that seems to hold the monopoly on sexu-

72

al use as well as the power to determine the value of sexual exchange. But in doing so, what extra pleasure she gives to the father, the man-father, who is thus (re)assured of having the penis! He will even have the leisure to invest in such lofty pursuits as making laws since *she,* at least, is upholding the value of the penis, maintaining its stock rating, keeping it from overspending in different specula(riza)tions. In an emergency, should it prove necessary, she will represent the penis. Her "phallicized" body will support its currency, prop it up, defend its exchange rate, guarantee its stock-holdings, while the father, the man, is busy with other investments. She is appointed to collect hommage and bring it back to its rightful owner.

The Penis = the Father's Child

The Primacy of Anal Erotism

"The feminine situation is only established, however, if the wish for a penis is replaced by one for a baby, if, that is, a baby *takes the place* of a penis in accordance with an ancient symbolic equivalence" ("Feminini-ty," p. 128). Whatever system of credit, or even usury, this formula has survived upon, perhaps one may still draw some profit from it. Though in this instance, it needs to be completed and its implications laid out: "Often enough in her combined picture of a 'baby from her father' the emphasis is laid on the baby and her father left unstressed."[59] But the baby-penis equivalence shows that "the ancient masculine wish for the possession of a penis is still faintly visible through the femininity now achieved" (p. 128).

(1) So, if the little girl, the woman, is to become "fully" a woman, the desire for a child must replace the wish to have a penis. The urge to procreate thus comes to supplant all the "other" phallic appetites. *The desire to have a child from the father takes the place of and excludes any possibility of her seeking out other modes of sexual relationship with the father, or with the father of the child.* This must be so if femininity is to be "normal" or "established." Woman has to want the penis purely and simply as the agent of (re)*production*—an ejaculator—and her seductive powers must be directed toward the child-penis, the *product* of copulation, if "sexual function" is to correspond exactly to the definition given by Freud.

---

[59](The *Standard Edition* differs significantly here from the French quoted by LI. "La femme, en désirant avoir un enfant, pense plus souvent à celui-ci qu'au père, dès lors relégué au second plan": "The woman, as she desires to have a child, thinks more often of it than of the father, who is henceforth pushed into the background."—Tr.)

Thus, "femininity" fades away before maternity, is absorbed into maternity: just possibly, there is even no more "penis-envy," as that was the ambiguous formulation of a trace of a desire for sexual pleasure. Of a memory of onanism? Of when she had something "like" a penis and could get some satisfaction from it. Which led to a wish to again "have something like it too." A bigger something, perhaps? But this hope-memory must fade, when confronted with the serious business of *(re)production.*

(2) That said, if the emblem of the phallus, the penis, is to be always present, re-presented in the object of desire, happiness is complete only if "the baby is a *little boy* who brings the longed-for penis with him" (p. 128).

(3) The child—and it is ardently hoped it will be a boy—appears merely to be a *penis-product and penis-substitute.* The contribution of woman's germ cells, the part played by her sex organs, her body, in the formation of the child, are, in this explanation of the sexual evolution of "femininity," totally ignored.

(4) This boy child is the sign of the seed's immortality, of the fact that the properties of the sperm have won out over those of the ovum. Thus he guarantees the father's power to reproduce and represent himself, and to perpetuate his gender and his species. What is more, the son, as heir to the name, ensures that the patrimony will not be squandered. And as heir, he also enriches the "house" by one more member.

(5) This conception of the "child" proves, on analysis, to derive from *anal erotism's primacy* over what is called genital sexuality. The child forms part of a series of substitutions: feces-penis-child. The penis, then the child, come to replace the stools: "The concepts *faeces* (money, gift), *baby* and *penis* [Freud's italics] are ill-distinguished from one another and are easily interchangeable."[60] The vagina—and even the womb? of which, paradoxically, no mention is made in this context—functions like the anus, rectum, and intestines. In fact "interest in the vagina, which awakens later, is also essentially of anal-erotic origin. This is not to be wondered at, for the vagina itself, to borrow an apt phrase from Lou Andreas Salome (1916) is 'taken on lease' from the rectum."[61]

Those Party to a Certain Lease

We need to look more closely at the two parties to this lease, at the rent paid, at who is endorsing the contract, at how long the lease is meant to

---

[60]"On Transformation of Instinct as Exemplified in Anal Erotism," *SE,* xvii:128.
[61]*New Introductory Lectures on Psychoanalysis,* Lecture xxxii, "Anxiety and Instinctual Life," *SE,* xxii:101.

run, etc. In this economy, woman's job is to tend the seed man "gives" her, to watch over the interests of this "gift" deposited with her and to return it to its owner in due course. The penis (stool), the sperm (seed-gift), the child (gift), all make up an anal symbolic from which there is no escape. One wonders, ultimately, if the standard underpinning the system is the penis? The sperm? Or "gold"? Values waver, falter, and the most productive, the most easily representable as (re)productive seems necessarily to carry the day. But, in fact, all these "equivalents" collect interest on the capital invested in the feces, which would remain the standard of value. As for woman, she will be the receptacle for the sperm (gift) injected by the penis (stool) and she forces the child (feces) out through the vagina (rectum). Thus she is apparently party to anal erotism. But except for her pregnancy, when she makes matter grow within her so as to have more jouissance after her delivery (?), woman's role seems to require only that she detach herself from the anal "object": the gift-child, just as she is required to give up the "fecal column" after coitus. Repeating, thus, her separation from the feces. But without pleasure. For the instincts correlated with anal erotism, instincts of aggression and narcissistic retention, are not allowed to her. She is not able to "decide between a narcissistic and an object-loving attitude . . . part obediently with (her) faeces, 'sacrifice' them to (her) love or else retain them for purposes of auto-erotic satisfaction and later as a means of asserting (her) own will." No "narcissistic clinging to anal erotism" for her.[62] In fact, if the penis re-presents the fecal mass, she has always already been "cut off" from it. Which would justify in her case "the comparatively lesser strength of the sadistic contribution to her sexual instinct . . . and make it easier . . . for the direct sexual trends to be transformed into aim-inhibited trends of an affectionate kind."[63] Everything is for the best: woman enters into the (re)production line with not the slightest desire to retain any auto-erotic satisfaction, any narcissism, any affirmation of her own will, any wish to capitalize upon her products. The work of gestation, of childbirth, of breast-feeding, of mothering, will be carried out with "not directly sexual trends" but with "aim-inhibited trends of an affectionate kind." Her only payment will be the, unconscious, satisfaction of finally possessing (?) a penis-equivalent. But Freud "had to face the problem of the later history of the anal-erotic instinctual impulses"—impulses he tells us elsewhere are very strong in the pre-Oedipus stage. And we still have to face that problem today.

---

[62]"On Transformation of Instincts as Exemplified in Anal Erotism," p. 130.
[63]"The Dissolution of the Oedipus Complex," *SE,* xix:179.

Woman Is/and Also Mother

(6) The conception and birth of the child repeat, reproduce, the question of beginnings. Of the relationship of woman—like and unlike man—to her beginning, to the time when her economy of the primal was established. Having a child could, conceivably, enable woman to work out her problems of "identification" with her mother, her first love "object," could insert woman into a specific economy that was both genealogical and specular. In this way, a woman becoming a mother will be *the Mother,* totally identified with maternity through a kind of murder of *her own mother* and through an obliteration of that relationship of *woman* to maternity that leaves her, for the present, as the place holder (*lieu-tenant*) of origin: phallic earth-mother. Or again she will be inscribed or will inscribe herself in this way, in an in-finite genealogical process/trial, an open count of the discount of origin: whereby she will be "like" her mother but not in the same "place," not corresponding to the same point on the number line. She will be her mother and yet not her mother, nor her daughter as mother, *with no closure of the circle or the spiral of identity.* Endlessly encircling the speculum of a primal place. Passing from inside to outside without ever, simply, being resolved, resorbed, reflected. And with this extra turn, this extra return, this additional twist, both open and closed, imprinted by each new "birth"—that is and is not identified with her mother, with maternity—she would no doubt be able to "play" her role of mother without being totally assimilated by it. In this way provision would be made for the subsistence of her female sexual desire.

But still it would be essential not to assign her simply to this function of maternity. Man would have to want more than to find his mother again and reproduce himself. More even than to provide her with the phallus that he will be also, in the person of his son. Man would have to be not too horrified and disgusted by his wife, his mother, as a "castrated" creature. Whence his need to go in for anal, fetishistic over-cathexis of his organ, and flight into real or fantasy homosexuality. The man-father would have to agree to share the holdings in sexual commerce, and especially in (re)productive potency. Etc.

All such unrealized "conditions" leave no past for sexual pleasure—no future either, if one sticks with Freudian theories. Sexual pleasure would be a point both pivotal and referential always already both "displaced" and "displacing," a re-mark both counted and counting, of *two* specific relationships to the "materiality" of beginnings—conception, birth— and to their primal images, shadows, fantasies or representations of origin. Two but obviously not two as the *sum of an addition:* nor two halves, two equal fractions, *the quotient of a division.* With each of these nonunits taking over from two like and unlike two couples. Indefinitely.

Forbidden Games

The specular conditions do not work in such a way as to allow a play of couples: this is Freud's refrain throughout this text and others. The castration of woman, penis-envy, hatred of the mother, the little girl's despisal and rejection of her sex/organ, the end of her (masculine) auto-erotism that results, the failure to explain the evolution of her anal erotism—except in terms of a "stunted penis"—are all signs that the appropriation of the specular, or speculative, process/trial is a victory for (so-called) masculine sexuality. They are signs of a specular process/trial which favors a *flat mirror* as most apt to capture the image, the representation, the auto-representation. This domination excludes the little girl from any discovery of the economy of her relationships with her mother, and with maternity. And Freud will deny that her attempt at "identification" with the mother—let us keep this term though we know already *that it cannot be a matter here of identity or nonidentity*[64]—could be an "expression," a stage in the evolution of what he labels "femininity." "It has not escaped us that the girl has wished for a baby earlier, in the undisturbed phallic phase: that, of course, was the meaning of her playing with dolls. But that play was not in fact an expression of her femininity; it served as an identification with her mother with the intention of substituting activity for passivity. *She* [Freud's italics] was playing the part of her mother and the doll was herself: now she could do with the baby everything that her mother used to do with her" (p. 128). One could obviously point out that a game—even of dolls—is never simply active or passive but rather frustrates that opposition by the economy of repetition that it puts "into play." And in this "game" of dolls, the little girl plays out the possibility of acting "like" her mother, "as if" she were the/her mother. A certain ludic potential would open up for her as regards maternity and mothering by means of this mimed rehearsal, repetition, re-presentation of her relationship to beginnings and to reproduction. But representing *herself* "as" mother, the game of maternity and mothering, is not an expression of femininity in Freud's opinion. To pretend, to act out, a relationship with the mother, with the maternal function, in Freud's opinion, is not feminine. No more feminine, for that

---

[64]It is because the female's relationship to the maternal, and indeed to itself, is so strange that the law of the identity principle might exemplarily come to question the reason at the basis of its value.

matter, than to represent oneself "as" a doll. To play with a representation of the self. *No fiction, no mimetic game, is allowed the little girl if it involves herself or her relationship to (re)production.*[65] Such games are "phallic."

On the other hand, the game with the doll-child that reveals the desire for the penis and the expectation of a child from the father is labeled "good," suitable for the "normal" evolution of femininity. Thus, playing with dolls will be either helpful or harmful to becoming a woman— "good" or "bad"—according to what it tries to act out. If the relationship to the penis, privileged representative of the phallus, is in control, if the doll-child "mimes" the penis-child, recalls the (re)production of the penis-child, then one is witnessing a true expression of femininity. But if in play the doll-child mimes the little girl, if in acting "like" the mother it mimes the process assigning the little girl the maternal or mothering role, then the doll-child behaves like a small male. The girl, let us repeat, has no right to play in any manner whatever with any representation of her beginning, no specific mimicry of origin is available to her: she must inscribe herself in the masculine, phallic way of relating to origin, that involves repetition, representation, reproduction. And this is meant to be "the most powerful feminine wish."

Hence "her happiness is great if later on this wish for a baby finds fulfilment in reality, and quite especially so if the baby is a little boy who brings the longed-for penis with him." What happiness indeed for the father, who recognizes in this boy-child, this son, his own likeness. The father is thus re-produced, re-presented, brought into the world again, mothered, desired all over again, through his wife who has become again, and more than ever, his mother. Here is the womb in which he may reproduce (himself) the re-producer. What a triumphant revenge for the anxieties of an Oedipus who *sees himself coming out* (*again*) from a womb he has himself fertilized. In this way he would close the phallic circuit and circularity, and verify his power to endow the woman-mother with a child-phallus—identical to himself—by means of a sex organ that is fetishized most effectively by woman's own "penis-envy."

The Hymen of Oedipus, Father and Son

Clearly he runs the risk that the story might go on and that this mother he has himself remade may prefer his "image" and surrender to the desire of the new Oedipus. Does the Oedipus-father lose his royalty thereby? Or does the parental strategy become more and more complex? But it is allowed, even desired. At least by the woman who prefers,

---

[65]Her assignment in fact is to re-produce the Phallus, even in its representation as penis. And a *second* copy of the original is always a "bad" copy.

Freud states, to give birth to a son rather than to a daughter. Woman is said to get more pleasure from reproduction of/for/by an other than from one that would bring her, in the imaginary or the imagination, more directly into play. She would find no satisfaction at all in re-producing herself. Her pleasure would be always already a function of her rejection, refusal of the self. . . . Therefore trying to re-present her-self, as a mother also, by playing the mommy with the doll-child would supposedly offer nothing femininely pleasurable. Whereas, being (re)made by the desire of Oedipus would be the "most powerful femi-nine wish." But who will be Oedipus? The father? Or the son? As she is forbidden all dealings with representations, as she does not understand very much—they say—about what is at stake metaphorically, the (so-called) real son is bound to win out. So where does that leave Oedipus-father? He will continue to repeat his little story with one more twist in the metaphorical spiral: his real mother is forbidden; his wife, who is like his mother, is allowed; she, "like" his mother, is the real mother of a son, his son, who is "like" him, and the two of them reenact for him, in front of him, the eternally displaced scene. The game goes on for ever and ever, sex is sublated for the eternity of its self-identity. While the "emphasis is laid on the baby" and the father is left "unstressed." But no matter. The son is remade by the father in his own likeness and woman is thereby inscribed in an economic calculus she has no control over. The proof of this is that "the ancient masculine wish for the possession of a penis is still faintly visible through the femininity now achieved." And besides, should we not "recognise this wish for a penis as being *par excellence* a feminine one"? The really important thing, surely, is for "femininity" to uphold and go on upholding the "ancient masculine wish for the possession of a penis." Is it not her lot in life to sustain the penis, to prevent it from drifting into analogical substitutions, from tearing up the anchor it affords for the whole system of generalizations? Thus the woman who is a man's woman must always keep this desire. This is what man asks her to perpetuate within his "house," as she remains unaware of the value her own sex organs might have for her.

"With the transference of the wish for a penis-baby onto her father, the girl has entered the situation of the Oedipus complex" (p. 129). The desires for identification with her mother, for copulation with the moth-er or the sister, for parthenogenesis, for reproduction of her "image," of herself (as) same, for auto . . . of all sorts, are eliminated. The remains of her libido—if any remains—are directed toward her father, the (father's) phallus-penis. Oedipus may come in if he wants to. The situation of the Oedipus complex has been achieved. As for the mother, the girl is increasingly hostile toward her "for she becomes the girl's rival, who receives from her father everything that she desires from him" (p. 129).

The (as it were) mothers of Oedipus, kept at a distance from the exchange of more complex values, are rivals for his real favors. The daughter blames her mother because she cannot be the daughter-mother. The mother blames the daughter because she cannot be the forbidden mother. That is the one most desirable, the mother still covered over by the veil of the hymen, the mother-to-be. The one who could be remade, once more, (like) his mother, if this were only possible. Daughter and mother are rivals before and after the event. And meanwhile father and son, Oedipuses both, spin out the metaphor, elsewhere. The metaphorical hymen.

But "for a long time, the girl's Oedipus complex concealed her pre-Oedipus attachment to her mother from our view." The desire of Oedipus has misunderstood, repressed, and censored, the libidinal attachment between the growing girl and her mother. He who desired woman only if she was *his* mother, or like *his* mother, could not realize the importance that the relationship to *her* mother might have to the girl growing into womanhood, or to the woman grown. He refuses to move out of *his* family, *his* genealogy. He won't even share with the mother his paternal rights over *his* daughter? Agreed, he will end up by admitting that this "pre-oedipal" attachment—preceding the oedipal or of a different nature?[66]—of the woman to her mother is "so important and leaves such lasting fixations behind it"! But he doesn't know what to make of it. "A long and difficult development?" of which the oedipal situation would be the "outcome"? "a kind of preliminary solution"? "a position of rest"? Oedipus has never had eyes for what is at stake here. He counts out his fantasies and so contradicts himself: outcome? preliminary solution? position of rest? haven? Which is it? He will end up losing sight of it altogether, by being unable to distinguish wife from mother, mother from wife. *Because it has neither "truth" nor "copies," nothing of its "own," this (so-called) female sexuality, this woman's sex/organ will blind anyone taken up in its question.* Therefore the gaze—and the theory, the *theória*—must be protected by being resolved into a phallomorphic representation, into phallic categories. By being considered, for example, only "in regard to" the shape of the male sex organ.

[66]Remember that the primal link between mother and daughter leads Freud to wonder if it is not necessary to "retract the universality of the thesis that the Oedipus complex is the nucleus of the neuroses" ("Female Sexuality," p. 226.)

The Deferred Action of Castration

Capitalism without Complexes

And so "we are now struck by a difference between the two sexes, which is probably momentous, in regard to the relation of the Oedipus complex to the castration complex" (p. 129). Let us see what it is. "In a boy the Oedipus complex, in which he desires *his* mother and would like to get rid of *his* father as being a rival, develops *naturally* from the phase of his phallic sexuality. The threat of castration compels him, however, to give up that [phallic?] attitude. Under the impression of the danger of losing his penis, the Oedipus complex is abandoned, repressed and, in the most *normal* cases, entirely destroyed" (p. 129).

But there will be no normal cases. The little boy will never cease to desire his mother. Freud never ceases—as we have already stressed—to insist upon this. The Oedipus complex will never be destroyed. Man will never cease to continue its scenography. By means of a trick, which can be called a *reason* if you like, but which one could already take by surprise, always, in every metaphorical process/trial. Woman will aid and abet this clever dodge, though ignorant of the stakes and of the price exacted from *her* to ensure that Oedipus's desire can be repeated.

So, after the disappearance of the Oedipus complex, "a severe superego is set up as its heir." What is this "severe" super-ego that results from the sham death of desire for the mother? It presides, Freud writes, over the formation of ideals, over the moral conscience and self-observation. . . . Better than *a* mother, then, is the working out of the *idea of the mother,* of the *maternal ideal.* Better to transform the real "natural" mother into an ideal of the maternal function which no one can ever take away from you.[67] And which will always constitute an *extra* for any woman-mother, an *additional womb*—one of ideas, ideals and theory. A reserve supply, perhaps, for whatever aporias may crop up in relations with all the women-mothers? Better than obedience to the single and therefore partial words spoken by individuals—fathers, for example—is the formation of a "moral conscience" that by reaching the essence and the universality of "things", prescribes, self-prescribes to man the proper behavior for every occasion. Transcendental laws, written "within," will make man both judge and defendant in the suit of his destiny, or even the world's destiny. Better than the gaze of the other, which is necessarily threatening because of its different viewpoint, is the subject's self-observation, the protective and reflexive extension of his "own" gaze.

---

[67]One could, however, interpret in this way the rivalries "to the death" for a theoretical idea: father and son are quarreling over who shall have the mother.

The Metaphorical Veil of the Eternal Feminine

Thus the—fictional—disappearance of the Oedipus complex would resolve itself into the individual's ability to make capital out of ideals and (thereby also) out of mothers, wives-mothers, laws, gazes. . . . Oedipus will have all the mothers he wants, all laws in his favor, and the right to look at anything. . . . all, or most, mothers, laws, views (or at any rate points of view). Oedipus will be rich and have no complexes about it. All he has given up is the desire for a woman, for a woman's sex/organ because in any case *that had no value.* His "super-ego," teeming with ideals and moral rules and self-reflective and self-representative gazes, will have taken woman away from him in exchange for an idea of woman, "femininity." The metaphorical veil of the eternal female covers up the sex/organ seen as castrated.

A "severe super-ego" takes over. . . . Because he cannot risk staking his organ, or his gaze, man comes up with ideas, and ideals, and notably sexual ones.

"What happens with the girl is almost the *opposite.* The castration complex prepares for the Oedipus complex instead of destroying it; the girl is driven out of her attachment to her mother through the influence of her envy for the penis and she enters the Oedipus situation as though into a haven of refuge. In the absence of fear of castration the chief motive is lacking which leads boys to surmount the Oedipus complex. Girls remain in it for an indeterminate length of time; they demolish it late and, even so, incompletely" (p. 129).

Why interpret the little girl's development and especially its relationship to the Oedipus complex, as the opposite—or "almost," more or less the opposite—of the boy's? As the opposite, the other side, reverse, of the masculine oedipal situation? Or its negative? Especially in the photographic sense.[68] Especially in the specular sense.[69] It seems that the same gaze, the same "mirror," the same specula(riza)tion is being used, that an attempt is being made to work out an *a contrario* representation of the process under discussion.

[68]Cf. "A Note on the Unconscious in Pyschoanalysis," *SE,* XII:264, where Freud further explains that "some of these negatives which have held good in examination are admitted to the 'positive process' ending in the picture." But woman is never admitted, except as that mirage of man called "femininity."

[69]"They are, these women, a product of our temperament, an image inversely projected, a negative of our sensibility": Proust, *Within a Budding Grove,* vol. 2, tr. C. K. Scott Moncrieff (New York: Random House, 1981), p. 955.

The Blind Spot of an Old Dream of Symmetry

Does "opposite" mean "placed over against something on the other or farther side of an intervening line; contrary in position"? Or does it mean "opposed," "hostile," or "harmful to," contrary like Mary in the rhyme or as as the dictionary develops the meaning?

This decisive moment in sexual structuring is then supposedly produced in the little girl's case as the "opposite" of the (so-called) masculine economy. Or so Freud would wish, as he thinks of sexual difference from within the realm of the same, and attributes all the properties (and improprieties) of the dictionary definition listed above to the sex "opposite" his own.

The Other Side of History

So "the castration complex [in the girl] prepares for the Oedipus complex instead of destroying it." Yet the female Oedipus complex cannot be thought of as the "same" complex as the boy's. It already assumes that the first cathexes, the first "tropisms" have been abandoned, rejected, and "hated." It assumes a break in contact with the original object, a turning away from the desire for origin. According to Freud, at any rate. And these operations are the result of the "castration complex" which, for the girl, is not a complex in the same way as for the boy since it is simply a matter (as it were!) of taking note of a "fact" or a *biological destiny*; "the accomplished fact of castration." This "castration" that Freud accounts for in terms of "nature," "anatomy," could equally well be interpreted as the prohibition that enjoins woman—at least in this history—from ever imagining, fancying, re-presenting, symbolizing, etc. (and none of these words is adequate, as all are borrowed from a discourse which aids and abets that prohibition) her own relationship to beginning. The "fact of castration" has to be understood as a definitive prohibition against establishing one's own economy of the desire for origin. Hence, the hole, the lack, the fault, the "castration" that greets the little girl as she enters as a subject into representative systems. This is the indispensable assumption governing her appearance upon the scene of "presence," where neither her libido nor her sex/organs have any right to any "truth" except the truth that casts her as "less than," other side, backside, of the representation thereby perpetuated.

In fact this desire for re-presentation, for re-presenting oneself, and for representating oneself in desire is in some ways *taken away from woman at the outset* as a result of the radical devalorization of her "beginning" that she is inculcated with, subjected to—and to which she subjects herself: is she not born of a castrated mother who could only give birth to a castrated child, even though she prefers (to herself) those who bear the penis? This shameful beginning must therefore be forgotten, "re-

83

pressed"—but can one speak at this stage of repression when the processes that make it possible have not yet come into being, and may, for this very reason, never come into being? Even if woman is sexually repressed, this does not imply that she actively achieved this repression[70]—in order to defer to a valid representation of origin. Therefore the girl shuns or is cast out of a *primary metaphorization* of her desire as a woman, and she becomes inscribed into the phallic metaphors of the small male. And if she is no male, because she sees—he says, they say— that she doesn't have one, she will strive to become him, to mimic him, to seduce him in order to get one: "The girl is driven out of her attachment to her mother through the influence of her envy for the penis and she enters the Oedipus situation as though into a haven of refuge." Like a skiff moored to a bollard that keeps it from venturing out to sea again. "In the absence of fear of castration the chief motive is lacking which leads boys to surmount the Oedipus complex." The girl indeed, has nothing more to fear since she has *nothing* to lose. Since she has no representation of what she might fear to lose. Since what she might, potentially, lose, has no value. She will therefore fear not the loss of her castrated sex organ but only the loss of *the love of her owner*: "In her, far more than in the boy, these changes seem to be the result of upbringing and of intimidation from outside that threaten her with a loss of love."[71] And the super-ego "cannot attain the *strength* and *independence* which give it its cultural significance". (Femininity, p. 129).

And indeed, if one reads what Freud writes elsewhere about the building of the super-ego, one can only conclude that the little girl, the woman, will be ill endowed in this regard also. The birth of the ego ideal has to be understood as a result of "an individual's first and most important identification, his identification with the father in his own personal prehistory."[72] Admittedly, as Freud explains in a note,"[73] this "father" can be a "mother" as long as the child is unaware of the difference between the sexes. And therefore, for the little girl—as Freud notes, having had the opportunity "to observe a young woman"—the supposedly phallic mother will provide the basis for structuring the ego ideal. But what becomes of this after the discovery of the mother's castration, that indispensable stage in "becoming a normal woman"? As we have learned,

[70]The same barrier that separates the "subject" from the "woman" is that which keeps the conscious and unconscious apart. Which is another way of perceiving the strength of the "virginity taboo", and of the censorship of the female "libido."
[71]"The Dissolution of the Oedipus Complex," *SE*, XIX:178.
[72]*The Ego and the Id*, *SE*, XIX:31.
[73]Ibid.

hate and rejection of the mother ensue. And of the ego ideal too, perhaps? Is there a collapse of that primary formation of super-ego?

"The super-ego is, however, not simply a residue of the earliest object-choices of the id; it also represents an energetic reaction-formation against those choices. Its relation to the ego is not exhausted by the precept: 'You *ought to be* like this [like your father].' It also comprises the prohibition; 'You *may not be* like this [like your father]—that is, you may not do all that he does; some things are his prerogative.' This *double aspect* of the ego ideal derives from the fact that the ego ideal had the task of repressing *the Oedipus complex;* indeed, it is to that revolutionary event that it owes its existence. Clearly the repression of the Oedipus complex was no easy task. . . . [The child] borrowed strength to do this, so to speak, from the father, and this loan was *an extraordinarily momentous* act. The super-ego *retains the character of the father.*"[74] Understand that the ego ideal itself is not without *ambivalence* and that this must aim to "retain the character of the father"; it appears in any case to derive its "strength" from him.

Here are yet more modes of constructing the super-ego that are unsuited to the formation of "femininity." And even if this description aims to "simplify the presentation" by considering only "the identification with the father," it is hard to imagine its female version or transposition. In fact, "the super-ego arises, as we know, from an identification with the father taken as a model."[75] Does this mean a woman could have a super-ego only by having a masculine attitude, "a powerful masculinity complex"? Again: "Every such identification is in the nature of a desexualization or even of a sublimation."[76] Now the father's penis, being an object of sexual envy, represents possible salvation for the castrated little girl who, by detaching herself from her mother, "enters the Oedipus situation as though into a haven of refuge." She is unable, then, to desexualize her relationship to her father, or even to the paternal model. Indeed, let us repeat, this would be unwelcome and unacceptable. She would be behaving like a man if she identified with the bearer of the penis: "When the girl's attachment to the father comes to grief later on and has to be abandoned, it may give place to an identification with him

[74]Ibid., p. 34. Freud italicizes the phrases "ought to be" and "may not be."
[75]Ibid., p. 54.
[76]Ibid.

✓ and the girl may thus return to her masculinity complex and perhaps remain fixated in it."[77]

Moreover "the question arises, and deserves careful consideration, whether this is not the universal road to sublimation, whether sublimation does not take place through the mediation of the ego, which begins by changing sexual object-libido into narcissistic libido."[78] Now the renunciation of the Oedipus complex, its repression and sublimation, can in the boy's case be interpreted in terms of narcissistic interests: "If the satisfaction of love in the field of the Oedipus complex is to cost the child his penis, a *conflict* is bound to arise between his *narcissistic interest* in that part of his body and the *libidinal cathexis* of his parental objects. In this conflict, *the first of these forces normally triumphs:* the child's ego turns away from the Oedipus complex."[79] One can read on and see how the whole oedipal problematic of the little boy is justifed in this way: "The object cathexes are given up and replaced by identifications. The authority of the father or the parents is introjected into the ego, and there it forms a nucleus of the super-ego, which takes over the severity of *the father* and perpetuates his prohibition against incest, and so *secures the ego from the return of the libidinal cathexis,*" "desexualization and sublimation of the libidinal tendencies," etc. All in all, the prohibition attaching to the Oedipus complex, the law it puts into play, the super-ego it puts into place, seem to function primarily as *narcissistic* protection for the little boy's penis, which had been endangered by *the discovery of the woman's, the mother's, castration:* "for if a woman had been castrated, then his own possession of a penis was in danger; and against that there rose in rebellion the portion of narcissism which Nature [!] has, as a precaution, attached to that particular organ."[80] So he will have to arm his penis with

✓ laws and ideals . . . reassure it by identification with the all-powerful, law-giving father, supply it with a severe super-ego, before it risks going out again toward, into, a woman's body. Whence the prohibition, the latency period, culture, morality, religion. For, when he discovers woman's castration—that necessary "pre-condition" for his castration complex[81]—the boy is seized by a panic similar to the one that, in later life, "the grown man may experience . . . when the cry goes up that Throne and Altar are in danger,"[82] and with similar illogical consequences. Let us not dwell on what amounts to an example of free associa-

[77]"Some Psychical Consequences of the Anatomical Differences between the Sexes," *SE*, XIX:256.
[78]*The Ego and the Id,* p. 30.
[79]"The Dissolution of the Oedipus Complex," *SE*, XI:176.
[80]"Fetishism," *SE*, XVII:148.
[81]"The Dissolution of the Oedipus Complex," p. 176.
[82]"Fetishism," p. 148.

tion, but merely note that the boy's principal purpose in the oedipal problematic is to safeguard and reinforce his narcissistic cathexis of the penis which his uncovering of the female sex organ has threatened. We should reconsider laws, ideals, morality, . . . in relation to that purpose.

The Submission of a Slave?

Meanwhile, one may emphasize that all this remains quite alien to the libidinal interests of the little girl. In her case, the castration complex does not serve to protect the narcissistic cathexis of her sex organ(s), but to subject it/them to a *total denarcissization!* That is to say, the aim is to make her accept the harsh reality of a sexual "mutilation" or "amputation." For the little girl, the woman, has to recognize the wound to her narcissism as a "scar."[83] She must resign herself to the "disadvantage" anatomy has in store for her, settle for the "sense of sexual inferiority" that results and "enter" into the Oedipus complex thanks to this "narcissistic sense of humiliation which is bound up with penis-envy."[84] She will (or theoretically would) have very little narcissistic ego for sublimation. But again one can infer from all this that the little girl's super-ego will be determined, above all, by a "childhood helplessness and dependence"[85] vis-à-vis the bearer of the penis. And the buildup of the super-ego following the Oedipus complex is compromised by the fact that she has no narcissistic interest in repressing her desire for her father, who is the only one who can possibly establish her narcissism—by a kind of phallic proxy, of course, and only if the father is willing. The girl's only way to redeem her personal value, and value in general, would be to seduce the father, and persuade him to express, if not admit, some interest in her. This in spite of the "horror" the father must feel for "the mutilated creature" or his "triumphant contempt for her,"[86] since women reawaken his castration anxiety. . . .

So this super-ego or ego *ideal,* "heir to the Oedipus complex,"[87] "answers to everything that is expected of the higher nature of man" from which derive "religion, morality and social sense—the chief elements in the higher essence of man." "The male sex seems to have taken the lead in all these moral acquisitions" which in some way only become part of woman's birthright through "cross-inheritance."[88] Phylogenesis will have to be examined if the paradox of woman's participation in the

---

[83]"Some Psychical Consequences of the Anatomical Differences between the Sexes," p. 253.

[84]Ibid., p. 254.

[85]*The Ego and the Id,* p. 35.

[86]"Some Psychical Consequences . . . ," p. 252.

[87]*The Ego and the Id,* p. 36.

[88]Ibid., p. 37.

superior values of humanity is to be interpreted. On this occasion, genetics has to come to the aid of history in accounting for the mystery of women's relationship to "culture," in justifying the fact that sometimes, *through chromosomal inheritance,* women can play some cultural role, even though nothing prepares, disposes, or authorizes them to do so. The super-ego, guarantor and producer of humanity's most noble values, is, it would seem, exclusively the product of chromosomes transmitted by males alone.

A Super-Ego That Rather Despises the Female Sex

One is not, however, to imagine, observe, understand, that women lack a super-ego. No. But it must be sought in an infantile submission to, or revolt against, the father or his substitute, that ensures for women that the ego ideal's function can never really be "interiorized" in the psyche. This solution would correspond to the age-old super-ego economy of the "normal" woman, at least in the West. Women do not make laws, even for themselves; that is not in accordance with their "nature."

But, all the same, many women are known to entertain acute, painful, paralyzing conflicts, in which the question of the role of the super-ego is unavoidable. No doubt in these cases the super-ego does not rise up against "objectionable impulses which remained outside the ego" in which "the sense of guilt is over-noisy but cannot justify itself to the ego. Consequently the patient's ego rebels against the imputation of guilt and seeks the physician's support in repudiating it."[89] Here the autonomous and "conscious" ego rebels and struggles against "*objectionable*" tendencies that are *outside it* and against a super-ego that is too cruel and demanding. For most women, things would not happen in this way. They would not be so much *guilty* as "ill." Mutilated, wounded, humiliated, overwhelmed by a feeling of inferiority that can never be "cured."[90] In sum, women are definitively castrated. Their guilt would remain mute: active, of course, but unutterable, ineffable, to be expressed only by the body. They would give themselves up to be punished—by the accomplished fact of castration—without knowing what they had done wrong, or even what they were suffering from, what they endured. As if "the object to which the super-ego's wrath applies has been taken into the ego through identification."[91] All this has happened, and is happening, quite unconsciously, of course: by identifying with the mother, and with

---

[89] *The Ego and the Id,* p. 51.

[90] Cf. for example "Anxiety and Instinctual Life," *New Introductory Lectures on Psychoanalysis, SE,* XXII:108–9.

[91] All the quotations from Freud in this paragraph and the following one are taken from *The Ego and the Id,* pp. 51–52.

woman, who turn out to be castrated. Does this account for the anger? If so, whose? Is it the anger of the little men that men claim women once were, or that of the big men themselves who supply women with a super-ego and serve as pitiless judges of those bodies that have no sex organ (exactly the same as theirs)? Usually, in any case, "the ego ventures no objection, it admits its guilt and submits to the punishment." In fact the ego would have no terms with which to defend itself as "the super-ego has obtained a hold upon consciousness." Women's "ego"— as has often been said in one way or another—is largely "unconscious" and subject to the "conscience" of fathers, men-fathers, which functions as her super-ego.

This is a strange economy, still to be explained fully. It may yet take the form called hysteria whereby, this time "the hysterical ego fends off a distressing perception with which the criticisms of its super-ego threaten it." And "we know that as a rule the ego carries out repressions in the service and behest of its super-ego, but this is a case in which it has turned the same weapon against its stern task-master." It would repress the super-ego itself and the guilt into the unconscious. But one knows how fragile is the hysterical ego, how fragmented, how it risks exploding and shattering at any moment. The operation described above can never constitute a definitive and systematic organization, even though it is repeated, or recurs, in sporadic fashion. With precarious repressions, the law-making fathers will keep the monopoly on "consciousness/conscience" and, calmly and coolly, will use rules and reasons to appease the conflicts of which they are the principal, secret cause.

For why is the woman's, the hysteric's, super-ego so "critical," so cruel? Several reasons might be adduced: its primitive character, the prohibition laid upon aggression in woman, whence the mortifying sadism of her super-ego; the relationship of women to the "mirror," to narcissism;[92] or again their relationship to language, discourse, laws, etc. Let us examine one reason that overlaps several others: *whatever works as a super-ego for women apparently has no love of women, and particularly of women's sex/organ(s).* It would in fact have been built up out of anxiety,

---

[92]In that the flat mirror reflects the greater part of women's sexual organs only as a hole. And the eye does the same, unless it gets "inside" (cf. Georges Bataille's *Story of the Eye,* tr. Joachim Neugroschel [New York: Urizen, 1977]). But even then the eye will be unable to take in the whole of the female sexual equipment with *one* look, as some of it will have remained "outside."

horror, disdain of woman's castration. A whole history opens up to reinterpretation. . . . So it will be necessary to take the time to develop this question of the super-ego. Every time Freud—and anyone else after him—falls back upon the unavoidable facts of anatomy, biology, or genetics, an important historical objective is thereby revealed and concealed. Or is it repressed? Or censored?[93]

An Indispensable Wave of Passivity

A Redistribution of Partial Instincts, Especially Sadistic-anal Instincts

Let us now "go back a little" and see how "as the second reaction to the discovery of female castration . . . a powerful masculinity complex" can develop.

[93]Thus you will have seen the oedipal triangle working in a mode of structuration that still belongs to the dialectic trinity. The *one* of the father (for which the male germ cell stands as security), the *one* of the mother (for which the female germ cell stands as security), and the *one* of the child (product of copulation). Preferably the child will be a son (the *one* of the penis) and in fact the whole structure will be in place only through him. But this *one* of the son can be *doubled* thanks to "bisexuality." Thus, the oedipal triangle, like the Hegelian dialectic, for example, will have brought in as many as four terms by the doubling of the third term, and by its ambivalent identificatory relationships with the other two. (Cf., for example, the third section of *The Ego and the Id:* "The Ego and the Super-Ego (Ego Ideal)," *SE,* XIX:28–39.) But if this doubling up already implies a process of relative negation, one of these "terms" will be the object of a negation of this *relative* negation, that is of an *absolute* negation: the "feminine" (in the woman that the mother also is because she is castrated, in the little boy, in the man). By being excluded-(*verworfen*)-as a result of this absolute negation, the fourth term—a mirror virgin of all *positive* (auto)reflection—will henceforth ensure the proliferation of fantasies for the one who becomes in/by this operation the (masculine) "subject." Who is also schizated, split and split again, of course, by the absolute negation of the fourth that he too once was. But henceforward "she" will only find herself again in the questions bearing on the structure of this split or *schize* of the "subject," which assures him an access to the "symbolic."

This will need to be put together with a text of Hegel's: "This negativitiy is the *restoration* of the *first immediacy,* of simple universality; for the other of the other, the negative of the negative, is immediately the *positive,* the *identical,* the *universal.* If one insists on *counting,* this *second* immediate is, in the course of the method as a whole, the *third* term to the first immediate and the mediated. It is also, however, the third term to the first or formal negative and to absolute negativity or the second negative; now as the first negative is already the second term, the term reckoned as *third* can also be reckoned *fourth,* and instead of a *triplicity,* the abstract form may be taken as a *quadruplicity;* in this way, the negative or the difference is counted as a *duality.* The third or fourth is in general the unity of the first and second moments, of the immediate and the mediated. That it is this *unity,* as also that the whole form of the method is a *triplicity,* is, it is true, merely the superficial external side of the mode of cognition": Hegel, *Science of Logic,* tr. A. V. Miller (London: Allen & Unwin, 1969, II:836, Hegel's italics.) It remains: to examine in depth the formal character of this quadruplicity.

"By this we mean that the girl refuses, as it were, to recognize the unwelcome fact and, definitely rebellious, even exaggerates her previous masculinity, clings to her clitoridal activity and takes refuge in an identification with her phallic mother or her father" ("Femininity," pp. 129–30). The options listed here are not readily compatible. For example, if it is the *fact* of castration the little girl refuses, the penalty she should pay would be to go into "delirium," but the other symptoms described give no suggestion of this. Or again: how can we reconcile on the one hand an *exaggerated masculinity* and on the other hand an identification with the *phallic mother;* phallic rivalry is played out between mother and man—in the same way, yet different, as between mother and father—but this does not justify the confusion of the modes of access to these representatives, or signifiers, of power, nor the failure to differentiate the identifications involved. And then again: is the persistence of *clitoridal activity* simply compatible with the identification with the phallic mother? Surely the goal of masturbation was to put the mother at a distance?

The statements that follow are even more obscure and curiously stitched together: "What can it be that decides in favour of this outcome? We can only suppose that it is a constitutional factor, a greater amount of activity, such as is ordinarily characteristic of the male" (p. 130). Why must there be an *outcome?* In which something gets *decided?* How are we to understand here, yet again, the appeal to a *constitutional factor* that truly seems to be the deus ex machina used to regulate, and justify, the fate handed out to woman, and women. As for the *activity ordinarily characteristic of the male,* might this not be what produces the outcome? Or is this another suitable point to stop and question and ferret out the precedence given to the active/passive polarity in the Freudian representation of the sexual economy? The next sentence would lead one to think so: "However that may be, the essence of this process is that at this point in development the *wave of passivity* is avoided which opens the way to the turn toward femininity" (p. 130). For this assertion to be understandable, it would have to be put in the context of, or conclusively compared to, a series of statements in which its implications are developed. We have already begun to do this, but let us summon up a few more fragments that are particularly explicit: for example, "it is not unimportant to bear in mind what transformations are undergone, during the sexual development of childhood, by the polarity of sex with which we are familiar. A first antithesis is introduced with the choice of object, which, of course, presupposes a subject and an object. At the stage of the pregenital sadistic-anal organization, there is as yet no question of male and female; the

91

antithesis between *active* and *passive* is the dominant one. At the following stage of infantile genital organization, which we now know about,
maleness exists, but not femaleness. The antithesis here is between having
a *male genital* and being *castrated*. It is not until development has reached
its completion in puberty that the sexual polarity coincides with *male* and
female."[94] Theoretically then, the active/passive opposition dominates
the pregenital sadistic-anal organization, during which there is still no
question of male or female. We may wonder, as a result, why this
opposition continues so insistently to shape the masculine/feminine polarity, to the point of providing its "psychological meaning." "The
antithesis active-passive coalesces later with that of masculine-feminine,
which, until this has taken place, has no psychological meaning."[95]
How, too, is it possible that, whereas at the sadistic-anal stage boys and
girls are alike, the active/passive polarity dominating that stage's instinctual economy should subsequently be *split in two,* with one term
assigned to the man and one to the woman? The same thing happens
with the terms subject/object or again, in the oral and phallic stages, the
polarities phallic sex/castrated sex. And all the components of the instinctual economy—see/be seen, know/be known, love/be loved, rape
the object/object (liking to be?) raped, . . . Pleasure/unpleasure? What
scenography of the couple, and coupling, is implied here?

The wave of passivity would therefore coincide with a *redistribution of
anal instincts*—and indeed of all the (so-called) partial instincts—, with
activity and passivity being attributed to man and woman respectively.
And with the fading, or indictment, of women's possessive, narcissistic,
and aggressive instincts. A fair number of statements seem to support
this hypothesis, some of which have already been quoted. But whereas
the "female constitution" is the habitual fall-back position from which to
explain the fate of woman's instincts, no justification can be found for the
fact that the little girl, *naturally,* has certain instincts in the pregenital
stages and that she, *naturally,* does not have them anymore later on. All
we learn is that "the comparatively lesser strength of the sadistic contribution to her sexual instinct, which we may no doubt connect with *the
stunted growth of her penis* [?], makes it easier in her case for the direct
sexual trends to be transformed into aim-inhibited trends of an affectionate kind."[96] Trends with passive aims? But what accounts for this reduc-

[94]"The Infantile Genital Organization," *SE,* XIX:145. Freud's italics.
[95]"Instincts and Their Vicissitudes," *SE,* XIV:134.
[96]"The Dissolution of the Oedipus Complex," *SE,* XIX:179.

tion in sadism, given that woman's penis has always already been "stunted"? Has a mere *look* been able to change her "constitution"? Perhaps it is more a question of a repression? But instigated by what? And why, from now on, label this operation a "wave of passivity," and at the same time account for it once again in terms of some anatomic-physiological process? And can it really be claimed, without the conniv-ance of powerful interests involving a certain misprision, that "maleness combines [the factors] of subject, activity and possession of the penis" whereas "femaleness takes over [the factors of] object and passivity" and of nonpossession, or impropriety, of the sex organ(s)? The vagina in fact is "now valued as a place of shelter for the penis" and inasmuch as it "enters into the heritage of the womb."[97] Of course, it has not escaped us that fundamental concepts of classical philosophy are being resorted to here. Enough to make Freud say that this state of things is so ancient as it find its legitimacy, its necessity, and even its rationality, in phylogenesis.

"There Is Only One Libido"

Femininity supposes, then, a "wave of passivity" and the transforma-tion of "direct sexual trends" into "aim-inhibited trends of an affection-ate kind." The installation of instincts with "passive aims," perhaps? So let us again read the text: "We have called the motive force of sexual life 'the libido.' Sexual life is dominated by the polarity of masculine-femi-nine; thus the notion suggests itself of considering the relation of the libido to this antithesis. It would not be surprising if it were to turn out that each sexuality had its own special libido appropriated to it, so that one sort of libido would pursue the aims of a masculine sexual life and another sort those of a feminine one. But nothing of the kind is true. There is only one libido, which serves both the masculine and the femi-nine sexual functions. To it itself we cannot assign any sex; if, following the *conventional* equation of activity and masculinity [which also happens to be the one Freud uses in his argument], we are inclined to describe it as masculine, we must not forget that it also covers trends with a passive aim. Nevertheless the juxtaposition 'feminine libido' is without any jus-tification" ("Femininity," p. 131).

There is only one libido. Libido would be the name—or password borrowed from the "genital" stage—given to the sexual instincts of the pregenital stages, and more specifically (at least in Freudian theory) to the sadistic-anal stage, which would have—would have had, would still have, will always have—the most irresistible, the most imperious, the most tyrannical force. There is only one libido and it could just possibly

97"The Infantile Genital Organization," p. 145.

be called "neuter": neither masculine nor feminine.[98] The anal instincts, and indeed any of the "partial" instincts, are sex-blind, according to Freud. However, anal erotism—to take up the most obvious example, at least as far as Freud is concerned—is possessive, narcissistic, constantly reacting offensively or defensively to the demands of other; it is aggressive toward the "object" that it tortures systematically whenever possible, that it would like to eliminate when its needs have been served or when its strength no longer relies on dominating and possessing the object: for anal erotism deals in death insofar as its own subsistence and the perpetuation of its pleasure allow.[99] It is always at war in order to have things, and have more things, and take things from others; in order to accumulate and build up capital, losing nothing.

In this relentless, exhausting, anxious "activity," in this merciless struggle for appropriation, for property, for the promotion and defense of territory, how can a minimum of repose, security, self-preservation, be guaranteed? They will be ensured by *the status assigned to woman in warfare*. Instinctual warfare. "Furthermore, it is our impression that more constraint has been applied to the libido when it is pressed into the service of the feminine function, and that—to speak teleologically— Nature [again!] takes less careful account of its demands than in the case of masculinity" (p. 131). Women may possibly be the occasion of war, or its booty, or its "object"—though not in a simple way, since what is principally at stake in war is the value of the penis for which woman can stand as the fetish guarantee—but they will be able to take no active part in it. They would always already have been conquered, "aim-inhibited in their instinctual trends" that have been converted into affection. They are havens of refuge and safety. They represent the total reduction of instinctual arousal. Therefore, the re-assurance of death. Soft, calm, painless. Swooning contentedly in the mother's womb. Welcome, relaxation, rest for the warrior. This would be the woman's function in this war set out in ritual phrases that sometimes sound like an exorcism. But even here women will be repressed, inhibited, oppressed, won't they? In their primary libidinal economy. The realization of their pregenital instincts—which, we are told elsewhere are "amazing" and "unexpectedly" comparable to the little boy's—will be checked, set adrift, turned into their opposite, in order to satisfy the instincts of men by a harmonious complementarity.

[98]Cf "we cannot even give the libido a gender," a phrase omitted from the French translation of "Femininity."

[99]Cf. "On Transformations of Instincts as Exemplified in Anal Erotism," and *The Ego and the Id*.

The Blind Spot of an Old Dream of Symmetry

Idealization, What Is One's Own

In this war, other *stores* will also be set up: the permanence of the booty and treasure. If what you want to get hold of, keep, accumulate, is perishable; if it can be taken away from you; if one look, for example, can change its value, then the toil and the war will be relentless and endless. Therefore, in place of the feces—decomposed/decomposable matter that is taken from you and that is subject to being appreciated by an other eye—will be substituted the *image, the specular production-re-production. Which is also speculative. The eye will ensure the recovery, and the mastery, of anal erotism. The mirror will idealize the product* that it will have introduced both into the field of optics and into an economy of re-production. Perhaps through a process of "sublating" the automatism of repetition? The "idealized" object will be the fecal mass—displaced before, and in front of—, the penis, or even the body; these serve as "frames" equally for all fetishistic representations, including femininity.

Possession is ensured, mastered, eternalized just as it is always already re-produced and therefore reproducible. Auto-erotism has become more autonomous, more powerful. And *invisible* as well, since it has entrusted itself to the eye and occupied the very site of sight. Of course, a mirror is needed. But this can be "interiorized," *put inside.* Representation can dispense with and supplant the role played in the real life of the senses by the mirror. Narcissus can even refine upon mirrors. . . . Other men, other penises, other discourses also are able to function as mirrors. Obviously, the risk of war continues. . . . So, woman perhaps? Yes, woman. No sex organs, no gaze, no desire for appropriation. Woman, re-duplicate of what man has staked upon desire. We have already seen that this role fell to woman. We shall, of course, need to come back to it.

Auto-erotism, particularly the anal kind, has thus found some "displacements," some positions, some goals that are more sublime, sublimated. In the service of the "noblest conquests of man," his ideals. It remains for him to ensure the preservation of his *seed* also, and of his relationship to auto-erotism. Which is masculine. This is obviously a more complicated business, especially because he can't reproduce his seed all on his own. Conflict with woman, and women, is likely to break out. It is on this point, one imagines, that the struggle with women for possession, for mastery of power, and for potency, is least avoidable. A whole strategy has to be worked out so that her, their, instincts remain inhibited . . . in their aims, so that women work at reproduction without pleasure or property rights over the product. So let us remember: the child will be the *penis-substitute,* desired by woman for this reason alone;

the longing for a child *of the same sex as the father,* in his likeness, will be attributed to women; man will retain a monopoly of activity in coitus; he will brand the product of coitus *with his own name;* although the woman has a duty to cater to the needs of the infant and satisfy his elementary wants, it is the father who will introduce the child, through identification with himself, *to the values* that are the most appreciated and prized; man-father will be the guarantor of the *systems of representation, ideals, public spirit, the practice of the law,* etc. And although woman remains indispensable in *materially* reproducing the child, she will have to submit as far as possible to man's reproductional projects. In fact this "teleology" is prescribed by "nature." And the "reason" for this libidinal repression in/of woman "may lie . . . in the fact that the accomplishment of the aim of biology has been entrusted to the aggressiveness of men and has been made to some extent independent of women's consent" (p. 131). The "sexual function", or reproductive function, that concentrates all the instincts into genitality, is therefore dominated by the sperm's attack upon the ovum, by man's attack on woman. And this biological imperative does not need her consent.[100]

The (Re)productive Organ

As for the penis, we learn that—in this final period of sexual evolution—it owes "its extraordinarily high narcissistic cathexis to its *organic* significance for the propagation of the species" and that "the catastrophe to the Oedipus complex . . . may be regarded as a victory of the race over the individual."[101] A problematic statement in more ways than one. For the penis has no great "organic significance for the propagation of the species," it is only a channel for the sperm and can even, conceivably, be done without. And to attribute its "extraordinarily high narcissistic cathexis" to this function may be considered symptomatic of the habit Freud's theory has of falling back upon organic processes. Freud himself was no neophyte in anatomy and physiology, so why does he misrepresent the fact that each sex has to be placed in a *twofold* economy—a *twofold* dialectic—*that of pleasure, as well as that of reproduction,*[102] even though he must find a reminder of this in the dualism of both female and male sexual organs? What *confusion of sexual functions* is he revealing here? And what advantage does he gain by losing sight of this? Perhaps that of

[100]This is another statement of the "categorical imperative" that Freud makes sexual pleasure submit to.

[101]"Some Psychical Consequences of the Anatomical Differences between the Sexes," p. 257.

[102]Unless for Freud, in what he describes and prescribes, there is only one pleasure: that of (re)production. Does anal erotism still prevail in the economy of (so-called) genitality?

96

ensuring, by some conjuring trick duly based on biology, the domination of the Phallus? In fact, at the end of sexual development, the phallic instincts—like all the so-called partial instincts—are subordinated to the "sexual function," or reproductive function, a function that Freud will, by reason of its "organic significance for the propagation of the species," subordinate to the penis. This is a curious syllogism, whereby the male is given back the power he had almost lost. Or almost shared? How strange to overturn and turn value over by first questioning the "phallic" in the name of reproductive priorities and then giving primacy to the phallus by virtue of its privileged role in reproduction. "Its extraordinarily high narcissistic cathexis" is justified on the grounds that it assures the "victory of the *race* over the individual."

On the other hand, "in girls the motive for the demolition of the Oedipus complex is lacking."[103] Yet it is unusual, in actual fact, for a daughter to have a child by her father, and she might, as a result, find some more practical uterine, if not vaginal cathexis preferable to a love for her father. This cathexis may obviously be ignored, refused, or denied. Just as the ovaries and the womb are denied any "organic significance for the perpetuation of the species" that might earn them an "extraordinarily high narcissistic cathexis."

Confirmation of Frigidity

One thing, however, that is not ignored completely—because it forms part of the field of therapeutic observation? of what passes for scientific objectivity?—is the "sexual frigidity of women" which "appears to *confirm* this disregard" and "is a phenomenon that is still insufficiently understood" ("Femininity," p. 132). Does it really confirm? Or is it not rather a symptom that tells us that woman's pleasure and the representation that can be made of it and that she can have of it, are—once again—too suppressed, repressed, obscured, or denied for her to be anything but "frigid." Even so, we would need to find out what the term "frigid" means in masculine discourse, and why women adopt it only with a sense of guilt, although they can rarely put their finger on why this should be. We would also need to examine the relationship between this "frigidity" and the aggressiveness that devolves upon the male in the sexual function, an aggressiveness that is exerted "independent of her consent." Perhaps female sexuality does not find its needs met by this violence, this rape, that "biology" supposedly demands of the male to ensure reproduction?

Sometimes frigidity is "psychogenic and in that case accessible to

---

[103]"Some Psychical Consequences . . . ," p. 257.

influence" (p. 132). That is, unless the historical repression is so great that this sexual *anaesthesia* can at best only be transformed into the equally symptomatic *hyperaesthesia* or the equally suspect *orgasmal fetishism*. And even these results would be limited to those privileged women who had received psychological treatment. The others, and indeed those same women, would remain entangled in a masochistic economy that certain psychoanalysts, male and female, do not hesitate to designate as the condition of woman's pleasure. These analysts thus ratify, or enact the status quo into psychic laws, and perpetuate it under the sanction of "normality." They become accomplices in their patients' lack of satisfaction, trying to reduce their anxieties and rebellions at their unsatisfactory lives by suggesting that satisfaction means liking what you have, that these women are "sick from dissatisfaction," that if they only wanted to give up a little bit of that pathological dissatisfaction they would be free of its burden. Etc.

"But in other cases," alas! frigidity "suggests the hypothesis of being constitutionally determined and *even* of there being a contributory anatomical factor." Even. . . .

Female Hom(m)osexuality

The "Constitutional Factor" Is Decisive

"The extreme achievement of such a masculinity complex would appear to be the influencing of the choice of an object in the sense of manifest homosexuality" (p. 130). The object choice of *a female* homosexual can only be determined by a particularly strong masculinity complex. "Analytic experience teaches us, to be sure, that female homosexuality is seldom or never a direct continuation of infantile masculinity." It should rather be interpreted as a regression "into her early masculinity complex" as a result of the "inevitable disappointments from her father" whom she has taken as an 'object' once she enters the Oedipus situation (p. 130). Obviously the significance of these disappointments must not be exaggerated; a girl who is destined to become feminine is not spared them either, though they do not have the same effect. And "the predominance of the constitutional factor seems indisputable" (p. 130). As might have been expected! Be this factor as it may, homosexual woman "play the parts of mother and baby with each other as often and as clearly as those of husband and wife"(!), attitudes which "will mirror" "the two phases in the development of female homosexuality." Would these two phases be, then, "a direct continuation of infantile masculinity" or a regression "into her early masculine complex"? Unless, of course, one of these alternatives, the second, corresponded to the identification with the father that comes after he has been renounced as an "object" of love? Other texts stress the possibility of this.[104] The essential thing, in any case, is to show that the object choice of the homosexual woman is determined by a *masculine* desire and tropism. The female libido is cut off from the active search for its instinctual "object-aims" and its primary "waves." It has in a sense neither aim (telos) nor origin (arche) of its own. The instincts that lead the homosexual woman to choose an object for her satisfaction are, necessarily, "male" instincts.

So we will read, in the argument developed in the text Freud devotes to a case of female homosexuality, that "in her behaviour towards her love-object," the homosexual woman " had throughout assumed the masculine part" and "had thus not only chosen a feminine love-object but had also developed a masculine attitude towards that object" (PCHW, p. 154). Furthermore "she changed into a man and took her mother in place of her father as the object of her love" (PCHW, p. 158). We read that, all the same, her "inversion . . . received its final reinforcement when she found in her 'lady' an object which promised to satisfy not only her homosexual trends, but also that part of her heterosexual libido which was attached still to her brother" (PCHW, p. 160), the same brother whom—after an unremarkable passage through the Oedipus complex—she "had begun to substitute for her father" (PCHW, p. 155). The unusually strong fixation to the lady could thus be explained by the fact that the latter's "slender figure, severe beauty and downright manner reminded her of the brother who was a little older than herself" (PCHW, p. 156).

Homosexual Choice Clearly Expounded

It seems that the phallic instinctual script is never written out so clearly as in the case of *female homosexuality:* in which a man desires the phallic mother, or another man. Something very obvious but usually unnoticed apparently becomes crystal clear when it shows up in women—that something being the pregnancy, in philosophical terms, of course, of *male homosexuality.* For this whole analysis is about male homosexuality. And Freud could doubtless have reminded us that, as far as the economy of desire goes, *miming*—acting, pretending—is capable of affording *an*

---

[104]Cf. particularly "The Psychogenesis of a Case of Homosexuality in a Woman," *SE,* XVIII:147–72. The "literary" qualities of this "story" and the ideological overdetermination of many of its statements are quite striking. (Page references to this essay—referred to as PCHW—will be made in the text.—Tr.)

increase in pleasure over simple discharges of instincts. He could have pointed out that acting "like" a man, desiring a woman who was "like" a man, just "as" a man does, would be the most satisfying performance of the phallic scenario. But he decides against this, unable to give up so easily the *natural basis* of desire. Therefore he will be on the lookout for the anatomical signs justifying his patient's—masculine—homosexuality. And although he is forced to admit that "there was no obvious deviation from the feminine physical type," that his patient was "beautiful and well-made" and had no "menstrual disturbance," he adds that she had "her father's tall figure, and her facial features were sharp rather than soft and girlish, traits which might be regarded as indicating a physical masculinity." However, "the psycho-analyst customarily forgoes a thorough physical examination of his patients, *in certain cases*[?]" (PCHW, p. 154).

A Cure Fails for Lack of Transferences

Be that as it may, "the analysis went forward almost without any signs of resistance, the patient participating actively with her intellect [thanks to her "intellectual attributes . . . connected with masculinity"], though absolutely tranquil emotionally" (PCHW, p. 163). Once, when Freud "expounded to her a specially important part of the theory, *one touching her nearly,* she replied in an inimitable tone, 'How very interesting', as though she were a grande dame being taken over a museum and glancing through her lorgnon at objects to which she was completely indifferent" (PCHW, p. 163). Indeed, that homosexual woman must have found Freud's explanations to be very like historical documents that did not touch her at all and left her all her emotional tranquility! As for the use of the lorgnon—the one through which he was looking at her perhaps?—as accessory or prop, responsibility for this has to be laid at Freud's door. It seemed, then, "as though nothing resembling a transference to the physician had been effected" (PCHW, p. 164). At any rate no transference that he recognized as such. None that fitted his theory of "transference," perhaps? Or else none that was practicable within his conception of a cure, and his ways of being, or not being, involved in it? The only hints of transference were supplied by dreams that "he did not *believe*" because they were "*false* or *hypocritical*" and intended to deceive the analyst "just as she habitually deceived her father" (PCHW, p. 164). Why this fear of being misled by the patient's unconscious? Or even by the "preconscious," if not the "waking conscious life" itself, which perhaps whispered their intentions in the dream? Why this fear of being "pleased" by a patient and later, as a result, "disappointed," "misled"?

Could it be that all these adventures would be unseemly in the dignified father figure that Freud intends to go on playing and that possibly covers up *his* transference? Therefore he made it clear to the person in question that he was perfectly aware that she wanted to make a fool of him, and he was right to do so since "after I had made this clear, this kind of dream ceased" (PCHW, p. 165). Thus the psychoanalyst can induce or forbid certain dreams. . . . As for the rest, the girl's parents were advised that "if they set store by the psychoanalytic procedure, it should be continued by a woman doctor" (PCHW, p. 164).

So here we have the homosexual woman shown the door by her psychoanalyst, because she refuses to allow herself to be seduced by the father quite as much as he refuses to become the surrogate object of her desire, which in this case would mean his being identified with a *cocotte*, a woman of "bad reputation," who "lived simply by giving her bodily favours" (PCHW, p. 161). Freud's well-brought-up, middle-class super-ego did not permit him such lapses. Or even let him admit that a "beautiful and clever girl, belonging to a family of good standing" might throw over her father (whom Freud knows and likes and is *paid* by) in favor of a whore.

Female Sameness

But isn't there a more unconscious, archaic, and "phylogenetically" remote stratum in Freud's super-ego that forbade him even more strongly to *identify with a woman*? Another good reason for sending the homosexual woman over to a female colleague while remaining skeptical about anything worthwhile coming out of the sessions of female analyst and female patient. For female homosexuality represented for Freud a phenomenon so alien to his imaginary economy that it could only be "neglected by psycho-analytic research" (PCHW, p. 147), and even neglected in the therapy of the homosexual woman patient. This is not to say that what Freud describes does not fit a certain "reality," or that his commentaries or explanations are simply "wrong." Many homosexual women can recognize themselves in this story or could at least try to find their bearings in it. Female homosexuality would nonetheless remain obliterated, travestied—transvestized—and withdrawn from interpretation. For nothing of the special nature of desire *between women* has been unveiled or stated. That a woman might desire a woman "like" herself, someone of the "same" sex, that she might also have auto- and homosexual appetites, is simply incomprehensible to Freud, and indeed inadmissible. Such an idea is rarely encountered in this phallocentric history, in which value is the prerogative of the penis and its equivalents. And in which it is not easy to be outside the system, "off the market." The claims advanced by female homosexuality are obviously not enough to raise doubts about the privilege of the phallus.

This does not mean, however, that woman's desire for herself, for the self-same[105]—a female self, a female same—is not be recognized. Does not have to discover a possible economy. That this desire is not necessary to balance the desire of the other. That the same-he and same-she do not have to be re-marked for her too if sexual difference is to be expressible without purely and simply incurring death: death of the ego, and therefore of the sexual instincts as well (to refer to a problematic developed by Freud but whose functioning he overlooks somewhat when he is describing the "development of a woman," in which the little girl would have to reject and devalue all representatives, male and female, and representations of her sex in order to turn her desires, her "envies," toward the only sex/organ: the masculine). The prohibition, the depreciation of the desire for the "self-same"—which women would perhaps promote, through their "masculine" phallic super-ego at any rate?—in the development of female sexuality would explain in large measure women's oft-lamented frigidity or lack of sexual appetite. But it could equally serve as an interpretive lever for many other accompanying or derived symptoms: lack of autonomy; narcissistic fragility or hypernarcissim; an incapacity for sublimation that does not exclude an "aethereal" erotism; at best difficult relations with the mother, and indeed with all women; lack of "social interest" and, more generally, of all sustained interest; depressions and chronic somatizations, etc. All these indicate the lack of an auto-erotic, homo-sexual economy. Or else, or as well as, *death drives*. The "active" enactment of which is forbidden for/in female sexuality. And this ban does not and cannot produce any results, any system of metaphor, any sublimation, simply because a dominant *specular* economy does not tally with female sexuality. The specular organization leaves, in no doubt different ways, both the female sexual function and the female maternal function in an amorphous suspension of their instinctual economy and/or shapes them in ways quite heteronomous to that economy. Their "economy" will be governed by the demands of drives—particularly sadistic or scoptophiliac ones—that only men can actually put into practice. Governed above all by the need to maintain the primacy of the Phallus.

---

[105]A self-same that would be "other" than the one that dominates the phallocentric economy of discourse and signifiers. It will be read by half-opening the "volume" elsewhere and otherwise.

So there will be no female homosexuality, just a hommo-sexuality in which woman will be involved in the process of specularizing the phallus, begged to maintain the desire for the same that man has, and will ensure at the same time, elsewhere and in complementary and contradictory fashion, the perpetuation in the couple of the pole of "matter."[106] Which can be defined as what resists infinite reflection: the mystery (hysteria?) that will always remain modestly *behind every mirror,* and that will spark the desire to see and know more about it. Which relates to the specular only indirectly, through what it offers, or does not offer, to be reflected and echoed by man's desire.

But woman devotes, it is insisted, very little cathexis to auto-erotism, auto-representation, auto-reproduction, even in homosexuality. The possibility that these might give her a specific sexual pleasure is little considered: the pleasure of caresses, words, re-presentations or representations that remind woman of her sex, her sex organs, her sexes.[107] would be little in demand, little interested or interesting, within a male heterosexual praxis, because it lacks masculine homologues. It would be a different, complementary or supplementary, sexual pleasure from that sought not only in heterosexuality but also in woman's implication within, or miming of, male homosexuality. There would also be a narcissistic well-being in acting out a regressive relationship with a "good" mother—despite Freud's somewhat incomprehensible insistence that such a relationship is exclusively associated with homosexuality, and, what is more, with the little girl's "virile" desire for (her) mother. Yet what exhilarating pleasure it is to be partnered with someone like oneself. With a sister, in everyday terms. What need, attraction, passion, one feels for someone, for some woman, like oneself. But might not this

---

[106]The assimilation and assignment of woman, the mother, to the pole of "matter" is traditional, as we know. It is found in Freud's work, including this essay on female homosexuality, where it is expressed more or less explicitly in the equally traditional question of whether homosexuality is "congenital" or "later-developed" (pp. 153 and 169), attributable to "physical" or "psychical hermaphroditism" (p. 154), to "body" or "character" (p. 170). And even though Freud is somewhat hesitant about positing the problem in this way, many of his statements prove how far his own views coincide with the traditional ones, particularly when it is a question of female sexuality. For example, we shall be told in this text that the independence of one of these factors from the other "is more evident in men than women, where bodily and mental traits belonging the opposite sex are apt to coincide" (p. 154). Woman's psyche, her personality, her "soul," correlate, in fact, better with organic factors than do man's. Perhaps she does not have a soul? People have doubted this in the past. Her homosexuality will thus be put down to her hormones, or her "hermaphroditic ovaries" (p. 172).

[107]The multiplicity of woman's erogenous zones, the plural nature of her sex, is a differentiating factor that is too rarely considered in the male/female polarity, especially as far as its implications for "signifying" practices are concerned.

feeling put an end to the little girl's "penis-envy," or encourage her "penis-desire"? Might it not give her back a phallic urge that was less greedy, frustrated, demanding, or . . . anorexic? But the need, the charm felt for one's like will be repressed, denied, turned into their opposites in what is labeled "normal femininity." In fact, they will only be barely hinted at in the interpretation of masculine homosexuality.

As for his homosexual woman patient, Freud will explain that "the *heterosexual* current" was "*deeper*" and in fact "was deflected into the manifest homosexual one." Woman's desire for her like is thus seen as "secondary," a "reactive formation" in some way to the disappointments her father had caused her, even though, it must be remembered, the little girl's first love object is her mother or else someone of her own sex. Even though Freud makes a point of forgetting this when he affirms about his patient that "from the very early years, therefore, her libido had flowed in two currents, the *one on the surface* being one that we may unhesitatingly designate homosexual. This latter was probably *a direct and unchanged continuation of an infantile fixation* on her mother" (PCHW, p. 168). The libidinal relationship with the mother is therefore more "on the surface" than her "deeper" heterosexual desire and it can "unhesitatingly" and without transformations be called homosexual. Thereby the primary purpose of female desire is *reduced* and *caricatured*. But woman's relationship with her origin must needs be canceled—as well as her original relationship with her mother and her sex, which is deemed to be "on the surface," "secondary," though "manifest"—if the domination of the Phallus is to be established. Emblem of the mastery exercised by and for man within *one* economy of origin. His own.

An Impracticable Sexual Relationship

An Ideal Love

This conception of female desire expounded by Freud—for which he is in some sense the spokesman—also seems to determine the woman's choice of her sexual partner: her "object choice." Let us forget that woman does not so much choose an object of desire for herself as she lets herself be chosen as an "object"; what is being rehearsed accounts for that "distraction" in the correct functioning of female (non) desire. "Where the choice is able to show itself freely, it is often made in accordance with *the narcissistic ideal of the man* whom the girl had wished to become" ("Femininity," p. 132). Really successful femininity cannot lay claim to being ideal or confer an ideal upon itself. It lacks a mirror *appropriate* for doing so. The narcissistic ideal for a woman will have been and theoretically is still the man she desired to become. Narcissism and her pact with the ideal would derive from phallic domination. Which woman has the task of supporting. Whence the fact that she will choose the man she would like to have been. And this, essentially, would satisfy the man's interests, for he would not have to step out of his *gender, ideally*. To woo, he would need only to correspond as closely as possible to the most perfect self-image, be as narcissistic as possible, an "absolute" model of narcissism. A woman would support that "model" with her "own" narcissistic project, and the model would thus have the advantage, and the excuse, of appeasing, satisfying, and, above all, healing, female narcissism. Which is necessarily wounded and humiliated by the accomplished fact of castration: since women has had a valid representation of her sex/organ(s) amputated.

Were It Not for Her Mother?

"If the girl has remained in her attachment to her father—that is, in the Oedipus complex—her choice is made according to the paternal type" (p. 133). This second solution, this "enclitic" choice of object, is a thornier problem. For woman shows that she has not succeeded in leaving her family. Whence the resurgence of infantile conflicts. And, by inheriting the little girl's desires for her father, the husband also becomes the butt of the *ambivalent* feelings, and therefore of the *hostility the little girl felt for her mother*. "The woman's husband, who to begin with inherited from her father, becomes after a time her mother's heir as well. So it may easily happen that the second half of a woman's life may be filled by the struggle against her mother, just as the shorter first half was filled with her rebellion against her mother" (p. 133). Even though, as the father, a husband could have expected a love and a desire totally lacking in ambivalence, in "struggles" and "conflict," even though this type of love was meant to guarantee conjugal happiness, it will nonetheless be troubled because of the resurgence of the maternal figure.

It is a little surprising, when you stop and think about it, to hear that a paternal transference onto the husband promises unalloyed marital bliss. That *thereby* one is assured that no ambivalent reactions, no difficulties of any kind will be experienced when the woman is deflowered, when she goes (back) through the fantasies or realities of being broken open, raped, when she lives through the anxieties and possible pain of pregnancy and childbirth. Not to mention her leaving her family home, setting up house in a new place, becoming inured to, or enslaved by, housework. What immense powers of *suggestion* the paternal authority must have if such achievements are to be laid at its door![108] Unfortunately, the mother—"her" mother—comes to disturb the conjugal happiness that had thus been "guaranteed." Woman's rebellions are never aimed at the paternal function—which is sacred and divine—but at that powerful and then castrated mother, because she had brought a castrated child into the world. Before she conformed to the established order, the little girl's primitive instincts could still be addressed to her mother. But the fact that the woman has not solved the problem of her relationship to her beginning, to her mother, to those of her own sex, affects her love relations. Or at least her first love relation, her first "marriage." As might have been expected. And woman's only way to rise above all these true-life stories, all the struggles she experiences, would be, apparently, to adopt a *masculine* narcissistic *ideal*. This choice, it is claimed, resolves, revokes, any war that may have been caused by rivalry between other ideals, other cover-ups, in the ideality of the lack of primal representation.

Or Her Mother-in-law?

"Another alteration in a woman's nature, for which lovers are unprepared, may occur in a marriage after the first child is born. Under the influence of a woman's becoming a mother herself, an identification with her own mother may be revived, against which she had striven up till the time of her marriage" (p. 133). A curious association leads on to the fact that this identification "may attract all the available libido to itself, so that the compulsion to repeat reproduces an unhappy marriage between her parents." So, identifying with the mother would lead to a repetition of the parents' marital problems. What is Freud exposing to interpretation? The unfortunate marriage of "his" parents? The inevitable failure of any match? The unhappy lot of any woman, even if she becomes a mother, in any marriage? And of the man as well, even if he becomes a father? What a strange way to talk of marriage, as something which, necessarily, wears the colors of misfortune. . . .

Squaring the Family Circle

As for the woman who becomes a mother, her motivation will remain forever the same: "the old factor of the lack of a penis has even now not

[108]Cf. in this regard "The Taboo of Virginity," *SE*, XI:191–208. One may wonder how hysterical suggestibility comes to be the indispensable correlative of the infallibly valid authority of the father's law. How the prohibition on *ambivalence* vis-à-vis the symbolic should have cast the feminine (desire) down into the unformulable imaginary, thus consecrating the "scission" between the poles of a pair and a break in contact in sexual relations.

lost its strength." As we see from the unavoidable fact that "a mother is only brought unlimited satisfaction by her relation to a *son; this is al-together the most perfect, the most free of ambivalence of all human relationships." Indeed "a mother can transfer to her son the ambition which she has been obliged to suppress in herself, and she can expect from him the satisfaction of all that has been left over in her of the masculinity complex" (p. 133). Thus, it is not so much the fact of be-coming a mother that would cause an "alteration in a woman's nature . . . after the first child is born," or at any rate that *simple* fact would not be enough to solve her conflicts, particularly with her hus-band: if she is a mother *like* her mother, mother of a daughter, the unfortunate relationship with her parents—who produced a daughter—will again threaten the union with her husband. But if she is mother to a boy—which, alas, did not occur in the relationship with her mother and which thus sets up or confirms for her, by her, the value of another "beginning"—then she will find, they will find, "unlimited satisfac-tion." For, thanks to her son, she will be recompensed for her narcissistic humiliation, she will be able to love the "bearer of the penis" "perfectly" and "without *ambivalence.*" He is the pledge of family harmony. For "even a marriage is not made secure until the wife has succeeded in making her husband *her child* as well and acting *as a mother* to him" (pp. 133–34). It is the coming of the boy, the birth of a son, that will solve the squaring of the circle.[109] The family circle. Since woman is thereby satisfied and proud to be inscribed in, and to perpetuate, the family tree of her father-husband. Thus, it is not the repetition, re-presentation, and representation of *her* relation to *her* mother that will be decisive in this matter. Nor her discovery of a specific specular relationship to the pri-mal, the interaction of a "speculum" around which the matrical function would turn and re-turn—in an excess/access to woman's sexual desire. Nor, again, the fact that motherhood might mean, for woman, the only possibility of being recognized as "potent." No. Her complete satisfac-tion must be pandered to indirectly. Phallically. By giving life to one who has the right to power, she wins the right to be perfectly happy. Proud of having willingly assisted in revealing her own anatomical in-feriority. An accomplice, in some way, of the destiny that her "own" womb re-enacts by perpetuating the domination of the penis and sperm. The only origin, or end, her pleasure may have is to resurrect, re-erect,

---

[109]You will have noted that to solve the squaring of this "circle of desire," woman's sex organs have been marked by a *double negation* (cf. note 93), but that she has to cathect the penis or value standard in a *doubly positive* way. This economy of duplication, possible thanks to the birth of the son, would guarantee her drives from all *ambivalence.*

forever, the male organ. Whence her disappointment if she gives birth to a girl. Which betokens: twofold humiliation, inglorious re-mark of her sex, inability to reproduce a "good copy" of the sex, that is, the penis. Henceforward, she is pushed back against her will into confronting an unsolved problem: the relationship with her mother.

But Freud will try as best he can to get around this problem, in the interests of all concerned. He posits *two phases* in the woman's identification with her mother. The first, "the *pre-Oedipus* one . . . rests on her affectionate attachment to her mother and takes her as a model" (p. 134). This description scarcely corresponds to Freud's earlier and admittedly partial and incomplete characterization of the little girl at the pre-Oedipus stage as a little man with rich sadistic-anal instincts—not to mention others—and thus aggressive, possessive, and still displaying amazing phallic activity. As far as the relations with the mother are concerned, let us recall: that the girl's wishes are "completely ambivalent, both affectionate and of a hostile and aggressive nature"; that she "wishes to get the mother with child" and "to bear her a child"; that she fears being killed or poisoned; that she reproaches her mother for having given her "too little milk—which is construed against her as a lack of love"; that the "next accusation flairs up when the next baby appears in the nursery," whence "the strength of these jealous impulses." One may add that "an abundant source of the child's hostility to its mother is provided by its multifarious sexual wishes . . . which cannot for the most part be satisfied"; that this hostility is increased when the mother forbids the child to masturbate; that "these early object-cathexes are regularly ambivalent to a high degree. A powerful tendency to aggressiveness is always present beside a powerful love"; or again that "any . . . intervention in the child's liberty must provoke as a reaction an inclination to rebelliousness and aggressiveness" and "even the mildest upbringing cannot avoid using compulsion and introducing restrictions." (All these quotations are from "Femininity," pp. 122–24.) However affectionate the little girl may be toward her mother in this first phase Freud alludes to, that affection is not lacking in ambivalence, aggressiveness, and hostility. As for taking her mother as a *model*, how could the little girl who is a little boy do so? At least unambiguously?

During the second, *oedipal, phase,* the desire to "get rid of her mother and take her place with the father" dominates. Now this phase coincides with the little girl's recognition of her castration and her subsequent entry into the Oedipus complex, wherein the little girl turns toward her father upon the discovery of her own and her mother's mutilation. So it is not a question of a simple wish to get rid of the mother in order to take her place alongside the father. The rejection of the mother—as well as the identification with her and the subsequent wish to get rid of her and replace her—seems to be a necessary precondition for that process of "becoming a woman" that relies upon the girl devaluing her own sex/organ(s). And therefore her mother's also. Now Freud, at this point in his argument, insists that "the phase of the affectionate pre-Oedipus attachment is the decisive one for a woman's future: during it preparations are made for the acquisition of characteristics with which she will later fulfil her role in the sexual function and perform her invaluable social tasks" (p. 134). This reasoning comes as something of a surprise after all we have read about woman's sexual development; here we are told that woman performs her "sexual function" better if she has renewed those ties with her mother that existed before the discovery of castration, that is before she recognized the specificity of her sex. Likewise, the statement does not tally well with what has been, and will be, said about woman's "social tasks." But perhaps we only need to follow Freud in his argument? Let him explain what he means? So: "it is in this identification too that she acquires her attractiveness to a man, *whose Oedipus attachment to his mother it kindles into passion*"! If woman wishes to attract man, she must identify herself with his mother. This act is required of her. And the castrating will result from the amputation of the whole of her earlier economy. Which will stand in for the, *female,* castration complex.

Thus woman is allowed to go back to the origin, as long as it is not her own. From this viewpoint—of expropriation, expatriation, and not reappropriation—the further back she goes the better. For example, to the *primary oral phase,* characterized by dependence, passivity, to her status as a newborn-object, fed, loved, valued, watched, . . . by the all-powerful other. Before the period of biting and other forms of aggression, obviously. Woman *will therefore act out regression* to that "stage." Here again, acting is mandatory since it allows the enjoyment of appetites and urges, with no risk or danger of death in the event of frustration. And because it gives her the opportunity to "play" *the part of the mother at the same time.* The husband's mother. Some relief from that enforced verisimilitude may perhaps be found in the relationship with the child she brings into the world. Whence the fact that "often it happens . . . that it is only his son who obtains what he [the man] himself aspired to"?

Generation Gap, or Being Historically out of Phase?

"One gets the impression that a man's love and a woman's are a phase apart psychologically." Obviously. But how? Does Freud mean by this that woman always remains at the pre-Oedipus "phase," whereas man would be fixed in the oedipal stage? Ultimately, there would be only one love for both of them: the *primal* one that takes the mother—one's own mother—as object. Whence marital conflict? Between mothers-in-law? And it would be the son who, at a much later stage, would bring woman into the Oedipus situation. She is finally oedipized by the son's desire. For his mother. Finally she is desired unequivocally. By her son. Whence the fact that the birth of a son is the primary condition of stability for the family group. The family is held together by the desire of Oedipus. Father and son.

But this statement of Freud's, at the very end of his life, contradicts the descriptions and prescriptions he continually made about the little girl's sexual development. How are we to understand this? As an implicit acknowledgment that female sexuality cannot be reduced to the categories developed to account for male sexuality? Including the castration complex? Including the Oedipus complex? As a realization that psychoanalysis still continues to ram its head against that "dark continent," femininity? Or else as discourse that necessarily contradicts itself when it deals with woman? Since contradiction is the characteristic operation of the unconscious that always inevitably upsets (conscious) discourse when the desire for/of woman is involved? Whence the irrationality of Freud's statement that woman would never be as likely to perform her "sexual function" as when she is—according to him—a "little man," as when she sticks to her primitive, pre-oedipal masculininity; even if he later regrets that the "love" of man and woman should be separated by a difference in psychological phases. Does this mean that a man might hesitate between the love for his wife-mother and that for his wife-daughter? Or his wife-son? A pederast Oedipus? Of course. Undecided whether he will appropriate the mother *as a sexual "object"* or *through identification*. Meanwhile, in the last analysis, the mother rejects her husband in favor of her son. Whose desire is less twisted.

This difference in psychological "phases" is equally, then, a difference in generations, or in relationship to generation, which woman, bound up as she is in the cultural systems and the property regimes that dominate the West, will be ill prepared to mediate, metaphorize, or "displace." In light of this divergence in psychological phases, one would be led to reconsider the specific ways woman and man are made to fit into the economy of (re)production and to reinterpret with this in mind the compelling role historical determinants have played in shaping the "psychological" and the theories meant to explain it.

Woman's Enigmatic Bisexuality

Of course, "what I have been telling you here may be described as the *prehistory* of woman." How reassuring and yet how disquieting! All has not yet been said about female sexuality. . . . But what we are told about her "prehistory" implies such a misprision, such a negation, such a curb on her instincts and primary instinctual representatives, and therefore such an inhibition, reversal of cathexis, or "conversion" of instincts as to bode ill for the history that follows.

"Taking its prehistory as a starting point, I will only emphasize here that the development of femininity remains exposed to disturbance by the residual phenomena of the early masculine period. Regressions to the fixations of the pre-Oedipus phases very frequently occur; in the course of some women's lives there is a repeated alternation between periods in which masculinity or femininity gains the upper hand" (p. 131). So what men call " 'the enigma of women' may perhaps be derived from this expression of bisexuality in women's lives." This bisexuality would then be analyzed as "early masculinity" on the one hand, and as the "beginning of femininity" through the acceptance of the "accomplished fact of castration," on the other hand. As valid phallicism, and castrated phallicism. Or, yet again, as a "masculine" desire for the mother, and "envy" of the father's penis.

In which case, does female bisexuality not figure as an *inverted recapitulation of the "program" masculine sexuality writes for itself?* As a projection, upside down and backward, of the end—the telos—of male sexuality's history? And the "*enigma* of women" would serve as a sign of his progression toward knowledge. Absolute knowledge. For his part, he would have to let into the forces of consciousness this nonknowledge that she seemingly perpetuates, this "unconscious" that has been allocated to her without her knowing it. For her, the knowledge would be absolutely "unconscious," nonknowledge, but he is able to decipher it to the extent that in some way or other he has tied woman down as the guardian of the negative. As she who ensures the possibility of an infinity of regression: of consciousness and sex. The death of consciousness (and) of sex is necessary to achieve a dialectical progression through phallic sublimation(?).

Thus woman's bisexuality, the undecidable quality of her sexual conditioning, the "unconsciousness" that marks her relationship to sexuate things, would constitute *the store of sexual difference* that woman keeps in nonknowledge for all the useful ends of idealization(s). "Female" bisexuality would evoke the wrong side, the backside, the other side, the over side, of *the matrix of history* (of what is called masculine sexuality), and all these sides would remain enigmatic. The enigma always needing to be interpreted in its "unconsciousness," whose repression must, for more reasons than one, be safeguarded. Woman would be the basis, the inscriptional space, for the representatives of the "masculine" unconscious. For the "unconscious" of the historical development (of sexuality). For her, that economy could rate only as "pre-history." And if one day her sexuality was recognized, if it did enter into "History," then his-story would no longer simply take place or have a place to take.

"Woman Is a Woman as a Result of a Certain Lack of Characteristics"

"In any case it is not my intention to pursue *the further behaviour of femininity* through puberty to the period of maturity. *Our knowledge, moreover, would be insufficient* for the purpose" (p. 131). The tale of women's sexual history is suspended before woman reaches adulthood. Before even the onset of puberty is touched on. Before, that is, the "discovery of the vagina," and the womb? Before woman leaves her family, changes her proper name, marries, has children, nurses them. All rather crucial stages. As are others. But, as far as this later development goes, "I will bring a *few features* together," tell you "of *a few more* psychical *peculiarities* of *mature* femininity, as we come across them in analytic observation," while noting that it is "not always easy to distinguish what could be ascribed to the influence of the sexual function and what to social breeding." These few features may be listed as followed (pp. 132 and 134):

(1) "Thus, we attribute *a larger amount of narcissism* to femininity, which also affects women's choice of object, so that to be loved is a stronger need for them than to love."

(2) "The effect of penis-envy has a share, furthermore, in *the physical vanity of women,* since they are bound to value their charms more highly as a late compensation for their original sexual inferiority."

(3) "*Shame,* which is considered to be a feminine characteristic *par excellence* but is far more a matter of convention than might be supposed, *has as its purpose,* we believe, *concealment of genital deficiency.*"

(4) "*Women have made few contributions to the discoveries and inventions in the history of civilization;* there is, however, one *technique* which they may have invented—that of plaiting and weaving. . . . *Nature* herself would seem to have given the *model* which this achievement *imitates* by causing the growth at maturity of the pubic hair that conceals the genitals. The step that remained to be taken lay in making the threads adhere to one another, while on the body they stick into the skin and are only matted together . . . we should be tempted to guess the unconscious motive for the achievement."

(5) "The fact that women must be regarded as having little sense of justice is no doubt related to the *predominance of envy in their mental life.*"

(6) "We also regard women as weaker in their *social interests*," no doubt because of "the dissocial quality which unquestionably characterizes all sexual relations."

(7) And women have "*less capacity for sublimating their instincts* than men."

(8) "A man of about thirty strikes us as a youthful, somewhat unformed individual. . . . *A woman of the same age, however, often frightens us by her psychical rigidity and unchangeability.* Her libido has taken up final positions and seems incapable of exchanging them for others. *There are no paths open to further development;* it is as though the whole process had already run its course and remains thenceforward insusceptible to influence—as though, indeed, the difficult development to femininity had exhausted the possibilities of the person concerned. . . . As therapists we lament this state of things, even if we succeed in putting an end to our patient's ailment by doing away with her neurotic conflict."

Very well. . . . But:

(1) An Ex-orbitant Narcissism

Does woman really have the option of "loving" or "being loved"? Even if we admitted that this description of the female choice of object in any way corresponded to reality. Femininity is instigated by a wave of passivity, by the transformations of the little girl's early instincts into instincts "with a passive aim" and by her perpetuating the "object" pole. When it really comes down to it, then, woman will not choose, or desire, an "object" of love but will arrange matters so that a "subject" takes her as his "object." The desirable "object" is always the penis, the phallus. Of the man (or) of the mother. Woman will therefore borrow from him or from them as much as she can, if she intends to sustain the "subject's" desire. If she wants him to love himself in her, (by the detour) through her. She is narcissistic, in fact, but only by phallic mandate, for, as we have seen, any narcissization of her own sex/organ(s) is completely out of the question. She is mutilated, amputated, humiliated . . . because of being a woman.

(2) The Vanity of a Commodity

Woman's physical vanity, which compensates for her original sexual inferiority, is said to be caused by "penis-envy." Let us accept the hypothesis. But, here again, *we may question whether woman has a choice of being or not being vain about her body* if she is to correspond to the "femininity" expected of her. Does not her sexual "usefulness" depend upon her being concerned about the qualities or "properties" of her body? If she is to solicit, support,and even swell the sexual pleasure of the male consumer. But he also demands reassurance about his possession of the standard of sexual values: whence the *essential* intervention of "penis-envy." Thus "femininity" is caught in a vicious circle; because she doesn't have "it," she must wish to have "it" since "it" is the guarantor of sexual exchange, but she doesn't have "it" so as to drive up, through her envy, "its" market rating as "general equivalent."

There is one problem, however; acting as if one had "it," pretending to have "it", in this kind of business, is a transaction that undercuts all the rates. Now woman cannot mime, pretend, any relation to *her own* sex organ(s) because she has been cut off from any access to idea, ideality, specula(riza)tion, and indeed a certain organic "reality." Therefore, since she really does not have the same sex organ that holds the monopoly on value, she will be particularly good at acting "as if" she had it, at "making believe" she has it. This is indeed what is required of her by man's castration anxiety and his fear of satisfying her instincts, even if we make no guesses as to what such a proposition might lead. The "physical vanity" of women, the "fetishization" of her body—a process patterned after that of the model and prototype of all fetishes: the penis—are mandatory if she is to be a desirable "object" and if he is to want to possess her. But no doubt she will in her turn seek to secure an increase in her price. The cosmetics, the disguises of all kinds that women cover themselves with are intended to deceive, to promise more value than can be delivered. Can they thus be seen as signs of a desire to appropriate the powers of the penis? Or at least to compete in the phallic economy by denying that they function under exploitation? Is there pleasure in this for women? Not much, not simply. This secondary, reactive forma-tion—"late compensation for their original sexual inferiority"—is always at the mercy of a look of depreciation and does not dress (or address?) the wounds of her past narcissistic humiliations, of her "congenital" inferiority; it does not alleviate the repression of her auto-erot-ism that is henceforth covered with shame. Even if someday she plays to perfection the role of femininity in all its bouregois perversity, it will in no way fill, will only deck with nothingness, this fault, this lack, of a specific specular economy and of a possible representation of her value, *for her and by her,* which could bring her into the system of exchange as something other than "object." This is not to say that she will not give them a run for their money, that she will not become a formidable rival in the marketplace of sexual equivalents, or that he will not fancy all the gold in the world has been set up as her capital. Or perhaps has been plated over her? Her body transformed into gold to satisfy his auto-erotic, scoptophiliac, and possessive instincts. . . .

(3) The Shame That Demands Vicious Conformity

But "shame" will remain as testimony to the deficiency of her genitals. Shame has doubtless become conventional, but still, its first goal was to hide the defective, imperfect parts of the female body. Shame will be the reminder, in reverse, of the compromise and the disavowal at work in the fetish. Though her body is beautiful and she is decked out in gold for him and by him, woman will still be reserved, modest, shameful, as far as her sex organs are concerned. She will discreetly assist in hiding them. Ensuring this *double game* of flaunting her body, her jewels, in order to hide her sex organs all the better. For woman's "body" has some "usefulness," represents some "value" only on condition that her sex organs are hidden. Since they are something and nothing in consumer terms. Are pictured in fantasy, what is more, as a greedy mouth. How can one trade on something so empty? To sell herself, woman has to veil as best she can how price-less she is in the sexual economy.[110]

(4) Women Have Never Invented Anything but Weaving

Whence the importance she vests in fabrics and cloth to cover herself with. This would explain the only contribution women have made to "the discoveries and inventions in the history of civilization"—weaving. Which is, however, more or less, an *"imitation"* of the *"model"* Nature gives in the pubic hair. Woman can, it seems, (only) imitate nature. Duplicate what nature offers and produces. In a kind of *technical* assistance and substitution. But this is paradoxical. Since Nature is all. But this "all" cannot appear as no thing, as no sex organ, for example. Therefore woman weaves in order to veil herself, mask the faults of Nature, and restore her in her wholeness. *By wrapping her up.* In a wrapping that Marx has told us preserves the "value" from a just evaluation. And allows the "exchange" of goods "without knowledge" of their effective value. By abstracting "products," by making them universal and interchangeable without recognizing their differences.[111] In a wrapping that Freud tells us serves to hid the difference of the sexes from the horrified gaze of the little boy, and the man. "We know how children react to their first impressions of the absence of the penis. They disavow the fact and believe that they *do* [SE, italics] see a penis, all the same.

---

[110]In fact it is as a body imprinted with the value of a penis-phallus that she is bought: that of the father or the pimp.

[111]Cf. *Capital*, Vol. I, Pt. I, ch. I, sec. 4.

They gloss over the contradiction between observation and preconception."[112]
Almost imperceptibly, the wrapping will have brought Nature and her
work into the fetishistic economy by hiding all she is capable of producing and preventing us from appreciating it. Beliefs and preconceptions,
from now on, are supported. And kept away from the contradiction of
observation.

But *the contradiction is already implicit in the veil* ["glossing over"] Freud
talks about, in the *duplicity* of that veil's function. Used to cover a lesser
"value" and to overvalue the fetish, it will equally serve to conceal the
interest afforded by what it claims to protect from devaluation: the interest, for example, one might take in the place of copulation; also, in an
other way, of conception. Or again it will fail to inquire how much
copulation might cost, for this is obviously difficult to calculate and
threatens the validity of the economy in place. If for no other reason than
that it cannot and could not, in any circumstances, be seen or known.
Thus challenging the systems of representation(s), of coining(s) of profits
and losses. Setting fire, it may be, to fetishes. Whence the need for
weaving to shield the gilded eyes from the possible incandescence of the
standard. Its (re)fusion at each copulation. A protective, defensive tex-
ture. A hymen whose usefulness needs to be re-evaluated, whether as a
"member-screen" or as "marriage." The "marriage" would be the *exclusive contract for the "use" of a certain value (of) wrapping*. The stakes in
this contract will be invested in a variety of places, thereby allowing for a
diversified portfolio. In woven goods, for example; sometimes figur-
atively woven. Into a mobilization, monopolization of sexual value for
the production of cloth, tissue, or text which abscond with its inner
prize, its inner fires (l'en jeu, l'en feu), and put them into the checking
account of a proper name, very often. One is referred, or turned back, to
the standards governing the possession of discourse, to God, the paradigm of all proper names/nouns, who (re)produces himself in a virgin
through the intercession of the word. Meanwhile woman weaves to
sustain the disavowal of her sex.

And this disavowal is also a fabric(ation) and not without possible
duplicity. It is at least double. *The woman and the mother do not double for
each other in exactly the same way*. The function of the wrapping is not the
same: a sheath does not enwrap in the same way as an amniotic membrane. "For example." Equally *heterogeneous* is the role of the "veil" that
serves to sustain the fetishist illusion. And that covers up *more than one*

---

[112]"Infantile Genital Organization," *SE*, xix:143–44. (The *Standard Edition* expression
"gloss over" is rendered in French by "throw a *veil* over," and the image of the veil is
echoed in the weaving-textile metaphor used in this passage of *Speculum*.—Tr.)

disavowal. And by stressing the disavowal of the mother's castration, one also disavows the risk of copulative combustion. By seeking to shield oneself from seeing that the mother has no penis, one will have already denied woman her sexual potency, the power of her jouissance. And of jouissance. By fetishizing the male organ. With which woman will be equipped, just possibly, after the consecration. The mother, once again, will have masked the woman. The veil also says: the matrical must (again) wrap up the vaginal. The membrane used to wrap up the goods, both to assist and to hide the work of (re)production, must close off and conceal the inner prize of pleasure. The inner fires. The threat to every fetishistic economy. To what veils everything more or less, in all systems of equivalents. Since the misprision of sexual difference remains, now and forever, their condition of possibility.

(5) A Very Envious Nature

"The fact that women must be regarded as having *little sense of justice* is no doubt related to *the predominance of envy* in their mental life." Given that woman has been unable to work out her envy in the way justice demands, she would indeed be unfamiliar with "the condition subject to which one can put envy aside." Woman's "envies" would not find an economy, a right, a system or law, to regulate the ways in which those envies could or could not be expressed. Indeed, the needs and desires of the little girl have remained "latent": curbed, inhibited, repressed, converted into hatred (of the mother), contempt (for the female sex), etc. All operations which, obviously, reinforce resentment, greed. instinctual tensions, but offer no way to measure them. The libidinal "catastrophe" represented by the little girl's discovery of castration results in "penis-envy" that will measure out, articulate the stages in "becoming a woman," and ensure their continuation.

But this "envy" is not simply to be read in terms of justice. *It sustains the cult of the fetish prototype.* And as such deserves to be interpreted as a *religious* tendency. "Mystic" values to which woman would be *predisposed:* by the suspension and censorship of her instincts; by all that remains enigmatic, obscure, and dark from her early childhood, her "pre-Oedipus" stage; by the revelation, also, of the male organ as signifier of omnipotence; by her marginality with respect to the systems of exchange; by her "passivity," even her "masochism," etc. A religious office to which she would be preordained, with which she would be entrusted. And all this has nothing to do with justice and might even oppose it. Veneration for the phallus defies the laws of the city, challenges their rulings and penalties. It doesn't give a fig about issues of legitimacy in men's conflicts. All it cares about is keeping the phallic emblem out of the dirt, covering over its dissoluteness, veiling its decay. Preserving it from derision, insignificance, and devaluation. Even if woman must die in the attempt, she will carry out her mission. Virgin? Her deed will be all the more exemplary. Condemned by the king? She will have shown all the more clearly the contradictions in the system. As the ruler's unworthy anger shows. For if woman does not religiously, blindly, support the attributes of power of the king, judge, or warrior, that power may well decline, or prove useless, since the real issue is always men's competition for power. That said, the patriarchal regime could scarcely be expected to tolerate Antigone's loud assertions about the mother's "phallic" empire, the rights of blood, her defiance of the king's scepter and the penis of his heir! In patriarchy, the revival of relations between mother and daughter always creates conflict.

To get back to justice or the "sense of justice," one might wonder how woman could possibly acquire it since *she is included in the exchange market only as a commodity.*[113] "If commodities could speak," they might possibly give an opinion about their price, about whether they consider their status just, or about the dealings of their owners. As for "modifying their envies" or knowing how to handle them justly, this seems difficult to manage. For even without speaking, "they cannot make their own way to market." They continue to rely on sustaining the "envy" of the buyers. Their "guardians." Who, of course, "must enter into relation one with another as persons, . . . reciprocally recognise one another as private owners. . . . This legal relation . . . secures outward expression in a contract . . . (whether legally formulated or no)." The "value" of the commodities in these more or less legal transactions is certainly crucial, but the commodities themselves have nothing to ask or say, no desire or need to express, no sale or purchase to make on their own account. At best they will be women mad about their bodies, which will make trade easier. By guaranteeing "envy." In a role assigned to woman that must be performed, even if it entails a few secondary accidents in order for the progress of established things to go smoothly.

In order, in this way, to perpetuate phallocentrism. For if woman did not want what he has, it would soon be obvious that the concentration on the phallus suffers from a certain ex-centricity. The problem is that woman often finds it hard not to claim access to the procedures of equivalency that are still limited by right to men alone, or at any rate to

[113](Expressions in quotation marks in the rest of this section are taken from Marx's *Capital,* vol. I, pt. I, ch. I, sec. 4, and ch. 2.—Tr.)

"masculinity," and whose practice is prescribed and re-marked by phallic hegemony. And ignorant, unaware of what she has earned by her merits, her value, by the potential specificity of her role in the exchange economy, woman will only be able to "envy" and demand powers equal, or "equivalent" to those of men. There comes, perhaps ineluctably, a moment when she will represent herself as the oppressed, the victim of penile narcissism, just so that she can get possession of those privileges. In a sexual revolt, or revolution that would simply reverse things and risk ensuring an everlasting return of the same. Thus, Freud is to a certain extent right in his opposition to the "feminists," except that the reasons he cites are questionable and testify to his failure to grasp the importance of the question.

(6) Society Holds No Interest for Women

And this is all the more true in that women's "social interests" are at stake. It could be conceded that sexual liberation is a demand, and notably a feminist demand, the terms of which have not infrequently been poorly expressed, ill judged, inadequately worked out. It is true these terms have lent themselves to irony and ridicule for such reactions come all too easily to privileged users of language who do not need to first acquire its use to then go on to subvert it. Nonetheless, the demands for social justice made by these emancipated women (or by those who at least hope to be emancipated) are not so easily eluded. Of course, it is still a matter, ultimately, of demanding the *same* prerogatives. Nonetheless, women have to advance to those same privileges (and to sameness, perhaps) before any consideration can be given to the differences that they might give rise to. For the fact that women are "weaker in their social interests" is obvious. The ambiguity, the double meaning, of that expression makes further comment unnecessary. And why, after all, should women be interested in a society in which they have no stake, which earns them interest only through the compulsory intervention of a third person who does hold a legal and de facto stake? Through "masculine protest"? Which risks earning them liabilities rather than . . . interest. Through masochism? On the social level, masochism offers little pleasure. In fact, how can one take part in social life when one has no available currency, when one possesses nothing of one's own to put in relation to the properties of the other, or others?

So . . . woman's weaker social interest "is no doubt derived from the dissocial quality which unquestionably characterizes all sexual relations. Lovers find sufficiency in each other, and families too resist inclusion in more comprehensive associations." Or again: woman's social inferiority *doubles* her sexual inferiority, and/or *reciprocally* so in a circularity it will be hard to get past, or out of. Thus, whereas one is aware of what social advantages woman sees herself refusing on the grounds of her "constitution," one forgets a little too easily the extent to which the estimates made of that constitution are themselves a factor in the social status allotted to women. Society, on the pretext of mimicking and assisting a nature for which it has itself provided the definition—we always go in circles—would "exert more constraint" upon women and take less account of femininity's "demands than in the case of masculinity." The result is that one cannot justify putting the words "female/social/interests" in the same phrase. Any more than "female/libido," perhaps? So why cite the "fact" that woman shows no interest in public affairs because she is more absorbed by sexual relations? because "lovers find sufficiency in each other"? Or the "fact" that women are often "frigid" as a function of their libidinal "destiny" and can rarely love anyone because of their penis-envy, etc.

All this is certainly very "obscure" and will remain so as long as "femininity" and the roles ascribed to it are not perceived to be both "secondary" formations and prescriptions that are "useful" to masculinity. Any other explanation that attempts to relate "femininity" to "woman"—constitution, biological destiny, castration, and even Oedipus complexes, frigidity, envy of the penis, and all the rest, vanity, shame, and weaving . . . —amounts to a set of statements so contradictory as to be surprising in a *masculine* argument. And the contradictions might possibly be explained by the lack of attention or interest (?) *Freud* devotes in this passage to the *social* dimension of sexual relations.

Marx defines man's relation to woman as an index of his relations to all his fellows, notably insofar as exploitation is concerned.[114] Whether they be considered as origin, practice, or reflection, sexual relations clearly cannot be dissociated from the general economy in which they operate. Equally clearly, when one thinks of women's weaker social interest in terms of preoccupations that are too exclusively sexual—and necessarily "a-social" therefore?—one is forgetting that to all intents and purposes the modes of sexual relation are determined by society and that thereby certain social structures are both perpetuated and initiated. Thus, if the social assignment allocated to women is the care and anxiety of sexual and amorous matters—as Freud's text assumes—then the question arises

[114]Marx, *Economic and Philosophic Manuscripts of 1844,* (London: Lawrence and Wishart, 1959), pp. 100–101.

as to which women he is talking about. Can his statement be extended to cover all societies, all classes? In other words, what *economic infrastructure governs Freud's conception of the role of woman?* Even as we take it as given that he reproaches woman for her lack of abilities—sexual, psychological, cultural, etc. Such misogyny can be understood as *an ideological bond that bails out* the current regimes of property.

For woman's work—which we may agree, provisionally, stands in a privileged relation to "love," "family," and "home"—has not always had the trait of reclusiveness and social isolation that Freud notes and that he sees as women's "weaker social interests," "social inferiority." Only with the advent of the *patriarchal family* and more particularly with the *monogamous individual family* does housekeeping lose its social character and limit itself to "private service." "The wife became the head servant, excluded from all participation in social production." And the succession of different property regimes—slave, feudal, capitalist—has not altered the fact that woman is possessed by the head of the family as a "mere instrument of production"[115] and reproduction. The marriage contract will often have been *implicitly a work contract,* but one that is not ratified as such by law, thereby depriving woman of her right to perfectly legitimate social demands: salary, work hours, vacations, etc. She is accepted on an "equal footing" in a home in which she takes care of the domestic chores in exchange for food, lodging, and clothes: an "au pair" wife. "The modern individual family is founded on the open or concealed domestic slavery of the wife. . . . In the great majority of cases today, . . . the husband is obliged to earn a living and support his family, and that in itself gives him a position of supremacy without any need for special legal titles and privileges. Within the family he is the *bourgeois* and the wife represents the *proletariat.*" (Engels, p. 137). As well as being an undeclared work contract, the marriage contract will also have disguised *a purchase agreement for the body and sex of the wife,* "who only differs from the ordinary courtesan in that she does not let out her body on piecework as a wage worker, but sells it once and for all into slavery" (Engels, p. 134). "Isn't a girl a commodity displayed for sale to whoever wants to negotiate her purchase and exclusive ownership? . . . *As in grammar two negatives make an affirmative, so one can say that in matrimonial morality two prostitutions pass for a virtue*" (Fourier, quoted by Engels, p. 135). Many

---

[115](Page references in the following section are to Friedrich Engels's *The Origin of the Family, Private Property, and the State,* New World paperback edition [New York: International Publishers, 1972], and are included in the text. The first quotation appears on p. 127.—Tr.)

analyses of this kind could be quoted. For example: "woman is a property acquired by contract: she is part of one's personal estate as possession gives title."[116]

This contract is usually drawn up between the father and the husband—like and unlike that between the customer and the pimp—with virginity being figured as a value over and above the dowry, in exchange for a certain capacity for work and a certain guarantee of potency demanded of the future husband (but no one will have neglected to make clear that these are also required of the bride, at least as far as the aptitude for work goes). Or else the whole deal will be arranged between the heads of two families as a function of their respective fortunes and ideological interests. In any case, *two men* will come to an agreement whereby the woman passes from one "house" to another and joins another "family circle." And as the father had to protect his daughter's virginity since this was a value necessary for her "exchange," the husband will have to keep his wife at home to ensure the concentration of his wealth in a single place, and its transmission by inheritance to his own children and no one else's. "Monogamy arose from the concentration of considerable wealth in the hands of a single individual—a man—and from that need to bequeath this wealth to the children of that man and of no other. *For this purpose, the monogamy of the woman was required, not that of the man,* so this monogamy of the woman did not in any way interfere with open or concealed polygamy on the part of man" (Engels, p. 138). "Monogamy and prostitution are indeed contradictions, but inseparable contradictions, poles of the same state of society" (Engels, p. 139). In fact these two poles are joined together in traditional monogamous marriage, a legal form of prostitution that is not declared as such and therefore, no doubt by negation, produces *moralism*. In any case, "families too resist inclusion in more comprehensive associations." Resist letting woman out of the house. And this keeps her in a state of economic dependence that justifies every kind of oppression. For example, the fact that "notwithstanding all the laws emancipating woman, she continues to be a *domestic slave,* because *petty housework* crushes, strangles, stultifies and degrades her, chains her to the kitchen and the nursery, and she wastes her labour on barbarously unproductive, petty, nerve-wracking, stultifying and crushing drudgery."[117] This state of things is essential to maintain the private nature of the appropriation of goods, to keep the nuclear family as society's economic unit: "The first class opposition that

[116]Balzac, *The Physiology of Marriage*.
[117]Lenin, "A Great Beginning," *Collected Works,* xxix, March–August 1919 (London: Lawrence and Wishart, 1965), p. 429. The italics are Lenin's.

appears in history coincides with the development of the antagonism between man and woman in monogamous marriage, and the first class oppression coincides with that of the female sex by the male" (Engels, p. 129).[118]

And it is never in the long-term plans of established power for oppressed persons (of either sex) to become interested in their social status or concerned about their "social inferiority." With the result that even if the economic role assigned to woman for centuries explains why she now pays little attention to "public" issues, one can be sure that powerful interests even today would like to distract her from such concerns. In the final analysis, is it these same interests that determine Freud's doctrine on woman's sexuality? Obviously Freud is right insofar as he is describing the status quo. But his statements are not mere descriptions. They establish rules intended to be put into practice. Therefore?

(7) A Fault in Sublimation

"We also regard women as having . . . less capacity for sublimating their instincts than men." Which gives a more absolute power to the (counter)transference to/of the analyst—father, man, husband—and makes it doubtful whether interpretation can offer any solutions.

It is assumed that woman, apart from a few exceptional individuals, has less aptitude than man for sublimation. That assumption is built into the very operation of sublimation, into its purpose, its conditions, its methods. And by falling back upon comparison—"less capacity"—Freud will once again have seen female sexuality as a *lesser version of masculine sexuality*. Now everything he has told us about becoming a woman explains why "femininity," even successfully achieved, cannot sublimate. For example, the super-ego in femininity works to impede sublimation. The mother, upon whom the primary identification is based, turns out to be castrated and therefore devalued; as for identifying with the "paternal prototype"—whether that be the "primitive" phallic

---

[118]Also: "With the division of labour, in which all these contradictions are implicit, and which in its turn is based on the natural division of labour in the family and the separation of society into individual families opposed to one another, is given simultaneously the *distribution,* and indeed the *unequal* distribution, both quantitative and qualitative, of labour and its products, hence property: the nucleus, the first form, of which lies in the family, where wife and children are the slaves of the husband. This latent slavery in the family, though still very crude, is the first property, but even at this early stage it corresponds perfectly to the definition of modern economists who call it the power of disposing of the labour-power of others. Divisions of labour and private property are, moreover, identical expressions: in the one the same thing is affirmed with reference to activity as is affirmed in the other in reference to the product of the activity": Marx and Engels, *The German Ideology,* in *The Marx-Engels Reader,* 2d ed., ed. R. C. Tucker (New York: Norton, 1972), pp. 159–60; italics in original.

123

mother or the father—, this is prohibited to woman twice over: the penis represents the object of desire that cannot be totally introjected since the super-ego which would result from that identification would be "masculine." Therefore woman will remain in *a state of childish dependence upon a phallic super-ego* that looks sternly and disdainfully on her castrated sex/organ(s). In its cruelty, woman's super-ego will favor the proliferation of masochistic fantasies and activities, rather than help build up "cultural" values. Which are masculine in any case.

Sublimation implies, also, the transformation of sexual libido into desexualized energy that can fuel the ego. Now, besides the fact that the definition of "ego" in woman is far from settled, the feelings of inferiority from which woman suffers and which are essential to the sexual and social role she is allotted do not promote the development of her narcissistic libido. Except through identification with male patterns (that result in her mouthing "masculine protests") or else through her willing agreement to represent the penis for man, to serve by proxy as its fetishistic basis and play the walk-on part of desirable "thing." Not surprisingly, such "things" have "less capacity for sublimating their instincts." We should also remember that woman has the task of maintaining the "object" end of the subject-object polarity of sexual difference; she will therefore be unable to perform the "substitution of objects" that occurs in the process of sublimation. Moreover, that sublimation is governed by social concerns in which she has no interest.

What is more, we know that the little girl's instinctual energy was curbed as a result of her "castration complex." Hence she will have little energy to invest in sublimating activities. Any remaining energy will go into her "attachment for her father . . . when repression has not been too strong." And of course we must always keep in mind the long, painful job of initiating femininity.

Is it necessary to add, or repeat, that woman's "improper" access to representation, her entry into a specular and speculative economy that affords her instincts no signs, no symbols or emblems, or methods of writing that could figure her instincts, make it impossible for her to work out or transpose specific representatives of her instinctual object-goals? The latter are in fact subjected to a particularly peremptory repression and will only be translated into a *script of body language*. Silent and cryptic. Replacing the fantasies she cannot have—or can have only when her amputated desires turn back on her masochistically, or when she is obliged to lend a hand with "penis-envy." There is no longer any question, even at this stage, of a system of fantasies that would correspond to

124

her own instincts, particularly her primary instincts. Nothing will be known about those, except, perhaps, in *dream*. Woman's desire can find expression only in dreams. It can never, under any circumstances, take on a "conscious" shape.

Enigmatic "somatizations," hysterical "dreams" in which we are supposed to see "the caricature of a work of art," as Freud puts it in *Totem and Taboo*. Woman's special form of neurosis would be to "mimic" a work of art, to be *a bad (copy of a) work of art*. Her neurosis would be recognized as a counterfeit or parody of an artistic process. It is transformed into an aesthetic object, but one without value, which has to be condemned because it is *a forgery*. It is neither "nature" nor an appropriate technique for re-producing nature. Artifice, lie, deception, snare—these are the kinds of judgments society confers upon the tableaux, the scenes, the dramas, the pantomimes produced by the hysteric. And if woman's instincts try to command public recognition in this way, their demand and de-monstration will be met with derision, anathema, and punishment. Or at least by belittling interpretations, appeals to common sense or to reason. A society has the duty to ban forgeries. And the hysterical woman who flaunts an appearance exceeding and defying the natural, the legally sanctioned mean, must be chastised. She must be curbed, humiliated, brought back to chastity, whether she likes it or not. Asceticism, decency, shame, are the forms of "sublimation" required of woman. Let us leave these forms "latent" for as long as it takes to get at least a hint of how *socially* pertinent sado-masochism is.

The proliferation of fake appearances put into circulation by the hysteric forces us to remember blood. Red blood. Woman, virgin and mother, represents the blood reserves. This natural source of profit—acknowledged as such in "prehistory" when the value of blood was recognized and even exhalted above all else—is denied, censored in favor of other goods and powers when patriarchy is established. Blood becomes covered over by other forms of wealth: gold, penis, child—we have already noted the system of possible equivalents in the anal economy. All these terms can be interchanged with "excrement" in the current imaginary of any "subject." Blood rights are so completely neglected that "consanguineous" is now defined as "sired by the same father" and, what is more, set in opposition to the word "uterine".[119] Sperm has capitalized the authority, the attributes, the product of labor, once associ-

---

[119](The definition of "consanguineous" that LI is using here is not usual in English, but the OED supports her point about the historical shift in the meaning of "blood relative": "MAINE, Anc. Law, V, (1870), 152. In the customs of Normandy, the rule applies to uterine brothers only . . . (in) England, the judges . . . extended it to consanguineous brothers, that is to sons of the same father by different wives"—Tr.)

ated with blood. But blood is not easily repressed. Its empire will be even greater as a result of the forgeries of maternal power that are to be turned out. Blood will play a major role in the sadistic and masochistic practices that are the mainstay of, almost, every "subject." He will be able to find pleasure only by opening up (again) the vein of blood. Red blood. By shedding blood (again). The blood of the mother. Wife or virgin. These forbidden tastes, sacred and impure, vicious, will reach consciousness only in the privacy of the bedroom, only in fantasy productions that are rarely discussed in public. It will be manifest only in the sheer strength of the sado-masochistic economy which expresses the desire to transgress the prohibition on bleeding and to overturn or deny the power of blood: man is cast as "active," woman as "passive." Man will beat the hysteric, for example, if for no other reason than that she needs to be brought back to the reality of "life." And this has already passed, of course, into the fake's pretence of self-sufficiency. Perhaps blood will have the freedom of the city, and the right to circulate, only if it takes the form of ink. The pen will always already have been dipped into the murdered bodies of the mother and the woman and will write in black, in black blood (like) ink, the clotting of its (his?) desires and pleasures.

But can any sublimation for blood lust be achieved? Does any socially recognized production exist that allows one to change all that blood lust implies? Or does a society—especially a society of leeches—depend upon a censorship of the attraction of blood? And, more specifically, does it depend upon a refusal to recognize the value of blood? Does valuing the one rely upon devaluing the other? *The history of sublimation is advanced by sublating the added-value of the forgery.* Therefore any effusion, or even transfusion, of blood will be taboo. Unless, of course, it has been pre-scribed by the City, or by Science—in what amounts to a pretense of setting the prohibition aside. Woman, who continues to keep the re-pressed elements in this prohibition alive, will therefore be rejected by society, under the pretext that she is anatomically inferior, castrated. And anything she produces will find a market only when it gains legit-imacy under man's name or auspices.

In the intimacy of the house, the privacy of the home, woman will hide away everything associated with blood. She will recognize its price only through humiliation and suffering. For the power of the female sex has to be conquered over and over again. The head of the family has to re-insure his potency. Every single day, therefore, he is enjoined to reappropriate the right to exploit blood and then, as a result, to go on to more sublime pursuits. The master is a vampire who needs to stay in disguise and do his work at night. Otherwise he is reminded that he is dependent on death. And on birth. On the material, uterine foundations of his mastery. Only if these be repressed can he enjoy sole ownership.

The wife, the mother, in different ways of course, will aid and abet this tyranny. Women's instincts are inhibited, turned back into their opposites, transformed into feelings of affection that will never manage to satisfy the sexual need which gave rise to them, as Freud has warned us. Such as the forms of "sublimation" that man, that society, demands of woman. *Libidinal continence,* in a word. Patient labor at instinctual self-destruction. Ceaseless "activity" of mortification. In this way, both by her and for her, the invisible work of death goes on. Relentlessly, woman reconnects the end to the beginning, though the end and the beginning are not *hers.* (Re)calling death in utero. But all this is *before her* conception in *her* mother and does not happen in any woman's real womb. Conception is depersonalized, impersonalized, universalized. All and nothing of the beginning and of the end. And meanwhile man projects the sublimation of beginning and end into immortal specula(riza)-tions.

(8) "La Femme de Trente Ans"

This discussion of the main features of female sexuality will end or suspend with a literary myth: Balzac's "La femme de trente ans." But here it will take a rather unexpected form. An unattractive form. Unless this simply shows the other sides of the seductive charms of that famous "woman of thirty."

"On the other hand I cannot help mentioning an impression that we are constantly receiving during analytic practice. . . . A woman of the same age (ca. 30), however, often frightens us by her psychical rigidity and unchangeability" (p. 134–35). Has she become assimilated to the patient work of death? Has she, moreover, become fixed in the representation of "femininity" prescribed for her? Is she a fetish whose corpselike beauty reflects a sexual indifference that has been won the hard way. "Her libido has taken up final positions and seems incapable of exchanging them for others." Her libido? What is this supposed to mean? There is no "female libido." But perhaps what libido she has has been so curbed, censored and finally inhibited that it can never function; perhaps woman does not have enough energy to change her condition. Especially since that condition is a result of social, economic, and cultural conditions and conditioning. These "final positions" Freud talks about could potentially be changed only by evolutions or revolutions of such importance that *one*

127

woman, even at the age of thirty, could not bring them about alone. Let us not forget in fact that so many different tasks are assigned to woman, so much work in the home, that she has little free time. Even if she had time, it would hardly be fitting for her to seek "inclusion in more comprehensive associations." Thus, at the age of thirty, married, mother of one, two, three . . . children, she has no more goals to pursue that would be acceptable to society. She can only carry on tirelessly with the same task. Perhaps she may have to accept that her husband has a mistress or two? This could lead her in the best of circumstances to reconsider or analyze her relationship to homosexuality. But these are not things one talks about, and it is not even certain that she herself will have the opportunity to say anything about it. Any more than about the even greater difficulties she will meet if she gets the desire to take one or more male lovers. She still has her son, you say? Yes, if her childhood dream has had the good luck to come true.

History and her story go on. . . . But what of "the paths open to further development"? "It is as though the whole process had already *run its course* and remains thenceforward insusceptible to influence—as though indeed the *difficult* development to femininity had exhausted the possibilities of the *person concerned*" (p. 135). As though the story was over? As though woman's history had never got further than prehistory?And, given that this "difficult development" to femininity has largely been the result of influences that are already fully operative—family, and patriarchal social power, phallocratic ideology "threatening her with a loss of love" if she does not submit[120]—the said "influences" demand only one thing of the woman of thirty, that she continue to satisfy them and be satisfied by them.

She is, however, quite unsatisfied. And this dissatisfaction will, in all probability, lead her to consult a therapist who will "lament this state of things" and fail to ameliorate it "even if [he] succeed[s] *in putting an end to [his] patient's ailment* by doing away with her neurotic conflict." Which is as much as to say. . . . The therapist's response is still surprising, all the same. The thirty-year-old woman may be accurately assumed to suffer from a hysterical psychosis, or neurosis, and to present to the analyst symptoms that are quite mobile and malleable. She no doubt expresses an anxiety of frustration that is in dire need of transference. For anyone still interested in such things, she is ideally susceptible to hypnosis and suggestion because of the fragility of her insertion into the symbolic system. All in all, *analytic practice might have been invented for her!* And not

[120]"Dissolution of the Oedipus Complex," *SE*, XIX:178.

for "the man of thirty" who will be predisposed by his socio-cultural involvement to obsessional psychoneurosis. But it seems that all that psychoanalysis can do for this woman is to confirm the "final positions" that her (?) libido has been forced to take up. The obsessional male—perhaps slightly paranoid?—strives to ease these female conflicts perhaps in order to maintain the status quo ante. Since he does not really want anything to change or evolve. He has no desire for woman to upset him in his sexual habits, his scoptophiliac and sadistic-anal instinctual economy, his narcissizing sublimations, his rather suspect respect for law and order. He does not want her to be anything but *his daughter,* whose gratifying fantasies of seduction it is his task to interpret, and who must be initiated into, and curbed by, the "reasonable" discourse of his (sexual) law. Or else he wants her to be *his mother,* whose erotic reveries he would take some pleasure in hearing, whose most secret intimacy he would finally gain access to. Unless again some very "unconscious" *homosexual* transference is tied in there, sotto voce.

But the really important thing is that no one should question the achievement of this "difficult development to femininity." Already that development will, alas!, have covered over and buried hysteria by a mimetic submission to the obsessional economy. And once again woman will support that economy, without every really being a party to it, without her sexuality ever being accounted for. She is reduced to a function and a functioning whose historic causes must be reconsidered: property systems, philosophical, mythological, or religious systems—the theory and practice of psychoanalysis itself—all continually, even today, prescribe and define that destiny laid down for woman's sexuality.

"That is all I had to say to you about femininity. It is certainly incomplete and fragmentary and does not always sound friendly. But do not forget that I have only been describing women *in so far as their nature is determined by their sexual function.* It is true that that influence extends very far; but we do not overlook the fact that an *individual woman* may be a *human being* in other respects as well"!

However, "if you want to know more about femininity, enquire from your own experiences of life [you men!] or turn to the poets, or wait until science can give you deeper and more coherent information."

SPECULUM

Any Theory of the "Subject" Has Always Been Appropriated by the "Masculine"

We can assume that any theory of the subject has always been appropriated by the "masculine." When she submits to (such a) theory, woman fails to realize that she is renouncing the specificity of her own relationship to the imaginary. Subjecting herself to objectivization in discourse—by being "female." Re-objectivizing her own self whenever she claims to identify herself "as" a masculine subject. A "subject" that would re-search itself as lost (maternal-feminine) "object"?

Subjectivity denied to woman: indisputably this provides the financial backing for every irreducible constitution as an object: of representation, of discourse, of desire. Once imagine that woman imagines and the object loses its fixed, obsessional character. As a bench mark that is ultimately more crucial than the subject, for he can sustain himself only by bouncing back off some objectiveness, some objective. If there is no more "earth" to press down/repress, to work, to represent, but also and always to desire (for one's own), no opaque matter which in theory does not know herself, then what pedestal remains for the ex-sistence of the "subject"? If the earth turned and more especially turned upon herself, the erection of the subject might thereby be disconcerted and risk losing its elevation and penetration. For what would there be to rise up from and exercise his power over? And in?

The Copernican revolution has yet to have its final effects in the male imaginary. And by centering man outside himself, it has occasioned above all man's ex-stasis within the transcendental (subject). Rising to a perspective that would dominate the totality, to the vantage point of greatest power, he thus cuts himself off from the bedrock, from his empirical relationship with the matrix that he claims to survey. To spec-ularize and to speculate. Exiling himself ever further (toward) where the greatest power lies, he thus becomes the "sun" if it is around him that things turn, a pole of attraction stronger than the "earth." Meanwhile, the excess in this universal fascination is that "she" also turns upon herself, that she knows how to re-turn (upon herself) but not how to seek outside for identity within the other: nature, sun, God . . . (woman). As things now go, man moves away in order to preserve his stake in the value of his representation, while woman counterbalances with the per-manence of a (self)recollection which is unaware of itself as such. And which, in the recurrence of this re-turn upon the self—and its special economy will need to be located—can continue to support the illusion that the object is inert. "Matter" upon which he will ever and again return to plant his foot in order to spring farther, leap higher, although he is dealing here with a nature that is already self-referential. Already fissured and open. And which, in her circumvolutions upon herself, will also carry off the things confided to her for re-presentation. Whence, no doubt, the fact that she is said to be restless and unstable. In fact it is quite rigorously true that she is never exactly the same. Always whirling closer or farther from the sun whose rays she captures and sends curving to and fro in turn with her cycles.

Thus the "object" is not as massive, as resistant, as one might wish to believe. And her possession by a "subject," a subject's desire to appro-priate her, is yet another of his vertiginous failures. For where he projects a something to absorb, to take, to see, to possess . . . as well as a patch of ground to stand upon, a mirror to catch his reflection, he is already faced by another specularization. Whose twisted character is her inability to say what she represents. The quest for the "object" becomes a game of Chinese boxes. Infinitely receding. The most amorphous with regard to ideas, the most obviously "thing," if you like, the most opaque matter, opens upon a mirror all the purer in that it knows and is known to have no reflections. Except those which man has reflected there but which, in the movement of that concave speculum, pirouetting upon itself, will rapidly, deceptively, fade.

And even as man seeks to rise higher and higher—in his knowledge too—so the ground fractures more and more beneath his feet. "Nature" is forever dodging his projects of representation, of reproduction. And his grasp. That this resistance should all too often take the form of rivalry within the hom(m)ologous, of a death struggle between two con-sciousnesses, does not alter the fact that at stake here somewhere, ever

134

more insistent in its deathly hauteur, is the risk that the subject (as) self will crumble away. Also at stake, therefore, the "object" and the modes of dividing the economy between them. In particular the economy of discourse. Whereby the silent allegiance of the one guarantees the auto-sufficiency, the auto-nomy of the other as long as no questioning of this mutism as a symptom—of historical repression—is required. But what if the "object" started to speak? Which also means beginning to "see," etc. What disaggregation of the subject would that entail? Not only on the level of the split between him and his other, his variously specified alter ego, or between him and the Other, who is always to some extent *his* Other, even if he does not recognize himself in it, even if he is so overwhelmed by it as to bar himself out of it and into it so as to retain at the very least the power to promote his own forms. Others who will always already have been in the service of the same, of the presuppositions of the same logos, without changing or prejudicing its character as discourse. Therefore not really others, even if the one, the greatest, while holding back his reserves, perhaps contains the threat of otherness. Which is perhaps why he stands off-stage? Why he is repressed too? But high up, in "heaven"? Beyond, like everything else? Innocent in his exorbited empire. But once you get suspicious of the reasons for extrapolation, and at the same time interpret the subject's need to re-duplicate himself in a thought—or maybe a "soul"?—then the function of the "other" is stripped of the veils that still shroud it.

Where will the other spring up again? Where will the risk be situated which sublates the subject's passion for remaining ever and again the same, for affirming himself ever and again the same? In the *duplicity* of his speculation? A more or less conscious duplicity? Since he is only partially and marginally where he reflects/is reflected? Where he knows (himself)? As likeness whose price can be maintained by the "night" of the unconscious? The Other, lapsed within, disquieting in its shadow and its rage, sustaining the organization of a universe eternally identical to the self. The backside of (self)representation, of the visual plane where he gazes upon himself? Therefore, resemblance proliferates all the more in a swarm of analogues. The "subject" henceforth will be multiple, plural, sometimes di-formed, but it will still postulate itself as the cause of all the mirages that can be enumerated endlessly and therefore put back together again as one. A fantastic, phantasmatic fragmentation. A destruc(tura)tion in which the "subject" is shattered, scuttled, while still claiming surreptitiously that he is the reason for it all. Is reason feigned perhaps? Certainly, it is *one*. For this race of signifiers spells out again the solipsism of him who summons them, convokes them, even if only to disperse them. The "subject" plays at multiplying himself, even deforming himself, in this process. He is father, mother, and child(ren). And the relationships between them. He is masculine and feminine and the relationships between them. What mockery of generation, parody of copulation and genealogy, drawing its *strength* from the same model, from the model of the same: the subject. In whose sight everything *outside* remains forever a condition making possible the image and the reproduction of the self. A faithful, polished mirror, empty of altering reflections. Immaculate of all auto-copies. Other because wholly in the service of the same subject to whom it would present its surfaces, candid in their self-ignorance.

When the Other falls out of the starry sky into the chasms of the psyche, the "subject" is obviously obliged to stake out new boundaries for his field of implantation and to re-ensure—otherwise, elsewhere—his dominance. Where once he was on the heights, he is now entreated to go down into the depths. These changes in position are still postulated in terms of verticality, of course. Are phallic, therefore. But how to tame these uncharted territories, these dark continents, these worlds through the looking glass? How to master these devilries, these moving phantoms of the unconscious, when a long history has taught you to seek out and desire only clarity, the clear perception of (fixed) ideas? Perhaps this is the time to stress *technique* again? To renounce for the time being the sovereignty of thought in order to forge *tools* which will permit the exploitation of these resources, these unexplored mines. Perhaps for the time being the serene contemplation of empire must be abandoned in favor of taming those forces which, once unleashed, might explode the very concept of empire. A detour into *strategy, tactics, and practice* is called for, at least as long as it takes to gain vision, self-knowledge, self-possession, even in one's decenteredness. The "subject" sidles up to the truth, squints at it, obliquely, in an attempt to gain possession of what truth can no longer say. Dispersing, piercing those metaphors—particularly the photological ones—which have constituted truth by the premises of Western philosophy: virgin, dumb, and veiled in her nakedness, her vision still naively "natural," her viewpoint still resolutely blind and unsuspecting of what may lie beneath the blindness.

Now is the time to operate, before all is lost. That is, plow again those fields which had been assumed cultivated once and for all, but which now turn out to have merely lain fallow, capable of products that choke anything growing in their soil. The "subject" must dig his foundations deeper, extend the underground passages which assured the edifice of his determination, further dig out the cellars upon which he raises the monument of his identification, in order to prop up more securely his "dwelling": the system of his relationship to self, the closure of his auto-repre-sentations, focus of his lonely exile as "subject." Man's home has indeed become these/his theoretical elaborations, by means of which he has sought to reconstruct, in an impossible metaphorization, the matrix and the way that would lead to or back to it. But by wishing to reverse the anguish of being imprisoned within the other, of being placed inside the other, by making the very place and space of being his own, he becomes a prisoner of effects of symmetry that know no limit. Everywhere he runs into the walls of his palace of mirrors, the floor of which is in any case beginning to crack and break up. This in turn serves, of course, to sublate his activity, leading him to new tasks which for a time will distract him again from his specular imprisonment. A diversion from the depths of his madness, pretext for an increase in attentiveness, vigilance, mastery. The reason for the quakes must be sought out, these seismic convulsions in the self must be interpreted.

But man only asks (himself) questions that he can already answer, using the supply of instruments he has available to assimilate even the disasters in his history. This time at any rate he is prepared to lay odds again, and, give or take a few new weapons, he will make the uncon-scious into a property of his language. A disconcerting property, admit-tedly, which confuses everything he had long since assigned meaning to. But that, it seems, is not the most important thing at stake. The really urgent task is to ensure the colonization of this new "field," to force it, not without splintering, into the production of the same discourse. And since there can be no question of using the same plan/e for this "strange" speech, this "barbarous" language with which it is impossible to conduct a dialogue—read, monologue—the discovery will be set out hier-archically, in stages. Will be brought to order. By giving here a little more play to the system, here a little less. The forms of arrangement may vary, but they will all bear the paradox of forcing into the same represen-tation—the representation of the self/same—that which insists upon its *heterogeneity*, its *otherness*.

Yet the fact that the dream can be interpreted only as a "rebus" should have persuaded the "reader" to turn it in all directions and positions, and not favor one type of inscription that would already prescribe a meaning to it: a linear, teleologically horizontal or vertical displacement, over a surface as yet unwritten, which it brands by cutting it up according to rules of repetition and recurrence, obeying processes that already para-lyze the "body's" system of gestures within a given graphic order, etc. Why not rather have recalled those "pictures" made for children, pic-tographs in which the hunter and hunted, and their dramatic rela-

137

tionships, are to be discovered *between* the branches, *made out* from *between* the trees. From the spaces between the figures, or stand-in figures. Spaces that organize the scene, blanks that sub-tend the scene's structuration and that will yet not be read as such. Or not read at all? Not seen at all? Never in truth represented or representable, though this is not to say that they have no effect upon the present scenography. But fixed in oblivion and waiting to come to life. Turning everything upside down and back to front. If, that is, the interpreter-subject did not desire "this" (the id) to continue sustaining the proliferation of images (of self), as a trompe-l'oeil backcloth for the same's show, for a theater of the identical.

Dreams are also riddles in that—during "sleep," and in order to "keep" asleep—they recast the roles that history has laid down for "subject" and "object." Mutism that says without speech, inertia that moves without motion, or else only with the motions of another language, another script. Dream pictography, dream choreography, phonography, and pornography which compensate for the present *paralysis* of the sleeper. Who will/would awake—perhaps?—only if the "child," faced with such "riddles," did not have the overweening desire to "see" an other and same figure and form than the one that is already present for him. If it were enough for him to be entranced, let us say, by a *double syntax,* without claiming to regulate the second by the standard of representation, of re-presentation, of the first. If he were not "wounded," threatened by "castration," by anything he cannot see directly, anything he cannot perceive as like himself. Did not feel, as a result, the need to invent a new "theory," yet another in the series of optical instruments which, by means of the second—or hundred and second—sighting, moves in around the "manifestations" of the unconscious, under the protection of technological distance. Prosthesis, which assists the horrified gaze to construct, laboriously, "consciously," concept by concept, the rationality of his repression. His established good. Session after session, in a procedure that is also regulated by visual—rememorative—laws, he repeats the same gesture reestablishing the bar, the barred. While all the while permissive, listening with benevolent neutrality, collecting, on a carefully circumscribed little stage, the inter-dict. The lines between the lines of discourse. But he restrictes himself to reframing, re-marking, or "analyzing" its contours, re-stratifying its stages, so that order, good "conscious" order, may prevail. Elsewhere.

Now, let us imagine—for what else is there to do when rereading Freud but imagine a response, or else admit one's inability to survey such

an imagination—let us imagine that man (Freud in the event) had discovered that the rarest thing—the most exciting as well as the most
scientifically rigorous, the most faithful to factual materiality and the
most historically curative—would be to articulate directly, *without cata-
combs*, what we are calling these two syntaxes. Irreducible in their strangeness and eccentricity one to the other. Coming out of different times,
places, logics, "representations," and economies. In fact, of course, these
terms cannot fittingly be designated by the number "two" and the adjective "different," if only because they are not susceptible to com-parison.
To use such terms serves only to reiterate a movement begun long since,
that is, the movement to speak of the "other" in a language already
systematized by/for the same. Their distribution and demarcation and
articulation necessitate operations as yet nonexistent, whose complexity
and subtlety can only be guessed at without prejudicing the results.
Without a teleology already in operation somewhere. But had the man
Freud preferred the play, or even the clash, of those two economies
rather than their disposition in hierarchical stages by means of one barrier
(or two), one censorship (or two), then perhaps he would not finally
have cracked his head against all that remains irreducibly "obscure" to
him in his speculations. Against the non-visible, therefore not theoriza-
ble nature of woman's sex and pleasure. Whatever the explorations he
attempts and which tempt him concerning this "dark continent," he
always refers back to some still blind and incomprehensible "horizon" of
investigation. And there, in what he recognizes as outside the range of
his systematic prospecting (beyond the self?), Freud is in fact indicating a
way off the historico-transcendental stage, at the very moment when his
theory and his practice are perpetuating, in the mode of enunciation and
the drama of enunciating, that very same stage, which we may now call
the *hysterico*-transcendental. Announcing by this re-mark, by this effect
of repetition—re-petitio principii—of recapitulation and, without his
knowledge, of mimicry, that his breath is privileged. And he is out of
breath.

For, when Freud reaffirms the incest taboo, he simply reannounces
and puts back in place the conditions that constitute the speculative matrix of the "subject." He reinforces his positions in a fashion yet more
"scientific," more imperious in their "objectivity." A demonstration he
clearly needed himself if he is to "sublimate" in more universal interests
his own desire for his/the mother. But as a result of using psychoanalysis
(his psychoanalysis) only to scrutinize the history of his subject and his
subjects, without interpreting *the historical determinants of the constitution of*

the "subject" as same, he was restoring, yet again, that newly pressed down/repressed earth, upon which he stands erect, which for him, following tradition though in more explicit fashion, will be the body/sex of the mother/nature. He must challenge her for power, for productivity. He must resurface the earth with this floor of the ideal. Identify with the law-giving father, with his proper names, his desires for making capital, in every sense of the word, desires that prefer the possession of territory, which includes language, to the exercise of his pleasures, with the exception of his pleasure in trading women—fetishized objects, merchandise of whose value he stands surety—with his peers. The ban upon returning, regressing to the womb, as well as to the language and dreams shared with the mother, this is indeed the point, the line, the surface upon which the "subject" will continue to stand, to advance, to unfold his discourse, even to make it whirl. Though he has barely escaped the ring, the vault, the snare of reconciling his end and his archives, those calls, resurgent, of his beginnings. Though that he-who-is-the-cause is barely keeping his balance. But since he now knows the reason for his wobbling. . . . And, after all, the acquisition of new riches is certainly part of this? Overdetermination, deferred action, dreams, fantasies, puns. . . . Language, by adopting its/these "annexes"—also ocular, uterine, embryonic—adds to its wealth, gains "depth," consistency, diversity, and multiplication of its processes and techniques. Was language once believed threatened? Here it is dancing, playing, writing itself more than ever. It is even claimed that language is "truer" than in the past, reimpregnated with its childhood. A consciousness yet more consciously pregnant with its relationship with the mother.

Whereas "she" comes to be unable to say what her body is suffering. Stripped even of the words that are expected of her upon that stage invented to listen to her. In an admission of the wear and tear on language or of its fetishistic denial? But hysteria, or at least the hysteria that is the privileged lot of the "female," *now has nothing to say.* What she "suffers," what she "lusts for," even what she "takes pleasure in," all take place upon another stage, in relation to already codified representations. Repression of speech, inter-dicted in "hieroglyphic" symptoms—an already suspicious designation of something prehistoric—which will doubtless never again be lifted into current history. Unless it be by making her enter, in contempt of her sex, into "masculine" games of tropes and tropisms. By converting her to a discourse that denies the specificity of her pleasure by inscribing it as the hollow, the intaglio, the negative, even as the censured other of its phallic assertions. By hom(m)osexualizing her. By perversely travestying her for the ped-erastic, sodomizing satisfactions of the father/husband. She shrieks out demands too innocuous to cause alarm, that merely make people smile. Just the way one smiles at a child when he shouts aloud the mad ambi-tions adults keep to themselves. And which one knows he can never realize. And when she also openly displays their power fantasies, this serves as a re-creation to them in their struggle for power. By setting before them, keeping in reserve for them, in her in-fancy, what they must of course keep clear of in their pursuit of mastery, but which they yet cannot wholly renounce for fear of going off course. So she will be the Pythia who apes induced desires and suggestions foreign to her still hazy consciousness, suggestions that proclaim their credibility all the louder as they carry her ever further from her interests. By resubmitting herself to the established order, in this role of delirious double, she abandons, even denies, the prerogative histrocially granted her: uncon-sciousness. She prostitutes the unconscious itself to the ever present pro-jects and projections of masculine consciousness.

For whereas the man Freud—or woman, were she to set her rights up in opposition—*might have been able* to interpret what the overdetermina-tion of language (its effects of deferred action, its subterranean dreams and fantasies, its convulsive quakes, its paradoxes and contradictions) owed to the repression (which may yet return) of maternal power—or of the matriarchy, to adopt a still prehistorical point of reference—whereas he might have been able also to interpret the repression of the history of female sexuality, we shall in fact receive only confirmation of the dis-course of the same, through comprehension and extension. With "wom-an" coming once more to be embedded in, enclosed in, impaled upon an architectonic more powerful than ever. And she herself is sometimes happy to request a recognition of consciousness thereby, even an appro-priation of unconsciousness that cannot be hers. Unconsciousness she is, but not for herself, not with a subjectivity that might take cognizance of it, recognize it as her own. Close to herself, admittedly, but in a total ignorance (of self). She is the reserve of "sensuality" for the elevation of intelligence, she is the matter used for the imprint of forms, gage of possible regression into naive perception, the representative representing negativity (death), dark continent of dreams and fantasies, and also ear-drum faithfully duplicating the music, though not all of it, so that the series of displacements may continue, for the "subject." And she will serve to assure his determination only if she now seeks to reclaim his property from him: this (of his) elaborated as same out of this (of hers) foreclosed from specula(riza)tion. The same thing will always be at stake. The profiteering will barely have changed hands. A barter solution that she would adopt out of the void of her desire. And always one step behind in the process, the progress of history.

But if, by exploits of her hand, woman were to reopen paths into (once again) a/one logos that connotes her as castrated, especially as castrated of words, excluded from the work force except as prostitute to the interests of the dominant ideology—that is of hom(m)osexuality and its struggles with the maternal—then a certain sense, which still constitutes the sense of history also, will undergo unparalleled interrogation, revolution. But how is this to be done? Given that, once again, the "reasonable" words—to which in any case she has access only though mimicry—are powerless to translate all that pulses, clamors, and hangs hazily in the cryptic passages of hysterical suffering-latency. Then. . . . Turn everything upside down, inside out, back to front. *Rack it with radical convulsions,* carry back, reimport, those crises that her "body" suffers in her impotence to say what disturbs her. Insist also and deliberately upon those *blanks* in discourse which recall the places of her exclusion and which, by their *silent plasticity,* ensure the cohesion, the articulation, the coherent expansion of established forms. Reinscribe them hither and thither *as divergencies,* otherwise and elsewhere than they are expected, in *ellipses* and *eclipses* that deconstruct the logical grid of the reader-writer, drive him out of his mind, trouble his vision to the point of incurable diplopia at least. *Overthrow syntax* by suspending its eternally teleological order, by snipping the wires, cutting the current, breaking the circuits, switching the connections, by modifying continuity, alternation, frequency, intensity. Make it impossible for a while to predict whence, whither, when, how, why . . . something goes by or goes on: will come, will spread, will reverse, will cease moving. Not by means of a growing complexity of the same, of course, but by the irruption of other circuits, by the intervention at times of short-circuits that will disperse, diffract, deflect endlessly, making energy explode sometimes, with no possibility of returning to one single origin. A force that can no longer be channeled according to a given *plan/e:* a projection from a single source, even in the secondary circuits, with retroactive effects.

All this already applies to words, to the "lexicon" (as it is called), which is also connected up, and in the same direction. But we must go on questioning words as the wrappings with which the "subject," modestly, clothes the "female." Stifled beneath all those eulogistic or denigratory metaphors, she is unable to unpick the seams of her disguise and indeed takes a certain pleasure in them, even gilding the lily further at times. Yet, ever more hemmed in, cathected by tropes, how could she articulate any sound from beneath this cheap chivalric finery? How find a voice, make a choice strong enough, subtle enough to cut through those layers of ornamental style, that decorative sepulcher, where even her breath is lost. Stifled under all those airs. She has yet to feel the need to get free of fabric, reveal her nakedness, her destitution in language, explode in the face of them all, words too. For the imperious need for her shame, her chastity—duly fitted out with the belt of discourse—, of her decent modesty, continues to be asserted by every man. In every kind of tone, form, theory, style, with the exception of a few that in fact rouse suspicion also by their pornographically, hom(m)osexual excess. Common stock, one may assume, for their production.

The (re)productive power of the mother, the sex of the woman, are both at stake in the proliferation of systems, those houses of ill fame for the subject, of fetish-words, sign-objects whose certified truths seek to palliate the risk that values may be recast into/by the other. But no clear univocal utterance, can in fact, pay off this mortgage since all are already trapped in the same credit structure. All can be recuperated when issued by the signifying order in place. It is still better to speak only in riddles, allusions, hints, parables. Even if asked to clarify a few points. Even if people plead that they just don't understand. After all, they never have understood. So why not double the misprision to the limits of exasperation? Until the ear tunes into another music, the voice starts to sing again, the very gaze stops squinting over the signs of auto-representation, and (re)production no longer inevitably amounts to the same and returns to the same forms, with minor variations.

This disconcerting of language, though anarchic in its deeds of title, nonetheless demands patient exactitude. The symptoms, for their part, are implacably precise. And if it is indeed a question of breaking (with) a certain mode of specula(riza)tion, this does not imply renouncing all mirrors or refraining from analysis of the hold this plan/e of representation maintains, rendering female desire aphasic and more generally atonic in all but its phallomorphic disguises, masquerades, and demands. For to dodge this time of interpretation is to risk its freezing over, losing hold, cutting back. All over again. But perhaps through this specular surface which sustains discourse is found not the void of nothingness but the dazzle of multifaceted speleology. A scintillating and incandescent concavity, of language also, that threatens to set fire to fetish-objects and gilded eyes. The recasting of their truth value is already at hand. We need only press on a little further into the depths, into that so-called dark cave which serves as hidden foundation to their speculations. For there where we expect to find the opaque and silent matrix of a logos immutable in the certainty of its own light, fires and mirrors are beginning to radiate, sapping the evidence of reason at its base! Not so much by anything stored in the cave—which would still be a claim based on the notion of the closed volume—but again and yet again by their indefinitely re-kindled hearths.

But which "subject" up till now has investigated the fact that a *concave mirror* concentrates the light and, specifically, that this is not wholly irrelevant to woman's sexuality? Any more than is a man's sexuality to the convex mirror? Which "subject" has taken an interest in the ana-morphoses produced by the conjunction of such curvatures? What im-possible reflected images, maddening reflections, parodic transforma-tions took place at each of their articulations? When the "it is" annuls them in the truth of a copula in which "he" still forever finds the re-sources of his identification as same. Not one subject has done so, on pain of tumbling from his ex-sistence. And here again, here too, one will rightly suspect any perspective, however surreptitious, that centers the subject, any autonomous circuit of subjectivity, any systematicity hooked back onto itself, any closure that claims for whatever reason to be metaphysical—or familial, social, economic even—, to have right-fully taken over, fixed,and framed that concave mirror's incandescent hearth. If this mirror—which, however, makes a *hole*—sets itself up pompously as an authority in order to give shape to the imaginary orb of a "subject," it thereby defends itself phobically in/by this inner "center" from the fires of the desire of/for woman. Inhabiting a securing mor-phology, making of its very structure some comfortable sepulcher from whence it may, possibly, by some hypothetical survival, be able to look out. (Re)g(u)arding itself by all sorts of windows-on-wheels, optical apparatuses, glasses, and mirrors, from/in this burning glass, which enflames all that falls into its cup.

But, may come the objection,—defending again the objective and the object—the speculum is not necessarily a mirror. It may, quite simply, be an instrument to *dilate* the lips, the orifices, the walls, so that the eye can penetrate the *interior*. So that the eye can enter, to see, notably with speculative intent. Woman, having been misinterpreted, forgotten, vari-ously frozen in show-cases, rolled up in metaphors, buried beneath care-fully stylized figures, raised up in different idealities, would now become

144

the "object" to be investigated, to be explicitly granted consideration, and thereby, by this deed of title, included in the theory. And if this center, which fixed and immobilized metaphysics in its closure, had often in the past been traced back to some divinity or other transcendence invisible as such, in the future its ultimate meaning will perhaps be discovered by tracking down what there is to be *seen* of female sexuality.

Yes, man's eye—understood as substitute for the penis—will be able to prospect woman's sexual parts, seek there new sources of profit. Which are equally theoretical. By doing so he further fetishizes (his) desire. But the desire of the mystery remains, however large a public has been recruited of late for "hysteroscopy." For even if the place of origin, the original dwelling, even if not only the woman but the mother can be unveiled to his sight, what will he make of the exploration of this mine? Except usurp even more the right to look at everything, at the whole thing, thus reinforcing the erosion of his desire in the very place where he firmly believes he is working to reduce an illusion. Even if it should be a transcendental illusion. What will he, what will they, have *seen* as a result of that dilation? And what will they get out of it? A disillusion quite as illusory, since the transcendental keeps its secret. Between empirical and transcendental *a suspense will still remain inviolate,* will escape prospection, then, now, and in the future. The space-time of the risk that fetishes will be consumed, catch fire. In this fire, in this light, in the optical failure, the impossibility of gazing on their encounters in flame, the split (schize) founding and structuring the difference between experience and transcendental (especially phallic) eminence will burn also. *Exquisite/ex-schizoid crisis of ontico-ontological difference.* What manner of recasting all economy will ensue? To tell the truth, no one knows. And, to stay with truth, you can only fear the worst. For you may fear a general crisis in the value system, a foundering of the values now current, the devaluation of their standard and of their regimen of monopolies.

The copulative effusion, and fusion, melts down the mint's credit with each moment of bliss. Renews and redistributes the accepted stakes: between two crises, two explosions, two incandescences of fetish mineral. And it is no easy matter to foresee whether, in that game, the one—the man?—who has recouped the biggest pile of chips will be the winner. It is equally possible to imagine that the one—the woman—who has spent her time polishing her mine will carry the day. Since the abrasion of the stores entrusted to the reflecting surface renders that surface more likely to set aflame the supplies and capitalizations of the one who, under cover and pretext of seduction, puts his riches on display.

145

But, will come the objection once again—in the name of some other objectality—we are not fed by fire and flames. Maybe. But then neither are we by fetishes and gazes. And when will they cease to equate woman's sexuality with her reproductive organs, to claim that her sexuality has value only insofar as it gathers the heritage of her maternity? When will man give up the need or desire to drink deep in all security from his wife/mother in order to go and show off to his brothers and buddies the fine things he formed while suckling his nurse? And/or when will he renounce (reversing roles so as better to retain them) the wish to preserve his wife/child in her inability, as he sees it, to produce for the marketplace? With "marriage" turning out to be a more or less subtle dialectization of the nurturing relationship that aims to maintain, at the very least, the mother/child, producer/consumer distinction, and thereby perpetuate this economy?

To return to the gaze, it will be able to explore all the inner cavities. Although, in the case of the most secret, it will need the help of ancillary light and mirror. Of appropriate sun and mirrors. The instrumental and technical exploitation of sun and mirror will have shown the gaze, proved to it, that those mines contained no gold. Then the gaze, aghast at such bareness, will have concluded that at any rate all brilliance was its own preserve, that it could continue to speculate without competition. That the childish, the archaic credit accorded to the all-powerful mother was nothing, was but fable. But how is one to desire without fiction? What pleasure is there in stockpiling goods without risks, without expenditures?

You will have noted, in fact, that what polarizes the light for the exploration of internal cavities is, in paradigmatic fashion, *the concave mirror*. Only when that mirror has concentrated the feeble rays of the eye, of the sun, of the sun-blinded eye, is the secret of the caves illumined. Scientific technique will have taken up the condensation properties of the "burning glass," in order to pierce the mystery of woman's sex, in a new distribution of the power of the scientific method and of "nature." A new despecularization of the maternal and the female? Scientificity of fiction that seeks to exorcise the disasters of desire, that mortifies desire by analyzing it from all visual angles, but leaves it also intact. Elsewhere. Burning still.

146

Korē: Young Virgin, Pupil of the Eye

And now there is no longer any difficulty in understanding the creation of images in mirrors and all smooth and bright surfaces. For from the communication of the internal and external fires, and again from the union of them and their numerous transformations when they meet in the mirror, all these appearances of necessity arise when the fire from the face coalesces with the fire from the eye on the smooth and bright surface. And right appears left and left right, because the visual rays come into contact with the rays emitted by the object in a manner contrary to the usual mode of meeting; but the right appears right and the left left, when the position of one of the two concurring lights is reversed; and this happens when the mirror is concave and its smooth surface repels the right stream of vision to the left side, and the left to the right. Or if the mirror be turned vertically, then the concavity makes the countenance appear to be all upside down, and the lower rays are driven upwards and the upper downwards.

—Plato

Every effort will have been made, however, to keep the eye, at least the eye, from being destroyed by the fires of desire. Wisdom, at its very beginnings, warns against looking directly at the sun, for fear of burning up the membrane at the back of the eye, screen for production and projection of forms in the eye's camera obscura. Finding an economy of light in all its dazzling brilliance, without risk of combustion and death, marks humanity's first steps into philosophy. And just as the sun, even in eclipse, must be observed only *indirectly, in a mirror* on pain of blindness, even so the spirit will serve as an additional reflector that helps us to look upon the Good. In the strictest sense, mortals cannot look upon Good.

(The epigraph is from Plato's *Timaeus,* 46a–c. All translations from Plato are from *The Dialogues of Plato,* tr. Benjamin Jowett, [Oxford: Oxford University Press, 1953]. "Young maiden, pupil of the eye," is the beginning of the *Greek-English Lexicon* [Liddell and Scott, 1968] entry for the word *korē.*—Tr.)

But the consuming contact of light will also be avoided by paying attention to *forms* alone. Vision protects itself from the risk of blindness by using daylight for the exact perception of "beings" and for the calculation of the relations and correlations "beings" have with their ideal inscription in the *psychē*. Direct vision means looking directly ahead, of course, but it also means doing so through an optical apparatus that stands between man and light and prevents light from *touching* him at all. Reason—which will also be called natural light—is the result of systems of mirrors that ensure a steady illumination, admittedly, but one without *heat* or brilliance. The everlasting correctness of things seen clearly, perceived rightly, has banished not only the darkness of night but also the fires of noon. The *epistēmē* begins its surveying, measuring, and calculating on the basis of *shadows* projected by/upon surfaces, screens, and supports. And the presence, the essence of forms (usually translated under the name of Ideas) will be determined only by the light that they have stopped, trapped, and that outlines them. The force of ideas, and their hold upon the memory, will be a function of the intensity of light that they are able to block or cut off. Their impress will be limited in ratio to their luminescence. The impact, the contact, of light is—at least implicitly—considered to be too close to the senses and to matter to constitute the main source of profit for the intelligible. Light is too corruptible, too shifting and inconstant to form the basis of the relationship to the self and to the All.

And the sun, in its incandescence, joins together with a burning glass (whose fiction the sun sustains, moreover, having always already swallowed, ingested the glass in its self-combustion) and sets the fleet of a whole nation aflame,[1] and must therefore topple from its place as model by which to establish the eternal laws of the City. This son/sun is still too close to the earth/mother, too absorbed in her world of passions, approximations, and touchings to serve as standard for measuring the father's ideal speculations. The sun may have pointed out, pinpointed, something of his power, may also have served the still empirical foundations of science, but the time comes nonetheless when he must fall once more below the horizon. His rays of light, flashing, burning, glaring, must cease to harry the Truth—*alētheia*—unchanging in the guileless virginity of the *logos*. The Words of the Father depend for their effect upon a measured and harmonious reflection of each part within the whole, untroubled by searchlights by night or eclipses by day. This rigorous distribution of each speck of brightness, of which only the

---

[1](Archimedes is reputed to have prevented the Roman forces from capturing Syracuse for three years by burning their fleet with the help of giant mirrors.—Tr.)

information is retained, is set up by relays of mirrors—as well as filters, lenses, paraphragms, camerae obscurae, projection and reproduction screens—which divide up "Being" as a whole into fragments suitable to each "being": mirror of the Good, origin of all specula(riza)tions; mirror of the spirit, differing according to the degree of wisdom of each existence; this *psychē*[2] is assisted by the mirror of divination of the liver; mirror of the eye in which the central point of vision—the *korē*—is the most purely reflecting; mirror of vocal flow, of the "current" of the voice in which the images of judgment are reflected. . . . A whole hierarchy of *katoptron* chills the light, shielding us from its touch and sight, its capacity to vary our perception of "forms," to make them move and flow free of their eidetic continuity. A mirror is their very source, after all, isn't it?

This is not to say that men will have no distrust of the properties of mirrors. That anyone playing with mirrors to create "false" beings, "illusions of reality," will not be accused of forgery. It will be made perfectly clear that the one may be confused with the other as a result of the *inversion* that mirrors effect. The specific properties of the *concave mirror* in this order of things is in fact given special emphasis: with a horizontal generatrix, a concave mirror does not affect the usual coordinates of vision. Does this imply that *man would see himself in it as he sees anyone else,* not as an other reflected self. Is the identification "as" like or same theoretically impossible? Is it impossible to account for the part played by symmetry? On the other hand, in a concave mirror with a vertical generatrix, man may be reflected *upside down.* The concave mirror's potential for setting things afire is not mentioned.

In fact, the refinements of theory brought to bear upon the ontic qualities of mirrors are not systematically carried over to the status of the being himself. The notion that, like a mirror, he might be *passed through* and have a *silver backing,* that he might reflect and be reflected in different ways, is in some sense denied. The Idea is intended to be real, independent of the art of mirrors. And yet the world from end to end is orga-

[2](It should be noted that "psyché" in French also means "cheval-glass."—Tr.)

nized as *mimēsis;* re-semblance is the law. Doesn't the universe work by coping defensively with light? Doesn't sameness of color and shape work to banish light's powers? To protect us from its potential ability to illumine, diffuse, touch, breed, transform? And warm? Nature, *physis,* is apprehended by (her) mirage, not by her dazzling radiance. Men freeze nature to understand her, they do not set her aflame. The names that will be given to her will be a series of ways—geometrical, arithmetical, logical—of cutting up her territory so as to make her relate to herself differently. Will man predicate her differently from himself? Is *alētheia* unveiled in the enumeration of her attributes? Does "being" (être) remain the store of brilliance from which the reason and logos of the philosopher attains ecstatic distance?

But the being that, from beyond the farthest heaven, resists being looked upon face to face, is even being itself here interpreted as referring to the infinity of light? Focused by some burning glass whereby God would gaze upon his glorious unity, merging even the discrimination of his (self-same) attributes? Or could being be the concentration, extrapolated from everything seen, of the blind spots by/in which the eye—and the eye of the soul—reflects and is reflected without seeing or being seen? Might it be this specularization of vision of/in the other that man cannot perceive at the moment of its production, or of his production? Holes by/in which he looks, and which the unveiling of Truth misses in its ontological presuppositions. Being is thus already caught up in a speculative economy, as a kind of *waste product,* if the ultimate good to which man claims to aspire is the reality of all being outside its constitution as appearance. Or again, is being the monopoly of light whose lightning flashes endanger the ever sensitive gaze of mortals, or is it already— always already—the profit-making principle of semblance? First and last cause of the proliferation of semblances in the ideal, is it yet closed in upon its invisible secret? "Origin" that interacts with Being, each covering over, disguising and supporting the other. Finally Being does not appear or even appear to appear. It slips away from the mind's grasp, even as it forms the foundation of mind. Is this the mystery—the hysteria—of Being? Hidden in its crypt where no one, however skilled in philosophy, has glimpsed it? Only at the rarest and highest moments of loving contemplation of the Good—or of the Beautiful?—will the wisest man receive some "intuition" that can barely be put into words.

Korē: Young Virgin, Pupil of the Eye

Here then, man does not yet have the plenitude of Being *within him,* but instead a whole range of theoretical tools (geometrical, mathematical, discursive, dialogic), a whole technique of philosophy and even of artistic practice, are being worked out to form a *matrix of appropriation* for man. And what he already terms "natural" or "more" natural is transformed—fissured, split all over again—by his speculations. This project is in fact admitted to be possible, but only barely, and its extent is left in the dark. "He" only talks about it as if he wanted to get rid of it: "There are many ways in which the feat might be quickly and easily accomplished, none quicker than that of turning a mirror [or a soul?] round and round—you would soon enough make the sun and the heavens, and the earth and yourself, and other animals and plants, and furniture and all the other things of which we were just now speaking, in the mirror."[3]

[3]*Republic,* Book x, 596e.

On the Index of Plato's Works: Woman

Alcibiades 120b: "Oh no, my friend, I am quite wrong, and I think that you ought rather to turn your attention to Meidias the quail-breeder and others like him, who manage our politics; in whom, as the women would remark, you may still see the slave's cut of hair, cropping out in their minds as well as on their pates; and they come with their barbarous lingo to flatter us and not to rule us."

Apology, 35a–b: "I think that such are a dishonour to the state, and that any stranger coming in would have said of them that the most eminent men of Athens, to whom the Athenians themselves give office and honour, are no better than women."

Gorgias, 512d–e: "May it not be that he who is truly a man must cease to care about living a certain time, and set little store by his life? Should he not leave all that with God, acknowledge that (as women say) no man can escape his destiny."

Meno 99d: "And the women too, Meno, call good men divine."

Phaedo 60a: "When she saw us she uttered a cry and burst out in true feminine fashion. . . . Socrates turned to Crito and said: 'Crito, let someone take her home.'"

Phaedo 116b: "And the women of his family also came, and he talked to them and gave them a few directions in the presence of Crito; then he dismissed them and returned to us."

Phaedo 117d–e: "What is this strange outcry? he said. I sent away the women mainly in order that they might not misbehave in this fashion, for I have been told that a man should die in peace."

Symposium 176e: "Then said Eryximachus, as you are all agreed that

(There are some slight differences in the section divisions between Jowett and the Budé version quoted by LI, and the order of sentences and clauses also frequently differs, but, as LI herself remarks in regard to the Freud, the basic points can be made regardless of the translation used.—Tr.)

drinking is to be voluntary, and that there is to be no compulsion, I move, in the next place, that the flute girl, who has just made her appearance, be told to go away and play to herself, or, if she likes, to the women who are within. Today let us have conversation instead."

Symposium 175b–e: "Love will make men dare to die for their beloved—love alone; and women as well as men. Of this, Alcestis, the daughter of Pelias, is a monument to all Hellas; for she was willing to lay down her life on behalf of her husband, when no one else would, although he had a father and a mother; but the tenderness of her love so far exceeded theirs, that she made them seem to be strangers in blood to their own son, and in name only related to him; and so noble did this action of hers appear to the gods, as well as to men, that among the many who have done virtuously she is one of the very few to whom, in admiration of her noble action, they have granted the privilege of returning alive to earth; such exceeding honour is paid by the gods to the devotion and virtue of love. But Orpheus, the son of Oeagrus, the harper, they sent empty away, having presented to him an apparition only of her whom he sought, but herself they would not relinquish, because he showed no spirit; he was only a harp-player, and did not dare like Alcestis to die for love, but was contriving how he might enter Hades alive; therefore they afterwards caused him to suffer death at the hands of women, as the punishment for his cowardliness."

Symposium 180d–181e: "For we all know that Love is inseparable from Aphrodite, and if there were only one Aphrodite there would be only one Love; but as there are two goddesses there must be two Loves. And am I not right in asserting that there are two goddesses? The elder one, having no mother, who is called the heavenly Aphrodite—she is the daughter of Uranus: the younger, who is the daughter of Zeus and Dione—her we call common; and the Love who is her fellow-worker is rightly named common, as the other Love is called heavenly. All the gods ought to have praise given them, but not without distinction of their natures; and therefore I must try to distinguish the characters of the two Loves. Now actions vary according to the manner of their performance. Take, for example, that which we are now doing, drinking, singing, and talking—these actions are not in themselves either good or evil, but they turn out in this or that way according to the mode of performing them; and when well done they are good, and when wrongly done they are evil; and in like manner not every kind of loving nor every Love is noble and worthy of praise, but only that which inspires man to love nobly. The Love who is the offspring of the common Aphrodite is essentially common, and has no discrimination, being such as moves the meaner sort of men. They are apt to love women as well as youths, and the body rather than the soul—the most foolish beings they can find are the objects of this love which desires only to gain an end, but never thinks of accomplishing the end nobly, and therefore does good and evil quite indiscriminately. The goddess who is the mother of this union is far younger than the other, and she was born of the union of the male and female, and partakes of both. But the offspring of the heavenly Aphrodite is derived from a mother in whose birth the female has no part,—she is from the male only; this is that love which is of youths, and the goddess being older, there is nothing of wantonness in her. Those who are inspired by this love turn to the male, and delight in him who is the more valiant and intelligent nature; anyone may recognize the pure enthusiasts in the very character of their attachments. For they love not boys, but intelligent beings whose reason is beginning to be developed, much about the time at which their beards begin to grow. And starting from such a choice, they are ready, I apprehend, to be faithful to their companions, and pass their whole life with them, not to take them in their inexperience, and deceive them, and make fools of them, and then run away to others of them. But the love of young boys should be forbidden by law, because their future is uncertain; they may turn out good or bad, either in body or soul, and much noble enthusiasm may be thrown away upon them. The good impose this law upon themselves of their own free will; and the coarser sort of lovers ought to be restrained by force, as we restrain or attempt to restrain them from fixing their affections on women of free birth."

Symposium 191b: "And when one of the halves died and the other survived, the survivor sought another mate, man or woman as we call them,—being the sections of entire men or women,—and clung to that."

Menexenus 237e–238a: "And a great proof that she brought forth the common ancestors of us and of the departed, is that she provided the means of support for her offspring. For as a mother proves her motherhood by giving milk to her young ones (and she who has no fountain of milk is not a mother), so did this our land prove that she was the mother of men, for in those days she alone and first of all brought forth wheat and barley for human food, which is the best and noblest sustenance for man, whom she regarded as her true offspring. And these are truer proofs of motherhood in a country than in a woman, for the woman in her conception and generation is but the imitation of the earth, and not the earth of the woman."

Cratylus 414a: "*Gynē* (woman) I suspect to be the same word as *gonē* (birth): *thely* (female) appears to be partly derived from *thelē* (the teat), because the teat is like rain, and makes things flourish (*tethelenai*)."

Cratylus 418b: "*Soc.* I will try to explain. You are aware that our forefathers loved the sounds ι and δ, especially the women, who are most conservative of the ancient language."

Cratylus 430b–431c: "*Soc.* I believe you may be right, but I do not rightly understand you. Please to say, then, whether both sorts of imitation (I mean both pictures or words) are not equally attributable and applicable to the things of which they are the imitation.

Crat. They are.

Soc. First look at the matter thus: one might attribute the likeness of the man to the man, and of the woman to the woman; and so on?

Crat. Certainly.

Soc. And conversely one might attribute the likeness of the man to the woman, and of the woman to the man?

Crat. Very true.

Soc. And are both modes of assigning them right, or only the first?

Crat. Only the first.

Soc. That is to say, the mode of assignment which attributes to each that which belongs to them and is like them?

Crat. That is my view.

Soc. Now then, as I am desirous that we being friends should have a good understanding about the argument, let me state my view to you: the first mode of assignment, whether applied to figures or to names, I call right, and when applied to names only, true as well as right; and the other mode, whereby that which is unlike is given or assigned, I call wrong, and in the case of names, false as well as wrong.

Crat. I suggest that may be true, Socrates, in the case of pictures; they may be wrongly assigned; but not in the case of names—they must necessarily be always right.

Soc. Why, what is the difference? May I not go to a man and say to him, 'This is your picture', showing him his own likeness, or perhaps the likeness of a woman; and when I say 'show', I mean bring before the sense of sight.

Crat. Certainly.

Soc. And may I not go to him again, and say, 'This is your name?'—for the name, like the picture, is an imitation. May I not say to him—'This is your name'? and may I not then bring to his sense of hearing the imitation of himself, when I say, 'This is a man'; or of a female of the human species, when I say, 'This is a woman', as the case may be? Is not all that possible—does it not sometimes happen?

Crat. I would fain agree with Socrates; and therefore I say, Granted.

Soc. For that I am grateful, my friend, if the fact is true; it is hardly necessary to persist in the dispute at present. But if I can assign names as

155

well as pictures to objects, the right assignment of them we may call truth, and the wrong assignment of them falsehood. Now if there be such a wrong assignment of names, there may also be a wrong or inappropriate assignment of verbs; and if of names and verbs then of the sentences, which are made up of them."

Republic I 329b–c: "How does love suit with age, Sophocles,—are you still the man you were? 'Peace', he replied; 'most gladly have I escaped the thing of which you speak; I feel I have escaped from a mad and furious master.'"

Republic II 360a–b: "Whereupon he contrived to be chosen one of the messengers who were sent to the court; where as soon as he arrived he seduced the queen, and with her help conspired against the king and slew him, and took the kingdom."

Republic III 387e–388a: "Then we shall be right in getting rid of the lamentations of famous men, and making them over to women (and not even to women who are good for anything), or to men of a baser sort, that those who are being educated by us to be the defenders of their country may scorn to do the like."

Republic III 395d–e: "Then, I said, we will not allow those for whom we profess a care and of whom we say that they ought to be good men, to imitate a woman, whether young or old, quarrelling with her husband, or striving and vaunting against the gods in conceit of her happiness, or when she is in affliction, or sorrow, or weeping; and certainly not one who is in sickness, love or labour."

Republic III 398e: "And which are the harmonies expressive of sorrow? You are musical, and can tell me.

The harmonies which you mean are the mixed or tenor Lydian, and the full-toned or bass Lydian, and such-like.

These, then, I said, must be banished; even to women who have a character to maintain they are of no use, and must less to men."

Republic IV 431b–c: "And now, I said, look at our newly created State, and there you will find one of these two conditions realized; for the State as you will acknowledge, may be justly called master of itself, if the words 'temperance' and 'self-mastery' truly express the rule of the better part over the worse.

On looking, he said, I see what you say is true.

Let me further note that the manifold and complex pleasures and desires and pains are generally found in children and women and servants, and in the freemen so called who are of the lowest and more numerous class."

Republic V. I would have to quote a large part of this book, but will limit myself to selecting a few fragments that indicate that in the ideal city woman will fulfill the same functions as man, as guardians of the State. But, apart from the fact that she will perform her duties *less well,* as a result of her inferior nature, she will also participate only insofar as she is the *same* as a man. This will give rise to a lengthy debate—which the reader should consult—on the definition of same and different in nature.

451b–c: "Well, I replied, I suppose that I must retrace my steps and say what I perhaps ought to have said before in the proper place. The drama of the men has been played out, and now properly enough comes the turn of the women, especially in view of your challenge."

451d–e: "Let us abide by that comparison in our account of their birth and breeding, and let us see whether the result accords with our design.

What do you mean?

What I mean may be put into the form of a question, I said: Are female sheepdogs expected to keep watch together with the males, and to go hunting with them and share in their other activities? or do we entrust to the males the entire and exclusive care of the flocks, while we leave the females at home, because we think that the bearing and suckling of their puppies is labour enough for them?

No, he said, they share alike; the only difference between them is that the males are regarded as stronger and females as weaker."

451e–452a: "Then if women are to have the same duties as men, they must have the same education? . . .

"Yes, and the most ridiculous thing of all will be the sight of women naked in the palaestra, exercising with the men."

454d–e: "And if, I said, the male and female sex appear to differ in their fitness for any art or pursuit, we should say that such pursuit or art ought to be assigned to one or the other of them; but if the difference consists only in women bearing and men begetting children, this does not amount to a proof that a woman differs from a man in respect to the sort of education she should receive; and we shall therefore continue to maintain that our guardians and their wives ought to have the same pursuits."

455b–e: "Let us say to him: Come now, and we will ask you a question:—when you spoke of a nature gifted or not gifted in any respect, did you mean to say that one man will acquire a thing easily, another with difficulty? the first, after brief instruction, is able to discover a great deal more for himself, whereas the other, after much teaching and application, cannot even preserve what he has learnt; or again, did you mean that the one has a body which is a good servant to his mind, while the body of the other is a hindrance to him? Would not these be the sort of differences which distinguish a man gifted by nature from the one who is ungifted? . . .

And can you mention any pursuit of mankind in which the male sex
has not all these gifts and qualities in a higher degree than the female?
Need I waste time in speaking of the art of weaving, and the preparation
of pancakes and preserves in which womankind is generally thought to
have some skill, and in which for her to be beaten by a man is of all
things the most absurd?

You are quite right, he replied, in maintaining that one sex greatly
excels the other in almost every field. Although many women are in
many things superior to many men, yet on the whole what you say is
true.

And if so, my friend, I said, there is no special faculty of administra-
tion in a state which a woman has because she is a woman, or which a
man has by virtue of his sex, but the gifts of nature are alike diffused in
both; all the pursuits of men can naturally be assigned to women also,
but in all of them a woman is weaker than a man."

456b: "Therefore those women who have such qualities are to be
selected as the companions and colleagues of men who also have them
and whom they resemble in capacity and in character?"

457a–b: "Then let the guardian women strip, for their virtue will be
their robe, and let them share in the toils of war and the defence of their
country; only in the distribution of labours the lighter are to be assigned
to the women, who are the weaker natures, but in other respects their
duties are to be the same."

457b: "Here, then, is one difficulty in our law about women, which
we may say that we have now escaped; the wave has not swallowed us
up alive for enacting that the guardians of either sex should have all their
pursuits in common; to the utility and to the possibility of this arrangement the consistency of the argument with itself bears witness.

Yes, that was a mighty wave which you have escaped."

457c–d: "The law, I said, which is the sequel of this and of all that has
preceded, is to the following effect,—'that all these women are to be
common to all the men of the same class, none living privately together,
and, moreover, that their children are to be common, and no parent is to
know his own child, nor any child his parent."

458c–e: "You, I said, who are their legislator, having selected the
men, will now select the women, and give them to them;—they must be
as far as possible of like natures with them; and they must live in common houses, and meet at common meals. None of them will have anything specially his or her own; they will be together, and will be brought
up together, and will associate at gymnastic exercises. And so they will
be drawn by a necessity of their natures to have intercourse with each
other—necessity is not too strong a word, I think?

158

Yes, he said;—necessity, not geometrical, but another sort of necessity which lovers know, and which is far more convincing and constraining to the mass of mankind.

True, Glaucon, I said; but now we can hardly allow promiscuous unions, or any other kind of disorder; in a city of the blessed, licentiousness is an unholy thing which the rulers will forbid. . . .

Then clearly the next thing will be to arrange marriages that are sacred in the highest degree; and what is most beneficial will be deemed sacred?"

459d–e: "Why, I said, the principle has already been laid down that the best of either sex should be united with the best as often, and the inferior with the inferior as seldom, as possible; and that they should rear the offspring of the one sort of union but not of the other, if the flock is to be maintained in first-rate condition."

460c: "They will provide for their nurture, and will bring the mothers to the fold when they are full of milk, taking the greatest possible care that no mother recognizes her own child;

Timaeus 42b–c: "He who lived well during his appointed time was to return to dwell in his native star, and there he would have a blessed and congenial existence. But if he failed in attaining this, at the second birth, he would pass into a woman, and if, when in that state of being, he did not desist from evil, he would continually be changed into some brute who resembled him in the evil nature which he had acquired."

Timaeus 76d–e: "From the combination of sinew, skin and bone, in the structure of the finger, there arises a triple compound, which when dried up, takes the form of one hard skin partaking of all three natures, and was fabricated by these second causes, but designed by mind which is the principal cause with an eye to the future. For our creators knew well that women and other animals would some day be framed out of men."

Timaeus 90e–91a: "Of the men who came into the world, those who were cowards or led unrighteous lives may with reason be supposed to have changed into the nature of women in the second generation. And this was the reason why at that time the gods created in us the desire of sexual intercourse."

Epistle VIII, 355c: "The usage that applies the term 'happy' to the rich is itself miserable, being a foolish adage of women and children, and it renders miserable those who put confidence in it."[1]

---

[1](*Thirteen Epistles of Plato,* tr. L. A. Post, Oxford: Clarendon, 1955.—Tr.)

How to Conceive (of) a Girl

Further, a boy actually resembles a woman in physique, and a woman is as it were an infertile male.

If we are to regard matter as the female desiring the male or the foul desiring the fair, the desire must be attributed not to the foulness itself, as such, but to a subject that is foul or female incidentally.

Here is an indication that the female does not discharge semen of the same kind as the male, and that the offspring is not formed from a mixture of two semens, as some allege. Very often the female conceives although she has derived no pleasure from the act of coitus; and, on the contrary side, when the female derives as much pleasure as the male, and they both keep the same pace, the female does not bear—unless there is a proper amount of menstrual fluid (as it is called) present.

And this is in fact what we find happening; for the natural substance of the menstrual fluid is to be classed as "prime matter" (prōtē hylē).

—Aristotle

But fire, in fact, what is that? A simple body, an elementary substance, that can be predicated on the basis of certain qualities. And light? The actual transparence of certain bodies that are potentially transparent: air, water, and many solids. Whereas at the beginning of epistemology, the philosopher was still marveling at such things as air, fire, and water, now they must be submitted to a rigorous scientific analysis so that their excessive power can be checked. They must be put in their place, within a general theory of being so as to lessen our fascination with them.

(The first, third and fourth epigraphs are from *Aristotle: Generation of Animals*, tr. A. L. Peck (Cambridge: Harvard University Press, 1963), pp. 103, 97–98, and 111. The second epigraph is from *Aristotle; The Physics,* tr. Philip H. Wicksteed and Francis M. Cornford (Cambridge: Harvard University Press, 1963), p. 93.—Tr.)

And, but, what of the *"first matter"*? What is this unknowable entity that has an existence in itself? Something that eludes the question "what is?" (*tode ti*). Might this not be the body of the mother, and the process of becoming flesh within the mother? Of becoming *phýsis* always already constituted as the *hypokeimenon* that defines the substance of man? Might it not be this bodiliness shared with the mother, which as yet has no movement of its own, has yet to divide up time or space, has in point of fact no way of measuring the container or the surrounding world or the content or the relations among all these? It cannot be shaped in any distinct mold. Fusion, confusion, transfusion of matter, of body-matter, in which even the elementary would escape any static characterization. In which same and other would have yet to find their meaning.

The state of existence of the "beginning" from which being will emerge and stand apart is not predicable; being traces its lineage back first to a male parent who already rejoices in a specific form, and then, if we go back over the causes of generation, to that father's desire and love for God: "origin" of pure property. For God, the intelligible will be identified with intellection, thus avoiding the aporia that may arise out of the boundlessness of a "first matter" as a result of her eternal and perfect autonomy. This being in the father is alien to all genesis. No future enters into the eternal present of its formation. But it is equally plenitude in action, and does not grow out of the soil of the past. It is activity that theoretically never needs to transform its power in order to achieve some goal—even if the goal were that of changing the other within it into sameness—since all accomplishment has always been contained within it. And neither does it move in *any place* within nature, it carries no notion of *extension,* either in its composition or in its surroundings, since extension would continue to emphasize its bodily relation to its mother/matter.

And if God—absolute (self)principle—*is,* in the very purity of conception, then he will be able to serve as paradigm—however grudgingly from his distant heaven—for the representation of all being, including the doubly aporetic representation of the fetus in the womb. Both the form of the fetus, which has always already been determined, and its existence, established and being prior to the woman bearing it, find an iron-clad guarantee in this Unbegotten being, this Origin beyond origins that produces them. Being itself, however, must not be assumed to be subject to process, specifically the process of generation, and it has no need to go on defining its substance out of the past and into the future. But already and henceforward, Being is credited with having been

161

shaped first, earlier than beginning itself even, in its relationship with its principle, its *telos* and, when we come right down to it, with the prime mover of the universe.

It is far from obvious that the "first matter" enjoys this ontological privilege since her weakness is perhaps the foundation upon which the supreme elevation (of) God is erected. By her failure to be defined or predicated, she serves as in(de)finite basis for the ontological promotion of each living thing. She is both radically lacking in all power of logos and offers, unawares, an all-powerful soil in which the logos can grow. This lack of awareness pushes deep down to the heaviest, weightiest point, that *still center, undifferentiated* and circular, whose admitted motive force seems to work on the *outer edge of its orbit.*

Every utterance, every statement, will thus be developed and affirmed by covering over the fact that being's unseverable relation to mother-matter has been buried. Once being has been constituted a priori, and matter has been sealed over again—as the *hypokeimenon* (sub-jectum) censored out of present existence—then man is free to wax eloquent about the struggles he has with the *hylē* and the *dynamis* though these fights are always already rigged. In fact, anything that is repeated so emphatically must always be suspected of being a kind of denial or refusal of awareness. And a philosophical discourse that will (claim to) take matter as such into consideration deserves to be attended to with special care. Somewhere it forgets or denies that its subject has already been disguised and travestied by a certain speculation. And the less we see and recognize the additional part played in the *physis* by the mirror, the more powerful and insidious is the fiction at work.

This matter—first held in suspension and suspicion—is already un-formed. The *physis* is always already being appropriated by a *telos*. This is true of the *plant,* or even of its *flower,* "for example." Even so, isn't a *logos* still necessary before the genus and species of the plant can be decided? Etc. The plant may indeed conform to her own purpose, but an other has to certify this. And that other must speak, and speak, more-over, as a philosopher. She may be fully herself and in herself, but an other has to declare that this is the case. Thus, her development is subject to definitions coming from an other. And if, in the unforeseeable future, she happened to unleash some nameless potency, it would not be up to her to judge whether or not this unpredictable event had occurred. *She* would not condemn the sudden unchecked appearance of the *physis* as a monstrosity, an aberration in the essence of plant life, a development that stands outside the category of plant, a natural crossbreed, or? . . . *She* would have no say in her own promotion into being. And if, through some impossible—in the aristotelian meaning of that word—realization of some as yet unknown essence, matter were to supplant or at least question the ontological development of man himself, overturning the premises that ensure his logic, then it seems likely that discourse would set out to prove that she was malformed. Probably discourse would demonstrate the a-teleology of a potency formed in that way, and capable of casting doubt upon the foundations of discursiveness.

The substance of the plant, like that of any (female) being, cannot move, or move beyond, the ontological status assigned to it. Once and for all. It is not capable of any less or any more. It must remain in its individuality and its numerical unity. Matter-potency is duly corseted in/by rigid categories that are laid down in the first instance by philosophy and subsequently by each of its scientific subsets that deal with the different kinds and species of Being. The meanings and directions of Being are always impervious to change, you understand.

The discoveries in the study of nature made by the physicist himself cannot modify what has been posited in the "Analytics." All that is specific to his field of analysis is already coopted by prescriptions that direct or interpret his findings. If he lays claim to contradict something the philosopher has said, this is because he doesn't know that Being has already been cut up into pieces and that as a result he can only take the attributes of one of nature's parts into consideration. Any contradiction can only be the result of not knowing this petitio principii, which prohibits Being from ever being defined by anything except the whole set of syllogistic premises.

These conflicts as to which takes prior place in the archive and which is to determine the space assigned to each within the theory are probably relevant to the question of the "infinite" and of the aporias that question constantly raises. If the prime mover didn't install a brake on the wheel of *infinite regression*, for instance, might not all substance risk hurtling into some formlessness of prime matter? It might be seduced into returning to the womb of the mother-earth where the identity of being with itself is endangered, or at least problematic. Therefore, access to the earth must be barred by developing an onto-theology at the very outset. Except in the case of God, who is alien to matter, this philosophical construct reduces the potential for generation, growth, change, and expansion for all beings. Everyone, in effect, is pulled up by the roots, deprived of the "body's" first resources, of the endless possibilities of being in space. Moreover, all must share the "place" that has been marked out and must keep each other in place. Hence, it is essential that no one outgrow the place allotted or the movements suited to his nature, that no new being should be added to the existing number for fear of encroaching on another's space or destroying it. No one must overflow his container, or make so much as a ripple. A motion or emotion. Which is "impossible" in a (suitable) place.

All that remains is for each person to realize his essence as perfectly as he can, to give full expression to his *telos,* within the limits ascribed him. This would involve a death struggle between individual entities, all intent upon appropriating the *dynamis,* if all had not been planned in advance by the philosopher in his supreme wisdom and distinterested generosity. Be it known that *God* alone rejoices in himself without reserve, and this only in heaven; he alone is unrelated to the mother–matter whom he knows not and has never known, in the perfection of his entelechy. As for *man,* who is by nature a slave, he is always changing in regard to the possession of his form. But to act will nonetheless be man's privilege over *woman,* whose relationship to substance is more *dynamis* within the system of differentiation which thus makes man and woman complementary, not rivals. Woman is closer to matter, then, and less able to take on her form according to the order of being. Is it up to man to help her to take possession of her form—and of herself?: Or does he rather use the opportunity to tap this potential for other ends of his own? In fact, the most valid acts in his eyes are certainly those in which *telos* and practice are combined. The perfect project would have no ulterior motive, simply the transformation of *energeia* into the produced object. Contributing to a woman's achievement of femininity—assuming this to be possible, for a man at least—necessarily means a detour, implies turning away from activity into a production that is merely secondary from the point of view of his ontological development. He should rather be concentrating on seeing, thinking, conceiving (not necessarily in the sense of engender), living, tasting happiness. In these movements alone is the end immanent in the action; hence these alone qualify as acts. In these the agent both produces and is affected by his energy, and energy is channeled back into itself, thus preventing it from ever flagging. Energy is neither expended nor expanded on moving some foreign substance, and the agent is never passively subjected to the activity of anything else—with the possible exception of the prime mover who sets the whole universe going. Thus, the wise man is motivated only to develop his own being, the being that is his cause and his goal, principle of his circular course through life that alone—it is said—would have in nature neither its beginning nor its end. Man's only "passion," therefore, is being. Yet if this is the garden man cultivates, where is the soil?

Woman, for her part, remains in unrealized potentiality—unrealized, at least, for/by herself. *Is she, by nature, a being that exists for/by another?* And in her share of substance, not only is she secondary to man but she may just as well not be as be. Ontological status makes her incomplete and uncompletable. She can *never* achieve the *wholeness* of her form. Or perhaps her form has to be seen—paradoxically—as mere *privation?* But this question can never be decided since woman is never resolved by/in being, but remains the simultaneous co-existence of opposites. She is *both one and the other.* She is at once decay and growth, for example, and this bodes ill for any resemblance she might have with the eternal. And the Eternal (as we may call it) has no truck with potentiality. She is equally *neither one nor the other.* Or is she rather between the one and the other—that elusive gap between two discrete bodies? between two real-izations of one body? Which implies that change can always come about, that somewhere anything could be redefined otherwise. Is she the reverse of the coin of man's ability to act and move around in the physical world we are calling "place"? Is she unnecessary in and of herself, but essential as the non-subjective sub-jectum? As that which can never achieve the status of subject, at least for/by herself. Is she the indispensable condition whereby the living entity retains and maintains and perfects himself in his self-likeness? Despite the risks of falling down into the "infinite," or of uncontrollable movements in the "void." Thus, this "lack of qualities" that makes the female truly female ensures that the male can achieve his qualifications. In order to take full possession of himself, man will need to take over not only the *potentiality* and *potency,* but also the *place, and all the little chinks* (re)produced in his ceaseless drive to transform anything different and still self-defining into his own likeness. And so on.

Thus, unaware of the bedrock of hysteria or of his reliance upon it, he goes on in(de)finitely moving in/on the body of his mother. She is merely a receptacle whose dimensions must be determined in case they prove threatening or in case she can no longer be overcome by the father's logic and assertion of precedence and prior existence. But he continues to feed on her undefinable potency of which *place* would be, some say, the most extraordinary store. Even intelligible matter would have some of this potency, no doubt, when it is predicated as having spatial *extension.* Furthermore, mother-matter affords man the means to realize his form.

Theoretically there would be no such thing as woman. She would not exist. The best that can be said is that she does *not exist yet.* Something of her a-specificity might be found in the *betweens* that occur in being, or beings. These *gaps* reopen the question of the "void," and thereby most commonly give rise to vigorous, horrified rejection and a move to plug the hole with speculative "tissues" and "organs." The perfectly natural evidence of the continuum is also brought into play here. Now, if everything is taken up with the realization of the *physis, woman has, and will have, no place and thus no existence.* This will be true even in her *privation* of being, which it is the essential task and ceaseless effort of dialectic and dialectic's indispensable intermediaries to bring or bring back to the fullness of the self's possession of substance.

Outside of this process is nothing: outside of this process is the nothing that is woman. She alone is in a position—perhaps?—to question her function in this all-powerful "machine" we know as metaphysics, in that omnipotent "technique" of onto-theology. She functions—still—as choice, but a choice that has always already been made by "nature," between a male pleasure and her role as vehicle for procreation. The latter role is most clearly apparent in "menstruation" which "belongs in the realm of the *prōtē hylē.*" By coming back to the cycle of the mother, at least in potentiality, one will have turned again to the first matter and her mysteries. But the male individual must take care not to slip back there. For his form is unlikely to profit thereby. It is rather by distance and separation that he will affirm his self-identity.

But what makes for the "primacy" he attributes to identity? This is the question Aristotle tried to elucidate in his ceaseless struggle with matter, and he resolves it only by postulating an "immanence" that corresponds to that of the logos. Freud also hammered away at this question in often contradictory statements. Now a clear-cut answer seems to be available; the primacy resides in the name(s) of the father, which is/are transcendent or immanent in his (as it were) natural development. Nonetheless, the *physis* must not cease to function. Indeed it must be openly admitted, at least in certain places, that *physis* has been travestied from the very beginning. Even in her sexuateness, she is the cloth of fantasy from which a logical order is still cut. The aporia of the "primary" identification of the "feminine" continues to break through the barriers created by logic, as they are built up.

Thus abandoned in her weakness, deformed and formless, the "female" is said to desire the "male" as ugly desires beautiful. This must not, however, be interpreted to mean that she is "essentially" ugly—that would be a grossly a-teleological conception—but only that she is ugly "accidentally."

But doesn't her whole existence amount to an "accident"? An accident of reproduction? A genetic monstrosity? For a human life takes its form only from its father, or more specifically from the male sperm, since the product of intercourse is not made up of the combination of sperm and ovum. *If this is so, how can a girl be conceived?* Except by chromosomal anomaly? In any case, she couldn't lay claim to any substance. Merely added to—or taken away from—essence, fortuitous, troublesome, "accidental," she can be modified or eliminated without changing anything in "nature."

Admittedly, because she is deprived of everything, "she" also wants to take possession of everything. And that has to be prevented, since anything she might thus attract to herself will be reduced to a mere reflection, shadow, fantasy, absence, of what it had been in its natural wholeness.

Une Mère de Glace

7. "We are thus brought back to the nature of that underlying matter and the things believed to be based upon it; investigation will show us that Matter has no reality and is not capable of being affected.

Matter must be bodiless—for body is a later production, a compound made by Matter in conjunction with some other entity. Thus it is included among incorporeal things in the sense that body is something that is neither Real-Being nor Matter.

Matter is not Soul; it is not Intellect, is not Life, is no Ideal-Principle, no Reason-Principle; it is not limit or bound, for it is mere indetermination; it is not a power, for what does it produce?

It lives on the farther side of all these categories and so has no title to the name of Being. It will be more plausibly called a non-being, and this not in the sense that movement and station are Not-Being (i.e., as merely different from Being) but in the sense of veritable Not-Being, so that it is no more than the image and phantasm of Mass, a bare aspiration towards substantial existence; it is stationary but not in the sense of having position, it is in itself invisible, eluding all effort to observe it, present where no one can look, unseen for all our gazing, ceaselessly presenting contraries in the things based upon it; it is large and small, more and less, deficient and excessive; a phantasm unabiding and yet unable to withdraw—not even strong enough to withdraw, so utterly has it failed to accept strength from the Intellectual Principle, so absolute its lack of all Being.

Its every utterance, therefore, is a lie; it pretends to be great and it is little, to be more and it is less; and the Existence with which it masks itself is no Existence, but a passing trick making trickery of all that seems

(This section consists of extracts from the Sixth Tractate, "The Impassivity of the Unembodied," from *Plotinus' Enneads,* tr. Stephen MacKenna, 2d. ed. rev. B. S. Page [London: Faber & Faber, 1956], pp. 201–222, reprinted by permission of Faber & Faber Ltd. The title is left in French as the play on the homonyms *mer/mère,* sea/mother, and the double meaning of the word *glace,* ice/mirror, have no exact English equivalents.—Tr.)

to be present in it, phantasms within a phantasm; it is like a mirror showing things as in itself when they are really elsewhere, filled in appearance but actually empty, containing nothing, pretending everything. Into and out of it move mimicries of the Authentic Existents, images playing upon an image devoid of Form, visible against it by its very formlessness; they seem to modify it but in reality effect nothing, for they are ghostly and feeble, have no thrust and meet none in Matter either; they pass through it leaving no cleavage, as through water; or they might be compared to shapes projected so as to make some appearance upon what we know only as the Void.

Further, if visible objects were of the rank of the originals from which they have entered into Matter we might believe Matter to be really affected by them, for we might credit them with some share of the power inherent in their senders: but the objects of our experiences are of very different virtue than the realities they represent, and we deduce that the seeming modification of matter by visible things is unreal since the visible thing itself is unreal, having at no point any similarity with its source and cause. Feeble in itself, a false thing and projected upon a falsity, like an image in a dream or against water or on a mirror, it can but leave Matter unaffected; and even this is saying too little, for water and mirror do give back a faithful image of what presents itself before them.''

. . . . . .

9. ''In answer: it must, first, be noted that there are a variety of modes in which an object may be said to be present to another or to exist in another. There is a 'presence' which acts by changing the object—for good or for ill—as we see in the case of bodies, especially where there is life. But there is also a 'presence' which acts, towards good or ill, with no modification of the object, as we have indicated in the case of the Soul. Then there is the case represented by the stamping of a design upon wax, where the 'presence' of the added pattern causes no modification in the substance nor does its obliteration diminish it. And there is the example of Light whose presence does not even bring change of pattern to the object illuminated. A stone becoming cold does not change its nature in the process; it remains the stone it was. A line does not cease to be a line for being coloured; nor, we may take it, does a surface; but might there not be a modification of the underlying mass? No: it is impossible to think of mass being modified by colour—for, of course, we must not talk of modification when there is no more than a presence, or at most a presenting of shape.

Mirrors and transparent objects, even more, offer a close parallel; they are quite unaffected by what is seen in or through them: material things are reflections, and the Matter on which they appear is further from being affected than is a mirror. Heat and cold are present in Matter, but the Matter itself suffers no change of temperature: growing hot and growing cold have to do only with quality; a quality enters and brings the impassible Substance under a new state—though, by the way, research into nature may show that cold is nothing positive but an absence, a mere negation. . . . Matter, therefore (the mere absence of Reality), cannot be modified: any modification that takes place can occur only in some compound of Matter and reality, or, speaking generally, in some agglomeration of actual things. The Matter itself—isolated, quite apart from all else, utterly simplex—must remain immune, untouched in the midst of all the interacting agencies; just as, when people fight within their four walls, the house and the air in it remain without part in the turmoil.

We may take it, then, that while the qualities that appear upon Matter group to produce each the effect belonging to its nature, yet Matter itself remains immune, even more definitely immune than any of those qualities entering into it which, not being contraries, are not affected by each other.

10. Further, if Matter were susceptible of modification, it must acquire something by the incoming of the new state; it will either adopt that state, or, at least, it will be in some way different from what it was. Now upon this first incoming quality suppose a second to supervene; the recipient is no longer Matter but a modification of Matter: this second quality, perhaps, departs but it has acted and therefore leaves something of itself after it; the substratum is still further altered. This process proceeding, the substratum ends by becoming something quite different from Matter; it becomes a thing settled in many modes and many shapes; at once it is debarred from being the all-recipient; it will have closed the entry against many incomers. In other words, the Matter is no longer there: Matter is destructible.

No: if there is to be a Matter at all, it must be always identically as it has been from the beginning: to speak of Matter as changing is to speak of it as not being Matter.

. . . . . .

11. I think, in fact, that Plato had this in mind where he justly speaks of Real Existents 'entering and passing out': these particular words are not used idly: he wishes us to grasp the precise nature of Matter's participation in the Ideas.

The difficulty on this point is not really that which presented itself to most of our predecessors—how the Ideas enter into Matter—it is rather the mode of their presence in it.

It is in fact strange at sight that Matter should remain itself intact, unaffected by Ideal-Forms present within it, especially seeing that these are affected by each other. It is surprising, too, that the entrant Forms should regularly expel preceding shapes and qualities, and that the modification (which cannot touch Matter) should affect what is a compound (of Idea and Matter) and this, again, not at haphazard but precisely where there is a need of the incoming or outgoing of some certain Ideal-form, the compound being deficient through the absence of a particular principle whose presence will complete it.

But the reason is that the fundamental nature of Matter can take no increase by anything entering it, and no decrease by any withdrawal: what from the beginning it was, it remains. It is not like those things whose lack is merely that of arrangement and order which can be supplied without change of substance as when we dress or decorate something bare or ugly.

But where the bringing to order must cut through to the very nature, the base original must be transmuted: it can leave ugliness for beauty only by a change of substance. Matter, then, thus brought to order must lose its own nature in the supreme degree unless its baseness is an accidental: if it is base in the sense of Baseness the Absolute, it could never participate in order, and if evil in the sense of being Evil the Absolute, it could never participate in good.

We conclude that Matter's participation in Idea is not by way of modification within itself: the process is very different; it is a bare seeming. Perhaps we have here the solution of the difficulty as to how Matter, essentially evil, can be reaching towards The Good: there would be (in this 'seeming') no such participation as would destroy its essential nature. Given this mode of pseudo-participation—in which Matter would, as we say, retain its nature, unchanged, always being what it has essentially been—there is no longer any reason to wonder as to how, while essentially evil, it yet participates in Idea: for, by this mode, it does not abandon its own character: participation is the law, but it participates only just so far as its essence allows. Under a mode of participation which allows it to remain on its own footing, its essential nature stands none the less, whatsoever the Idea, within that limit, may communicate to it: it is by no means the less evil for remaining immutably in its own order. If it had authentic participation in The Good and were veritably changed, it would not be essentially evil.

In a word, when we call Matter evil we are right only if we mean that it is not amenable to modification by The Good; but that means simply that it is subject to no modification whatever.

This is Plato's conception: to him participation does not, in the case of Matter, comport any such presence of an Ideal-Form in a substance to be shaped by it as would produce one compound thing made up of the two elements changing at the same moment, merging into one another, modified each by the other.

In his haste to his purpose he raises many difficult questions, but he is determined to disown that view; he labours to indicate in what mode Matter can receive the Ideal-Forms without, itself, being modified. The direct way is debarred since it is not easy to point to things actually present in a base, and yet leaving that base unaffected: he therefore devises a metaphor for participation without modification (a plastic material, gold, moulded into various patterns), one which supports, also, his thesis that all appearing to the senses is void of substantial existence and that the region of mere seeing is vast.

Holding, as he does, that it is the patterns displayed by Matter that cause all experience in material bodies while the Matter itself remains unaffected, he chooses this way of stating its immutability, leaving us to make out for ourselves that those very patterns impressed upon it do not comport any experience, any modification in itself.

In the case, no doubt, of the bodies that take one pattern or shape after having borne another, it might be said that there was a change, the variation of shape being made verbally equivalent to a real change: but since Matter is essentially without shape or magnitude, the appearing of shape upon it can by no freedom of phrase be described as a change within it. On this point if one must have 'a rule for thick and thin' one may safely say that the underlying Kind contains nothing whatever in the mode commonly supposed.

But if we reject even the idea of its really containing at least the patterns upon it, how is it, in any sense, a recipient?

The answer is that in the metaphor cited we have some reasonably adequate indication of the impassibility of Matter coupled with the seeming presence of images not present.

But we cannot leave the point of its impassibility without a warning against allowing ourselves to be deluded by sheer custom of speech.

Plato speaks of Matter as becoming dry, wet, inflamed, but we must remember the words that follow: 'and taking the shape of air and of water': this blunts the expressions 'becoming wet, becoming inflamed'; once we have Matter thus admitting these shapes, we learn that it has not itself become a shaped thing but that the shapes remain distinct as they entered. We see, further, that the expression 'being inflamed' is not to be taken strictly: it is rather a case of becoming fire. Becoming fire is very different from becoming inflamed which implies an outside agency and, therefore, susceptibility to modification. Matter, being itself a portion of fire, cannot be said to catch fire. To suggest that the fire not merely permeates the matter, but actually sets it on fire is like saying that a statue permeates its bronze (and 'statufies' it).

Further, if what enters must be an Ideal-Principle how could it set Matter aflame? But what if it is a pattern or condition? No: the object set aflame is so in virtue of the combination of Matter and condition.

But how can this follow on the conjunction when no unity has been produced by the two?

Even if such a unity has been produced, it would be a unity of things not mutually sharing experiences but acting upon each other. And the question would then arise whether each was effective upon the other or whether the sole action was not that of one (the form) preventing the other (Matter) from slipping away?

. . . . . .

13. Further, they must explain in what sense they hold that Matter tends to slip away from its form (the Idea). Can we conceive it stealing out from stones and rocks or whatever else envelops it?

And of course they cannot pretend that Matter in some cases rebels and sometimes does not. For if once it makes away of its own will, why should it not always escape? If it is fixed despite itself, it must be enveloped by some Ideal-Form for good and all. This, however, leaves still the question why a given portion of Matter does not remain constant to any one given form: the reason lies mainly in the fact that the Ideas are constantly passing into it.

In what sense, then, is it said to elude form?

By very nature and for ever?

But does not this precisely mean that it never ceases to be itself, in other words that its one form is an invincible formlessness? In no other sense has Plato's dictum any value to those who invoke it.

Matter (we read) is 'the receptacle and nurse of all generation'.

Now if Matter is such a receptacle and nurse, all generation is distinct from it, and since all the changeable lies in the realm of generation, Matter, existing before all generation, must exist before all change.

'Receptacle' and 'nurse'; then it retains its identity; it is not subject to modification. Similarly if it is (as again we read) 'the ground on which individual things appear and disappear', and so, too, if it is 'a place', a 'base'. Even the description which is censured as implying a ground to the Ideas does not attribute any state to it but probes after its distinctive manner of being.

And what is that?

This which we think of as a Nature-Kind cannot be included among Existents but must utterly rebel from the Essence of Real Beings and be therefore wholly sometimes other than they—for they are Reason-Principles and possess Authentic Existence—it must inevitably, by virtue of that difference, retain its integrity to the point of being permanently closed against them and, more, of rejecting close participation in any image of them.

Only on these terms can it be completely different: once it took any Idea to hearth and home, it would become a new thing, for it would cease to be the thing apart, the ground of all else, the receptacle of absolutely any and every form. If there is to be a ceaseless coming into it and going out from it, itself must be unmoved and immune in all the come and go. The Entrant will enter as an image, the untrue entering the untruth.

But at least, in a true entry?

No: how could there be a true entry into that which, by being falsity, is banned from ever touching truth?

Is it then a pseudo-entry into a pseudo-entity—something merely brought near, as faces enter the mirror, there to remain just as long as the people look into it?

Yes: if we eliminated the Authentic Existents from this Sphere, nothing at all now seen in sense would appear one moment longer.

Here the mirror itself is seen, for it is itself an Ideal-Form of a kind (has some degree of Real Being); but bare Matter, which is no Idea, is not a visible thing; if it were, it would have been visible in its own character before anything else appeared upon it. The condition of Matter may be illustrated by that of air penetrated by light and remaining, even so, unseen because it is invisible whatever happens.

The reflections in the mirror are not taken to be real, all the less since the appliance on which they appear is seen and remains while the images disappear, but Matter is not seen either with the images or without them. But suppose the reflection on the mirror remaining, and the mirror itself not seen, we would never doubt the solid reality of all that appears.

If, then, there is, really, something in a mirror, we may suppose objects of sense to be in Matter in precisely that way: if in the mirror there is nothing, if there is only a seeming of something, then we may judge that in Matter there is the same delusion and that the seeming is to be traced to the Substantial-Existence of the Real-Beings, that Substantial-Existence in which the Authentic has the real participation while only an unreal participation can belong to the unauthentic since their condition must differ from that which they would know if the parts were reversed, if the Authentic-Existents were not and they were.

14. But this would mean that if there were no Matter nothing would exist?

Precisely as in the absence of a mirror, or something of similar power, there would be no reflection.

A thing whose very nature is to be lodged in something else cannot exist where the base is lacking—and it is the character of a reflection to appear in something not itself.

Of course, supposing anything to desert from the Authentic Beings, this would not need an alien base: but these Beings are not subject to flux, and therefore any outside manifestation of them implies something other than themselves, something offering a base to what never enters, something which by its presence, in its insistence, by its cry for help, in its beggardom, strives as it were by violence to acquire and is always disappointed so that its poverty is enduring, its cry unceasing.

This alien base exists and the myth represents it as a pauper to exhibit its nature, to show that Matter is destitute of The Good. The claimant does not ask for all the Giver's store, but it welcomes whatever it can get; in other words, what appears in Matter is not Reality.

The name too (Poverty) conveys that Matter's need is never met. The union with Poros, Possession, is designed to show that Matter does not attain to Reality, to Plenitude, but to some bare sufficiency—in point of fact to imaging skill.

It is, of course, impossible that an outside thing belonging in any degree to Real-Being—whose nature is to engender Real-Beings—should utterly fail of participation in Reality: but here we have something perplexing; we are dealing with utter Non-Being, absolutely without part in Reality; what is this participation by the non-participant, and how does mere neighbouring confer anything on that which by its own nature is precluded from any association?

The answer is that all that impinges upon this Non-Being is flung back as from a repelling substance; we may think of an echo returned from a repercussive plane surface; it is precisely because of the lack of retention that the phenomenon is supposed to belong to that particular place and even to arise there.

If Matter were participant and received Reality to the extent which we are apt to imagine, it would be penetrated by a Reality thus sucked into its constitution. But we know that the Entrant is not thus absorbed:

Matter remains as it was, taking nothing to itself: it is the check to the forthwelling of Authentic Existence; it is a ground that repels; it is a mere receptacle to the Realities as they take their common path (of emanation) and here meet and mingle. It resembles those reflecting vessels, filled with water, which are often set against the sun to produce fire: the heat rays prevented, by their contrary within, from being absorbed are flung out as one mass.

It is in this sense and way that Matter becomes the cause of the generated realm; the combinations within it hold together only after some such reflective mode.

. . . . . .

15. . . . But the Reason-Principle operating upon Matter is external to it only in a very different mode and sense: exteriority in this case is amply supplied by contrariety of essence and can dispense with any opposite ends (any question of lineal position); or, rather, the difference is one that actually debars any local extremity; sheer incongruity of essence, the utter failure in relationship, inhibits admixture (between Matter and any form of Being).

The reason, then, of the immutability of Matter is that the entrant principle neither possesses it nor is possessed by it. . . .

In that example, no doubt, the mental representation—though it seems to have a wide and unchecked control—is an image, while the Soul (Mind) is in its nature not an image (but a Reality): none the less the Soul or Mind certainly stands to the concept as Matter, or in some analogous relation. The representation, however, does not cover the Mind over; on the contrary it is often expelled by some activity there; however urgently it presses in, it never effects such an obliteration as to be taken for the Soul; it is confronted there by indwelling powers, by Reason-Principles, which repel all such attack.

Matter—feebler far than the Soul for any exercise of power, and possessing no phase of the Authentic Existents, not even in possession of its own falsity—lacks the very means of manifesting itself, utter void as it is; it becomes the means by which other things appear, but it cannot announce its own presence. Penetrating thought may arrive at it, discriminating it from Authentic Existence; then, it is discerned as something abandoned by all that really is, by even the dimmest semblants of being, as a thing dragged towards every shape and property and appearing to follow—yet in fact not even following.

. . . . . .

16. An Ideal-Principle approaches and leads Matter towards some desired dimension, investing this underlie with a magnitude from itself:

Matter neither has the dimension nor acquires it; all that shows upon it of dimension derives from the Ideal-Principle.

Eliminate this Ideal-Form and the substratum ceases to be a thing of magnitude, or to appear so. . . .

In a word, though Matter is far extended—so vastly as to appear co-extensive with all this sense-known Universe—yet if the Heavens and their content came to an end, all magnitude would simultaneously pass from Matter with, beyond a doubt, all its other properties; it would be abandoned to its own Kind, retaining nothing of all that which, in its own peculiar mode, it had hitherto exhibited. . . .

That a thing essentially devoid of magnitude should come to a certain size is no more astonishing than that a thing essentially devoid of heat should become warm: Matter's essential existence is quite separate from its existing in bulk, since, of course, magnitude is an immaterial principle as pattern is. Besides, if we are not to reduce Matter to nothing, it must be all things by way of participation, and magnitude is one of those all things.

In bodies, necessarily compounds, magnitude—though not a deter-mined magnitude—must be present as one of the constituents; it is im-plied in the very notion of body; but Matter—not a body—excludes even undetermined magnitude.

17. Nor can we, on the other hand, think that Matter is simply Abso-lute Magnitude.

Magnitude is not, like Matter, a receptacle; it is an Ideal-Principle: it is a thing standing apart to itself, not some definite mass. When it desires to abandon its station in the Intellectual-Principle or in the Soul and assume (physical) magnitude, it gives to its images (the material forms)—aspir-ing and moving towards it and eagerly imitating its act—a power of reproducing their states in their own derivatives. The Magnitude which has gone forth to the image-making stage has recourse to the Absolute Magnitude and carries with it the likeness of Matter, and so by extending Matter enables it, devoid though it be of all content, to exhibit the appearance of Magnitude. It must be understood that spurious Magni-tude consists in the fact that a thing (Matter) not possessing actual Mag-nitude strains towards it and has the extension of that straining. . . .

Matter takes on what we conceive as extension; it is compelled to assume a relation to the All, and gathered under this Idea and under Mass, to be all things—in the degree in which the operating power can lead the really nothing to become all. . . .

All is perceptible by virtue of this origin in the Intellectual Sphere but all is falsity since the base in which the manifestation takes place is a non-existent. . . .

Matter is manifested in this sphere as Mass by the fact that it mirrors the Absolute Magnitude; Magnitude here is the reflection in the mirror. Matter must go as one total thing wherever the image (of the Idea) calls it; it is everywhere submissive—the material of determination and not the determined thing itself; what is, in its own character, no determined thing may become determined by an outside force, though, in becoming thus determined, it does not become the definite thing in question, for thus it would lose its own characteristic indetermination.

. . . . . .

18. . . . The image of magnitude cannot appear on any basis of equality in a small mass—it is, after all, an image of Magnitude: yet it aspires to the full presentment of that Absolute Magnitude and approaches it as nearly as the company of its inseparable associate (Matter) will allow: thus it confers Magnitude upon that (=Matter) which has none and cannot even muster up the appearance of having any, and the visible resultant exhibits the Magnitude of mass.

Matter, then, wears Magnitude as a dress thrown about it by its association with that image of Magnitude to whose movement it must answer; but it does not, for that, change its Kind; if the image which has clothed it were to withdraw, it would once again be what it permanently is, what it is by its own strength, or it would have precisely the Magnitude lent to it by any other form that happens to be present in it.

The (Universal) Soul—containing the Ideal Principles of Real-Beings, and itself an Ideal Principle—includes all in concentration within itself, just as the Ideal Principle of each particular entity is complete and self-contained: it, therefore, sees these principles of sensible things because they are turned, as it were, towards it and advancing to it: but it cannot harbour them in their plurality, for it cannot depart from its Kind; it sees them, therefore, stripped of mass. Matter, on the contrary, destitute of resisting power since it has no Act of its own and is a mere shadow, can but accept all that an active power may choose to send. In what is thus sent, from the Reason-Principle in the Intellectual Realm, there is already contained a degree of the partial object that is to be formed: in the image-making impulse within the Reason-Principle there is already a step (towards the lower manifestation) or we may put it that the downward movement from the Reason-Principle is a first form of the partial: utter absence of partition would mean no movement but (sterile) response. Matter cannot be the home of all things in concentration as the Soul is: if it were so, it would belong to the Intellectual Sphere. It must be (like the Soul) all-recipient but not in that partless mode. It is to be the Place of all things, and it must therefore extend universally, offer itself to all things, serve to all interval: thus it will be a thing unconfined to any moment (of space or time) but laid in submission to all that is to be.

. . . . . .

19. The Ideal Principles entering into Matter as to a Mother affect it neither for better nor for worse.

Their action is not upon Matter, but upon each other; these powers conflict with their opponent principles, not with their substrata—unless the substrata are taken as comprised with the entrant forms. . . .

This, I think, is why the doctors of old, teaching through symbols and mystic representations, exhibit the ancient Hermes with the generative organs always in active posture; this is to convey that the generator of things of sense is the Intellectual Reason-Principle: the sterility of Matter, eternally unmoved, is indicated by the eunuchs surrounding it in its representation as the All-Mother.

This too exalting title is conferred upon it in order to indicate that it is the source of things in the sense of being their underlie: it is an approximate name chosen for a general conception; there is no intention of suggesting a complete parallel with motherhood to those not satisfied with a surface impression but needing a precisely true presentment; by a remote symbolism, the nearest they could find, they indicate that Matter is sterile, not female to full effect, female in receptivity only, not in pregnancy: this they accomplish by exhibiting Matter as approached by what is neither female nor effectively male but castrated of that impregnating power which belongs only to the unchangeably masculine.

. . . And If, Taking the Eye
of a Man Recently Dead, . . .

As a result, it is manifest that a painting is immediately formed . . . on the inner surface of the brain that looks toward its concavities. And from thence I could easily take that picture as far as a certain little gland situated more or less in the middle of those concavities which is properly the seat of common sense. I could even go further and show you how it may at times pass from there along the arteries of a pregnant women into some determined member of the child in her womb and form there those birthmarks which are cause of such wonderment to all Learned Men.

—Descartes

If the premises of reasoning are *necessary* in the work of Aristotle, if the infinite has to be canceled in favor of the prior status of a substance that ensures that the relation of subjectum to predicate is applied *across the board,* with no space left for indeterminacy, it is the conclusion that emerges as irrefutable in Descartes. The *singular* at *one point,* at this point, has become necessary in reconstructing the whole, and lays down the general grounds whereby the *universal* may be re-affirmed within a system of doubt methodically applied to every object. But the singular, it must be admitted, is of a *particular* kind here: it is the thinking substance that, moreover, turns back upon itself and fastens up the circle of (its) subjectivity.

Once the primary identification has been achieved,—at least within the argument developed here—the possibility arises not only that the

(Both the epigraph and the title of this essay are taken from the Fifth Discourse of Descartes's scientific treatise on refraction and telescopes, *La Dioptrique,* found in René Descartes, *Oeuvres et Lettres,* ed. André Bridoux, [Paris: Pléiade, 1937], pp. 216 and 205. The *Discourse on Method* was written as a preface to the three scientific treatises on meteors, dioptrics, and geometry.—Tr.)

subject exists as such but that its condition of being results from self-reflection. This will all happen, of course, in the *wink of an eye* and will remain elusive. But doesn't that just prove that reality is involved here? Flowing, restless reality. Or that what is now founding the subject's existence and reflection works like the backing of a mirror that has been introjected, "incorporated," and is thus beyond perception; it can barely be intuited because it has no reflections of its own, and then only when speculative activity itself is suspended? If the "I" can desist from specific cerebration—from conceiving some clear-cut thought but also from attending to images or sensations that may be represented to its mind (esprit)—then, *for a moment,* it perceives itself as the *matrix* of everything that is thought (within it). The "I" exists over and above the day-to-day material of perception and is assured of being throughout everything and beyond everything. Whatever else, other than itself, may happen. By this flash of awareness, the philosopher will be required to trace himself *a path, a way,* which he *freely decides* to follow, as opposed to letting himself be swamped (by those images), in a flood of dreams or even of doubts in which he can neither swim nor wade. Much less think. Since the ground threatens every minute to shake the present certainties of the subject, *it must not be allowed any power of specularization. The basis for representation* must be purged of all *childish* phantoms or fantasies or belief or approximations. Anything picked up, accepted, and repeated without proof. About the other, the Other. Saying "no" to everything is the crucial way to be assured that one is really (like) oneself. Otherwise, there will always be doubts about what relates to the self and what to the other. About the reflections others might have in the self, and the self in the Other. Such unending, recurrent suspicion paralyzes all activity. So it is best to push suspicion as far as it will go, to the last of its implications, and then judge the results and put an end to the corrosive urge to put every certainty to the test.

If generalization there be here, it is to be found in hyperbolic doubt, in the systematic questioning of everything. Everything can be put in doubt, (it is) I (who) doubt(s), therefore (it is) I (who) am. The relation to the universality of being of the thinking and speaking "I" is then assured. *Undoubtedly.* But he took good care not to suppose, not to presuppose, that some other "I" might be doubting too. The most he is prepared to do is wonder whether the Other might not take a devilish pleasure in making him doubt everything. The "I" is still a child, an in-fans, when it comes to manipulating logic, with a touch of the adolescent when, on the contrary, self-identity has to be re-affirmed all over again. Representation here is auto-affective, auto-affecting solipsism. It embroiders its dream of potentiality alone in its chamber, indifferent, at least for a while, to the rest of (its) history that is still being woven. All alone, with an ever cautious *negativism,* it cuts up and reworks the *subject's links to his archives.* And *to his process/trial of engendering.* Once upon a time, something related to genesis and becoming used also to appear and even to precede the specific predicates attributed to the substance, the sub-jec-tum. But now, by a stroke of almost incredible boldness, it is the singular subject who is charged with giving birth to the universe all over again, after he has brought himself back into the world in a way that avoids the precariousness of existence as it is usually understood. Once *the chain of relationships, the cord,* has been *severed,* together with ancestry and the mysteries of conception, then there is nothing left but the subject who can go back and sever them all over again whenever he likes. In a speculative act of denial and negation that serves to affirm his autonomy. By means of a verb (to think) that, as if by chance,—or is it necessity?—can do without an object if need be, can also be predicated as an absolute, though at the price of some austerity, some effort of the will. Speculation is "pure," and as intransitive in its process as "to live" or "to be."

And that will have been possible only because, when the "I" thinks about something, the object of its thought is in fact itself, a self constituted as the virtual *passive* both in the present and past tenses. *This is the basis for (its) representation.* The process of thought (cogitationes) is made relative to the object of thought (cogitatum) that thinks them. The crucial thing in fact is to decide who, *here and now,* is representing or being represented. *The rest or remainder* will follow. Later. And if the objection is raised that you have to "breathe" before you think, and therefore exist, such naivete will elicit the retort that, whether or not I am breathing, if I am not aware of breathing, nothing can prove to me that I am in fact doing so. Therefore, that I exist. My certainty of being, even though it cannot precede predication, will make do, if need be, without my breath. And if my body and all material things, and even the sky, the earth, even other minds, fail to afford the proofs I can have or wish to have of them, my "spirit" (âme) is enough for me to live in complete security since, *if all else fails, it has the power to deny everything.* Even the truth of what it thinks. For, even if my "spirit" were wholly subject to illusion, it would continue in its being, provided it knew it was being misled. Really?

And what if illusion were constitutive of thinking? Not in the sense that the cogitationes "fail" to correspond to (their) objective reality, but in that whereby illusion would serve as fiction of proof of the cogitatum itself, as coming to the same thing as the entity who is now thinking (himself)?

The Eye of a Man Recently Dead

The unity and simplicity of the subject, of the cogitans and cogitatum—a sham. What if, therefore, the crucial thing to do were rather, or especially, to conclude that the other exists—and the self in the other—from the fact of thinking? What if I thought only after the other has been inserted, introjected, into me? Either as thought or as a mirror in which I reflect and am reflected. And if the thoughts that I have received from the other, or the others, are put in doubt by a solipsistic gesture which already calls its own validity into question, the fact that the mechanisms of thought and the "thinking tissue" are necessarily constituted by the other and appropriated by me does not seem to upset this "subject" in the affirmation of his lonely existence. Any more than the fact that I cannot reflect or be reflected unless I use a reflecting screen.[1] Such optical considerations are examined in specific treatises. *Already outside ontology.*

The same thing applies to the discussions of woman and women. Gynecology, dioptrics, are no longer by right a part of metaphysics—*that supposedly unsexed anthropos-logos whose actual sex is admitted only by its omission and exclusion from consciousness,* and by what is said in its margins. And what if the "I" only thought the thought of woman? The thought (as it were) of femaleness? And could send back this thought in its reflection only because the mother had been incorporated? The mother—that all-powerful mirror denied and neglected in the self-sufficiency of the (self) thinking subject, her "body" henceforward specularized through and through. The "I" would go so far as to reinvent the whole of language—if he could—in order to avoid confusing the only laws he recognizes as constitutive of his existence with the laws received from his fathers. For the latter assure him only of academic certainties that are already completely out of date for his present existence.

Abandoned is any heritage that leaves him *guilty of all thought.* Nothing is taken for granted in a fit of scruple whose application across the board is on the same scale as what he is cutting himself off from, as his refusal of anything not his same self. "Essentially." Here is a *vicious circle* in which cause and effect are confused in a collapse of all foundations, an erasure of all beginnings, a distrust of all memories, of all stories. Of all

[1](In the experiment with a fresh eyeball described at the beginning of the Fifth Discourse of the *Dioptrics,* Descartes explains that a piece of thin white paper or eggshell must be placed at the back of the eye to form a screen for the reflections of the objects outside the camera obscura.—Tr.)

183

imaginations, all sensation. He doubts even the difference between sleep and waking, the two being defined as an almost fetal lethargy and the vigilant consciousness of the mature man that he is.

Nonetheless, the "I" thinks. Or so he thinks. This is the "fixed point" amid these uncontrollable vortices. The "I" thinks, therefore it is. A verb, a verbal process/trial serve as premises for existence, re-create "being" just as it was about to succumb, drowning in deep water, with nothing and no one to hold on to. Not even its own thoughts since these are known to be very confused before birth as the spirit (âme) at that period is so entwined with matter that its only concern is with receiving impressions. But *such a regression* can and must be avoided by holding on to clear and distinct ideas, *here and now*. And the first such idea to present itself is—at this moment—that "I think." Building on this seed, this germ cell of truth, and on the development of a "natural" light—though you really must not ask me right now where it comes from and how it came into being, in case I lose hold of it, and so on indefinitely—the "I" will confer existence upon itself. Being without any copulation? The "I" therefore "copulates" without copulation in/of its ancestors: major or minor. The "I" therefore "is," without any "all" or "if" or "but"; these will appear later in the birth process when the "I" is assured as the only foundation under-lying its representation. The "I" reifies itself, attests to itself in a reality that is eminent from the word go. Reality is formally and objectively demonstrable as thinking substance. It follows immediately that: the "I" is in him who cogitates, here and now, without any possible flaw in his proof. Short of not thinking. And that is impracticable, even for the man in the street or the man in error. From the time of his conception he thinks (himself). Doubt, even extended to the whole universe, reveals that blind spot where he conceived (himself) without realizing it, camera obscura of representation (of the world) which, stripped of all pictures, ex-sists in its in-sistance. The eye of the spirit gives up all the various sights that are presented to it or forced upon it and thus reveals itself at last to be an *organ of sight* that has forfeited the body—if only for one, scientifically controlled, wink of the eye—, cut itself off from the body in order to see into it better. That is, in clear and distinct fashion, without the profusion of nerve impulses that jumble the parts of the body and the environment all up together: sensations, imaginations, memories, . . . these need to be suspended during the aseptic procedures accompanying this surgical dissection. Henceforward, the gaze has no "object" that its perception as of one *behind the scenes* could still, at last, see. The eye/ "I" (of the spirit) is closed to the charms of seductively deceptive things and, once its mechanism has been analyzed, it will frame and reproduce only what is technically set up in front of it.

For this new "subject" that enters the world again greedy for scientific powers, any (other) fantasy, and (other) dream, disturbing the precision of his theoretical instruments, must be frozen—any "passivity" of senses that are still natural and therefore uncontrollably open to impressions from silent, forbidden matter. At least for as long as it takes to make a decisive move. To focus the lens definitively. The "I" thinks and it will be, and you will be, whatever its photographic apparatus has zoomed in on, providing that apparatus is not opened so hyperbolically wide or closed so tight that there is nothing to be seen. The in(de)finiteness of a speck—a *yellow* spot nonetheless—will redefine the horizon of knowledge. In this ascetic ellipsis of the body—or of everything but the *yellow?*—the "I" believes its field of operations has been simplified, cleansed of all stains: dreams, insanities, disordered passions. Sicknesses of a limited understanding that will have to be taken into account, but later. And clearly and distinctly. Withdrawn into a strict deprivation of all exercises of the sensibility and the imagination, the subject will observe the world like the pilot of a ship taking to the open sea where nothing determines the perspective but the limitless *nothing to be seen.* Turning inward, therefore, back into himself, the subject will set out again, will start to trace his way, buttressed by this (almost) *nothing to have.* Despite it all, "I think," therefore *I have being.* A lack is turned into an excess of power, into an all-powerful *matrix* that will make him lucidly reconsider to what and to whom he owed his life.

So this sea where he is, or at least seems to be, lost, that overwhelms him on every side and so puts his life in danger, what is she? Considered coldly, she consists of an *extended corporeal thing.* Probably immense. Which explains why the gaze at least is drowned, saturated in her. But from this place where he is now assured of existing, he can cut the sea into any number of pieces, subject her to any number of visual angles, inscribe her in an even vaster space in order to draw a line around her: a map of the world. The "I" can subject the sea to a whole range of techniques that will transform her into an *object of use:* into a means of transport, for example. Nature can at the very least be useful to the "subject" as he moves about. Nonetheless, he must harden his heart to the glorious assault of her colors, to the fascination of her sheer size, to the seduction of her smells and sounds. Let him, above all, not want to smell, feel, or drink her. Such impulses would obviously be mistakes, for the subsistence of his own body as well. Let him therefore call upon his will, *which also has no bounds,* and disdain such ultimately secondary modes of being in order to concentrate on the sea's essential attribute: extension. And, armed as he now is, he will succeed in this. Even if he is obliged to repeat the operation of multiplication *indefinitely.* Even if he has to make his fractions complex, *double* them in fact, as a function of *the curved nature of her lines.* But this will not upset the plan(e)s of our surveyor-subject, or drive him away from an art of *geo-metry* in which he excels, applying it with arrogant confidence in the more and more *twisted* spaces that had hitherto been out of reach of mathematical prospection, given over to the imaginative fancies of man. The "I" thinks, therefore this thing, this body that is also nature, that is still the *mother,* becomes an extension at the "I" 's disposal for analytical investigations, scientific projections, the regulated exercise of the imaginary, the utilitarian practice of technique.

"I think," therefore. But at the price of clearing away all thought, razing to the ground all objective reality for my ideas. "I" think, but about whom? About what? And, in some manner, what for? And who will give me something to think about, and think about rightly, in this existence in which I am at present confirmed. And *confined.* Leaving me hungry for something other than my single certainty of being. When it comes down to it, who will replace, or substitute for everything and everybody I have given up in order to be? I am a fixed point that cannot forever remain *in suspension.* This pure and simple reiteration of being as point risks in the end seeing its distinctness fade away, while at the same time the form of an empty idea, exhausted and infuriated by a total lack of object, or even part-object, would swell in(de)finitely. This form will threaten the disembodied plat-form of my certainty if I fail to find a respondent capable of satisfying it and whose perfection will, moreover, be guaranteed by its total innocuousness as far as I am concerned. By this I mean both that the infinitely perfect does not need me in order to exist in its full autonomy and that it can no longer deceive me or itself on pain of losing its absolute value. And my desire for this ideal assures me clearly and distinctly that this is rigorously impossible.

I think, therefore God is: infinite being who at every moment gives a new impetus to the formation of my subjectivity and, what is more, confers upon my words the truth of the objective realities that they aim for in ideas. God nourishes my words, ever and again, with the inexhaustible breast-phallus of his all-powerful understanding. God is, but it is the "I" that by thinking has granted him that essence and existence that the "I" expects from God, in a piece of reasoning conducted according to an order that thwarts ignorant men's belief in revelation. *The son,* after busying himself with his own genesis, *reproduces (for) himself,* "on the third day," a "father-mother" to his own specifications. Or *in his own image?* He creates the infinite bonus that is demanded by his lack of, and therefore his inability to perceive, the perfect existence, by his disappointment that the subject's capacity to constitute himself must be exercised over and again because of his failure to resorb matter's extension into thought.

Thus he has not been able to reduce the organism by/in his speculative system. No matter how often it is split up, the organism still has to be taken into account and remains impenetrable, resistant, and opaque to the intellectio. But the "I" can nonetheless exploit it with a little cunning. *He can machine it into detached pieces* and then carefully analyze its mechanisms and principles of functioning, its cogs, its springs. He will devote all this scientific knowledge to the service of a will whose potential is known but whose impetuous moves can mislead you. So it is important not to be thoughtlessly influenced by any joy, sorrow, passion, . . . Not that these are reprehensible in themselves, but they might mislead a mind (esprit) that is still confused, lacking in lucidity, that must be brought back to reason at all costs. Otherwise it might experience "phantom limb" problems such as arise when a limb has been amputated—though, it must be stressed, this in no way detracts from consciousness—or suffer from a thirst that corresponds to no real need. Above all, of course, he risks putting his life in danger by failing to detect the poison hidden in the most tempting dishes. For examples. God should not be blamed for all this, as these faults and tricks in man's nature are the result of his mixed composition, of his not being only a spirit (âme). And God who did not create him in confusion is in no way responsible. He remains, in fact, the guardian of the immutable truths that we recognize in ourselves when we do Him allegiance.

But how are "bodies" supposed to behave *among themselves?* Optimally, they should act to preserve each individual as well as the harmony of the set of all the parts. If possible, they must live in *peaceful co-*

subsistance. Each body must try to move without disturbing either the mobility or the repose of the others, without affecting their motivation to move around—perfection happily consists in using free will to *raise* the spirit to the contemplation of eternal truths—or to keep their feet firmly anchored to the ground. Clashes begin, obviously, when *two bodies move toward each other.* Should one not presume that the ideally natural tropism would lead them to head *in a straight line,* one after another, pushing into one another and thus transmitting to each other the divine impulse that is their originary motivation? So, when two bodies meet, a rapid calculation is needed to estimate their relative speeds and masses, and to establish a correlation with the direction they are moving in. There follow all kinds of laws to predict the force and nature of the *impact.* The important thing is for each one to continue on its way according to the order of the universe. Thus they are unable to stop each other or in fact to join together—for the simple reason that two parties cannot stand in the same place, with the exception of God and the angels, for fear of throwing a monkey wrench into the world's works. But, on the other hand, they cannot stay so far apart from each other as to leave space for a vacuum, though the vacuum is always to be understood as being full of body and only empty in regard to one's expectations of its being filled with other things.

For if there were really a vacuum, "nature" of her own volition would close over, sealing the two lips of that slit. And if you raise the objection that God can surreptitiously empty a *vase*—for example—of its contents, thus leaving it devoid of anything that would justify *opening its neck,* I shall retort that *my conception finds that distasteful,* and that anyway God cannot possibly fail to satisfy *the principle of non-contradiction.* But this is to respond to the fancies of ingenuous souls who have yet to consider the properties of *imaginary spaces.* And matter, although indefinitely *extendable and divisible*—into innumerable but contiguous parts, so that continuity is not forfeited—is, as a whole, all of a piece. And space is, as a whole, constant and immutable, even though subordinated to the diversity of its parts. Even if matter seems to produce heterogeneous movements, these are to be interpreted as necessary to *the homogeneity of the whole.* This is the case with those *irregular vortices* and that *subtle matter* that slides as a result in the *narrow* corridors that open as they are whirled around. For all bodies must both be separated—with each one occupying the space corresponding to it, and no possibility of confusion between them—and juxtaposed as in the working of an enormous *machine* where each piece is essential to move the whole. Movement is thereby unceasing and lasting. And very useful.

The Eye of a Man Recently Dead

All this has been conceived and reconstructed on the basis of the certainty I had that my representation was the only firmly established value, the only thing that could not fail me in this world where everything I feel is perpetually the slave to change. This is true not only in my own experience of the outside world but also according to what most people say. I lived, therefore, as if in the middle of vortices, or an earthquake, full of unrest, racked and jerked around, going hither and thither without any order, shaken from all sides even in my brain—though you will probably be dubious about that, since my brain would thus be outside the influence of my will—, unable even to fix my gaze on any one thing. Thus it became necessary for me to take *one fixed point* from which to begin all over again: closing my eyes, blocking my ears, turning away from all my senses, even ridding my thoughts of all images of bodily things. Moreover, I had to refuse to imitate the ancients whose moment is—here and now—past, and to take my stand instead upon those modern sciences that can greatly modify our way of conceiving. Thus was I reborn, cleansed of those fables and material impressions that darken the understanding of children. And if, for a long time, I wondered if this also were a dream, I now know how to tell dreams from waking. And I concluded therefore, supported by proof, that this could not be a matter of dreaming. In fact, what is usually taken as reality is a fiction, and vice versa. For the confusion of *real object* and *virtual object* may persist even in one who has faced up to the laws of optics. Unless one is to suppose, with a certain lack of generosity and esteem for mankind, that a mind (esprit) may deliberately pretend?

But it cannot be cast up at me as an ethical failing that, from the blind spot where—with evil intent?—I anchored my skiff, I was able to see that when my representation comes back to me, it theoretically forces me at the very least to be doubled—turns me and representation upside down, moreover, and deforms us in all sorts of other ways, such as *size*. By putting up with the fact that the whole world has always presented itself to me *upside down* and therefore should be subjected to doubt from top to bottom, I have *no doubt* been saved from realizing that in my thought I am subject—the "I" is "subject"—to/of reversal itself. I shall remain in ignorance of the fact that, in this embrace of truth that I covet above all else, I am seeking, in simplest terms, to be united with *an image in a mirror*. This is how I am. At last alone, copula. I-me, coupled to-

189

gether in an embrace that begins over and over again. And fails equally often, because of the glass that separates us. God at least leaves me the hope that it will be different. One day.

And if, by chance, such good will seems laughable, let it be known that the faculty of laughter in man is only a fourth-degree characteristic, just as, and in a quite other way, the body is not essentially defined by touch and impenetrability, but instead by extension.

La Mystérique

Take a concave mirror and put it next to a dry and inflammable material; then expose the mirror to the rays of the sun; the dry material will catch fire and burn because of the heat of the sun and the concavity of the mirror.
—Ruysbroeck the Admirable.

Woman is the most noble way to address the soul, and it is far nobler than virgin.
—Meister Eckhart

The Word was made flesh in order to make me God.
—Angela of Foligno.

La mystérique: this is how one might refer to what, within a still theological onto-logical perspective is called mystic language or discourse. Consciousness still imposes such names to signify that other scene, off-stage, that it finds *cryptic*. This is the place where consciousness is no longer master, where, to its extreme confusion, it sinks into a dark night that is also fire and flames. This is the place where "she"—and in some cases he, if he follows "her" lead—speaks about the dazzling glare which comes from the source of light that has been logically repressed, about "subject" and "Other" flowing out into an embrace of fire that mingles one term into another, about contempt for form as such, about mistrust for understanding as an obstacle along the path of jouissance and mistrust for the dry desolation of reason. Also about a "burning glass." This is the only place in the history of the West in which woman speaks and acts so publicly. What is more, it is for/by woman that man dares to enter the place, to descend into it, condescend to it, even if he gets burned in the attempt. It is in order to speak woman, write to women, act as preacher

(The French title's economy and richness cannot be matched in English. Four elements are fused in LI's neologism: mysticism, hysteria, mystery, and the femaleness ["*la* mystérique"] fundamental to the previous three.—Tr.)

191

and confessor to women, that man usually has gone to such excesses. That he has accepted the need to take the detour through metaphors that can scarcely be called figures. That he has given up his knowledge in order to attend to woman's madnesses. Falling—as Plato would say, no doubt,—into the trap of mimicking them, of claiming to find jouissance as "she" does. To the point when he can no longer find himself as "subject" anymore and goes where he had no wish to follow: to his loss in that a-typical, a-topical mysteria. Where it will already have been noted—to the amazement of all—that the poorest in science and the most ignorant were the most eloquent, the richest in revelations. Historically, that is, women. Or at least the "female."

But how is this done? Given that the horizon line is already drawn, and drawn, in fact, by the "subject" who defines himself at the same time, in a circularity that knows no end except the return, over and over again, upon itself/himself. The problem is to break down the walls around the (male) one who speaks, sees, thinks, and thereby now confers being upon himself, in a prison of self-sufficiency and a clarity made of the shadows of denial. The task is to go back through the house of confinement and the darkness of the night until once again he feels the light that forms and other speculative veils had shrouded from his gaze in an effort to weaken its white heat. All this left man hungry and thirsty. At least sometimes, at least in some places. Even now.

But as the eye is already guardian to the reason, the first necessity is to slip away unseen. And in fact without seeing much either. In a blind breaching of the philosopher's closed chamber, from the matrix of speculation in which he had cloistered himself in order to consider everything clearly. The "soul"[1] escapes outside herself, opening up a crack in the cave (une antr'ouverture) so that she may penetrate herself once more. The walls of her prison are broken, the distinction between inside/outside transgressed. In such ex-stasies, she risks losing herself or at least seeing the assurance of her self-identity-as-same fade away. This will probably not happen all at once, since she is already caught, enve-

---

[1](For almost the next page the pronoun "elle" is repeated, at increasing distance from its apparent antecedent "l'âme." Rather than adopting the conventional strategy of repeating the word "soul" at judicious intervals and otherwise using "it" and related forms, I have hypothesized that LI is not *naming* a specific entity but evolving something unnamed but essentially female, and I have therefore adopted the pronoun "she" without further nouns.—Tr.)

loped in various representations, in different configurations and chains that lead her, bit by bit, back to her unity. To resembling what she would ideally be in her own form, or substance. And the road she will have to take in order to flee the logic that has framed her thus is not nothing. Moreover, she doesn't know where she is going, and will have to wander randomly and in darkness. And her eye has become accustomed to obvious "truths" that actually hide what she is seeking. It is *the very shadow of her gaze* that must be explored. Night for all sensible, all solar vision, a blaze of light that would make the sun itself repent its self-conceit. Night, above all, beyond the mind's speculation, beyond theoretical contemplation, even that centered upon Being itself. And if man once thought that straight vision could allow him to escape the opaque barrier that every body presents to the light, now, in his impetuous desire, he is plunged into the darkness that a supposedly enlightened gaze had projected in its very rings and reversals.

Yet, in this nocturnal wandering, where is the gaze to be fixed? The only possibility is to push onward into the night until it finally becomes a transverberating beam of light, a luminous shadow. Onward into a *touch* that opens the "soul" again to contact with divine force, to the impact of searing light. She is cut to the quick within this shimmering underground fabric that she had always been herself, though she did not know it. And she will never know it or herself *clearly* as she takes fire, in a sweet confusion whose source cannot at first be apprehended. She is torn apart in pain, fear, cries, tears, and blood that go beyond any other feeling. The wound must come before the flame. But already there is delight and longing in this torment, if she has entrusted herself to a skill subtle enough in its strength. Though the path she is cutting is a difficult one, she is impatient to set everything else aside and pleads to go on. But she cannot specify exactly what she wants. Words begin to fail her. She senses something *remains to be said* that resists all speech, that can at best be stammered out. All the words are weak, worn out, unfit to translate anything sensibly. For it is no longer a matter of longing for some determinable attribute, some mode of essence, some face of presence. What is expected is neither a *this* nor a *that*, not a *here* any more than a *there*. No being, no places are designated. So the best plan is to abstain from all discourse, to keep quiet, or else utter only a sound so inarticulate that it barely forms a *song*. While all the while keeping an attentive ear open for any hint or tremor coming back.

For how does one chart a course in this ignorance that can gain enlightenment only from the embrace of fire? No doubt we must edge our way through narrow doorways and along knife-edge paths, dark and terrible, squeeze painfully between two walls, wedge our bodies through slits in order to move into the full light of the caves to be explored. Endless open space, hung emptily between here and there, dizzying height, steep ascent, even retreat—all these lie ahead perhaps. But how does one tackle these things, even if one felt passionately about them, if there is no sense of *vocation?* No directing goal is in sight, no cause can be taken for a point of reference. No "natural light" is available to help us along this path that has already been erased and eroded in the confusion with those reflecting walls of the "soul" which she had made her own in the cold reasonableness of optics. The light is out in this night, a strange awakening is vaguely expected while everyone sleeps; and the higher mental faculties are in a deep slumber, the understanding in a virtual stupor. What is beginning to happen takes place in such secrecy and deep oblivion that no intelligence, no common sense, can have precise knowledge of it. A faraway solitude reigns in this silent touching, which yet is moved to its very depths. And which can so easily be distracted, disturbed in its still uneasy suspense. No decision can break in. All is passive waiting, unpremeditated abandon. Refusal of any willed, concerted activity that could stand in the path of "grace." Expectant expectancy, absence of project and projections. Unbearable sweetness and bitterness, aridity, dizzy horror before the boundless void. Just an elusive memory that flees representation, re-presentation, repetition. Even in dream.

A gulf that opens up ahead, moves away, strains, never knowing or imagining (itself) in its unfathomable nakedness. An abyss that swallows up all persons, all names, even proper names. For in fact all properties (and proprieties) will have to be shed to continue this penetration. Love, wish, affection, delight, interest, profit must all go as they are still related to a self-as-same, clothing it in a surplus value whose deceptive and treacherous charms are felt only by one who has yet to experience union in its most outrageous nakedness. Its lack of any marketable asset except this desperate immodesty. This "simplicity" stripped of all attributes that will soon sink to the bottom of the bottomless, engulfing the last dwellings of the soul to/in infinity. Turning the soul's chambers, her den, upside down so as to lead her to that abyssal source that she could never have found otherwise. For the soul was closed up over the possesion of a knowledge which made her quite obtuse, particularly in her claims to the immaculate state that no creature had yet been able to pierce or undo. And which is mixed in a jouissance so extreme, a love so incomprehensible, an illumination so unbounded that un-knowledge thereby becomes desire. Nothing has a price in this divine consumation and consumption. Nothing has value, not even the soul herself, set apart from standardization, outside the *labor* market. The soul spends and is spent in the margins of capital. In a strictly non-negotiable currency, an expenditure without accountability, in the resources of its loss. At least so far. Or perhaps for ever. Even simple counting hinders her fall into the abyss of her prodigality, her madness, expansion and dissipation of self. At the final reckoning, the richest person will certainly be the one who has most depleted the stores. But even saying that is being too calculating, too logical even in this reversal of all known economics. No more measure(s) should be taken. We must reach the final dispossession of the last imaginary retreat into pure objectivity: the "I" calculated and therefore still knew *where* it stood. Reference points, drafting plans to survey this extension, this mother-matter—all these are henceforward taken from mastery. All surfaces and spatial constructions also collapse in a conflagration that pushes further and further back the depths of a gulf where now everything is burning. Fire flares up in the inexhaustible abundance of her underground source and is matched with an opposing but congruent flood that sweeps over the "I" in an excess of excess. Yet, burning, flowing along in a wild spate of waters, yearning for even greater abandon, the "I" is *empty* still, ever more empty, opening wide in rapture of soul.

But alone and without help, alas! the soul cannot prevent herself from being buried and sealed off in her crypt. Hidden away, she waits for the rapture to return, the ecstasy, the lightning flash, the penetration of the divine touch. These come intermittently, briefly, rarely, hastily, and the soul is left in great sorrow. She is all comprehension and consent, but her two lips, parted to receive other embraces, soon become dry and re-tracted over their mourning, if the wait is too long. No voice is hers to call, no hands can fill the open hungry mouth with the food that both nourishes and devours. Abandoned, the soul can barely keep faith. No image, no figure alleviates such mortal absence. No picture, no portrait, no face could serve to ease the waiting, even if they were available in this lack of all defined form. Finding the self imposes a *proximity* that knows no aspect, mode, or figure. No metaphors can designate the radiant splendor of that touch. Any intermediary would risk deferring the fleet-ing *moment* of its coming. Not even a supportive, evocative *milieu* can sustain, prepare, or recall its intuition. Any addition or adornment might cosset the touch into a complacency incompatible with the difficult trail it must blaze. Like a bolt from the blue.

But can life go on in such violence, however sweet it may be? Does one not die from dying, or die from not dying? How to decide at a time of earthshattering jouissance and pain? Swooning, fainting, bones and flesh torn apart with a crack that covers up the sound of all words of remission. Fire and ice freeze and singe without respite, and nothing lies between their endless, alternating intemperance. Without spring or autumn, morning or evening. The implacable harshness of midday in summer, midnight in winter, mingling their extremes with no lull, no neutral interval in the switch from one to another. *Everything is relentlessly immediate* in this marriage of the unknowable, which can never be evaded once it has been experienced. In a deeper unity than the still, already, speculative unity that underlies the sense of these wrenching contradictions. The bottom, the center, the most hidden, inner place, the heart of the crypt to which "God" alone descends when he has renounced modes and attributes. For this most secret virginity of the "soul" surrenders only to one who also freely offers the self in all its nakedness. This most private chamber opens only to one who is indebted to no possession for potency. It is wedded only in the abolition of all power, all having, all being, that is founded elsewhere and otherwise than in this embrace of fire whose end is past conception.

Each becomes the other in consumption, the nothing of the other in consummation. Each will not in fact have known the identity of the other, has thus lost self-identity except for a hint of an imprint that each keeps in order the better to intertwine in a union already, finally, at hand. Thus I am to you as you are to me, mine is yours and yours mine, I know you as you know me, you take pleasure with me as with you I take pleasure in the rejoicing of this reciprocal living—and identifying—together. In this cauldron of identification will melt, mingle, and melt again these reversing matrices of our last embraces.

But how to remember all this if the fire was so fierce, the current so strong as to remove all traces? If everything has become fire and water and nothing remains but a burning shimmer and flowing stream? If the brazier was so deep as to erase all memory of the path of touch that still guides us in our ecstatic transports? If nothing remains but/of an incandescent hearth that none can reach?

Unless this "center" has also always been of glass/ice too. Mirror made of matter so fluid, so ethereal that it had already entered and mingled everywhere? What if matter had always, already, had a part but was yet invisible, beyond the senses, moving in ways alien to any fixed reflection. What if everything were already so intimately specularized that even in the depths of the abyss of the "soul" a mirror awaited her reflection and her light. Thus I have become your image in this nothingness that I am, and you gaze upon mine in your absence of being. This silvering at the back of the mirror might, at least, retain *the being* (l'être)—which we have been perhaps and which perhaps we will be again—though our mirage has failed at present or has been covered over by alien speculations. A living mirror, thus, am I (to) your resemblance as you are mine. We are both singular and plural, one and ones, provided that nothing tarnishes the mirrors that fuse in the purity of their exchange. Provided that one, furthermore, does not exceed the other in size and quality. For then the other would be absorbed in the One (as) to infinity.

When I look upon you in the secret of my "soul," I seek (again) the loss of specularization, and try to bring my "nature" back to its mirroring wholeness. And if "God" had already appeared to me with face unveiled, so my body shines with a light of glory that radiates it. And my eyes have proved sharp enough to look upon that glory without blinking. They would have been seared had they not been that simple eye of the "soul" that sets fire to what it ad-mires out of its hollow socket. A burning glass is the soul who in her cave joins with the source of light to set everything ablaze that approaches her hearth. Leaving only ashes there, only a hole: fathomless in her incendiary blaze.

Thus "God" has created the soul to flare and flame in her desire. And if beyond this consummation He/she endures, it is because He/she is nothing but adoration of that warmth, passion for the hearth that none can appropriate, light suited to that lone mirror, *and* its virtual reduplication. *Or* again because this has been explained—by the theological, teleological imagination—as the mutual attraction of the father and the son felt in a loving breast—thereby rescuing the "soul" of man from being completely lost to that attraction. Man's identity in the hommologous, his reason in hommosexuality was preserved by the interpretation. But such conceptions of the mind do not lead to "God's" finest excesses. For "God" goes beyond all representation, however schematic in its approximation.

And perhaps He has chosen *her* body to inscribe His will, even if she is less able to read the inscription, poorer in language, "crazier" in her speech, burdened with matter(s) that history has laid on her, shackled in/by speculative plans that paralyze her desire. Sometimes even the "soul," in a kind of sensuality of reason, deprives her of tremendous good fortune by leaving her in ignorance of the extremes of jouissance. Her "soul" is at fault vis-à-vis the body because, in its elevation and revelation of her, it seems not to have understood that physical ills are always an obstacle to the highest good. That the delicacy and sensitivity of the "body" have great importance, that the division of the "heart" of man is the fault, the crack, in which love is lost in controversies that merely scratch the surface of the problem.

But the path she follows to bring together and revive this wide, wild, unwary space that she is (on) earth will be more savage and cruel than if she could simply fall back right now upon a "soul" that was a kind of cocoon, swathing the most secret self and folded over the specula(riza)tion of its source. But she is still darkness to herself through and through, nor does she understand the world surrounding her. In this undifferentiated blindness she will be able to achieve distinctness only by a certain number of cuts, severings. She gives herself up to "others" only after she has effected this separation from everyone and from her habits, in which pain enables her to feel herself again and to gather her strength. This strength soon becomes exalted in such a flood of potency that she is taken to be possessed. Therefore she is condemned by confessors or inexperienced voyeurs who are horrified to see or hear her fall stricken to the ground, toss and turn, shriek, grunt, groan convulsively, stiffen, and then fall into a strange sleep. They are scandalized or anxious at the idea of her striking herself so terribly, thrusting sharp points into her stomach, burning 'her body to put out the fire of lust, searing her whole frame, using these extreme actions both to calm and to arouse her sleeping passions. The explosion of these passions strikes whoever witnesses them dumb. In their apollonian wisdom, witnesses are persuaded to try any devilry that will drive back these furies, which now she can no longer contain. Hiding them one moment, flaunting them the next. Intending to keep them secret, not able to do so always, or anymore, when these violent attacks go through her, though alien to her. Sometimes they shake her, at other times they leave her prostrate, pale, like a dead woman. Stretched out, once again, (on) the ground. In the dark. Always without consciousness.

But a "God" already draws near in these/her fainting states. What does it matter that all judge her mad if the "prince of the world" has noticed her and if henceforward he will be her companion in solitude. She awakes full of joy, only to fall back into new torments. For how, in one's unworthiness, can one keep doubt at bay? How could "God" reveal himself in all his magnificence and waste his substance on/in so weak and vile a creature as woman? She has so often been humiliated, and every particle in her being seems but decay and infection. *Waste, refuse, matter.* Thus she will abase herself over and again in order to experience this love that claimed to be hers, and pass again through those imaginings that forbid her to respond. She takes on the most slavish tasks, affects the most shameful and degrading behavior so as to force the disdain that is felt toward her, that she feels toward herself. And perhaps, at the bottom of the pit, she finds her purity again. In this way, the blood, the sores, the pus that others clean away and she absorbs will wash her clean of all stain. She is pure at last because she has pushed to extremes the repetition of this abjection, this revulsion, this horror to which she has been condemned, to which, mimetically, she had condemned herself. She is chaste because she has faced the worse perversions, has prostituted herself to the most disgusting acts, the most filthy and excessive whims. She has been redeemed in all her purity within this absence of all representations of her that now obtains, in this void, empty even of repulsion, this nothingness of soul that she knows herself to be. And she has left the others behind, disconcerted, unable to follow her that far. Unable to go and see.

And if "God," who has thus re-proved the fact of her non-value, still loves her, this means that she exists all the same, beyond what anyone may think of her. It means that love conquers everything that has already been said. And that one man, at least, has understood her so well that he died in the most awful suffering. That most female of men, the Son. And she never ceases to look upon his nakedness, open for all to see, upon the gashes in his virgin flesh, at the wounds from the nails that pierce his body as he hangs there, in his passion and abandonment. And she is overwhelmed with love of him/herself. In his crucifixion he opens up a path of redemption to her in her fallen state.

Could it be true that not every wound need remain secret, that not every laceration was shameful? Could a sore be *holy?* Ecstasy is there in that glorious slit where she curls up as if in her nest, where she rests as if she had found her home—and He is also in her. She bathes in a blood that flows over her, hot and purifying. And what she discovers in this divine passion, she neither can nor will translate. At last, she has been authorized to remain silent, hidden from prying eyes in the intimacy of this exchange where she *sees* (herself as) what she will be unable to express. Where she sees nothing and where she sees everything. She is closed over this mystery where the love placed within her is hidden, revealing itself in this secret of desire. In this way, you see me and I see you, finally I see myself seeing you in this fathomless wound which is the source of our wondering comprehension and exhilaration. And to know myself I scarcely need a "soul," I have only to gaze upon the gaping space in your loving body. Any other instrument, any hint, even, of theory, pulls me away from myself by pulling open—and sewing up—unnaturally the lips of that slit where I recognize myself, by touching myself there (almost) directly.

And in the rapturous vision of the place of your joyous expansion and mortal ecstasy, *a lightning flash has lit up the sleeping understanding within me.* Resisting all knowledge that would not find its/my sense in this abyss. Now I know it/myself and by knowing, I love it/myself and by loving, I desire it/myself. And if in the sight of the nails and the spear piercing the body of the Son I drink in a joy that no word can ever express, let no one conclude hastily that I take pleasure in his sufferings. But if the Word was made flesh in this way, and to this extent, it can only have been to make me (become) God in my jouissance, which can at last be recognized. Now the abyss opens down into my own self, and I am no longer cut in two opposing directions of sheer elevation to the sky and sheer fall into the depths. I know, now, that both height and depth spawn—and slit—each other in(de)finitely. And that the one is in the other, and the other in me, matters little since it is in me that they are created in rapture. *Outside of all self-as-same.* Never the same, always new. Never repeated or repeatable in their transports of joy which can never be counted or determined by measurement. Indeed they are (or it is) eternal because immense. Mystery, me-hysteria, without determinable end or beginning. More intimate than the "soul" even. Crypt for the reciprocal sharing of the abyss between "her" and God. Into which she will have to (re)descend in order to find, at last, the quietude and rest in herself-God. She is transformed into Him in her love: this is the secret of their exchange. In her and/or outside her, as, in her jouissance, she loses all sense of corporeal boundary. Her distance from herself is all the greater because the fire was more deeply "inward." Because the deepest summit of her cave has been touched. Her remoteness in ecstasy, the flights of her soul, are all the greater because they reach further into that absence of soul that she is.

How strange is the economy of this specula(riza)tion of woman, who in her mirror seems ever to refer back to a transcendence. Who moves away (for) who comes near, who groans to be separated from the one who holds her closest in his embrace. But who also calls for the dart which, while piercing through her body, will with the same stroke tear out her entails.[2] Thus "God" will prove to have been her best lover since he separates her from herself only by that space of her jouissance where she finds Him/herself. To infinity perhaps, but in the serenity of the spacing that is thus projected by/in her pleasure. At present that pleasure is still hemmed in by representations—however metaphysical—and by pre- scriptions—still ethically onto-theological—which determined it (and her) and thus limit their extension. And if she does not feel raped by God, even in her fantasies of rape, this is because He never restricts her orgasm, even it is hysterical. Since He understands all its violence.

Thus (re)assured of the complicity of this all-powerful partner, they/she play(s) at courtship, kneeling in self-abasement at one moment, adorning themselves with gold and diamonds the next, touching, smell- ing, listening, seeing, embrac(s)ing each other, devouring, penetrating, entering, consuming, melting each other. She is trusting as a dove, ar-

---

[2](In her famous vision of the Flaming Heart, Saint Teresa of Avila wrote: "I saw an angel close by me, on my left side, in bodily form. He was not large, but small of stature and most beautiful—his face burning, as if he were one of the highest angels, who seem to be all of fire. I saw in his hand a long spear of gold, and at the iron's point there seemed to be a little fire. He appeared to me to be thrusting it at times into my heart and to pierce my very entrails; when he drew it out, he seemed to draw them out also, and to leave me all on fire with a great love of God. The pain was so great that it made me moan, and yet so surpassing was the sweetness of this excessive pain that I could not wish to be rid of it. The soul is satisfied now with nothing less than God." Quoted by Victoria Sackville-West in *The Eagle and the Dove* [London: Doubleday, 1944], p. 94.—Tr.)

rogant as a queen, proud in her nakedness, bursting with the joy of such exchanges. Her divine companion never tires of praising her and encouraging her (auto)eroticism that has so miraculously been rediscovered. Her confessor will not always lend an approving ear to this, especially if he lacks experience in such things. But what does that matter, she knows that she can no longer be mistaken. It is enough to know that "God" loves for her to live, and die.

And if someone were to object that, with the Good thus within her, she no longer needs to receive it, she would reply in her ateleological way, that, for her, the one doesn't rule out the other.

Paradox A Priori

What can be more like my hand or my ear, and more equal in all points, than its image in the mirror? And yet I cannot put such a hand as is seen in the mirror in the place of its original: for if the original was a right hand, the hand in the mirror is a left hand, and the image of the right ear is a left ear, which could never serve as a substitute for the other. Here are no inner differences that any understanding could think; and yet the differences are inner as far as the senses tell us, for the left hand cannot be enclosed in the same boundaries as the right (they cannot be congruent) notwithstanding all their mutual equality and similarity; the glove of the one hand cannot be used on the other.

In the dark I orient myself in a familiar room when I can seize on a single object whose position I can remember. Here obviously nothing helps me except the capacity of determining positions by a subjective ground of distinction. For I do not see the objects whose position I should find, and if someone had played a joke on me by putting on the left what was previously on the right while still preserving their relationships to each other, I could not find my way in a room with otherwise indistinguishably equal walls. But I soon orient myself through the mere feeling of a difference between my left and right sides.

—Kant

It sometimes happens that the sun causes the earth to shake underfoot, and people fear being knocked over, or thrown sickeningly downward into the pit, or even flying off into the void. To reestablish the balance that has been so dangerously disturbed, the philosopher decides that from now on nature overall will be put under the control of the human spirit and her origins will be based on her necessary obedience to the law. So the ground will now rest upon a transcendental ceiling that is propped

(The epigraphs are from (1) *Prolegomena to Any Future Metaphysics That Will Be Able to Present Itself as a Science,* tr. Peter G. Lucas [Manchester: Manchester University Press, 1953], sec. 287, p. 42; (2) *Critique of Practical Reason,* tr. and ed. Lewis White Beck [Chicago: University of Chicago Press, 1949], sec. viii, 135, p. 295.—Tr.)

up by the forms and rules of representation and is thus unshakable. To build this construction, man was, of course, obliged to draw on reserves still in the realm of nature; a detour through the outer world was of course indispensable; the "I" had to relate to "things" before it could be conscious of itself. But this initial period of cooperative creation is forgotten in an arrogant claim to sovereign discretion over everything.

This is the first instance of the passage from sensation to understanding whereby—not unmysteriously—a schematism arises that will never do justice to the sensible world. For the most sophisticated faculty of the senses, the imaginary, will remain the slave of understanding. Anything conceded to nature is immediately and imperiously taken back and will be found useful only insofar as it ensures more rigorous dominion over her. Thus, the function of the transcendental schema will be to negate an intrinsic quality of the sensible world, and this irremediably. Nature is foreclosed in her primary empirical naivete. Diversity of feeling is set aside in order to build up the concept of the object, and the immediacy of *the relationship to the mother* is sacrificed. The intuition of the transcendental aims, under some vague and undetermined generality, to unify all the various sensations that take place or have taken place. In this way the multiplicity of unlabeled sensations is blacked out, reduced to a single entity that can be used to legislate—in the cruelty of understanding—the bond to the empirical matrix, or, in other words, to *hysteria.* It is crucial that we never know the transcendental object as such lest we recognize it and reject the almost matrical effectiveness it has in veiling our perception of all phenomena and structuring their (re)appearance. The object cannot be known, therefore, for the simple reason that it allows that conceptual *window* to be put in place in which nothing is seen *per se* but whose frame enables all the rest to be intuited. The role played by the object will be rediscovered (and rediscovered as a *gap*) only by questioning the time taken to circumscribe the space or else the *extension* in this way. By questioning, that is, the *logical* time taken for the object to constitute itself as the imperative mediation between those empirical intuitions that lead to confusion and as the regulation of the empirical into universal a priori categories. By questioning the *third term,* which is very much the creature of the second and required to purge itself of the first term that had once nourished its affection, on the assumption, no doubt, that it remains homogeneous with the first term by its very temporality. With this restriction: that the temporality is in fact not the same but that of a transcendental *property/propriety* that alleviates the horror of the inchoate and unpossessable as well as the disgust for the misshapen refuse that will be excreted under the form of matter. Henceforth such schemas will regulate the imagination of the scene in all kinds of indirect ways that remain *pure representations* for all that. This does not mean that the mind has simply given itself the object that it sees—that would be to claim the intellectual intuition possessed only by the Supreme Being—but rather that the mind has taken this way of defining the a priori conditions whereby it apperceives objects and whereby those objects that it represents to itself spontaneously will be *properly conceived.* Their possible materiality will appear only subsequently in a kind of failure of their apprehensible form, in a conclusion that the mind cannot foresee and that defiles the purity of the intuition. However grounded in the senses the intuition may be, it is nonetheless framed a priori by space and time. Space and time, in turn, are to be viewed as forms of the outer sense or of the internal sense that organize and thereby subsume a diversity that is ridiculous in its confusion of feeling, whether it comes from an outside world peopled with objects which thereby receive their specific geographical destination, or from an inner world under the control of changes that can henceforth be analyzed in function of time. But which time?

For if, already, we know which time was needed to produce the window through which we see the universe, to frame the space whereby the infinite is determined a priori, always already defined in/by the subjectivity of man, we have still to learn that the *space-time of specularization* is implicit in the intuition of space. And even if, conceptually, my right hand and my left hand, or my hand and its image in the mirror, are rigorously the same, or the same thing, this would not be true for the intuitive character of space in which *the paradox of symmetry* was taken into account. Thus already a mirror turns out to support the apprehension of objects. Are we to assume that a mirror has always already been inserted, and speculates every perception and conception of the world, *with the exception of itself,* whose reflection would only be a factor of time? Thus extension would always already be re-staged and re-projected by the subject who, alone, would not be situated there. Does the subject derive his power from the appropriation of this non-place of the mirror? And from speculation? And as speculation constitutes itself as such in this way, it cannot be analyzed, but falls into oblivion, re-emerging to play its part only when some new effect of symmetry is needed in the system. By some recourse to the imaginary, perhaps, that is both other and the same?

The aim this time is to prevent the irreconcilable gap between the sensible and the supersensible from opening up into a chasm. The connection between them will be found in the *reflecting* judgment that (re)produces the feeling of pleasure between (two) other things—the faculties of knowledge and desire. But since both pleasure and pain are *necessarily* linked to desire—which finds its basis in reason—a practicable intermediary, a priori in its principle, is needed to connect the natural concepts with the concept of liberty. This go-between, destined to become specular, will be at least doubly effective. Either the "mirror" has already been defined as inclusive of the object it must mirror, or it simply re-determines that object's intrinsic quality by framing it. Or the mirror does not "know" the "object" proposed and has to constitute a general reproducible matrix while reflecting it. This requires the mirror to re-think it/himself, re-reflect it/himself, so as to be able to subordinate to its/his unity and to the unity of its/his law this new *diversion* of nature which affronts it/him and threatens to shatter and *divide* it/him. This does not mean that the mirror must understand all the caprices of nature—it/he happily leaves that task to the possible intervention of an all-powerful intellect—but it/he needs at the very least a system that helps it/him to deal with nature. Since it/he cannot completely control her, he will give it/himself principles of control that will operate in the experiences it/he has of her. It/he will act "as if" at least a divine intelligence contained the secret of the order followed by nature's sometimes unpredictable empirical laws. "As if" all that diversity were directed toward a higher unity—*a bigger mirror?*—which it/he also should strive to conform to, even without any knowledge of it. Yet the effect of the mirror is already felt in the difference of the pleasures or pains arising out of his relations to certain objects in nature.

Let us take the "example" of his *relations with women*. Anyone who has done the experiment can attest that not every woman arouses the same kind of attraction in a man. Thus, the first woman may appear *pleasing,* the second *beautiful,* another, in very rare instances, may achieve the *sublime.* This indicates that one woman or another has touched different properties in the man's mind. Interpretation of this can be useful both in pursuing the critical analysis of the mind's functioning and in helping the man make the pertinent choice. For all these charms, in the end, rest on (only) the inclination that the man has *within him* for women. Thus he will find pleasing the woman who immediately arouses his sensuality. But, by unilaterally awakening desire or the need for satisfaction, and thus provoking an interest that can be perceived directly, that woman risks wearying a man very quickly, even though she is necessary for the realization of the great design that nature has inscribed in the difference between the sexes: *procreation.* But it is nonetheless permissible to enjoy that difference in ways more sophisticated, more worthy of a cultivated man. And the sight of a *woman's beauty* affords a true *pleasure* to the imagination and the intellect. Such no doubt is the purpose of a man's relation to such an "object," assuming that he stops to contemplate it disinterestedly, without any representation of a goal—a need?—to be satisfied directly. For then, without his knowledge, that vision *feeds* those inconceivable faculties of knowing that are at work in the reflective judgment and that demand the fullness of aesthetic feeling if they are to live and grow. Thus one can understand the formal subjective purpose of what may be called the "woman-object." She will be asked to be *not simply pretty*—too much obvious symmetry is unexciting—*nor too recognizably female*—the intellect might then reduce her to some concept—*nor too virtuous*—this might arouse reason alone and provoke nothing but a little painful respect. Poised in suspense between the faculties of the male subject, woman cannot be decided about, and her beauty serves to promote the free play of mind. And of course what matters is not the existence of the object—*as such it is indifferent*—but the simple effect of a representation upon the subject, its reflection, that is, in the imagination of a man.

Besides, reason finds *interest* in this ultimately contingent agreement between the productions of nature and the *disinterested* pleasure he takes in looking at them. The intensity of the pleasure is all the more rational in that it will reflect (on) the capacity of matter herself, at her most *fluid* and therefore *archaic,* to produce beautiful forms even where the human eye penetrates too rarely to reflect them effectively: that is, *at the bottom of the sea.* In those inaccessible chasms, one part of matter splits off or even evaporates and thus makes all the rest precipitate and solidify in the form of *crystal.* This cannot be laid at the door of submission to the mind or even to some goal that nature herself might have adopted. Its/this power is rather *ateleological* and *accidentally* appropriate to the harmonious exercise of man's faculties. Indeed, such things overwhelm the intellect, but, by exceeding the concept, they theoretically engender an echo in the Idea whereby almost-intuition would reestablish an *almost*-nature. It seems that the Idea represents (itself) indirectly (in) these free productions of matter. This play of *analogies,* in which indetermination will always have acted, boundlessly *enlarges* the mode of conceiving and/or rescues the imaginary from the schematic.

Nature has also proved useful, we are told, in elaborating a spiritual plus that will not surrender to the sensible for all that but will be interpreted as a *symbol* of a *supersensible* unity of all the faculties, as corresponding to a point of concentration in the supersensible. *Center of a mirror? Of a psyche?* The place where all reflections converge? But who, up to this point, is looking at what? Or what has forced whom to reach this point of concentration where everything meets without determination or limits—resource of subjective harmony. What *extra* ingredient in the formal rigor of the faculties could have brought them into agreement? What or whom is he moving away from as he looks? The "soul" again, and most profoundly: focus and unity of the subject, authorizing and even conducting—in a secret never entirely uncovered, in a *mystery intractably obscure and hidden*—the free union between him and himself. That union is dreary and dead in its tastefulness and is anyway hypothetical unless it receives life from a "soul," which is as much as to say *from matter: its genius.* An appeal is now launched to another genius, one that will, himself, respond, a second time, by asserting his synthetic and genetic rule and by producing a *meta*-aesthetic. Meanwhile, he waits for that other genius—a son?—to come into the world and perhaps wed him in the medium of their shared taste.

Thus ideas—or Ideas—or reason can be presented in different ways in sensible nature. In the interests of the beautiful, or natural symbolism, presentation is *positive* but *indirect,* and is realized by *reflection.* In genius, or artistic symbolism, presentation is *positive* but still *secondary,* and is brought about by the creation of *another nature.* And if that positivity has become possible—though at the price of *touching* the sensible world only indirectly and at second hand—this is because the passage through the sublime has already taken place, installing a *negativity* in the unmediated relation with nature. In fact it would be more correct to say that the negativizing operation is re-installed or repeated—*again for the second time*. For schematism already practiced negativism in that it formed a screen or obstacle in the path of immediate contact, which favors only *one kind* of (so-called) direct relationship—projection. But no doubt *passion* still went beyond this formal framework; sometimes its enormous pent-up energies burst out and re-projected themselves upon everything in nature that remains unformed or deformed, as if, when faced with the non-specularizable, imagination suffered a violent urge that pushed it to the worst extremities. But, unable to understand it nonetheless, imagination falls back upon itself, marked, as it were, with the negative of its power. In all naivete, it might thus believe itself inferior to nature, impotent or maimed in comparison with nature's sovereign greatness and potency. But a little analysis will prove that the imagination owes its weakness instead to its desire for reason to reunite the in-finite of the sensual world into one whole, and that its powerlessness is relative only to the Idea it forms about that world. Contradiction would thus operate *within* the subject between the demands of his reason and the more limited power of his imagination. Thus unevenness gives rise *to pain:* the proof of an *insufficient dimension*.

But in the end this pain will make a new pleasure possible. For in its confrontation with the "too small," and in order to avert the possibility of contempt, the imagination will surpass itself by representing the inaccessibility of the rational Idea. Its "not possible" enables the negative to open up and separate within, thus making the presentation of the infinite possible. In this way, the imagination's boundaries disappear, it enters into abstraction (of the sensible world) and thus, however negative the world or the imagination may be, the "soul"—still—is enlarged. All of nature is contained in the (let us say) *blank vastness* of the soul, place of—virtual—supersensible gathering and uniting. Beyond measurement, yet harmonized by the intervention of a spacing in negativity, the "soul" solves the disagreement between the imagination and reason. However, the "soul" has both to support and to be supported by a movement toward the birth of a *culture*. It cannot ex-ist only in separation, in the dizzy abstraction of the infinite. Though speculated in an indeterminate manner, it must re-determine itself practically. The negative at work in knowledge must be coordinated dialectically with the realization of desire. Such is the sublime dynamic which predestines man to be (only) a moral being.

Is this the end result of a pain arising from a complex that is sometimes too big? The principle "noli tangere matrem" locates its economy of reason and desire in the *categorical imperative*. Fear and awe of an all-powerful nature forbid man to touch his/the mother and reward his courage in resisting her attractions by granting him the right to judge himself independent, while at the same time encouraging him to prepare himself to continue resisting dangers in the future by developing (his) culture. Culture, also, is based upon this *abyss* that reason represents for the imaginary. That reason knows it replaces the imaginary by the sleight of hand of a transcendental illusion will not translate into awareness of the specular pulse which puts it into an infinitely receding perspective. The fact that "God" never appears as an object of possible presentation does not prevent the process of Idea from moving in His direction. It remains true that, since nature's immensity is turned into the inaccessibility of the final goal, *the paradox of a kind of symmetry has been evaded. One kind of difference,* inverted in the mirror, will never be analyzed. Is this because that difference could not be mirrored as object? If so, this is precisely how it under-lies the very functioning of the "object," which is, finally, the functioning of desire—i.e. the desire *to turn inside out the girdle,* the sheath, which enfolds representation *in* the subject. This is not achieved without pain. Or without a *remainder*. But provided that space is resorbed into time, there is still hope that the mind can perfect this operation at some point in the boundless future.

All this works, of course, provided the original evil, which still continues to draw man into the passion of the sensible world, does not drag him too far into transgression of the law. Like a new Adam succumbing to a *mysterious* seduction in the company of some nondescript Eve or other, and thereby sullying his primal innocence. But since he *freely* consented to sin, it follows that he equally has the native capacity to rise up to the good. And such is the order of duty, which enjoins him to root out such tendencies and undergo a radical *conversion*. Thus, this *fundamental perversion* must be transformed into *pure respect*. To do so in no way involves an appeal to the grace of "God." Man's own strength is enough, providing he has not too deeply buried the resources that were his native gifts. The archetype of moral intention in all its purity is, of course, that son of God whose mother remained forever a virgin. Who was begotten, that is, without the shame of copulation. He is the model (as it were) sent down from heaven to men, re-clothed in humanity, and by his doctrine, by his virtuous actions, and above all by his sufferings, he shows us how it is possible to be absolved by "God" of original sin. By his sweet sorrow—sweet snare!—the son redeems man. By his death he pays man's debt to "God." Triumph is his, the crucified, whose agony bears witness for all to see of the fate that awaits all good men here below. His glory lies in the humiliation to which he is nailed by the violating instrument of con-version. And this sacrifice, for a while longer, will be made by faith, by *belief.* By an imaginary excess that goes beyond the knowledge of intellect, that has not yet been reabsorbed in a purely moral legislation, that has yet to bow to the imperative of practical reason which demands a public liberty of conscience if it is to proceed without unfortunate side effects.

But no society, whether monarchical or oligarchic or democratic, has allowed this. One must rather think of some kind of *family* community. It might work under the direction of an invisible moral Father represented by his Son and honored by all its members through Him, thus forming a cordial, voluntary, universal, and lasting association. Should such a group need a few rites and rituals—ritual *chastisement* for example—this is only to be expected, given the weakness of human nature, the time needed to make people aware of the need to act out of duty, given humankind's quest, now and forever, for some *pleasure-pain* along the path toward a greater perfection. The form of such rewards-punishments will, in each case, be inspired *directly* by "God," the supreme lawmaker of reason. Natural reason, in its strictest form. The divine character of the command is granted only as a *bonus jouissance,* supplementing what the "I" already recognizes as a duty. The *voice* of the Father—or of the proscribed mother?—is an extra revelation and reward, but an indispensable extra, at least when it speaks within. A kind of tip. *A bonus of relief and release* for the freedom of the subject, who thereby once more gives himself the right to impose his law on everything around him. What does the subject care for self-love and other inclinations, for these have, after all, surreptitiously taken their revenge within the sovereignty of the consciousness. The less consciousness feels itself deliberately chosen, the more arrogant it becomes, the more confident of its own strengths which the critical side of consciousness likes to call its limits. In its own refusal of blindness, consciousness is blinded by all knowledge that does not find its cause in the mind itself. Thus, lucidity gives rise to illusion as well as illumination since, each time its system wanes, it re-metabolizes a mystery, rising up over and again by some new reflection of the source of light. With the help of a glass, sometimes unsilvered, or of a pane blackened with smoke.

Thus we can imagine the subject building his house, room by room. And the house is virtually complete: firm foundation, clear title, cellar, stairs, dining room, dressing room, den, study, corridors, doors, windows, attic. . . . The fact that it is divided up into different parts in this way is of small matter, provided that each part is subordinated to the whole and never lays claim to being a whole itself, for *that* would not allow man to give a distinct shape to the mystery—*or the hystery*—that is walled up in this harmonious domestic structure. The (female) not-all will (not) represent each stage in that demarcation of living space whereby the subject comes into being, but not the final unity that is to be made out of the units, for woman/women cannot hold the purpose that forms the mind. Women are only useful in part, as openings-mirages that reflect this a priori proposition needed for the mind's/his *foundation:* i.e., the seduction of *the whole of nature*. Woman will constitute the imaginary sub-basement that shores up the mine, will act as man's guiding thread in his various relationships with the many faces of the sensible world. These relationships aim to overcome the sensible in/by schematism and categories; by disinterested contemplation of natural beauty, which the detour through "woman" clears of narcissistic profit; by reenforcement of vitality as a result of nature's sublime ability to burst free and set free; by abstraction in the feeling of infinity engendered by nature's limitless grandeur; by the elaboration of a work in which it is sometimes difficult to decide how far the symbolic is mimicking the free production of nature; by amoral autonomy which is self-empowering in its practice, finding its guarantee only in a Father who exists solely in a desire to exercise law freely over everything.

And, in the suffering made necessary by his pleasure, shall we place Kant next to Sade? Or, if the subtlety of his mind is given one quarter turn of the screw more—in or out—next to Masoch? Such a notion can still arouse interest in a system that is so set in the ice of formalism; both together, or neither simply one nor the other. The lawgiver is the cruel instrument implementing the rule, of course, but he is also forced into a painful respect for Nature (some of whose laws escape him), into suspending his feelings in the sight of beauty, and even into resenting that the pain of separation still stings. The circle is squared, but no object of desire can be defined, unless once again it be that search for the remains of a relationship with the mother. In himself? Outside himself? But now everything has moved inside the house the subject has made, or is. And whether the scene seems set inside, or outside, whether in his room or in his study, sometimes enjoying a fire fancied to be burning in baroque curls of smoke or else gazing out through the/his window at the still in(de)finite space of the universe, the action is always inside his house, his mind. And what or who can now put it outside? Only a messenger of revolution perhaps? Or else the fact that this hearth is made of glass and that those glasses—rather tarnished by age, their brilliance dimmed, having always in fact been unsilvered or blackened by smoke—mirror so deadly a boredom that, whatever one's firm intent, one might finish by wishing to die—to die of love, were that still possible—rather than have things just go on. Forever.

The Eternal Irony
of the Community

On the one hand, the uterus in the male is reduced to a mere gland, while on the other, the male testicle in the female remains enclosed within the ovary, fails to emerge into opposition, and does not become an independent and active cerebrality. The clitoris moreover, is inactive feeling in general; in the male on the other hand, it has its counterpart in active sensibility, the swelling vital, the effusion of blood into the corpora cavernosa and the meshes of the spongy tissue of the urethra. The female counterpart of this effusion of blood in the male consists of the menstrual discharges. Thus, the simple retention of the conception in the uterus, is differentiated in the male into productive cerebrality and the external vital. On account of this difference therefore, the male is the active principle; as the female remains in her undeveloped unity, she constitutes the principle of conception.

'In the case of the eye,' says *Sömmerring*, 'it seems that the arteries are continued in finer branches, which no longer contain red blood. These branches pass initially into a similar vein, but finally into veinlets carrying red blood.'

—Hegel

The purpose that moves blood relatives to action is the care of the *bloodless*. Their inherent duty is to ensure *burial for the dead*, thus changing a natural phenomenon into a spiritual act. One more step (into negation) and we see that it is the task of womankind, guardian of the blood tie, to gather man into his final figuration, beyond the turmoil of contingent life and the scattered moments of his Being-there. Man is thereby raised into

(The epigraphs are taken from Hegel's *Philosophy of Nature*, ed. and tr. M. J. Petry [London: Allen & Unwin, 1970], pp. 175 and 123 respectively. Hegel's discussion of Sophocles' *Antigone*, upon which much of this essay is closely based, can most easily be found in English in *Hegel on Tragedy*, ed. Anne and Henry Paolucci [New York: Doubleday, 1962], pp. 260–73.—Tr.)

the peace of simple universality. In essence, woman has to take it upon herself over and over again, regardless of circumstances, to bury this corpse that man becomes in his pure state. She has to enable man to sublate a universality that smacks too much of the natural, or so it would seem, by affirming—for this is pure truth restored—that death is merely the peace of/and universality of the conscious essence of self. Man is still subject to (natural) death, of course, but what matters is to make a movement of the mind out of this accident that befalls the single individual and, in its raw state, drives consciousness out of its own country, cutting off that return into the self which allows it to become self-consciousness. Just as man must strive to make this negativeness into an ethical action by sacrificing his life for the city—in war for example—so woman must be that external and effective mediation that reconciles the dead man with himself *by taking upon herself the operation of destruction* that the becoming of mind cannot manage without. Thus woman takes this dead being into her own place on his return into the self—a being that is universal, admittedly, but also singularly drained of strength, empty and yielded passively up to others. She must protect him both from all base and irrational individuality and from the forces of abstract matter, which are now more powerful than he. Shielding him from the dishonoring operation of unconscious desires and natural negativeness—*preserving him from her desire, perhaps?*—she places this kinsman back in *the womb of the earth* and thus reunites him with undying, elemental individuality. To do this is also to reassociate him with a—religious—community that controls the violent acts of singular matter and the base urges which, unleashed upon the dead man, might yet destroy him. This supreme duty constitutes the divine law, or *positive* ethical action, as it relates to the individual.

Yet, on the other hand, human law places a negative meaning upon this individualism. In fact each member of the city has a right both to a living and to Being-for-itself, wherein the mind finds its reality and its being-there. But the mind is at the same time the strength of the whole, and hence it gathers *these individual parts* into *one negative entity*. The mind reminds the parts that they are dependent upon this totality and that they owe their *life* to it entirely. Thus any associations—such as families—that one assumes have been founded primarily to serve individual ends, whether the acquisition of personal wealth or the search for sexual pleasures, invite a war that may disrupt their intimate life and violate their independence since these threaten to shatter the whole. All those who persist in following the dictates of individualism must be taught by the government to fear a master: death. They must be prevented from sinking into the neutral Being-there, from regressing into the inner world of the senses, from ecstatically entering a world beyond, lacking all predicates that can be appropriated by the self of consciousness. *The cult of the dead and the cult of death* would thus be the point where divine law and human law join. And also that point where, at least on the higher ethical level, the relationship between man and woman is possible.

This unsullied relationship takes place only *between brother and sister.* They are the same blood, but in them blood is at rest and in balance. Thus they do not desire each other, they have neither given nor received this Being-for-the-self from each other, they are free individualities vis-à-vis each other. What is it, then, that impels them to unite so that finally one passes into the other? What meaning does each have for the other that draws them thus into this exchange? Is it recognition of *blood?* Of their common allegiance to the power of the *same blood?* Could it be their complicity in the permanence, the continuance of blood that a matriarchal type of lineage ensures in its purest and most universal being? In this sense the family of Oedipus would be quite exemplary because the mother of the husband is also his wife, thus re-marking the blood tie between the children of that union—including Polynices and Antigone. Furthermore, the uncle—the mother's brother—will in this family be the representative of an already patriarchal power. Or is it rather that brother and sister share in the *same sperm,* thus giving consanguineity an (other) equilibrium, ridding it of its own magic passion but counterbalancing it with another? In fact, however, the sperm does not join with the blood (though it was long thought to do so) but with the ovum: had this copulation been given its full weight and "effectiveness," it would already have irremediably shattered the unity of mind and ethical substance. Moreover, copulation takes place only in the impure mingling of the marriage of husband and wife. Are we then to seek this pact between sister and brother in a *common name,* in the notion that their co-uterine attraction is matched by their submission—represented by the patronymic—to symbolic rules that might be supposed to carry the potency of blood one step further and already to raise the family community to the types of laws in force in the city?

Thus, for one instant, brother and sister would recognize each other in their single self, each able to affirm a right that is achieved through the power each has when balanced in/by the other; the power of red blood and of its reabsorption, its sublation into a process of denominating—i.e., of semblance. An ideal distribution would hypothetically occur in which the (ethical) substance of matriarchy and of patriarchy would coexist, contributing their own subsistence to each other, in a peace without alloy, a relationship without desire. The war of the sexes would not take place here. But this moment is mythical, of course, and the *Hegelian dream* outlined above is already the effect of a dialectic produced by the discourse of patriarchy. It is a consoling fancy, a truce in the struggle between uneven foes, a denial of the guilt already weighing heavily upon the development of the subject; it is the delusion of a *bisexuality* assured for each in the connection and passage, one into the other, of each sex. Yet both sexes, male and female, have already yielded to a destiny that is different for each. This is so even if rape, murder, breaking and entering, injury, were still, in appearance at least, in general at least, suspended between brother and sister. But in fact such is not the case, as Hegel admits when he affirms that the brother is for the sister that possibility of recognition of which she is deprived as mother and wife, but does not state that the situation is reciprocal. This means that the brother has already been invested with a value for the sister that she cannot offer in return, except by devoting herself to his cult after death.

Certainly, in the work of Sophocles, which marks the historical bridge between matriarchy and patriarchy, things are not yet that clear. No decision has yet been made about what has more value. On the one hand, *blood is no longer pure* in Sophocles: the father, at least for a time, was king; the king thereby affirms his rights as father, as well as the complicity between family (patriarchal) power and that of the State. And tragedy enacts the punishment that is incurred by a taste for blood. On the other hand, *the privilege of the proper name is not yet pure:* the power of the father's name, had its right already been in force, should have prevented Oedipus from committing murder and incest. But this is not what happens. Moreover, the fact that each sister and brother has a double also indicates that this is still a transition in which the extremes—which will later be defined as being more masculine or more feminine: i.e., Eteocles and Ismene—seem almost like caricatures. Now, whereas Ismene is termed a sister because she shares *the same blood* as Antigone, and whereas Polynices is termed a brother because he was born of *the same mother,* Eteocles is brother because he is the son of *the same father and the same mother.*

These things can be stated in other ways. *Ismene* seems indisputably a "woman" in her weakness, her fear, her submissive obedience, her tears, madness, hysteria—all of which in fact are met with condescending scorn on the part of the king. Ismene is subsequently shut up, as a punishment, in the palace, the house, with the other women, who are all thus deprived of their freedom of action for fear they may sap the courage of the most valiant warriors. For *Antigone* things are less simple, and the king himself fears she may usurp his manhood—"Better be beaten, if need be, by a man, than let a woman get the better of us."[1]—if she does not pay for her insolence with death. Antigone does not yield to the law of the city, of its sovereign, of the man of the family: Creon. And she will choose to die a virgin, unwedded to any man, rather than sacrifice the ties of blood, rather than abandon her mother's son to the dogs and vultures, leaving his double to roam in eternal torment. Better to die than to refuse service to the divine law and to the attraction she feels for the gods below. There her jouissance finds easier recognition, no doubt, since her allegiance to them frees her from the inventions of men. She defies them all by/in her relationship to Hades. In her nocturnal passion she acts with a perversity which has nothing in common with the wretched crimes that men stoop to in their love for money, or so the king says. Indeed she boasts of this, stating publicly that she had rather die than give up such practices. And that, moreover, *between her and the king, nothing can be said*. She alone among the Cadmeans, *the literates*, reasons thus. At least out loud. In this way, she becomes the voice, the accomplice of the people, the slaves, those who only whisper their revolt against their masters secretly. Without friends, without husband, without tears, she is led along that *forgotten path* and there is *walled up* alive in *a hole* in the rock, shut off forever from the light of the sun. Alone in her crypt, her cave, her den, her womb, she is given just enough food by those who hold power to ensure that the city is not soiled and shamed by her decay. She is alone in confronting the underground god in order to see—again—if she will survive that solitary ritual.[2] But love, for her, has far too many fatal representations for her desire to recover from such punishments. However guiltless, she feels she bears the burden of her mother's fatal marriage, feels guilty for being born of such terrible embraces. Thus she is damned, and by consenting to a punishment she has not merited and yet cannot escape, at the least she accepts on her own

[1](Sophocles, *The Theban Plays*, "Antigone," tr. E. F. Watling [Penguin Classics, 1947], p. 144.—Tr.)

[2]("I'll have her taken to a desert place/Where no man ever walked, and there walled up/Inside a cave alive, with food enough/To acquit ourselves of the blood guiltiness/That would else lie upon our commonwealth./There she may pray to Death, the god she loves/And ask release from death or learn at last/What hope there is for those who worship death." Ibid., p. 147.—Tr.)

account the death knell of her jouissance—*or is mourning itself her jouis-sance?*—by killing herself. Does she thus anticipate the decree of death formulated by those in power? Does she duplicate it? Has she given in? Or is she still in revolt? She repeats, in any case, upon herself the murderous, but not bloody, deed of her mother. Whatever her current arguments with the laws of the city may have been, another law is still drawing her along her path: identification with her mother. *But how are mother and wife to be distinguished?* This is the dreadful paradigm of a mother who is both wife and mother to her husband. Thus the sister will strangle herself in order to save at least the mother's son. She will cut off her breath—her voice, her air, blood, life—with the veil of her belt, returning into the shadow (of a) tomb, the night (of) death, so that her brother, *her mother's desire,* may have eternal life. She never becomes a woman. But she is not as masculine as she might seem if seen from an exclusively phallic viewpoint—for it is tenderness and pity that have motivated her. Rather, she is a captive of a desire whose path has reached a dead end, has never been blazed. And did she seek the relationship with the mother in *Polynices* because he was the more feminine of the brothers? The younger? Or at any rate the weaker, the one who is rejected. The more irritable and impulsive one, who in his anger will seek to open the veins of his blood again. He who is armed for/by the love of a woman, married, unlike his siblings, and through that foreign match condemning his sister to die buried alive. At least in his passion for blood he has annulled the right of his brother—*Eteocles*—to command, has destroyed his brother's—his elder's?—relation to power, reason, property, the paternal succession. And has, with the same blow, killed himself.

Yet the government's mode of action remains unchanged. Another man was ready to take up the challenge: *Creon.* He also is alone—like Antigone—but he has the instrument of the law. Desperate he is, no doubt, but he yet claims that all power is his alone. Though he has brought son and wife to utter destruction, he climbs back onto the throne, without love, and the scepter remains in his hands. Death-stricken he is, and/but regulating his practice rigidly. Inflexible in his severity. Implacable in his reasons. His fragile strength, as apt to be broken as to break, demands that he fear pleasure, domination by women, the passion of youth represented by his son, the plots of the people, the slaves' revolt, even the gods (who are still controlled and divided by desires), soothsayers, therefore, and finally the "elders." He defends his privilege of being the sole safeguard of speech, truth, intelligence, reason—the fairest of all possessions—though at the same time he raves a little wildly in his relations with the gods and with women, for example. And in this mass grave of all the members of his family—Ismene is set aside in a golden prison which a change of ruler in fact risks transforming into a simple private home—in this general outflowing of blood, he thus (thereby) remains *one*. But nonetheless, he is *broken* between a self-sureness that is now only misfortune—is he not a superfluous man, weighed down by unbearable destiny, for whom everything and everybody has become equally contingent?—and the rigid sovereignty of a Being-for-the-self empty of content (of the substance of blood), an omnipotence alien to itself. A man who receives his personal power only by exercizing a right that has resolved all (blood) ties between individuals into abstract universality. Soon a God, but a god without any desire but that of submitting everyone to the law of blood congealed in the status of semblance: the Ego.

This is a necessary moment in the development of the mind, but Hegel expresses almost melancholic regret of/in this passage, and the dream of going back to that attraction to the/his sister which is unmingled (by blood). Back to the time when the species and genus had, it seems, not yet come into being, and when that unity, that individuality, *that still living, blood subject* simply took place. And in the nostalgia aroused by this return into the past. Hegel reveals his desire for a relationship that is certainly sexuate but does not need to pass through the realization of sexual desire. Desire intervenes to break the harmony unified in its blood cycle, in which brother and sister are theoretically between the phases—still relatively undifferentiated in their animality—of blood's circulation: inspiration/expiration, fluidity/hardening, apprehension/resorption of an outside. Thus one (male or female) would breathe out while the other would begin to breathe in, he/she would be becoming red blood while the other would return to self in his/her veins, he/she would affirm atomic individuality as cell(s) while the other would remain lymph, he/she would return to the earth in the form of carbon at the very moment when the other is rousing from torpor and taking fire, etc. But perhaps they are already irremediably separated throughout that process called *digestion*. For if the female one can recognize herself in the male one, who has therefore supposedly assimilated her, the reverse is not necessarily true. And if Antigone gives proof of a bravery, a tenderness, and an anger that free her energies and motivate her to resist that *outside* which the city represents for her, this is certainly because she had digested the masculine. At least partially, at least for a moment. But perhaps this will have been possible only at the time when she is mourning for her brother, just long enough to give him back the manhood he had lost in death and to feed his soul therewith. And to die in the act.

Already, then, the balance of blood has been upset, changed, dissolved. And the unadulterated happiness that is to be had from digesting one's own substance, from giving oneself fluidity, from breaking into one's own movement, from giving birth to oneself, is not shared equally between male and female, brother and sister. But, as long as the sister goes on in her living unity she can be the self-representative basis of that substance—the blood—that the brother assimilates in order to return to the self. She can guarantee that the son develops for himself (pour soi), independently of the couple that made him: she is *the living mirror*, the source reflecting the growing autonomy of the self-same. She is the privileged place in which red blood and its semblance harmoniously (con)fuse with each other, though she herself has no right to benefit from this process. And the different recognition that the city pays to their auto-speculation, the one in the other, has always already perverted their union, although sometimes a public re-mark is needed to make it obvious that the one must eliminate the other.

Thus male and female will be split further and further apart. The wife-mother will henceforward become more and more associated with nourishing and liquefying *lymph,* almost *white* while she loses her blood in cyclic hemorrhages, *neuter and passive* enough in her matter for various members and organs of society to incorporate her and use her for their own subsistence. The man (father) will persevere in developing his individualization by *assimilating* the external other into and for the self, thus re-enforcing his vitality, his irritability, and his activity; a particular triumph is experienced when man absorbs the other into himself in his intestine. The Father-king will repeat the rupture of (living) exchange between man and woman by sublating it into his discourse. Blood is burned to cinders in the writing of the text of law whereby man produces (himself) at the same time (as) the double—differently in him, in his son, and in his wife—and the color of blood fades as more and more semblances are produced, more atoms of individual egos, all bloodless in different ways. In this process some substance is lost: blood in its constitution of a living, autonomous subjectivity.

At the heart of the dialectic is hypochondria, melancholia. It can be linked to a clot of blood, cruor, reminiscent of the bloody calvary that set it on high, or else to the last froth left by an in(de)finite liquid which opens up the cup of its chalice even in Absolute Mind. Such clots and lymph, had they been able to close up wounds without weeping fluids, would have left the mind (only) to stony solitude and innocence. Assuming that the stone referred to serves to close off and mark the space in which femininity dies.

Thus we must go back to the decisive ethical moment which saw the blow struck producing a wound that no discourse has closed simply. The harmonious relationship of brother and sister involved a (so-called) equal recognition and nonviolent co-penetration of two essences, in which femininity and masculinity achieve universality in human and divine law. But this mutual agreement was possible only for as long as *adolescence* lasted and neither was impelled to act. A prolongation of childhood, a kind of Eden shielded from war and blessed by the household gods. But these idyllic and/because *immaculate* loves of childhood could not last. And each will soon realize that his or her equal is also his or her worst enemy, negation, and death. For the rule of law is impossible in a situation of mutual sharing in which one has as much value as the other, is equitably the same. In such circumstances consciousness could not recognize its simplicity or that wholeness which is the pathos of its duty. It must therefore make up its mind to act in accordance with that part of the ethical essence which has become apparent to it—that is, to the part which would correspond to its natural allegiance to one sex. Thus, without realizing it, consciousness finds itself embroiled willy-nilly in the rape of the other, who is henceforward injured by the partial character of such an operation. It is immediately clear, however, that the particular individual is not guilty or at fault. He is but the ineffective shadow acting on behalf of a universal self. And in fact, whatever his lack of personal responsibility, he will pay for his crime by finding that, subsequently, he is cut off from/in himself. In any event, he becomes conscious of that scission whereby the other side is now revealed to him in opposition and enmity. A dark potentiality that has always been on the watch comes suddenly into play when the deed is done: it catches the consciousness of

222

self in the act—the act of also being, or having, that *unconsciousness* which remains alien to it but yet plays a major role in the decision consciousness takes. Thus the public offender who has been killed turns out to be the father, and the queen who has been wedded is the mother. But the purest fault is that committed by the ethical consciousness, which knew in advance what law and power it was disobeying—that is to say, necessarily, the fault committed by femininity. For if the ethical essence in its divine, unconscious, feminine side, remains obscure, its prescriptions on the human, masculine, communal side are exposed to full light. *And nothing here can excuse the crime, or minimize the punishment.* And in its burial, in its decline into ineffectiveness and pure pathos, the feminine must recognize the full measure of its guilt.

What an amazing vicious circle in a single syllogistic system. Whereby the unconscious, while remaining unconscious, is yet supposed to know the laws of a consciousness—which is permitted to remain ignorant of it—and will become even more repressed as a result of failing to respect those laws. But the stratification, on top/underneath, of the two ethical laws, of the two beings-there of sexual difference—which in fact have to disappear as such after the death of brother and sister—comes from Self, of itself. The movement by which the mind ceaselessly sublates necessity, climbing to the top of its pyramid more easily if the other is thrust deeper down into the well. Thus the male one copulates the other so as to draw new strength from her, a new form, whereas the other sinks further and further into a ground that harbors a substance which expends itself without the mark of any individualism. And it is by no means sure that the rape to which she continues to be subjected is visible in broad daylight, for the rape may equally well result in her retreating down into a crypt where she is sealed off. Or else in the resurgence of an "essence" so different, so other, that even to expect it to "work on the outside" reduces it to sameness, to an unconscious that has never been anything but the unconscious of someone conscious of human law alone. Which is as much as to say that the crime can easily occur unnoticed and that the operation may never be translated into a fact. Unless each of these/its terms is doubled so radically that *a single dialectic is no longer sufficient to articulate their copulation.* For if it is asserted that the one character and the other are split into a conscious and an unconscious, with each character itself giving rise to that opposition, there remains the question of how it will be possible to *translate* the laws of the unconscious into those of the conscious, the so-called laws of God into the laws of philosophy, the laws of the female into those of the male. What will be the passage of their *difference* in the subsequent movement of the mind? Or rather, how will that difference be resolved? How does the mind acquire, in a variation of deferred action (après-coup), the right to make laws and official statements about (the) matter, when a certain process of statement has already excluded difference in its desire to return to sameness? This problem can be approached in another way: the masculine will be able to retrace the path of his discursive law, but it is also the role of the masculine to prescribe the law for the female, since she can have no knowledge (of it) for herself. And the fact that, ideally, each is both unconscious and conscious does not in practice prevent the conscious from being identified as masculine, whereas the unconscious remains fixed on the female side, repressed as a result of the impossibility of differentiating the maternal. This implies that masculinity—in man and possibly in woman—will to some extent be able to dialecticize its relationships and identificatory allegiance to the maternal, including a negativization of female singularity, but this would not true for femininity, which is aware of no difference between itself and the maternal, or even the masculine, except one that is mediated by the abstract immediacy of *the* being (as) or by the rejection of *one* (as) being. The female lacks the operation of affirming its singular and universalizable link to one as self.

Woman has no gaze, no discourse for her specific specularization that would allow her to identify with herself (as same)—to return into the self—or break free of the natural specular process that now holds her—to get out of the self. Hence, woman does not take an active part in the development of history, for she is never anything but the still undifferentiated opaqueness of sensible matter, the store (of) substance for the sublation of self, or being as what is, or what he is (or was), here and now. There is a doubling of a present of utterance in which present is already no more, has already passed into the universal, when woman appears in that *quasi-subjectivity* that is supposedly hers. And that cannot be possessed as consciousness of self. In her case "I" never equals "I," and she is only that individual will that the master takes possession of, that resisting remainder of a corporeality to which his passion for sameness is still sensitive, or again his double, the lining of his coat. Being as she is, she does not achieve the enunciatory process of the discourse of History, but remains its servant, deprived of self (as same), alienated in this system of discourse as in her master and finding some hint of her own self, her own ego, only in another, a You—or a He—who speaks. Her own will is shattered so afraid is she of the master, so aware of her inner nothingness. And her work in the service of another, of that male Other, ensures the ineffectiveness of any desire that is specifically hers.

But, when woman renounces her claim to desire, external things are positively molded, their forms are determined by a self that is not re-marked by any individual pathos or by any contingent arbitrariness, things in which the mind might intuit itself as objectal reality. This would be the final meaning of the obedience demanded of woman. She is merely the passage that serves to transform the inessential whims of a still sensible and material nature into universal will.

Woman is the guardian of the blood. But as both she and it have had to use their substance to nourish the universal consciousness of self, it is in the form of *bloodless shadows*—of unconscious fantasies—that they main-tain an underground subsistence. Powerless on earth, she remains the very ground in which manifest mind secretly sets its roots and draws its strength. And self-certainty—in masculinity, in community, in govern-ment—owes the truth of its word and of the oath that binds men to-gether to that substance common to all, repressed, unconscious and dumb, washed in the waters of oblivion. This enables us to understand why femininity consists essentially in laying the dead man back in the womb of the earth, and giving him eternal life. For the *bloodless one is the mediation that she knows in her being,* whereby a being-there that has given up being as a self here passes from something living and singular and deeply buried to essence at its most general. Woman can, therefore, by remembering this intermediary moment, preserve at least the soul of man and of community from being lost and forgotten. *She ensures the Er-innerung of the consciousness of self by forgetting herself.*

But at times the forces of the world below become hostile because they have been denied the right to live in daylight. These forces rise up and threaten to lay waste the community. To turn it upside down. Refusing to be that unconscious ground that nourishes nature, womanhood would then demand the right to pleasure, to jouissance, even to effective action, thus betraying her universal destiny. What is more, she would pervert the property/propriety of the State by making fun of the adult male who no longer thinks of anything but the universal, subjecting him to derision and to the scorn of a callow adolescence. In opposition to the adult male, she would set up the strength of youth possessed by the *son*, the *brother*, the *young man*, for in them, much more than in the power of government, she recognizes a *master*, an *equal*, a *lover*. The community can protect itself from such demands only by repressing them as elements of *corruption* that threaten to destroy the State. In fact these *seeds* of revolt, in principle, are quite powerless, are already reduced to nothing by being *separated from the universal goal* pursued by the citizens. Any community has a duty to transform these too immediately natural forces into its own defenders by inciting the young men—in whom the woman's desire takes pleasure—to make war upon each other and slaughter one another in bloody fights. It is through them that the still living substance of nature will sacrifice her last resources to a formal and empty universality, scattering her last drops of *blood* at a multitude of points which it will no longer be possible to gather up in the intimacy of the familiar cave.

And if, in those *points*, the *sperm*, the *name*, the *whole individual* can find a representing basis that allows them to rise up again and recover, blood in its autonomous flow will never re-unite again. But the eye—at least in the absolute—would have no need of blood to see with, anymore perhaps than the Mind to think with.

Volume-Fluidity

So woman has not yet taken (a) place. The "not yet" probably corresponds to a *system of hysterical fantasy* but/and it acknowledges a *historical condition*. Woman is still the place, the whole of the place in which she cannot take possession of herself as such. She is experienced as all-powerful precisely insofar as her indifferentiation makes her radically powerless. She is never here and now because it is she who sets up that eternal elsewhere from which the "subject" continues to draw his reserves, his re-sources, though without being able to recognize them/her. She is not uprooted from matter, from the earth, but yet, but still, she is already scattered into x number of places that are never gathered together into anything she knows of herself, and these remain the basis of (re)production—particularly of discourse—in all its forms.

Woman remains this nothing at all, or this all at nothing, in which each (male) one seeks to find the means to re-plenish the resemblance to self (as) to same. Thus she moves from place to place, yet, up to the present, it has never been she that was dis-placed. She must continue to hold the place she constitutes for the subject, a place to which no eternal value can be assigned lest the subject remain paralyzed forever by the irreplaceableness of his cathected investments. Therefore she has to wait for him to move her in accordance with his needs and desires. In accordance with the urgency of the economy in operation. She is patient in her reserve, her modesty, her silence, even when the moment comes to endure violent consummation, to be torn apart, drawn and quartered. Enough of

(LI's title is "L'incontournable volume." "Contourner" means to trace an outline or shape, and also to distort, twist, or evade.—Tr.)

227

the stitches closing her vagina are taken out, sexuality is permitted her—but as a mother only?—to allow him to penetrate her body again, in the hope of finally losing his "soul" there. Such corruption is too calculated, and he risks ending up more of a child, and thus more enslaved, than ever. Meanwhile, her shining raiment, her gleaming skin conceal the disaster within, hide all that devours and rends her body. *A female one,* thus, at least as far as the eye can see; the striking makeup, the motherly role she plays, cover up the fact that she is torn to pieces. Fragments: of women, of discourse, of silences, of blanks that are still immaculate (?) . . . Everything thrust aside wherever the "subject" seeks to escape from his emprisonment. But even as he struggles to fracture that specular matrix, that enveloping discursivity, that body of the text in which he has made himself a prisoner, it is Nature he finds, Nature who, unknown to him, has nourished his project, his production. It is Nature who now fuses for him with that glass enclosure, that spangled sepulcher, from which—imaginary and therefore absent—she is unable to articulate her difference. Thus she allows herself to be consumed again for new speculations, or thrown away as unfit for consumption. Without saying a word. Scarcely does she try to promote her usefulness or ensure her exchange value by means of a few gadgets; the latest brilliant novelties put into circulation by men and only a little warped by her faintly baroque frivolity.

Everything has to be (re)invented to avoid the *vacuum.* And if the place is plowed over again in this way, it is always in search of the lost roots of sameness. Because, on the horizon, a hint was appearing of a "world" so inconceivable, so other, that it was preferable to go back underground rather than witness so dizzying an event. Although the mother represents only a mute soil, a mystery beyond metaphor, at least she is still *pregnant.* Obviously, you will find opaqueness and resistance in the mother, even the repulsiveness of matter, the horror of blood, the ambivalence of milk, the threatening traces of the father's phallus, and even that hole that you left behind when you came into the world. But she—at least—is not nothing. She is not this vacuum (of) woman. This void of representation, this negation of all representation, this limit set on all present representations (of self). The mother is pulled apart, indeed, but by the child being born or tearing at the breast. He can believe this at any rate. That gap, break, or fault, then, is well known to him since he has made use of it and closed if off in his systematics. It is not the gap (of) woman, which he defends himself against by changing her into a mother, or which he combats, in his effort to block any "other," by means of the protective veil of a language that has already changed even its evasions into fetishes.

Woman is neither open nor closed. She is indefinite, in-finite, *form is never complete in her*. She is not infinite but neither is she *a* unit(y), such as letter, number, figure in a series, proper noun, unique object (in a) world of the senses, simple ideality in an intelligible whole, entity of a foundation, etc. This incompleteness in her form, her morphology, allows her continually to become something else, though this is not to say that she is ever univocally nothing. No metaphor completes her. Never is she this, then that, this and that. . . . But she is becoming that expansion that she neither is nor will be at any moment as definable universe. Perhaps this is what is meant by her insatiable (hysterical) thirst for satisfaction. No one single thing—no form, act, discourse, subject, masculine, feminine— can complete the development of woman's desire. And for her the risk of maternity is that of limiting (herself and her desire) to the world of *one* child. By closing herself up over the unit of that conception, by curling around that one, her desire hardens. *Perhaps it becomes phallic through this relationship to the one?* And likewise a femininity that conforms and corresponds too exactly to an idea—Idea—of woman, that is too obedient to a sex—to an Idea of sex—or to a fetish sex has already frozen into phallomorphism. Is already metabolized by phallogocratism. Whereas what happens in the jouissance of women exceeds all this. It is indefinite flood in which all manner of developments can be inscribed. The fullness of their coming into being is hinted, is proclaimed as possible, but within an extension swelling outward without discernible limits. Without telos or arche. Provided that it is not already phallic. That it has not already submitted to the prescriptions of a hommosexual imaginary and to its relationship to the origin, to a logos that claims to lead the potency of the maternal back into the same—to Sameness—in itself and for itself.

But woman is not to be resolved like that. Except in her phallosensical capitulations and capitalizations. For (the) woman neither is able to give herself some meaning by speech nor means to be able to speak in such a way that she is assigned to some concept or that some fixed notion is assigned to her. Woman is not to be related to any simple designatable being, subject, or entity. Nor is the whole group (called) women. One woman + one woman + one woman will never add up to some generic entity: woman. (The/a) woman refers to what cannot be defined, enumerated, formulated or *formalized*. Woman is a common noun for which no identity can be defined. (The/a) woman does not obey the principle of self-identity, however the variable x for self is defined. She is identified with every x variable, not in any specific way. Presupposed is an excess of all identification to/of self. But this excess is no-thing: it is vacancy of form, gap in form, the return to another edge where she re-touches herself with the help of—nothing. Lips of the same form—but of a form that is never simply defined—ripple outwards as they touch and send one another on a course that is never fixed into a single configuration.

This will already have taken place without the consent or assent of any object, or subject. This is an other topo-(logy) of jouissance. Alien to masculine self-affectation that has seen there only its own negative—the death of its logic and not its alter(n)ation in a still undefined copulation. Man's auto-erotism presupposes an individualization of the subject, of the object, and of the instrument appropriate(d) to jouissance. If only for an instant, for the time it takes to switch. (The/a) woman is always already in a state of anamorphosis in which every figure becomes fuzzy. A state of cyclic discontinuity closing in a slit whose lips merge into one another. Thus she cannot *repeat herself* nor produce herself as something *quite other* in pleasure, for the other already within her affects her, touches her without ever becoming either one or the other (male or female). The separation of this unforming contact cannot be formulated in the simplicity of any present. And since she has never raised herself up to that simple present, woman remains (in) her indifference. Remains what he undertakes to rape and rend. What he acts to speak for and touch, here and now. Even if to act is to feel again. For to be (the/a) woman is already to feel oneself before anything else has specifically intervened. She is beyond all pairs of opposites, all distinctions between active and passive or past and future. But this surreptitious self-affection is not overt, cannot be expressed in words. It is *true* that women don't tell all. And even if one begs them to speak, if he begs them to speak, they will or would never express anything but the will and the word of the "subject" who rapes and robs them of their jouissance. Women have already lost something more intimate—something that finds no communion in "soul"—and "gained" only propositions in exchange. They are already dominated by an intent, a meaning, a thought. By the laws of *a* language. Even in their madness, which turns language upside down and inside out. Telling all for the/a woman has no meaning or has no one meaning, since she cannot express this nothing that affects her, in which she is always already touched. This is the "nothing to tell" that history—History—duplicates by removing both it and her from the economy of discourse.

Thus (the/a) woman may, in a pinch, be a signifier—even below the line—in the logical system of representations and representatives-repre-senters, of the "subject." This does not mean that, as this signifier, she may in any way recognize herself. Or even that man, as representer of the power (of the) phallus, corresponds for her to any meaning, except perhaps that of her exclusion from herself. For man is placed in such a way as to re-mark the distance, the separation, in which she finds herself, but the "subject's" imprisonment in the autarchy of his metaphorical system implies that, even when such "re-marking" occurs, it does so only in the context of that contiguousness in which she is contained, retained, in her jouissance, and which steers her away from her own course in order to articulate a phallic whole: her function henceforward will be as *hole*. And for her, metaphor will continue to work as violation and separation, except if, *empty of all meaning that is already appropriate(d)*, she keeps open the indefinite possibilities of her jouissance—that is, God, the design introducing a "figure" that resists using its allegiance to an individual as a firm foundation. A figure that still has extension, but that does not break up into more and more comprehensive forms. God, whose desire is a closed book to mere expertise, left to/in ignorance. Perhaps because He refuses hatred? Yes, if hatred comes from the partic-ular character of knowledge. In which each one, male and female, would try to get the *best bit* of knowledge, and struggle to use his spec-ul(ariz)ation to tear apart the representation of the other, thereby pre-serving the power (of) truth of the spectacle upon which he/she gazes. Denying the fiction of the mirror that lies beneath. But, for someone who knew everything, rivalry in appropriate (self)knowledge would be meaningless. Woman certainly does not know everything (about her-self), she doesn't know (herself to be) anything, in fact. But her rela-tionship to (self)knowledge provides access to a whole of what might be known or of what she might know—that is to God. And here again, by duplicating that speculative condition as a kind of caricature, that is, by excluding it—except as phallic proxies—from all individual science, from the appropriation of all knowledge (of self), "History" has manipu-lated the desire of woman—who is forced to function as an object, or more rarely as a subject—so as to perpetuate the existence of God as the stake in an omniscience quite alien to its determination. God is adored even as He is abhorred in his power. And because God has been set aside in/by female jouissance, He will bring horror and aversion down upon it, because of its "un-likeness," because its "not yet" defies all comparison. And if in the attention the "subject" now devotes to defining woman's sexuality, he aims to become identical to the being—the Being—of the other—the Other?—and seeks to resorb otherness into Sameness, wanting that, the Id, her, and her . . . knowledge in order to be more like Self, to act more like Self, woman can only reply: not . . . yet. And in fact, in one sense, in this sense, never.

For man needs an instrument to touch himself with: a hand, a woman, or some substitute. This mechanism is sublated in and by language. Man produces language for self-arousal. And in the various forms of discourse, the various modes of the "subject's" self-arousal can be analyzed. The most ideal of these would be philosophical discourse, which gives privileged status to "self-representing." This mode of self-arousal reduces the need for an instrument to *virtually* nothing—to the thought (of) the soul: soul defined as a mirror placed inside whereby the "subject," in the most secret as well as most subtle way, ensures the immortality of his auto-erotism.

Sciences and technologies also need instruments for their self-arousal. And to some extent they are thereby freed from the "subject's" control, and risk depriving him of a fraction of his solitary profit, competing with him in a bid for their autonomy. But thought still subsists. At least for a while, for as long as it takes to think (oneself) woman. Is this the last resource available to the self-arousal of the "subject" as such in/by language? Or is it rather a small opening in his vicious circle, in the logos of sameness? If machines, even machines of theory, can be aroused all by themselves, may woman not do likewise? Now a crisis breaks out, an age in which the "subject" no longer knows where to turn, whom or what to turn to, amid all these many foci of "liberation," none rigorously homogeneous with another and all heterogeneous to his conception. And since he had long sought in that conception the instrument, the lever and, in more cases than one, the term of his pleasure, these objects of mastery have perhaps brought the subject to his doom. *So now man struggles to be science, machine, woman, . . . to prevent any of these from escaping his service and ceasing to be interchangeable.* But he will never quite manage to do this as in none of these things—science, machine, woman—will form ever achieve the same completeness it does in him, in the inner sanctuary of his mind. In them form has always already exploded. Indeed it is in this way that form can take pleasure in herself—in edges touching each other—or sustain that illusion for the other. Whereas the "subject" must always re-exhibit (his) form in front of the self in order to taste its possession once more. The master in his pleasure is enslaved to his power.

When the/a woman touches herself, on the other hand, a whole touches itself because it is in-finite, because it has neither the knowledge nor the power to close up or to swell definitively to the extension of an infinite. This self-touching gives woman a form that is in(de)finitely transformed without closing over her appropriation. Metamorphoses occur in which there is no complete set, where no set theory of the One is established. Transmutations occur, always unexpectedly, since they do not conspire to accomplish any telos. *That,* after all, would rest on the assumption that one figure takes up—sublates—the previous one and dictates the next one, that there is *one* specified form, that becomes *another.* But this happens only in the imaginary of the (male) subject, who projects onto all others the reason for the capture of his desire: his language, which claims to designate him perfectly.

Now, the/a woman who doesn't have *one* sex organ, or a unified sexuality (and this has usually been interpreted to mean that she has no sex) cannot subsume it/herself under *one* generic or specific term. Body, breasts, pubis, clitoris, labia, vulva, vagina, neck of the uterus, womb, . . . and this *nothing* that already gives pleasure by setting them apart from each other: all these foil any attempt at reducing sexual multiplicity to some proper noun, to some proper meaning, to some concept. Woman's sexuality cannot therefore be inscribed *as such* in any theory, except indirectly when it is standardized against male parameters. The clitoris achieved some success in that way since it was not thought of in terms of apartness, even from the other pleasures. The same thing, among others, occurred with motherhood. Both the clitoris and motherhood, like, indeed, every aspect of female desire, were assigned meaning through auto-representations of the (so-called) male sexuality. And these necessarily serve as models, units of measurement, and guarantees of an economic step in exactly the right direction. This is apparent even in the essential *trinitary* structure: the subject, the object, the instrument-copula that links them together. Father, Son, and Holy Ghost. The womb of mother-nature enables the (male) one to join up with the (so-called) other in the matrix of a discourse. It will even be possible, by playing upon negativity with skill and varied success, to extend this so-called family circle to include four terms, four members. The fourth, by its absence, its dumbness, its death, its *glass,* smooths out the exchanges between the three others. But it is always the same discourse that develops, more and more brilliant, though at the price of a little inflation. The (male) subject collects up and stitches together the scattered pieces of female merchandise (scattered in silence, in inconsequential chatter, or in madness) and turns them into coins that have an established value in the marketplace. What needs to be done instead, of course, if she is to begin to speak and be understood, and understand and express herself, is to suspend and melt down all systems of credit. In every sense. The credit, the credibility, that sustains all the current forms of monopoly, needs to be questioned. Otherwise, why speak about "her," since the only currency she provides or enjoys is her silence?

But is it really a question of *her* in all this, even now? Or is it just the mother again? Is this revival of interest anything but the anxious search for something still good to eat in a world that is starved by the dictates of increased productivity and the threat of overcrowding? In the last analysis, isn't this a return to the mother's milk, to the generosity of her blood, to the richness of her womb, with its specifically territorial connotations? Is this regression? In order to extract new profits. New modes of subsistence. Or is it the mystery of a sex that takes pleasure in "nothing" (except when that sex also limits itself to an anal-oral fantasy system, consuming the "phallus" it has nourished and enabled to reproduce), a sex that finally allows a disillusioned desire to see past the "veil" which once masked that strange "thing"—the pleasure of merging endlessly with the other, of touching and absorbing each other without any privileged identification? Whereby neither one (male or female) nor the other is assumed as a term, any more than is their passage into each other—a passage which is nothing, or which is that something taken away from the circularity of movement looping back upon itself, or that apartness which always already refers to a (male or female) other.

The other can come into play in all kinds of ways providing that there is no imposition of rigid forms: of being, having, speaking, thinking. For that inflexibility will always sever the exchange; fixing and freezing the apartness between the two into a one. This *one* may henceforward be identified, repeated, counted, serialized, transformed in the process— even be summed up into a finite One, but this will no longer have any beneficial effect. Once its unformable apartness has been defined as a *one,* the sexual rapport will have lost the jouissance of its in(de)finite exchange in the other. Of course, other pleasures can be substituted for it, notably the pleasure of exchanging truths or quips with one's peers. For, if the affirmation of the *one* is sustained only by that formal rigor, then what *other* could possibly respond to such an absolutely ingrained notion? Castration will turn out to have been merely a negation of the other implied by sexual difference, taking the form of screens, prisons, cells, stases in relationships, and thereby reverting to its repression. This would apply in discourse as well, of course, wherein each atom of meaning finds its force of truth in being unique in extension and comprehension; using the self-identity of that assertion to define its spatial distinctness from others, but also and at the same time, decisively cutting up the whole matter of language, the whole of speculation, and, moreover, of the "blanks" in discourse. Those things that are not said or said between the lines since they have already been given meaning. Even in the silence of the other, who says nothing (but) what the "subject" has already told her to say. The "subject" will thus be able to exploit the other, fragment her, speculate her—and find in her nothing but the same sameness? This male other will serve only to duplicate his own identity in a different way.

Woman has also been asked to serve in this manner. Sometimes the reduplication is assumed to operate upon a chaotic substance that the "subject" claims to form, sometimes upon the effectiveness of a negativity representing a hollow whole that is still to be determined in the future, sometimes upon the repetition of an assertion which, though designed to be instantaneous, requires nonetheless to pass back through/ in the other. But within this increasingly subtle duality of meaning in all its properties, *the redoubling which has already taken place, but in a quite other manner, in woman has been evaded.* The female will be placed beyond the pale of language, and thus will at least win an ambivalent respect for her virginity—that taboo of frontiers which gape open at the outer limits of the will and the power to say everything. Opening onto another "world" of which nothing but that gaping slit is known. Giving rise to the anguished fear of trespassing without a password, with no possibility of a challenge, no rights set out in writing, no toll to pay, no strict limit between a before/after, outside/inside, familiar/foreign, . . . speakable/unspeakable. When the father, again, takes it upon himself to legitimize the transaction by allowing for the *bonus* that is due him, he will thereby have reduced the feminine to the maternal, the go-between without property or propriety who gives him access to the den where he mines his wealth. That wealth may take the form of a family, a tribe, a community, a people. The go-between has already been exported *inside* the father's territory. And the possibility of closeness, of a touch, without reserve, to the point of ecstasy, has been excluded from the conception (of property). Here the two has already been reduced to the one, even in the various modes of its difference. The very close no longer moves out toward the irreducibly far, within a nothing that can be appropriated.

Except perhaps in God still. In the heavenly beyond, whose qualities, powers, names they have attempted to enumerate by exploiting chastity, but without coming to the end of its duplicity. . . . God (of) that band that would secretly appear at the opening of a diabolical pleasure? In order to fill the gap, says one, in order to take pleasure, says the other. In order to take the pleasure of the other—or of the Other—in its redoubling into nothing that is known. Still . . . God, that entity par excellence, that radically autarchic unity, that universality and eternity now and always, that procreator of all nature, that sacred name of names, they say. That sex (of) nothing at all in his absolute fluidity, plasticity to all metamorphoses, ubiquity in all things possible at once, invisibility— who has not ceased to heed women, though silently, in their most secret, covered places. God knows women so well that he never touches them directly, but always in that fleeting stealth of a fantasy that evades all representation: between two unities who thus imperceptibly take pleasure in each other. And if "God" has been conceived as a perfect volume, a closed completeness, an infinite circle as far as extension extends, it is certainly not as a result of women's imagination. For this passion for an origin that coils around neatly, even at the risk of biting its own tail, for a house (or whore house?) carefully shut away so that the "thing" may perhaps (come to) pass, for a womb that is sutured together over/in its inwardness, is not women's passion. Except, occasionally, in their maternal phallicism or their impotent mimicry. Their "God" is quite other, as is their pleasure. And since his death has always already taken place, at least in this "world," it is not about to occur. But of course women will not say so, because there is nothing there to expose. Or to know (and this can be written differently according to the expectation of its impossible [re]production).

For the/a woman, two does not divide into ones. Relationships defy being cut into units. And when "she" hangs on so desperately to the one, even to the point of putting a capital letter for *one* god made Man, it is only so as to repeat that value "she" has a right to upon the exchange market—the value of no value. That nil, that zero, that moving decimal place which is the basis and seal of all accountability. This is not to say that she has no price for each individual male, unless she is understood to be beyond price because she establishes the foundation for the economy's validity. The economy is always vulnerable to the fission of its elementary particle, its unit of trade, by this more-or-less nothing that can upset the market rates. The fact that until recently it has been his prerogative to take his bearings in the child is no doubt attributable to the need to represent things to himself in the same terms. More or less. To bring them down to the *same units,* even if that way accounts are already made more complicated: with two producing the one in order to merge and cancel each other out in their couple. Reproducing another one, in whom he no longer recognizes himself. Does this second (of the) one belong to the mother? Then he may be called Polynices, and he will be reprojected from the city as the law knows it. And if the one who comes into the world in this manner is a girl, such a thing is so inconceivable that it has to be erased immediately for fear of disrupting market rates: she is (only) her mother, or another boy to be reduced to the youthful condition of asexuality, a-sex (held in reserve in case values eventually crash) or nothing. In any case nothing that can be shown to people except in her death, (or) her imprisonment behind the door of the house.

And there almost nothing happens except the (re)production of the child. And the flow of some shameful liquid. Horrible to see: bloody. *Fluid* has to remain that secret *remainder,* of the one. Blood, but also milk, sperm, lymph, saliva, spit, tears, humors, gas, waves, airs, fire . . . light. All threaten to deform, propagate, evaporate, consume him, to flow out of him and into another who cannot be easily held on to. The "subject" identifies himself with/in an almost material consistency that finds everything flowing abhorrent. And even in the mother, it is the cohesion of a "body" (subject) that he seeks, solid ground, firm foundation. Not those things in the mother that recall the woman—the flowing things. He cathects these only in a desire to turn them into the self (as same). Every body of water becomes a mirror, every sea, ice. Otherwise he has to creep up on them from behind. He eyes their heights and depths from a fortress that closes at the back: suture of a hole which assures the "subject" of his rebirth in pure and simple matter that the form of the Father's spirit will fashion, if he has not already done so, according to his logic. Thus he is protected from that indecent contact: woman. Preserved from any possible assimilation into that shapeless flux that dampens, soaks, floods, channels, electrifies, lights up the apartness in the blaze of its embrace. Without common measure with the one (of the subject).

To keep himself from dissolving completely, he will still have recourse to the *speculum*. Giving up his plans, his neat outlines, his univocally framed shape, his calculations of proportions established once and for all, his immovably reflected unit(y), he will try to come to terms with the curves of the mirror. This does complicate the relationships to self (as same). But perhaps it is not impossible to analyze those curves, with the help of those instruments he now has in his arsenal. Everything, then, has to be rethought in terms of curl(s), helix(es), diagonal(s) spiral(s), roll(s), twirl(s), revolution(s), pirouette(s). Speculation whirls round faster and faster as it pierces, bores, drills into a volume that is supposed to be *solid* still. Covered with a hard shell that must be fractured, trepanned, split open, explored in its hidden heart. Or belly. Whipped along, spinning, twirling faster and faster until matter shatters into pieces, crumbles into dust. Or into the substance of language? The matrix of discourse? The mother's "body"? He takes them apart to examine them, to gaze upon their (and his) smallest atoms, and spaces in atoms. Searching everywhere for some possible hidden vein of gold, for some extra potency, which may guarantee the value of the "subject" and thus perpetuate his exchanges in property. The child gets a rather lower rating in this new system: too much time is taken (re)producing it. The woman-mother who is being worked over in detail by the "subject's" specula(riza)tions no longer has the leisure to shut herself off for the duration of a pregnancy.

But, if the reserves stored in that volume were to run out also, would he have to turn once again to the instrument that spawned him? And indeed forged him? Would he have to admit that he was already fundamentally different from what he claimed to seduce, that until now he has touched nothing? Nothing not already known. That, by fabricating an apartness of his own, he has failed to cope with the one that—already—

existed. Must he admit that, at best, he has merely reached the other side, the backside of his projections? Been perhaps beyond the symmetry of a reflection? Or of an inversion? Finding in the blind alley of specular, speculative negative entropy the need for a growth which, at each moment in his reproduction in sameness, must drill further down or further up.

The/a woman never closes up into a volume. The dominant representation of the maternal figure as volume may lead us to forget that woman's ability to enclose is enhanced by her fluidity, and vice versa. Only when coopted by phallic values does the womb preclude the separation of the lips. It is the subject who must be charged with confusing the one with the other by reducing the contact between them in his desire. For if she (or they, both female) were at once to be two but not divisible into one(s), how would he find his bearings? How could he worm his way in between them, into their womb(s). The other must therefore serve to mirror the one, reduplicating what man is assumed to know already as the place of (his) production. "She" must be only the path, the method, the theory, the *mirror,* which leads back, by a process of repetition, to the recognition of (his) origin for the "subject."

But the woman and the mother are not mirrored in the same fashion. A double specularization in and between her/them is already in place. And more. For the sex of woman is not one. And, as jouissance bursts out in each of these/her "parts," so all of them can mirror her in dazzling multifaceted difference. Is she therein more complete than in the whole? If so, it would mean that this protean pleasure can be broken down into shards, pieces of *a* mirror. This may in fact be true at times; moreover in the polymorphic games of reflection, of inversion, perversion, it may even be satisfying. But that way lies once again the pleasure of the hommologous, not that of a sexuality in which many heterogeneous elements fuse, and fuse again, and confuse, as the ice sparkles and flames up from/in its apartness. To gather them together in some unit(y) of specula(riza)tion, some summation arising out of their pleasures, has nothing—yet—to do with all that burns and gleams without end or limit in the blazing embrace of those fiery hollows.

Speculum of the Other Woman

The/a woman cannot be collected into *one* volume, for in that way she risks surrendering her own jouissance, which demands that she remain open to nothing utterable but which assures that her edges not close, her lips not be sewn shut. And, admittedly, the history of this return upon herself has dispossessed her. She remains outside the circularity of a thought that, in its telos, turns to his ends the cause of his desire: she is the unconscious basis of that attempt to find metaphor for an originary matrix in the sphere of intimacy with self, of nearness to self, of a "soul" or a mind. She is still the whole of a place that cannot be gathered into a space and is only a receptacle for the (re)production of sameness. Yet, at the same time, she is forced to serve many functions, torn apart, drawn and quartered in the service of the specific unit(y) of a field, a name, a sex, a gender, that are devoid of all possibility of touching again. Opaqueness of matter, fleeting fluid, vertiginous void between two, a mirror in which the "subject" sees himself and reproduces himself in his reflection, a shutter set up to allow the eye to frame its view, a sheath-envelope that reassures the penis about the mark made by its solitary pressures and imprints, a fertile soil to bear his seed. . . . Never is she one, either male or female.

Unless she competes with the phallosensical hommologue that even today fills itself with gold in order to spawn more and more offspring to occupy, saturate, and exploit to its own profit the productiveness of this gap, this nothing. Nothing, that is, that is as yet known *in truth*. And, in *one sense,* ever.

PLATO'S *HYSTERA*

The myth of the cave, for example, or as an example, is a good place to start.[1] Read it this time as a metaphor of the inner space, of the den, the womb or *hystera,* sometimes of the earth—though we shall see that the text inscribes the metaphor as, strictly speaking, impossible. Here is an attempt at making metaphor, at trying out detours, which not only is a silent prescription for Western metaphysics but also, more explicitly, proclaims (itself as) everything publicly designated as metaphysics, its fulfillment, and its interpretation.

The Stage Setup

So let us make reading the myth of the cave our point of departure. Socrates tells us that men—*hoi anthrōpoi,* sex unspecified—live *underground,* in a *dwelling formed* like a *cave.* Ground, dwelling, cave, and even, in a different way, form—all these terms can be read more or less as equivalents of the *hystera.* Similar associations could in fact be made for *living, dwelling* for a certain time or even for all time, in the *same place,* in the *same habitat.*

As the story goes, then, men—with no specification of sex—are living in one, same, place. A place shaped like a cave or a womb.[2]

---

[1](As previously noted, all quotations from Plato refer to the Jowett translation. Because the passage under consideration, Republic VII, 514–517a, is brief, I have given section references only when confusion seemed likely.—Tr.)

[2](Throughout this essay, LI weaves a sequence of puns based on homonyms and rhymes of the word *antre*—cave, or den. The most prominent rhyme is *ventre*—womb. Another important one is *entre*—between, which gives the complex pun *antr-ouverture* used at times by LI instead of *entr-ouverture*—gap or half-opening. Unfortunately this sequence of word-plays has no simple equivalent in English.—Tr.)

Turned Upside-down and Back-to-front

The entrance to the cave takes the form of a long passage, corridor, neck, conduit, leading upward, toward the light or the *sight of day,* and the whole of the cave is oriented in relation to this opening. Upward— this notation indicates from the very start that the Platonic cave functions as an attempt to give an orientation to the reproduction and representation of something that is always already there in the den. The orientation functions by turning everything over, by reversing, and by pivoting around axes of symmetry. From high to low, from low to high, from back to front, from anterior to opposite, but in all cases from a point of view in front of or behind something in this cave, situated in the back. *Symmetry plays a decisive part here*—as projection, reflection, inversion, retroversion—and you will always already have lost your bearings as soon as you set foot in the cave; it will turn your head, set you walking on your hands, though Socrates never breathes a word about the whole mystification, of course. This theatrical trick is unavoidable if you are to enter into the functioning of representation.

So men have lived in this cave since their childhood. Since time began. They have never left this space, or place, or topography, or topology, of the cave. The swing around the axes of symmetry necessarily determines how they live, but they are unaware of this. Chained by the neck and thighs, they are fixed with their heads and genitals facing *front, opposite*— which in Socrates' tale, is the direction toward the back of the cave. The cave is the representation of something always already there, of the original matrix/womb which these men cannot represent since they are held down by chains that prevent them from turning their heads or their genitals toward the daylight. They cannot turn toward what is more primary, toward the *proteron* which is in fact the *hystera.* Chains restrain them from turning toward the origin but/and they are prisoners in the space-time of the pro-ject of its representation. Head and genitals are kept turned to the front of the representational project and process of the *hystera.* To the *hystera protera* that is apparently resorbed, blended into the movement of *hysteron proteron.* For *hysteron,* defined as what is behind, is also the last, the hereafter, the ultimate. *Proteron,* defined as what is in front, is also the earlier, the previous. There is a fault in the *hysterein* which is maintained by the *proterein,* or more exactly here by the *prosō,* the forward, the *prosōpon,* the opposite, the face, the visage, the physiognomy, the *blepein eis prosōpon,* or even the *protasis*—maintained by links, by chains that are, as it were, invisible. Thus keeping up the illusion that the origin might become fully visible if only one could turn around, bring it into one's field of vision, facing one's face, if only it were not artificially turned away. One is able only to look ahead and stretch forward. Chains, lines, perspectives oriented straight ahead—all maintain the illusion of constant motion in one direction. Forward. The cave cannot be explored in the round, walked around, measured in the round. Which means that the men all stay there in the same spot—same place, same time—in the same *circle*, or circus ring, the *theatrical arena* of that representation.

Special Status for the Side Opposite

And the only thing they can still do is to look at whatever presents itself before their eyes. Paralyzed, unable to *turn round or return* toward the origin, toward the *hystera protera*, they are condemned to look ahead at the wall opposite, toward the back wall of the cave—the back which is also the front, the fore—toward the metaphorical project of the back of the cave, which will serve as a *backcloth* for all the representations to come. Heads forward, eyes front, genitals aligned, fixed in a straight direction and always straining forward, in a straight line. A phallic direction, a phallic line, a phallic time, backs turned on origin.

This project, or process, by which the *hystera* is displaced, transposed, transferred, metaphorized, always already holds them captive. The transposition of the anterior to the posterior, of the origin to the end, the horizon, the *telos*, envelops and encircles them; it is never susceptible of representation, but produces, facilitates, permits all representations since all are always already marked, or re-marked, in the incessant repetition of this same work of projection. Which yet is impossible, or cannot be completed at least. The *hystera*, faceless, unseen, will never be presented, represented as such. But the representational scheme and sketch for the *hystera*—which can never be fulfilled—sub-tends, englobes, encircles, connotes, overdetermines every sight, every sighting, face, feature, figure, form, presentification, presence. Blindly.

Certain men, then—sex undetermined (?)—are chained up in/by this transposition of the *hystera*. In no position to turn their heads, or anything else. Unable to turn, turn around, or return.

A Fire in the Image of A Sun

They have been given a *light*, however. It comes from a *fire* burning at a distance, behind and above them. A light indeed, but artificial and earthly. A weak light, and one that offers the eyes poor visibility, far from ideal conditions for seeing and being seen. Its distance and particularly its position in relation to the prisoners control the play of shadow in a specific way. It is a light that gives little light. That produces only shadows, reflections, fantasies, all of which are bigger than the *objects* figured in this way. Given the light's situation in relation to these objects, to the prisoners, to their gaze. And given the light's exposure in the earth. A fire, then, burns at a distance, behind the men and above them. *Like* the natural daylight, sunlight—afar, behind, above (at least in this place)—but meant to be only an artificial, artful reproduction of sunlight *inside* this translation, reversal, projection of the *hystera.* A fire lighted by the *hand of man* in the "image" of the sun. A *topographic mime,* but one whose process of repetition, reproduction, is always already multiply doubled up, divided, scaled down, demented, with no possible recourse to a first time, a first model. For if the cave is made in the image of the world, the world—as we shall see—is equally made in the image of the cave. In cave or "world" all is but the image of an image. For this cave is always already an attempt to re-present another cave, the *hystera,* the mold which silently dictates all replicas, all possible forms, all possible relation of forms and between forms, of any replica.

The Forgotten Path

Thus, in that cave, inside that cave, burns *a fire* "in the image of" *a* sun. But there is also *a path,* no doubt made in the image of the conduit, neck, passage, corridor which goes up (or rather would go down) out of the cave toward the light of day, toward the sight of day. Gallery, sheath, envelope-passage, enveloped, going from the daylight to the underground grotto and its fire. A conduit which is taken up and re-produced *inside* the cave. A repetition, representation, figuration re-enacted within the cave of that passage which we are told leads in and out of it. Of the path *in between.* Of the "go-between" path that links two "worlds," two modes, two methods, two measures of replicating, representing, viewing, in particular the sun, the fire, the light, the "objects," and the cave. Of this passage that is neither outside nor inside, that is between the way out and the way in, between access and egress. This is a key passage, even when it is neglected, or even especially when it is neglected, for when the passage is forgotten, by the very fact of its being reenacted *in* the cave, it will found, subtend, sustain the hardening of all dichotomies, categorical differences, clear-cut distinctions, absolute discontinuities, all the confrontations of irreconcilable representations. Between the "world outside" and the "world inside," between the "world above" and the "world below." Between the light of the sky and the fire of the earth. Between the gaze of the man who has left the cave and that of the prisoner. Between truth and shadow, between truth and fantasy, between "truth" and whatever "veils" the truth. Between reality and dream. Between. . . . Between. . . . Between the intelligible and the sensible. Between good and evil. The One and the many. Between anything you like. All oppositions that assume the *leap* from a worse to a better. An ascent, a displacement (?) upward, a progression along a line. Vertical. Phallic even? But what has been forgotten in all these oppositions, and with good reason, is how to pass through the passage, how to negotiate it—the forgotten transition. The corridor, the narrow pass, the neck.

Forgotten vagina. The passage that is missing, left on the shelf, between the outside and the inside, between the plus and the minus. With the result that all divergencies will finally be proportions, functions, relations that can be referred back to *sameness*. Inscribed, postulated in/by *one, same unit(y)*, synthesis or syntax. Dictating silently, invisibly, all the *filial* resemblances or differences. Even if it seems possible to name what articulates them, or see it represented: sun, for example. Or truth. Or good. Or father. Or phallus? For examples. Thus pointing to the so-called spring, or source, at the heart of difference? or at its womb? which would theoretically guarantee its action, especially its action as quite other. Or Other. But whatever assures the functioning of difference in this way is always already foreign to the multiple action of difference, or rather differences, because it will always already have been wrapped away in verisimilitude, once the neck, the corridor, the passage has been forgotten. License to operate is only granted to the (so-called) play of those differences that are measured in terms of *sameness* or that kowtow to analogy, of different analogies re-marked in the unrepresentable, invisible process of translating the *hystera*. It is within the project encircling, limiting the horizon in which the *hystera* is made metaphor, that this dance of difference is played out, whatever points of reference outside the system and the self are afforded for relating them one to another, bringing them together, making them metaphor. For metaphor—that transport, displacement of the fact that passage, neck, transition have been obliterated—is reinscribed in a matrix of resemblance, family likeness. Inevitably so. Likeness of the cave, likeness(es) within the cave, likeness(es) of the transfer of the cave. Likeness(es) of copies and reflections that have a part to play in the cave. Where man, *ho anthrópos*—sex unspecified, neuter if you will (*to genos?*) but turned to face only straight ahead—cannot escape a process of likeness, even though he re-presents or re-produces himself *as* like. He is always already a captive of repetition. Everything is acted out between rehearsal and performance, repetition and representation, or reproduction. Particularly since the representation designated as presence, or the presence making an appearance as representation, makes men forget, in an other or like act of forgetting, the foundation it rises out of. And unveiling so-called presence is merely entering into another *dream*. Which is always the same, even when it finds support in the visible, even if it pursues itself, with eyes wide open, in broad daylight, backed up with proofs of objectivity. This dream of sameness will end up in the fancy—or the inference, or indeed the deduction—that the neck, passage, conduit, that has been obliterated and forgotten, can be nothing but the one, the same, penis. Simply *turned inside out,* or *truncated*. For examples. One supposition is not explored: that it might possibly be a matter of a mirror both like and unlike. A concave mirror perhaps? Made to reflect a mirror both like and unlike. Let us say a convex mirror? But suppositions like that would certainly raise a few problems. With regard to the "object" of reflection, angles of divergence, and unforeseen error in focusing. These obviously could be played with to produce new differences, still within the pursuit of an old dream of symmetry that would in turn be complicated if it began to calculate and predict their effects. All through the re-intervention of the mirror or mirrors which, we must remember, is only one means of repetition among many. This is one representation of repetition, though a privileged one no doubt, and interpretation has still to get to the bottom of it, to see behind its mask of an unrepresentable desire for likeness.

But we're getting ahead of ourselves, and ahead of the story that Socrates has already put together so that things unfold in the right order. He guides you surefootedly along a well-blazed trail, according to a tried and true method. No surprises, no cracks are to be feared. He plays it all back *in reverse,* as it were, and with a certain irony, retracing his steps, confident of the destination, skirting all obstacles. The only risk you run is of finding yourselves at the end more cunningly enslaved than at the outset. Understudies in a mime that you yourselves confirm.

Paraphragm/Diaphragm

A path in this cavern runs *between* the fire and the prisoners. Reenactment *on the inside* of this scene of the conduit, passage, neck, leading to the sight of day. This path conforms to the topography of the other path, and a fire in the image of the sun or a sun hangs over it. Now it seems that along this similarly sloping track, a *little wall, teikhion,* is raised, barring the road, the way, the passage. A small wall, a wall-ette, *built* by man, that cannot be crossed or breached, that separates and divides without any possibility of access from the *other side*. The diminutive, "i," in the word *teikhion* is usually translated by little, or low, but it could also be rendered as thin, light, wholly unrelated to the massive walls around a city, for example. The wall of a private house or home: *teikhion*. A wall

248

that Plato in fact compares to a *curtain,* or *veil, hōsper ta paraphragmata.* A little wall "like" a curtain, or a curtain "like" a little wall? Which referent is primary in this analogy? No simple decision can be arrived at. This wallcurtain swallows up the conjuror's sleight of hand; this wallcurtain stands in the way, barring the path, by/for artifice. It is artfully, artificially fashioned by human hand. This wallcurtain or restraining wall or balustrade prevents the men who have raised it from having access to the back of the cave. Here the backcloth of representation.

Inside Plato's—or Socrates'—cave, an artificial wall curtain—reenactment, reprise, representation of a *hymen that has elsewhere been stealthily taken away,* is never, ever, crossed, opened, penetrated, pierced, or torn. Neither is it always already half open. The fragility, the tenuousness, or even transparence evoked by the diminutive—*teikhion*—and perhaps by the curtain comparison, relies upon the wholeness of this partition—an *inner* facade that not only reduces the opposition of inner and outer in scale as far as possible, but also reverses them—without any retrospective effects or pro-jects.

On one side, then, men pass, move about freely, we are led to believe, they are led to believe, restricted only by the ban on advancing further into the cave. On the other side, prisoners are chained up facing the back of the cave—a hollow space that is just as *closed off* as the wall curtain will remain *intact*—, backs to the fire, to the balustrade, to the men moving about behind it, and to the instruments of their prestige. Their backs are also turned, of course, to the origin, the *hystera,* of which this cave is a mere reversal, a project of figuration. Without cracks. A prison that these men can have no measure of, take no measures against, since they are restrained by other, or like, chains or images of chains from turning back to the opening of this grotto, from walking around to examine its topography, its deceptive pro-ject of symmetry. The a priori condition of the illusion governing and structuring this drama in mime. Fictive representation of the repetition that leads, and can only lead, to the contemplation of the Idea. Eternally fixed.

Chains, then, prevent the prisoners from turning around toward the entrance to the cave, as well as toward the origin. And toward the sun, the fire, the path running up to it, the wall curtain, the men moving about behind it and the "objects" they use in their tricks. Behind them is all this, and they are forbidden not only to look at it but to move toward it. And this makes possible a certain number of *permutations* as well *as confusions as to the function,* the functioning, *of what is behind,* and what behind is. Invisible.

The Magic Show

Behind them are men. And they are doubly behind: behind them and behind the partition. But this *twofold* distance can in no way be unfolded into twice one is two, for the division operated by the partition *within* the cave is never transgressed.

Between the prisoners and those men who are situated *behind,* some kind of show will be put on provided one accepts that the "little wall" or "curtain" that in other instances cannot be crossed may be leant over, looked over. Sublimated perhaps? The show will take place over the wall, if the "objects" are *raised high enough.* But this wall is not supposed to be very high. At least it has been usual to translate thus in terms of verticality the "i" diminutive in *teikhion* and perhaps the *hōsper ta para-phragmata.* So the wall will be got over. But not really. It won't be climbed or leaped. The men, the men's "bodies," will remain beind this screen. But by thrusting their bodies *high enough,* the men will succeed in getting across the screen some symbol, reproduction, fetish of their "bodies" or those of other living animals. It is this erected effigy of their bodies whose shadow, produced by the fire burning behind and above, will appear in profile upon the posterior side of the cave, in its new role as projection screen. Between these *two screens* that are not twice one— the screen that reproduces and multiplies cannot be added up with the screen that subtracts and divides—, the chained men are on show/at the show.

Their eyes are dim, it is true, but if they were not looking, fascinated, rapt in fascination with what they see opposite them, then the projected shadows, the reflections, phantoms, would lose the attraction of their appearances, the reality of their phantasmic power. Those shadows come from the interception of the firelight by the effigied emblem—immortalized in its deathly duplication—of men whose ancestor seems successfully to have raised *above a screen-horizon* this prestigious fake, *this lasting morphological impress.*[3] What cunning and utterly convincing necromancers these are who sacrifice (even themselves) to the greatness of their specters and thereby rob, rape, and rig the perspicacity of their public, blinding it with their exhibitions. Here are stealthy sandmen, working in the half-light of mid-night. Solar masks. But they are cut off from the stage by a curtain that, here, is opaque. Hidden from the eyes they charm but equally kept away from seeing their own show, the effects of their

[3](In translating "simulacre" I have preferred "fake" to the usual "simulacrum" because "fake" seems to convey that note of moral condemnation Plato has when talking of the life of the body. The word "impress" translates "estampage," a pun meaning both branding, stamping (the male form places a stamp upon the female matter) and also swindling, fleecing.—Tr.)

own sorcery. Their clearsightedness is busy in the wings with modeling
the form of their replica(s) into the very fiction of verisimilitude. They
form artful attributes, eclipsing the light of the fire—the sun's image?—
which etches their shadows on the back of the cave. Copy cats copied in
their turn by reflections that steal out of reach of the miracle-workers.

The deception, the make-believe, works on at least *three* levels here.
Let us for a moment (pretend to) fix our attention upon that number.
Obviously this three cannot be interpreted as three times one. The magician, whose position behind and/or in front already cries out to be analyzed in terms of *doubling-back,* substitutes for himself the instruments of
his power, which are deceptive because they claim to be such perfect
copies. Already a man's gaze is lost in them. By intercepting light that
allows for clear vision, these deceptive figures are doubled by their own
shadows. Fiction engenders fiction. Projections, reflections, fantasies.
But of whom? of what? Of the prisoners too, between the fire and the
surface that reproduces the images? The wall face works all too well. It
multiplies all by itself. The protagonists don't understand what is going
on. No one knows any longer who is the deceiver and who the deceived.
How are the parts being cast? To whom or what is the projection to be
attributed? All aid and abet a simulation that continues unaided and
whose cause always already goes back earlier, ever backward into the
cloud-filled future past of ever darkening projects.
Meanwhile, on that set-up stage of men's representation, we find a
minimum of two men: the two only seem to be the product of an addition—and/or one or the other of them is half—but which half? half of
what? since the whole business is based on indivision—effigied, half-
blinded, half robbed-raped, half cut in on the deal. These two men, twice
two halves of men to the *n*th power (or power renounced?) *uphold the
process of mimēsis* from each side of a wall curtain in which their strat-
egems are lost in infinite regression. This facade doubles, redoubles,
infinitely reverses the opposition of inner and outer, all within the symmetrical closure of this theater.
Such operations of division can always be played with and played back
to provide some stake in this game that is always already rigged. Endlessly giving the game away. Betting, on nothing, till kingdom come.
Mortgaging into insolvency this twisted cave of Plato's—or Socrates'.
And no one will take his cave away from him, even counting with
imaginary numbers. For in this cavern the tricks are many and can never

be reduced or added up or multiplied simply together, although the numerous different parts being played advance the size and authority of the effects in effect. Each time in these plural operations of deception, the passage from imitating to imitated, from present to past, is withheld. Dazzling trompe-l'oeil!

A Waste of Time?

The show is also a pass-time. Thus, the repetition of origin, or the origin of repetition, only gives an illusion of being arrested in its symmetrical reproduction—Plato's *hystera*. Representation only stops repetition by extrapolation. Sameness is prescribed and reenacted therein, but it is also held in reserve and lives on in a primordial presence that will determine all replicas but will never be exhausted. There is always some *to spare*. Over and above—*auxiliary to being*—any withdrawal that will be made. In the meantime, between time.

But time is still there all the same, held in suspense. The fiction that man and his copy are equivalent immortalizes time's attributes. Thereby putting the sun in eclipse, though the sun provides the rhythm of the calendar too: day/night, seasons, years. Like and unlike, like returning as unlike. Fetishes and ghosts will thus argue over dead time. And penumbra. O! *Impoverished present, copula in effigy only, statement in a state of rigor mortis.* Who can parse subject and predicate, or their doubles, when all are doubly dead? This makes for no deed of title, of course, since the doubling up is obviously not twice one death, but perhaps an attempt to share out what is commonly known as death. The fission of one between two deaths, the spacing out of one dead between two. The effraction within a death cave. And the operation is necessarily one of indivision.

This is not all. The reenactment within the cave of the path which might lead in, out of, or back to it, that access and egress from the cave, condemns the two-way movement of its use, the beat of its opening/closing. A ban on pulsations, rhythmic intervals that are unlike and yet again the same. The artifact of the path, and the partition *within* the grotto cannot, of course, take over this function. The partial, man-made opening of a division/multiplication merely perpetuates and indeed lends credit, ad infinitum, to the cave's reversing operation and thus sustains the snare constituted by its symmetrical pro-ject and the closure of its representation. It always operates *inside* the cave. It re-marks the breaking into fractions, speculates on its potency, tries to anticipate the split, the bar, and to take advantage of it. Sometimes by breaking and entering. But always *inside*. All such interventions *defer penetration*. They contract to penetrate, but never in fact come through. For the wall curtain

remains impregnable. And never will the *paraphragma* offer a sure replacement for a certain *diaphragma*.

We are really wasting our time with this show, which is intended as a
preliminary education in reminiscence. There is the odd hitch in the
system, of course. For the holes, cracks, tears—in the *diaphragma* for
example—or the faults and failings of the *hysterein* must, in their turn, be
re-marked, reinscribed. Particularly in the memory. Which is not to say
that they will or can be represented, but that by their very elimination,
their very reserve, they will set up the economy of that representation.
Even in the term used to designate its goal, its ultimate profit—*a-lētheia*—, not forgotten, without the veil of forgetfulness. The *negative and
negating* constituent of *alētheia* must not be left out of consideration. Thus
the outlawed element—called the slave and the repressed in other symbolic systems—rules without appeal or recall the very text that outlaws
it. This becomes clear if we question its overdetermination, and unmask
the figures, forms, signs, that ensure its present coherence.

A Specular Cave

Such an enterprise is never simple, but it will be simpler here than
elsewhere because of the plural relationship this scene has to origin. Here
is theater, text, that has yet to reflect or reflect upon its perspective. Here
the properties of the eye, of mirrors—and indeed of spacing, of space-
time, of time—are dislocated, disarticulated, disjointed, and only later
brought back to the perspective-free contemplation of the truth of the
Idea. Idea eternally present, postulated by the separation, the dismem-
bering of, on the one hand, the "amorphous" but insistent anteriority of
the *hystera,* that unrepresentable origin of all forms and all morphology,
and, on the other hand, the dazzling fascination of the Sun—image of
Good—who must be there across the way if we are to see good/well.
Eidos, ever identical to itself, like unto itself, ensuring the identity of
repetition, ensuring that what may be repeated is, while at the same time,
in a dialectical trick we must come back to, constituting itself as matrix—
in front, turned inside out and backward—, origin in its turn, as well as
cause, invisible, of all proper visibility. Outside the perception of the
mortal eye, positioned opposite and above, vertically (is this phallicism
squared?), here is the light of evidence by which all vision will have to be
polarized if it is to remain clear, in a right appreciation of "beings," in a

straight and true direction: *orthotēs*. Harmonious conjunction and in fact confusion of the *hystera* and the sun in an *ecstasy of copula*. Invisible and indivisible ideality—whose distinct parts can never be seen (again) on inspection—cause and pole, whether inverted or not, of the straightness of vision. Being, one, simple, unalterable, beyond analysis, permanent. Is this the extrapolated—or even sublimated?—replica of an *insoluble primal scene?*

But there, in the *apaideusia* of the cave, Being is tested by being split up into offspring, copies, and fakes. These disperse and miniaturize the potency of the gaze. Of mirrors. Of eyes "like" mirrors, that are not, always already, broken and articulating the break, but rather are artificially disjointed and divided into properties offering an illusion of analysis, and addition, and multiplication, up to the highest power. The unit!

Thus a bony cavernous socket encloses the eye. An inside-out socket, in this case, in which the gaze is swallowed up in a vault. Projection sphere for the *hystera protera:* the *hystera* that has been inverted and turned backward by Plato. An enclosure, veil-wrapping of the originary blind incarceration, which has been turned over to become the circus and backdrop of representation. A motionless retina, a reticulum without nerves, a mere concave surface, reflecting light and shadows. An opaque rearview mirror. *Light off.* A horizon that blocks light, and sight into the bargain. Limiting the view but ensuring the reproduction by *reflection* of what is claimed to take place behind. The painted figure, the fake, the seductive fantasy will serve to intercept retroactive effects whose twists and turns will be kept not only from the men chained up, staring in captive fascination at the wall opposite them, but also from the magicians, eternally hidden by the screen from their own stratagems. That screen is not even unsilvered glass. It is better thought of as the back of the mirror(s). Or as a *water-tight* bulkhead, as a *paraphragma* impervious to all blows, even in retrospect. A fiction, a fictive fission both before and after the fact. An attempt to master the blow in its division and duplication. Cutting, dismemberment. An operation with an excess of terms and *remainders*. Indefinitely. The protection screen is fit to engender (only) the replica, the replica of the replica. Indefinitely. The screen that subtracts, divides and defends, sends back phantasmatic off-spring by projection—as remainders, over and above—onto the screen that reproduces and multiplies. Such products are good enough for blind eyes to gape at. Clearsightedness works on the sly, from the wings. There are twice two half-gazes. A wide-eyed gaze, an averted gaze.

The *paraphragma* is also an eyelid. Built of stone. A veil permanently drawn, never open by so much as a crack. An inorganic, mineral mem-brane. A dead tissue, dead like all the others delimiting or dividing this scene; and they *organize* this representation artfully. Stiff, rigid mem-branes, *frozen* by the "likes" or "as ifs" of evocation and figuration that have always already got in the way. Consisting in/by the inter-position of a certain *speculum* which, *naturally* has already been enveloped. Every-thing on the inside here is already re-silvered. Closed up, folded back upon some kind of specular intuition. *A specularity of intuition that has yet to reflect its perspective and has yet to be interpreted into an intuition of spec-ularity.* No mirror offers itself to be seen and read in this speleology. And the truth of what we see depends on this.

But this cave is already, and ipso facto, a speculum. An inner space of reflection. Polished, and polishing, fake offspring. Opening, enlarging, contriving the scene of representation, the world as representation. All is organized into cavities, spheres, sockets, chambers, enclosures, simply because the speculum is put in the way. The operation is abortive—naturally—since only reflection is safe and spawns misbegotten freaks, abortive products before and after the fact. This cave intercepts the games of copula in a miming of reproduction and in each figuration of the inner space the image of the Sun engenders sham offspring. This mime simulates offspring beyond appeal and recall, pretends to defer them by/for some kind of anamnesia. Irretrievably. For has reminiscence not always already engaged in rapturous contemplation of the Idea? The eternally present Idea? Target, or vanishing point, and death, that domi-nates this preliminary education. Existence from the beginning but de-void of any family context. A margin outside inscription which like a star both guides and at the same time strikes to the ground, frames and freezes all forms of replicas, all possible relation between the forms of replicas. Limning and limiting the show, the dialogue, the language outside time or place in its extrapolation of light. Or else stealthily open-ing it up into an abyss of blinding whiteness at every step, or letter, or look. *Matrix. Or given the name of matrix. Yet virgin of presence.* Ravishing anything which has yet to be targeted and measured. Or which seems that way, at least. The projection screen is a mirage that conceals the part played by the mirrors that have always already produced and framed it "as such."

This accounts for the fact that they all remain motionless in that enclosure, fixed in the being-prisoners attitude they have been cast for, *frozen* by the effects of symmetry that they do not realize are directing this theater of remembrance. The prison that holds them is the illusion that the evocation and the repetition (of origin) are equivalent. They sit riveted by the fascination of what they see opposite. By the semblance of what is apparently taking place behind and by its projection which, by pretending to be immediate presence, presentation, steals the economy of both before and after the fact. Foils the interaction of relationships between repetition and representation, or reproduction, and perverts its prescriptions and balances. The end, the unrepresentable Idea, guarantees that replicas and copies are engendered and conform, and the fiction of the being-present masks the ancestry of its reproduction-production, with repetition left over and to spare. Time, space-time are side-tracked by a symmetrical process ordering representation elsewhere, or correlatively, are seduced, captivated, caught, in the lustrous glow of the Idea, of the Sun. *Brilliance of silver-backing in suspension.* Surety—of daylight?—put up and never paid back. Preventing metaphor and phony analogies from drifting away. *Sun, anchor of origin.* Closing off and arresting the cycle of phallic scenography and its system of light metaphors in an *unreflected* glare. Everything in this circus will sustain the blinding snare. Fetish-objects, wall curtain, screens, veils, eyelids, images, shadows, fantasies are all so many barriers to intercept, filter, sift the all-powerful incandescence, to charm and shield the eyes while at the same time displaying and recalling, even from behind such masks, its own cause and goal. The gaze is ringed by a luminous, infinitely reverberating blindness. By a dazzling orbit.

The Dialogues

One Speaks, the Others Are Silent

"While carrying their burdens, some of them, as you would expect, are talking, others silent." As you would expect. Really and truly? Yes, you would expect it, given the systems of duplication, the rules of duplicity, that organize this cave. For if everyone talked, and talked at once, the background noise would make it difficult or even impossible for the doubling process known as an echo to occur. The reflection of sound would be *spoiled* if different speakers uttered different things at the same time. Sounds would thereby become ill defined, fuzzy, inchoate, indistinct, devoid of figures that can be reflected and reproduced. If everyone spoke, and spoke at once, the silence of the others would no longer form the *background* necessary to highlight or outline the words of some, or of one. Silence or blanks function here in two ways to allow replication. *Of likeness.* (Note that these two ways cannot be analyzed into twice once; the silence of the magicians cannot simply be added to that of the back of the cave.)

And moreover the *echo*—which mythology has linked to a woman who dies a virgin for love of Narcissus—would be hindered by the fact that these enchanters talked to each other. The interference of speech, of what goes on and gets across in conversation, could no longer be reduced to that *neutral* blank, that *neutral* silence which allows words and their repetition to be discriminated and separated out and framed. This is how the illusion is sustained that there are specific terms for each thing and each one, which can be reproduced as such. Thus, the present of production-reproduction would be destroyed not just because the effects of retroaction had become so complex but even more because of the part played in the drama of interventions by factors of pluridetermination and overdetermination. This would apply in the hiatus, the supposed break and joint between a present and a past—an imitating and an imitated, a signifier and a signified—whereby the present takes up, repeats, *specularizes,* the past which is defined as a present that has taken place. But it would equally work to open up this present or past, spread it out, unfold it in the suspense of insoluble, unresolvable correlations, between a preterit and a future perfect tense, as well as between a future perfect and a preterit. If these "men carrying burdens" talked to each other, at least at this point in Socrates' tale, they would interpret and unmask the mimetic function that organizes the cave.

So some speak and others are silent. Someone or other speaks, the others do not. Thus the possibility of the replica is set up. Unless, that is, the silent offer that possibility by taking the place of a reflecting screen.

And so it goes in Plato's *Dialogues,* even the ones that mimic a conversation on mimesis. As you might have expected. Naturally. The phrase *hoion eikos* immediately translates, betrays, and conceals the question of a mimicry of sound and language within the economy of exchanges, notably verbal exchanges. And it will be a long time before the backing behind this apparent "naturalness" begins to be questioned, before the problem is raised about the relationships between mimicry, representation and communication. But the hysteric—derived from *hystera*, as you might have expected—will deceptively, covertly, bring up the forgotten dilemma.

"You have shown me a strange image, and they are strange prisoners," he says. Here the "image" previously *described* is reframed as image. The summary, somewhat in the manner of a retort, gives support for belief in a "good" mimesis in language. And inscribes, furtively, surreptitiously, silently, through the indirection of a so-called fanciful reproduction, through the credibility of equivalence vested in that repeat, the place, the illusion of a place, the delusion of a place of transcendental significance. Working out of sight and, perhaps, out of speech, this place is claimed to dominate, exceed, and guarantee discourse. Glowing bright and white, the "truth" of the Idea therein reserves itself, keeps itself in reserve, in store, as the—extrapolated—source of sight. Of night. Of the economy of relationships between white and black, as well as between white and white, black and black. Between whites, blacks, and sight. What we define "as" meaning is made possible in this way, as are the signs that seem to mark it in a privileged way and to (re)produce it. The system is an extrapolation of the *white* light that cannot be seen as such but allows us to see and gives us an awareness of the black. Black plays no further part; its guarantee is suspended; or rather has always already been staked elsewhere in the writing of the text that will neither be seen nor mimed, *in truth*.

Like Ourselves They Submit to a Like Principle of Identity

"They are like ourselves," he replied. As you might have expected. Naturally. Why should the process of likeness stop or be contradicted here? Why should those telling, representing the scene, not be equated with those they are talking about? Why should they not serve to endorse the conformity of their words? Unless it is that they have been set up as equivalents by the identity, the principle of identity, governing their discourse. Or that they come by this "likeness"—they who are like ourselves who are ourselves alike—through a regulated alternation of replicas in which interference and the background noise of the conversation are turned down, right from the start. The "we" and the "I replied" would have no other strategic aim than to disguise and sustain at one and the same time the priority or the apriorism of sameness.

"They are like ourselves," I replied. And just as we believe that mime, even if indirectly, can take us back into reality and imagine that we evoke and recall it even in the language of figures, so also have they failed to take the measure of that fiction constituted by the reversing projection of the *hystera protera* or to take measures against it. Yet this project prescribes and overdetermines, in silence, the whole system of metaphor. Shutting it in, like the "prisoners" in Plato's cave. Chained up like ourselves—I might say—backs to the origin, staring forward. Chained up more specifically by the effects of a certain language, of certain norms of language that are sometimes called *concatenation,* or chain of propositions, for example.

"Do you think they"—any more than ourselves?—"have seen anything of themselves and of one another, except the shadows which the fire throws on the opposite wall of the cave?" Never have these "prisoners" *envisaged* anything but the reflections, shadows, fancies of objects that are (always already) made, represented-reproduced (always already) behind them. And this thanks to the light of a fire burning not only behind them, but also (always already) behind the "objects" that are manufactured and produced by the magicians. The fire is said to be artificial, a firework in the image of the sun. That is also behind. This setup in which the *hystera* is reversed fuels the confusion between a certain origin defying representation and the daylight, the good clear light of representation. The confusion between fire and light, the fire of the origin and the light of day. Fire comes in only as light, lit in the image of the sun. There is *one* fire, *one* sun, and moreover the one somehow comes out of the other. The sun sires fire, as a bastard son, in an artful retroversion of genealogy. Seeing (daylight) would become the single cause of origin. Forgotten is the force used to pivot the scene around axes of symmetry, ignored is that fission, that split—or pseudo-split—that duplicity which is already ahead of the game and in which the Sun would theoretically be Father, God, procreator of all. Or at least everything

acted out on this stage. The other, and the move from the female one to
the other, are forgotten upon this theater of representation where light,
which lets us see, holds center stage. And the scene *incurs a debt* when it
reproduces the other scene, and the passage, corridor, neck, leading in
and out of it. That passage joins the two scenes together, but not, of
course, by merely swiveling around axes of symmetry.

Provided They Have a Head, Turned in the Right Direction

In Plato's cave, men—sex unspecified—gaze at shadows projected
opposite them on the back of the cave. The fire behind produces nothing
but shadows and gazes fascinated by shadows. And whether it be
through their own eyes or through the eyes of their companions, the
men can see only the projection of the light of the fire striking "objects,"
"figures," that are always already manufactured. Behind.

What else could they see, considering that every one of them is kept in
that same position? They are seated, looking fixedly across from them,
backs to a supposedly like origin, one and the same, and to the path
reenacted within the cave, to its partition, to the magicians, to the instruments of their prestige, and to their spells. Which are of course always
the same. Thus the men can *see* the same images, shadows, fancies,
through the eyes of others. Within this *twisted* cave of Plato's, all are
identical to, identified with, prisoners who are the same and other. The
community of men is caught in the snare of a symmetrical project that
they could only glimpse by turning their heads. But these men are
chained above all by the intractibility of repetition, by the overdetermination of the one by the other, which both fascinates and escapes
them. No sun will ever reduce this overdetermination to an exact truth
of perception, to a "nature" clearly seen.

The most striking effect of their being thus forced to keep their heads
still all their lives seems to be to set up the scene of representation, since
this depends upon the side, the face, the figure, the gaze being turned in
the right direction around some axis or pivot. And the confusion about
position and orientation, of opposite and behind, front and back, seems
to breed fakes and fancies that *good sense and proper orientation* could clear
up. What is more, the head has to be correctly turned, and modeled (for
that turn), and styled, moved in the right way—which is the wrong
way. The head is turned around to suit the illusion *on the opposite side* that
the prisoners stare at. It would take a general, comprehensive survey to
get back to the true, to remember the truth that we have been artificially
led away from. You would have to have completed the whole circuit, by

in fact doing two half-circuits, or circles. For it is an illusion that you can close the circle, return to the same point, the same "truth." The truth of sameness, which has always already artfully prescribed the detour needed for its re-cognition. Yet it takes advanced gymnastics to reduce the turn away from origin and back to the sun and come up with a propaedeutic that puts a ring around the truth. And when difference dodges and twirls between two poles, process and project plunge down, destroying a truth that orders them. Viciously. The axis authorizing this pirouette, dominated in the vertical plane by the sun, dazzles us into neglecting the break effected by that volte-face, and the reduction of its ellipse.

Thus there is *one single upright,* standing straight and erect, with the stage pivoting around it, and its relation to the sun, the solar tropism, apparently determines the correct orientation. *One* spindle *only* rises toward *one* sun, but it has always already been tricked and truncated by the duplicity of a project that relies upon its function and its functioning, as such. *One single spindle,* but one that always runs the risk of being fractured should the foundation collapse under some dream of symmetry that has artificially struck its joints together and disguised its piecemeal construction. For taking the detour that includes the back of the cave, the road out of the cave and the (so-called) return to the sun also involves taking a few other lines, routes, tracks that cannot be traced back to the unit(y) without incurring liabilities. Even if the unit(y) were that of a direct route, or of a correct orientation. The end of the story will show this.

What Is = What They See, and Vice Versa

"Then, if these prisoners were able to talk to each other—*dialegesthai*—about what they see, don't you think that they would call—*nomizein*—what they see what is—*ta onta*—?" "Inevitably." *Ananke.* The peremptory affirmation of this inevitability attests to another vicious circle (other and yet the same) that supports and confirms the maneuverings to get around its aporias. And just as it was natural, probable that among the magicians certain should speak—or a certain one should speak—and others be silent, so it is essential to re-mark, reduplicate, replicate the necessity of the relationship between, on the one hand, the possibility of talking to each other and, on the other, of giving the name "beings" to what one sees as beings. It has been demonstrated earlier that sight is the same for all the men in chains, and in fact for all of us who are identical to them as they are to each other.

A whole conception of language here halts—or runs up against—the illusion of a system of metaphor, a meta-metaphor, postulated by the preexistence of the truth that *decides* in advance how conversation, interventions, will develop. These "inters" are dictated by a specular genealogy, by a process of images, reflections, reduplications which are rated in terms of their conformity, equivalence and appropriateness to the true that is meant to be uncovered. These "inters" can be calculated or combined as proportions of a more or less correct relation to the sameness (of the Idea); they are always cross-referenced with the ideal of truth which determines their enumeration, their measure, their analogic and dialectical pertinence and, as a consequence, the order, the hierarchy, the subordination of the interventions by which differences are regulated and declinable as more or less "good" copies. Copies, that is, of the same, the identical, the one, the permanent, the unalterable, the undecomposable. The Being. Whose names, representations, and figures,—along with their differences, their intervals, their syntax and dialogic—re-mark, signpost, stagger the divisions of the *gap,* which is always to be *reduced,* between the appearance of truth and the truth that it veils.

The A-lētheia, a Necessary Denegation among Men

Once the possibility of a conversation has been framed and unalterably fixed in position then the *alētheia* that has secretly helped to set all this up will soon put in an appearance, in the dialogue at least, and be named a pawn in a game and on a chessboard. In fact, of course, *alētheia* not only is the game's main stake but also determines its layout, its principles, and its modus operandi. *Alētheia* will come into play when *denomination* occurs but in fact, silently, it has determined the whole functioning of the language, its terminology, its syntax, its dramatization. Yet this exorbitant power is hidden in the fact that it is *also* used as metaphor and evoked and recalled. Not without the assistance of a (de)negation: the word is *a-lētheia.*

When the thing that determines all the logic and affirmation of discourse can successfully be expressed therein by means of *a (de)negation,* this enormously enlarges the scope of the game underway. As long as the efficacy of that operation is never queried. As long as no one seeks to interpret how equivocal is the *formality* by which veils are theoretically lifted, notably the veils of oblivion, error, and mendacity. Of fantasy. As long as no measure is taken of the fact that using representations in utterance (even if it be) by means of negation/denial, in order to repeat what tacitly determines them, does not undermine that domination but in fact increases its weight and reinforces its status. Such repetition entails the interminable developments of a discourse that is predicted, enveloped, rolled up in its project, and whose modes of exposition, demonstration, and transformation will be nothing but different versions of its deeds of credit. But their function as *simulations* will itself never be unveiled as *cause,* even, or especially, if it is designated by the term *unveiling.*

The economy of this optical jiggery-pokery now demands that the *alētheia* be named. We will have to wait only for the next trick of deduction, or the next paragraph. But this particular paragraph is really worth its weight in *gold,* for it under-lies the whole Socratic dialectic: nothing can be named as "beings" except those same things which all the same men see in the same way in a setup that does not allow them to see other things and which they will designate by the same names, on the basis of the conversation between them. Whichever way up you turn these premises, you always come back to *sameness.*

Even Her Voice Is Taken Away from Echo

"And suppose further that the prison had an echo which came from the other side." From the wall facing them, blocking their view, circumscribing the gaze, the show, the scene. What if the back of the cavern, that project reversing the unrepresentable origin, that backcloth for all representations, had, moreover, an echo? The fantasies it would permit—to which it would offer its reflecting screen, the polished whiteness of its surface—would emit sounds, the words pronounced by the magicians. By those men who carry effigies, placed between the opening of the cave, its fire, its path on the one hand and the partition, the prisoners, the back of the cave, on the other hand. The shadow-reflections of their marvelous tricks, which trace and outline both themselves and the *silent virginity* of the back of the cave, begin to speak, we are told, eclipsing the staggered artificial system of their productions-reproductions. Shadows of statues, of fetish-objects, these and none other would henceforth be named truth—*to aléthes*—by the men in chains. Projections of symbols for men's bodies, raised high enough so that they show over the top of the little wall so as to dominate and sublimate it—though the wall has been raised in the cave artificially—would, theoretically, be the only possible representation of the truth for the prisoners because they provide, in addition, the echo of the words pronounced by the same men. The echo is possible because of the reflecting property, the so-called *virginity and muteness of that back of the matrix/womb* which a man, an *obstetrician,* turned round, backward and upside down in order to make it into the stage, the chamber, the stronghold of representation.

In all events, the womb has been played with, made metaphor and mockery of by men. At least *three* men, if this time you count the stage director. But this three is only apparently a sum. And the one nearest the back of the cave, the one with the heaviest chains, the one bound with the strongest fascination to the depths of that crypt, will be so strongly persuaded that the shenanigans of the other are the truth that he will lose all the senses that the "others" pretend still to control. But at this point in the drama, as quite often in fact, it is hard to decide who is weaving the web of illusion and who is caught in it.

But before everything goes mad in this cave, to a point where a possible resumption of the dialectic would demand that the way out of it be considered, at least for an exemplary prisoner, there is this: The projections of the statufied emblems of men's bodies will be designated by the term *truth* only if they can be lent voices, *echoes* of the words pronounced by the magician-imagemakers. Thus, to state everything quite clearly, only the effigies of men's bodies, the words of men, the gaze of men— whose sex is no doubt undetermined, except in the formalization of their gender?—will be available to decide on what is true and false and to make the question of the *parousia* of truth unavoidable. All of this demands, of course, that both a *paraphragm* and the *back* serve as virginal and mute screens and thus keep the strategies operating successfully. It is indispensable to keep magicians and prisoners permanently separated by means of an impenetrable partition, and to offer fantasies and voices the reliable assistance of the furthest wall of the cave. These two screens must come into play, must figure between the (at least two, two halves of) men if the relation acted out between them is to include the question of truth, is to allow truth to make an appearance.

But of necessity—*pollē anankē*—truth will be unequivocally obvious only if the emission of sounds is made an attribute of the fantasies. Sound (*phōnē*) gives fantasies a character of pure and immediate presence that masks the artificial mechanisms, the reduplications, the repetition-reproduction procedures, to say nothing of the obliterations that *contrive* their elaboration. If it speaks, the semblance will represent truth, even if everything was excluded. Sound—taken away from Echo here or elsewhere—indicates the presence of truth, which requires the privilege enjoyed by the *phōnē*. Truth and *phōnē* sustain and determine their mutual domination, at least when it is a matter of ensuring the present existence, the presence of the existence of the *alētheia*. Of establishing once and for all the *parousia* of the idea (of) truth, of the ideal of truth. Given that this is so, some concession, some appeal in fact, must be made to that *elementary matter, the air*. At least to the extent to which the element will already be disturbed, subjected to rhythm, number, and harmony, already altered mimetically. Trans-formed into sounds which, once elaborated into language—whether in lexicon or syntax—will immediately be enslaved to the idea of verisimilitude. Thus sound's only prerogative is to function as a relay station, a detour that is indispensable in guaranteeing the previous existence of the *alētheia,* which will henceforth take command of all "beings," including voices. Once founded and named, the power of truth will enslave and eclipse the instrument that established its authority. Truth will exist, an eternal presence, without that material element, reduced to the medium of one of its manifestations: the realization of voice.

A Double Topographic Error, Its Consequences

Now, in that cave, let us not forget that this *parousia* rests on the indirect authority of men's words, heard by men and lent to fantasies which men produce and see. Moreover, it is men who lend credit to the *parousia* as such, specifically when they name it. This is how the system and the transactions of the recognition of truth operate. And, let us note, its justification is to sanction, organize, regulate, and arbitrate the relationships between men, particularly by means of theorization. And this is so in the *polis* as well as in the cave. An ideal of truth is in fact necessary to under-lie and legitimize the metaphors, the figures used to represent the role of women, without voice, without presence. The feminine, the maternal are instantly *frozen* by the "like," the "as if" of that masculine representation dominated by truth, light, resemblance, identity. By some dream of symmetry that itself is never ever unveiled. The maternal, the feminine serve (only) to keep up the reproduction-production of doubles, copies, fakes, while any hint of their material elements, of the womb, is turned into scenery to make the show more realistic. The *womb,* unformed, "amorphous" origin of all morphology, is transmuted by/for analogy into a circus and a projection screen, a theater of/for fantasies. The little wall, the *paraphragm*—a replica within the cave of a diaphragm that has been secretly eliminated elsewhere—enables, perpetuates, gives added range and relief to representation by artificially opening up a division/multiplication *within* the cave, by infinitely scaling down the opposition of external/internal as well as by resorting to the theurgic, astrological device of putting them into infinite regression, in order to keep up the attractions of the shows parading past the wall. Like an impenetrable eyelid, this paraphragm makes magicians and darkroom disappear. It is a veil that will not tear, will certainly never open but will distract the eye from its function. *A screen that sets men gazing in different directions*—some gazing "off," into the wings/some gazing in fascination—preventing them from glimpsing each other, from mingling, taking each other's measure, except by means of the *interposed object-fetish* that captures and hides the light. Twice two half—or halved?—gazes are blinded so as to give infinite scope to the show.

As for the *path,* that reproduction *within* the cave of the passage, conduit, neck that rises—or should, rather, descend—out of the crypt toward the light of day, toward the sight of day, if that path is given a metaphor or a name, it remains nonetheless in the very back, *shrinking away* from the scene being played out. It has been led astray once again. *Forgotten, set back, and then set further back again,* both included within and excluded from the cave. Serving, of course, by its slope to ensure the fire's glow but seeing very little traffic up to now. It is just possible to envisage, or deduce, that the path has been occasionally trodden by the magicians. But the attention of the protagonists is not directed toward it, is in fact turned away from it. Indeed the path's position in the cave betrays a *double error,* a *double faux-pas,* on the part of the play's director, despite all his expertise in mimicry. So we are forced to understand, and conclude, that the error is a necessary part of the *parousia* of truth, which relies on *this path's being included within the theater* of representation and at the same time *thrown back onto the other side of the paraphragm.* As a result of some ill-placed mimetic scruple or of some fallacious exhaustion contributing to the scene's closure, the path must have its appropriate copy *within* the cave, but it must have neither access to nor function in the process of reproduction-production that takes place on that scene. It seems clear that this path is not the way out to daylight and that the journey to the presence of truth takes advantage of topographic gaps which will never be taken into consideration.

Equally unaccounted for is the whole sexual scenography of which the gaps are a privileged symptom. And no explicit terms will be used to make the prisoners understand that they are taking the false for the true, like untutored children. The objection that will be raised to counter their "opinions" is never traced back to its premises or related to the sexual economy which it simultaneously conceals and upholds. That objection will be based upon a failure to differentiate between a "good" and a "bad" mimesis, between a "faithful" reproduction of the truth—a copy that allows truth to appear underneath the mask—and the fantasies, fakes, shadows, copies of copies of objects which are already artificially fabricated, mimed, and merely to contemplate which leads to madness.

The madness of the "men in chains," for example. Such men are not even in a position to take the measure of their insanity—*aphrosunē.*—since they are under the spell of magic tricks and have nothing to oppose or compare to them, no "other" truth, nothing truer, no "vision" of truth. They are still in that state of *apaideusia* which does not allow fakes and copies, reduplications of the truth, to be distinguished from truth itself.

But this truth, which it is madness to fail to recognize—madness being a kind of excess, of drifting away from all relation to truth, unpegged to truth's standard—would always already have covered over, erased (or sublimated?) the scene of another, forgotten, "truth" or "reality," whose fate is secured and sealed by the discourse of Socrates. The *alētheia* in the very negation/denial that it speaks, may be interpreted as the affirmation of a possibility of reviewing what has been forgotten within an economy of representation that prescribes its neglect. The *a-lētheia* would theoretically function henceforth as *the bond offered as security for what has been forgotten* in the Socratic dialectic from the dawn of Western photological systematics, as the representation of representation which keeps the sun from the place(s) of its tropical beat(s). Forcing the sun in some manner to spin around, to turn eternally in its own orbit, forever to return to the same point in the circle where it would always already have been placed in order to keep every system in order, including, paradoxically, its own. The sun is fixed, frozen, the keystone supporting the whole—phallic—edifice of representation that it dominates, illumines, warms, makes fertile, and regulates by scattering its beams everywhere. No return is possible. No reverberation is powerful enough to bend the sun in its course, modify the autarchy of its fire. And the sun itself is assumed to have no other need or desire than to move in a circle, to come back upon itself, whatever heliotropism it has produced elsewhere. Attracting everything to itself, never deviating from its path. Indefinitely circumscribing the earth, offering the rhythm of days and nights, seasons, years. Of time, which always comes back to the same thing. At least for those things that are supposed to measure time, to record it, repeat it, close the cycle. Immutable periodicity of sameness. Background against which differences will be marked, and referred back inevitably to sameness. Separations can be measured by the inevitable return of the same. The sun is caught in an *eternal pendular isolation* as it describes the orb of the representable, the visible world, and distinguishes ideas

Speculum of the Other Woman

from copies, from fakes. And also as it determines what is proscribed in the theater of representation.

The Avoidance of (Masculine) Hysteria

A Hypnotic Method

How can these prisoners, for whom nothing exists but fakes, but words associated with projected shadows, how can these men hallucinated by voices whose tricks of reproduction-production they cannot hear, fascinated by spectacles whose mimetic techniques they are incapable of evaluating, how can these madmen, these children deprived of all education be freed of their chains and cured of their insanity? And, again, what forms will that insanity take before the men escape the *apaideusia* that keeps them in the cave, ignorant of the difference between true and false?

Each time that one of the men is (or is in the story) freed of his bonds and forced, all of a sudden, to get up, turn his head, start to walk, and turn his eyes toward the light, all these actions will cause him pain, and the glare of the fire will (supposedly) prevent him from seeing the "objects" upon whose shadows he had earlier gazed.

Only one man is freed at a time. Someone—an undefined, dumb "someone"—will shed his prisoner's chains and henceforth move freely. If he could. But those chains in actual fact are merely doubles, figures, representations of an immobility, a lethargy resulting from the sympathetic magic of the cave and the spells of the magicians. Even when his bonds are loosed, the prisoner will (or would) still be stiff and numb, frozen into holding his earlier position, hamstrung, bewitched still by what is happening on the opposite wall—since all the movement, all the action and acting takes place on the projection screen—if he were not suddenly forced—by someone, a *male* someone or other—to get up and stand on his feet, whether he likes it or not. This *anastasis* will cause him pain. Hitherto such verticality and phallicism had been restricted to the *protasis,* to keeping the gaze, the head, the body, facing straight ahead, straining forward. This *proterein* alleviates and disguises the lack of the *hysterein* whose measure these prisoners have never been able or willing to take. Since, then, they have been chained up within the project of making metaphor of the *hystera*—the matrix of this scene of representation—it is only after resistance and pain that the man or men will be set

268

on their feet in the cave and will begin to walk around it, and thus be torn out of the continuity of a *hysterical sleep or dream*. Their movements are still forced, as if they were sleepwalkers obeying the *hypnotic power* of a teacher who has to cure the numbness, induce the stiff joints to bend, even if it is painful to do so. The body is tied in knots by the charm of the spectacle unfolding on the back wall of the cave, and that paralysis is not remedied without difficulty. Particularly when it comes to those effects that are most essential in maintaining the spell: the inability to turn around or return toward the supposed place of origin in order to take official cognizance of the analogic fiction that under-lies that representation. *Stupor, astasia, narrowing of the field of vision,* privileged orientation toward the opposite wall—all these are necessary if the deception is to work, and Socrates decides *all of a sudden* to mix them up, putting an end to the beliefs of these prisoner children of the *hystera*.

The man is forced to get up, turn his head and walk. As if that were possible, all at once, without recourse to another trick: the *suggestive force* of a tutor who pays no heed to the resistance of the "body" to this brutal change of tropism. Thus all these acts will hurt and, obliged to look up, both overhead and backward, toward the light of the fire, the prisoner-child will be blinded by the fire's glare, and his dazzled eyes will no longer be able to make out the "things" whose shadows he had earlier gazed at. And no doubt the eye does not pass without transition from darkness to the brightness of a torch since it has been harmed, put out, in the night.[4] But yet how would he see, from the outset, what had always been kept out of his sight, forbidden to his gaze? Does one all of a sudden and by a kind of pedagogic fiat, however philosophically justified, displace the *horizon* which determines perspective, points of view, and which limits the gaze? Especially when this involves turning the whole field of vision around and including what had hitherto been kept *at the back* and had enabled all vision to occur, on condition no one ever clapped eyes on it. Dazzled by the brightness of the fire, the captive from the back of the cave will equally find his senses reeling from the sudden need to spin around, pivot. For a long time he will suffer an irreducible diplopia from two irreconcilable points of view, and one cannot be made to take precedence over the other without the loss of some flame. Either let Truth carry the day against deceitful appearances, or else, claiming once more to reverse optics, let us give exclusive privilege to the fake, the mask, the fantasy because, at least at times, they mark the nostalgia we feel for something even more true.

We will continue to waver indecisively before this dilemma unless we

---

[4] *Timaeus*, 45–46.

interpret *the interest, and the interests,* involved here. Who or what *profits* by the credits invested in the effectiveness of such a system of metaphor, in such patterns of squares and definitions of the pawns in the game, in the attribution of these differential criteria to the pieces of the chessboard, in that *hierarchy* of values as stake, rules, and reward in the game? What that we should question has been *forgotten,* not about a truer truth, a realer real, but *about the profit that under-lies the truth/fantasy pair?* And what tribute is being levied to pay for what has been forgotten? as it continues to exist at the price of complications that make the game more and more complex, subtle, vertiginous and, in the last analysis, interminable. And it is never in the interests of any referee to declare the foul, blow the whistle.

But we are still in the cave, and there a master seeks to convert to the truth, or at least to the truer, one prisoner who seems unwilling to give up his ravings, his *aphrosunē.* "And then conceive someone saying to him that what he saw before was an illusion, *phluarias,* but that now when he is approaching nearer to being, *tou ontos,* and his eye is turned toward more real existence—*pros mallon onta*—he has a clearer vision—*orthoteron blepoi.*" What if he were assured that now his gaze was turned in a straighter direction, and was therefore clearer, more able to take stock of beings? He would reply, as you may guess, being the child he is, that what he saw before was truer than what is being pointed out to him now!

(A Hypnotic Method) That Buries and Forbids "Madness"

Thus, in this den, where we still are, the tragedy is played out between him who holds the truth and him who holds the fantasy. But the one who has the power to prohibit madness is neither of these and he gives the name of "madman" to *his* "other"—or *his* "one," that is, to whatever is foreign to him, whatever in/for him is now and forever alienated. Truth here must reign supreme and has always already distinguished true from false. Truth's empire permits no hint of indecision between these alternatives. Thus, of the two men—the two halves of men/man—the one is on the right lines, sees clearly, thinks aright, while the other is a deranged child, misled by fakes. Unreasonable, oblivious, unaware. Therefore it is incumbent upon one of the parties to lead the other back onto the straight and narrow, temper his stupidity, destroy his dreams. This will be done by a display of strength in which "madness" will not simply disappear on command but will rather be subjected to prohibition, denial, leaving a clear field to law, discourse, which are discrete and have neatly delineated categories and dichotomies, with nothing left unaccounted for outside themselves. The arbitrariness of this decision is justified in terms of an *other life* that has to be recollected. For in the present life, that of the child in the cave, what could induce anyone to choose as the more visible, the more true, and ultimately the more valuable something that is merely named and that is intended to replace something else that has charmed your whole life? And in fact isn't it a kind of rambling bewilderment, of delirium, to give up the certainties of the past at the insistence of a teacher? Whether those certitudes be "sensible," fantastic, or phantasmatic. As soon as one begins to pay attention to the procedures and goals of this authoritarian pedagogy one ceases to be sure what madness or lunacy is exactly. One can no longer decide what, or who, is more, or less, "mad."

And if we have to hammer the point home, note this also. The "things" that the captive is told have more being and are more true—such as the objects whose mere shadows he had been accustomed to seeing—these "things" are not now to be acknowledged simply as the beings, now present, whose mere projection had been enough to produce that fascinating fantasy. Far from it. None of the scenographic, cinematographic apparatus is "unveiled" to him. Not the tricks of the director, not the architectonic of the cave, not the cunning of the magicians, not the mechanism of projections, not even the principle of the moving pictures, to say nothing of the principle of the echo. And it is only through some *new hocus-pocus, of reason* if you like, that the teacher forces him to see in those little "statues" alone the cause—less disguised, truer, closer to being—of what had once captivated him. For, in making his demonstration, the teacher only lifts the veil in order that he may subsequently better conceal the motives of desire, the different kinds of tropisms, even the effects of giddiness you get from swinging from the chandelier-Idea. The fixture-fixation.

Thus in his daze, the man free of chains and enchantments, free to turn his head, will have only a blurred perception of what is shown him. And he will decide that, all in all, what he contemplated earlier was clearer than this blindness and confusion. "And you may further imagine that his instructor is pointing to the objects as they pass and requiring him to name them,—will he not be perplexed?"

Who wouldn't be? What the prisoner had been used to call "beings"—*onta*—designated what he had always seen. More precisely what they, he and the others (like him), had always seen, to the exclusion of anything else. All other vision had been impossible or forbidden them. Faced with these same "shadows," these men identical among themselves apparently gave the name "beings" to what they saw, in the hypothesis of a conversation. And it was necessarily so. They would not have been able to speak among themselves had they not signified each thing by a "proper" name/noun (however arbitrary), that is to say, by a nonequivocal term. The paradigm of all proper names/nouns is Being, or else Truth. The being of Truth or the truth of Being. No discourse, no dialogue will escape that law. Not even in this myth, which serves the philosopher. The names that man, or men, had pronounced must have been referred back to, standardized against, the truth, or they could not have understood each other.

But suddenly, in the name of truth, the prisoner is unchained, disenchanted, turned away from what he had considered true, from what he, and the others, had designated by the name of truth, and he is required to say what these things are that had always been behind him and of which he had previously seen only the shadows. How could he obey, given that for these new "beings"—if beings they be for him, coming as they do almost from another world—he has no appropriate term, no agreed-upon or suitable denomination, since he looks upon them all on his own and has lost his point of view on the true, on being, as a result of being forced to turn around? Outside of language, outside of convention and communal recognition, outside of identical perception that can be identified within a set of procedures for conversation with others who share his view, these things *are* for him *nothing*. Or they are *strange*. Strangeness, the *stranger*. In any case he does not have the means to distinguish them—*apokrinesthai*. They are nothing he is in a position to delineate or define adequately in words.

Now these "things"—assisted, of course, by the whole seductive art of stage direction—certainly sustained his interest and, one may say, his community of interests with the (like) others, but they also have more being in their univocal simplicity and make him see more clearly: or so the tutor tells him. In comparison with them, all he had seen before was illusion. He is going to introduce them by force into an economy of values in which, *as such,* they used to have no function, no place. Or at any rate none that is or can be designated by the prisoner. The assertion is that from now on nothing may be named or understood but those objects. And that assertion is no longer validated through conversation but takes the form of peremptory instruction. The relation to truth will no longer be organized through the *identity of posture*—and imposture—of gaze, of point of view, of "shadows," an identity imposed upon the men chained up in the cave, but instead *through the discourse of a master who is supposed to guarantee the pertinence of the analogies,* the adequateness of the relations between each "being" and the truth.

The perception of the prisoner will henceforth go through the propositions of the master. It will be regulated according to the logos, the logic, of the philosophy tutor. The result will be that if the more "present" also represents what has more being—*given that everything immediately perceived was only a projection*—this surplus of being or of truth is herewith prescribed by professorial fiat based upon an earlier life, which one should feel guilty for having forgotten, and by the necessity of a new project, a *telos* that allows the relations between men to be regulated. But this "surplus of truth" does not function by bringing into play something in excess of what the chained men had hitherto perceived as "beings." Whatever inveigling charm this *surplus* may have, it marks a break with the preceding economy, which must be abandoned as childishness, dreams, insanity. One must turn (around) toward something else, cut short the childish beliefs and language, make a clean break between fantasies and reality. In some way it is necessary *to forget in order to remember what is truer.*

But this transition implies a jump. A fault, a split, which cannot be crossed without risk. One may lose one's sight, one's memory, one's speech that way. And one's balance. Going across in this way is, moreover, a one-way trip. It denies the chain of connections and all retrovision, all retroaction. It will take the life of anyone who dares to move through in reverse. But it's a matter of life and death whichever way you look at it. This is the price paid for the *reason* to which the prisoner is now converted.

A Remainder of Aphasia

His conversion is not without *suffering, dizziness, dazzlement.* And even *aphasia.* For, just as he is unable to recognize what is shown him as more real, so the prisoner cannot name these "things": he is struck dumb until he has been taught to say what he *must* say. This discourse of "more" truth does not arise as a result of an increase in speech over and above the man's past words, but rather out of the *conversion of language* also. And that cannot be brought about simply by adding a few apt terms, but demands a transformation of the process of discourse. We move on to new chains that are irreducible to the preceding ones. It is necessary to learn to speak (again), and specifically to distinguish, to index, to name. And all according to a law that prescribes not a displacement toward "more" truth—for then truth would represent some value, some *x*, whose *interest*, whose *meaning* would be assigned from the outset, by a capital decision. The law of this "new" discourse challenges what was previously designated as "beings" on the grounds that it had been founded upon the commonality of (so-called) immediate and sensible certainties. The law lays an inter-dict upon the return back, obliterates all retro-cession. And orders man to take the definitive step away from fantasy, dream, childhood. Away from desire? From *hysterical* desire at any rate. For all of these are *nothing*. So that he may turn to wisdom. The wisdom of the master. And of mastery.

But whereas the cunning of the director and of the magicians, their use of ellipse and eclipse for example, once held the prisoner fascinated, now another disappearing trick will entrance and captivate the (so-called) free man. The non-visible, the non-appropriable, the non-propertied, are evaded within the economy of truth, of proper meaning and proper noun. From the trickery of magic we move on to the trickery of authority. For example. Authority will not be seen or measured or designated in the discourse of truth. The passion that under-lies it is thereby laid under proscription.

The Misprision of Difference

Two pieces of sleight of hand that are never unveiled compete in the process of representation. A split tears open the arche of presence. And because that division is irreconcilable, it undermines from time immemorial the serenity of wisdom, of philosophy. Even if it has always already extrapolated the copula. At the zenith of transcendence. The Idea, the Being, the Idea (of) Being mask *the dehiscence* of an origin that is never recognized as (product of) copulation. Being stands on high, offstage, in a so-called life before or after the present life, in a deceptive supplementarity to life, and there it referees the life and death rivalries between the representants and representations of origin. Even though it has been decided that these struggles will die out in the Sun, that light will conquer darkness and truth fantasy, that *the father* in other (?) words will hold the monopoly on procreation, will alone sow the "good" seed and be able to give it a "proper" name, nonetheless, underground, in the dim light of the cave, or else in the *captive consciousness of the child*, the fight will go on. The second birth, secondary origin, renaissance or reminiscence of truth will never, simply, defer the *hysterical tropism*. The discourse of reason, solar and paternal metaphor, will never oust the fantasy structure of the cave completely.

Twice two half-origins, two half-turns in relation to origin, two half-detours away from origin will continue to claim a monopoly on truth (of origin), to compete for primacy in reproduction. But there is no reduction of the gap, the rift between the bewitching spell of the cave and the logic of reason, between the earth's attraction and the sun's allure. Between the more maternal and the more paternal, whose—sexual—difference will never have been considered as cause and necessary condition for copulation. Obviously, neither the coming together of two entities in copulation, nor its product, can be counted in two halves. Neither halves "of man/men," nor sex organs/sexes, nor representation(s), nor language(s). Copulation cannot be divided in this way. Unless control is already being wielded by the fixed idea of the same—Being—which has to be rediscovered, reunited, and re-produced. For better rather than for worse, for good rather than for ill, in truth rather than in fake. That is to say, in Idea(s). Being not simply a-sexuate or trans-sexuate. This is not to say that it explicitly re-marks one sex, or the other. Rather it maintains the partition without allowing itself to be cleaved by the difference at work there. For Being's domination requires that whatever has been defined—*within the domain of sameness*—as "more" (true, right, clear, reasonable, intelligible, paternal, masculine . . .) should progressively win out over *its* "other," its "different"—its differing—and, when it comes right down to it, over its negative, its "less" (fantastic, harmful, obscure, "mad," sensible, maternal, feminine . . .). Finally the fiction reigns of a simple, indivisible, ideal origin. The fission occurring at the beginning, at the time of the primitive conjunction(s) is eliminated in the *unity of concept*.

Eternal archive of the Idea. Birth pushed further and further back into an infinity where all differences, and differings, fuse in a blind contemplation.

The Unreflected Dazzle of Seduction

And so this prisoner, already suffering from dizziness, confusion, and various algias resulting from the brutal twist around he has been forced to make, "if he is compelled to look straight at the fire itself, will he not have a pain in his eyes?" Accustomed to the half-light of the grotto, to the darkness of the back of the den, to the mid-night of the underground projections, he is suddenly, brutally, forced to look straight at the light, the fire, the glowing "source" of the fantasies that once entranced him. How could those eyes endure having such a vision, such an illumination forced upon them? How could they not "turn away," flee the light, in order to return to that perhaps less elevated and more deeply buried spectacle that they were able to contemplate without difficulty, that they can look upon without being blinded? And, consequently, will the man not conceive that what he is used to seeing is clearer than this "light" that is being shown him, indexed for him, by gesture or word as the "reason" whose partial concealment once entranced him?

From one half-turn to the other, he is probably completely at sea now, unable to see where to go. What should be put in front? What left behind? Where is the side facing, the facade, the face? And the behind? Or the *proteron,* the *hysteron.* And the *hystera?* Whom or what to trust? And the force of habit, the resistance of repetition, of the representation of the repetition that he knows, sends him back to his previous posture, visions, and voices. Better to be misled by fakes than to lose one's sight by opening the eyes to the flame of truth.

Particularly since the truth that they claim to unveil to him now is not simply that of the seductive fantasy. *Since there is not, and will not be an alētheia of seduction.* But the fire, like the sun, may put one on the wrong track here. Especially if one is a prisoner who doesn't know any better, having been chained up since childhood at the back of a cave. He is still unaware that the fire has always already served some theoretical fiction. He has not yet learned to steal/veil sun and fire in a "good" system of metaphor that regulates his gaze according to the *lack* of image. Fire that will have the unbearable glare of a light that is too bright, too immediately present, too close for ocular metabolism. The *hybris* of nature irrupts violently. Something as yet unsighted, unsurveyed—or which seems so at least—dazzles the man's eyes. Makes him turn back to his chamber. To his phantoms. To his dreams. Which can pleasurably be considered the only possible (sensible) certainties.

Two ways of escaping, of covering over, the *hybris* of nature respect and reject each other at the same time, each tugging at the veil of truth and almost tearing it. For the prisoner who knows nothing of the art of dialectic and the powers of the ideal, the intolerable part of nature, *physis,* would be the blinding brilliance of the fire, the sun. The philosopher, on the other hand, who has already bent light to his logos, cannot tolerate the sympathetic magic of the shadowy vault of fantasies, the hallucination, the "madness." A certain natural violence must be resorbed into wisdom. By means of those changes in direction, those half-turns, of a *plus* or a *minus* of truth. In this system, truth is everywhere, and also nowhere. There is an artificial comparison of these "appearances" of the originary, which have not simply to appear—particularly not in a demonstration in which some will defeat others—but to join up and become articulate(d). The truth is everywhere thanks to the lure, the alluring privilege given to a "bonus." A sharp rise in values occurs, but no *actual appearance*. Two faces would have been necessary each time to make an evaluation. A natural monstrosity. Of course. Truth nonetheless carries the day by means of a comparative sleight of hand that excludes any appeal to a "natural" standard. The degrees of kinship, the resemblances or differences in relationships, the parallels, the confrontations, the estimates of usefulness and price, etc., will be regulated by processes intrinsic to the logos. "Nature" will be solved in this way. By means of comparisons, analogies, metaphors which claim to make her present, to represent her, with a "bonus" of truth if you like, but you could equally say with a "bonus" of fantasy. By eclipsing her.

But natural violence does not submit without difficulty. Without the physical pain of that prisoner-child, for example. Without his vertigo. His blindness. As well as his *indecision,* his *uncertainties,* his *turnings back* to recover something of his previous tropism, of his past passions. Of his ground. Of his den. After all, he knows nothing else, not even in what a state of reversal, of symmetric topsy-turviness, he had once been held. In the *hystera.* He is still unaware of the still virtually hysterical projection that has served as backdrop to his representations, his dreams, his fantasies, his beliefs, his judgments. To his doxosophy. Out of these still hysterical reminiscences he is now suddenly being torn; he is being told to forget them and to reenter the order of the law. The law of the "bonus" of truth.

But the *hystera* does not allow itself to be reduced, or even seduced, thus. Even by means of argument that is reasonable, a (so-called) more appropriate word. The ear may surrender in this way, but the womb will not be conquered. In fact, a half-turn more is perhaps *one more* reversal, but it is not *a reversal of reversal.* Even if the interacting effects of symmetry, the metaphors in circulation, the modifications of tropisms are calculated in a more complex way, together with the ellipses and elisions, this does not mean that a complete sweep (of the horizon as well) has been effected, or that a circle has brought reason to its sense(s), after hysterical wanderings. It does not mean that the prisoner has found truth itself (as same) after his geotropic extravagances. One half-turn more will never bring you back to where you were before: to the cave, the earth, the mother, the *hystera.* Before birth, which, moreover, is conception. The half-turn resolves anything that still recalls the time in the womb into phantoms, baby tricks, idle chat, or even into nothing. It erases all trace of intrauterine life. And if this is the project that has to be carried through if we are to return to a more essential, ideal birth, at least this half-turn does not defend it, except surreptitiously. A dizzy deception answers to the optical illusion of the fakes and to the pass-time of the eternity of the Idea. Of Being. Fictive murder of the detour through life.

But then where are the phantoms? Everywhere? Is the body of the man waking from a spell nothing more than a shadow? He at least runs the risk of this being so if he gives up those recollections of the mother and the womb. If he seeks to banish his "fantasies" of origin and to abort his own beginnings, his own story. Don't you think that, having been foolish (*aphrōn*), he risks becoming demented (*paranous*)?

The "Way Out" of the Cave

The "Passage"

And now, what if someone—*tis*, an anonymous someone of the *male* gender—were further to brutalize the man whose chains he had earlier taken off, by forcibly dragging him, against his will, with a *hybris* contrary to his "natural" bent, along the "steep and rugged ascent" out of the grotto, and holding "him fast until he is forced into the presence of the sun himself"? What if the unknown did not let go of the man, but prevented him from springing away or running off, until he had carried out his personal project of tearing the man away from the shadow of his former home and dragging him into full daylight? Don't you think that the man treated this way, man-handled, lacerated perhaps, "saved" in this manner, would be "pained and irritated"?

So some accomplice, some acolyte-obstetrician, some faceless, nameless hack, of whom we know only that he is male, will with a firm hand forcibly extract the prisoner-child, against his will, from his previous home. Will thrust him out of the den, forcing him along the rocky track full of obstacles that can tear and mutilate flesh, up the steep slope, the vertical shaft, out of the place where he has always dwelled, and into the light of day. Will tear him away from the underground chamber, his stronghold, in order to lead him to the sight of the sun, keeping an authoritative and relentless hold on him during the savage climb. The man thus vigorously dragged outside will (probably) not be pleased, but will be filled with suffering and indignation. Someone, to sum up, will (probably) act in such a way as to bring the poor fool (back) onto the paths of reason. What does "in such a way" mean?

A Difficult Delivery

It may be imagined—in fact you have already been told—that this same "someone" has first twisted the chained man round, turning him away from the farthest wall of the cave, so as to direct his gaze, his head, his body, toward the statues and the fire, and also toward the opening of the grotto: thus imprinting the man with a rotational movement that anticipates his exit from this chamber, this room or womb. It may also be supposed that, by making him move forward in his prison, the man has brought the prisoner progressively nearer to the path leading from inside to outside, and even that, by leading him into this corridor, this narrow pass, this neck, the man has made him suffer as much as a result of the difficult passage as by the sudden change of place to which he is subjected. But out of what dwelling and into what other dwelling is the prisoner being moved? And what transition can this be? And again, what lies beneath such an approach to *childbirth*?

And, since we are invited, and are attracted by the show, let us meanwhile not lose sight of the facts, the realities, the "beings." Already the prisoner was no longer in a womb but in a cave—an attempt to provide a figure, a system of metaphor for the uterine cavity. He was held in a place that was, that meant to express, that had the *sense* of being *like* a womb. We must *suppose* that the womb is reproduced, reproducible, and reproductive by means of projections. That it is already subject to the laws of symmetry and analogy which, theoretically, would have given it the *form* of a grotto, would have transformed it into a cave. By/for representations. The farthest wall of that den would serve both as a horizon-limit and as a backcloth for projection.

This "like" or "as if" of the cave is based on artifice, on a mechanism that is fictional among other things, but the prisoner is unaware of all this: whence his imprisonment in that unique dwelling, trapped in a single metaphorical project. But one must admit that the obstetrician, at least the anonymous assistant—bringing being into the world, if you like—is equally blind to the *twisted, reversed, inverted* character of this "prison." Unless he is just pretending ignorance? Since he claims to bring the prisoner out of the cave as out of a womb, according to the techniques of childbirth. Neglecting the "like" and "as if" that have always already been at the bottom of such scenography. Not calculating the effects of turning around and backward which have already made that scene the way it is. No doubt the prisoner, the child, is made to twist around before he is pushed out, but there is no twisting of the theater of representation from which, *as such,* he cannot so easily escape. Even by means of philosophical fiat. The instructor conducts the operation in this way "as if" the enclosure of the cave were the womb. An "as if" like this obviously cannot begin to suspect or even sublimate the fundamental "as if" of the scene of the cave. And he, or they, seem to have forgotten the staging or at least he—the scriptwriter—claims to disguise the part it plays and to discount its retroactive effects.

But isn't he himself caught in the net he has spread, captured by something more powerful than his dialectical line of argument? Caught so fast that, to escape—for he wants to "get out"—he can resort only to *jumping* into an *other* life. Whence the recourse he has to an *other* birth, an *other* origin. Both of them ideal. But the harmoniously calculated relationship to these *others* will not get round the break in contact, the crack in progression or regression that become(s) imperative. The passage from one to the other will (or would) from now on only be managed by introducing proportions, the special prerogative of a few initiates—initiators—whose silence, secrecy, and concealment—especially in the wings of the stage—most probably guarantee its effectiveness. *Magical* effectiveness. For they themselves seem almost caught in their own traps, almost lost in their own relations. Arithmetic comes in handy for lighting the path into and out of the earth, the mother. Neck, corridor, path, which do not allow themselves to be reduced and seduced by rational measures. Or even by less than rational, by quite imaginary measures. In fact everyone so far is well and truly chained up by this mimodrama, caught in mimicry. And in hysteria. So one more trick will only be able to *simulate* a way out. But there will be no escape from what has held one captive. And even as the prisoner was fascinated by the magicians' tricks and a slave to those of the stage director,—or else to the latter's errors and failures of understanding, notably of a topographic kind—the wise man, the philosopher will be crazy to believe that he can thus escape the uterine dwelling and leave it behind him once and for all, so as to gaze upon the earth in the open air, in the pure natural light, having finally and unequivocally unveiled the cause of all that had hitherto fixed his attention, charmed his eyes, determined his tropism. "Jumping" out of the perpetual sympathetic magic of the vault for projected shadows, perceived through backward vision, and into the eternally present ecstasy of the Sun (of the) Idea. Out of the attraction he has always felt for the familiar, into the peremptory affirmation that cognition and re-cognition can occur only through/in what has been defined as such by (the discourse of) truth. Truth is unveiled by/for him, face to face, instantly, without the shadow of a doubt or the intervention of any mirror, and with the full force of law. Passing from the fluid darkness, from the shimmering imprecision of reflections, from the phantasmagorias of the *doxa* to the neat, clear-cut, immutable, unambiguous categories that characterize, divide up, classify, and order everything, every "being," according to rational intuition, in the clear and distinct intelligibility of the *nous*. But, by this conversion, has *aphrōn* become *paranous?*

Then Whence and How Does He Get Out?

So the man will be ejected from the cave by force. From the cave in fact? Or perhaps from an other, a *third place?* Through another *third,* way out? That in some way eclipses the two others. Or all the others? A way out without an opening through which he could have entered? Except in fantasy? Or in words? For the passages through which he might have been introduced or inserted have been eliminated, obliterated, stopped up, in order to ensure the domination of the Truth. The path is virtually forgotten, and indeed impracticable for the privileged type of projection which assumes reversal, retroversion. In two half-turns, detours, they will have pretended to roll the man up in the matrical, or its surrogate, covering both up, circumscribing, surrounding them by symmetrical operations. Putting analogical envelopes and wrappings that are more manageable in their place. For such envelopes allow one to (as it were) get in and (as it were) get out in a more decisive fashion, and they will keep the agreed and agreeable forms. The man will be brought out by a path he could never have got in by, out of somewhere he never lived. Leaving behind a place that he entered not by projection but in ways difficult to decide and calculate, through passages that cannot be reduced to a simple ideal elaboration. Still in the *apaideusia,* which one must "get out of" once and for all. Whence the miming of practices and *topoi* that in fact cannot be reproduced, duplicated, imitated, except in fiction. And there will be an attempt to fix what has been imitated in function of an extrapolated law of meaning prescribing the faithfulness, the conventions, the economy of the imitator. The authoritarian pre-existence of such an order masks the aporias that it evades.

So he will get out. He gets out. But obviously not from the place he has (or may have) been put into. And to refer to what has already been established, not from Plato's cave. Thus, he has not passed back over the *teikhion,* the wall curtain, any more than he was (would have been) able to cross it beforehand. A paraphragm forbids its limits from being crossed—forbids the seed, the gaze, light rays, and all bodies, all "beings" except ideal beings. The wall is an artifact necessary to representation, or at least to this one, and it forms an *impermeable* barrier to absolutely all matter. Perhaps it has (may have) been put up—as a balustrade dividing the cave, its prisoners, its gazes, its *topos*—after the prisoners have been let in. This is conceivable. Perhaps the "back" of the cave has been closed off so that men's bodies may live there. Very well. But how does one break clean through that opaque, water-tight partition in order to return, or turn away from, or be torn away from the depths of that crypt? Unless one is a phantom? Unless what is involved is a *faked* appearance on the "other" side? A *semblance* of appearing outside? But then where are the phantoms? And the fakes? Outside? Or inside? Or do they proliferate as a result of the/this demarcation of outside and inside, of the intervention of an artificial paraphragm that sets inside/outside in opposition, *everywhere*. A cave where/whence even men's bodies would appear to be merely illusory, breeding nothing but ghosts. White or black. Solar phantoms or sepulchral shadows. More, or less, good.

A World Peopled by Ghosts

Now a ghost has never been stopped by a wall, or even a door, much less by a curtain or a veil. A ghost doesn't even re-mark (on) them. But you can check his ghostly credentials by seeing how easily he can cross any partition, separation, division, interval, between two homes, places, times, space-times. Without effort. He is unaware of all differences. Barriers, separations, differences are necessary, however, if ghosts are to exist, and go on existing. The barriers include, of course, those which forbid crossing over from death to life, from life to death. The ghost transgresses these established borders. Nothing holds him in check. Hence the fear, the repression, the laws that partition off the different dwellings. In order to protect against the "apparitions," which go from strength to strength as a result. The defenses against the phantoms breed phantoms, and vice versa. There is no end to it. This cave produces more ghosts than any other, even if they are sometimes clean, clear, even sunlit ghosts. Washed of their uterine contaminants and their graveyard corruption. White, like any self-respecting ghosts. The very idea (of the) phantom is everywhere, but it will be purged of its rather frightening character, its awesome associations with death and the "body." When it comes right down to it, what is needed is for there to be nothing but phantoms. No more distinctions between phantoms and non-phantoms. Between life and death, death and life. Underground and open-air dwellings. Between mother and father, "if you like." Let everything and everyone be formalized and illustrated in the heaven of eternal ideas. With just a few fetish-statues, fallen shadows, wretched cast-offs of a former life remaining to be raised, re-suscitated, to their ideal essence.

But it is not proper to alert just anyone to the "paradise" that awaits him, to tell just anyone how it will be in the other life. And, just possibly, there will not be an "other" life. So it is necessary, once again, to fake an exit, and a painful, harrowing, even wounding exit for the body of the prisoner who is already dizzy and dazzled and afflicted with arthritis pain and various other ailments. Curiously, the misadventures of the "body" will be dwelt upon. And whereas not a word will be said about the impossibility of passing through the paraphragm, which can be crossed only by sublimation—but once you have sublimated the body all you have left is air, smoke, vapor, ghost—much stress will be laid on the various stages in the adventurous climb out of the cave.

Certainly nothing will be said about the *path* within the cave, nor of the *teikhion*. Once these have been re-presented *within* the den, their access, or excess, was, or theoretically would be, eliminated. So by the wave of the wand which makes even the magicians themselves disappear, the path and the *teikhion* no longer block the way. Or at least one doesn't want to know, see, or recognize anything about them. Suddenly the only path is the one that goes from the earth to the sun. But that one is full of traps, it is rocky and rugged, it can wound, tear, cut. And you have to keep a firm hold on a man if he is to consent to pass that way. (Keep as silent as you see fit, but you will always end up admitting in some way, perhaps by one little extra adjective—an equivocal one of course, like *trakheias*—what you didn't want to, couldn't, say.) This corridor is thus supposedly full of sharp edges and points, and the man will pass (back) through it only with pain and anger. And if someone did not push him along—some *one* of the masculine gender—he would refuse the ordeal. He would prefer to remain in, or perhaps on, the earth, the mother, but avoid associating with her regularly. For her company is represented to him, here, as thorny, pregnant with danger.

The Time Needed to Focus and Adjust the Vision

Impossible to Turn Back (or Over)

At this point in the story someone gets the man out, by pulling rank—despite his "pain and irritation." And forces him to see daylight. But "having reached the light, his eyes blinded by the glare of the sun, he would be unable to look at what is shown to and designated to him now as true things." The philosopher-acolyte agrees that this is so, and explains immediately that it is only a matter of "becoming accustomed." The man has to *focus* his vision and *adjust* it to these new conditions. Does this need to close the ocular diaphragm distract attention from the problem of the paraphragm? The theory is that this is all a matter of *time*. Of transition, and *progressive* transition this time. Of a transference perhaps? It is necessary to wait, to take one step at a time, to be patient and methodical. This is the approach encouraged by the stage director, by the philosopher, who is arranging the curricula of ignorant children, still ruled by impulse and needing to be accustomed to the ways, the laws, of reason. So let us follow how this art of formation, of transformation—by elevation—is put into practice.

It is the opinion of the wise man, the obstetrician, that the man "will look more easily, with the least difficulty, at shadows first of all. Secondly at the reflections in the water of men and other things. Only then the objects themselves. Then, raising his eyes toward the light of the stars and the moon, he will contemplate the constellations and the firmament itself more easily during the night than the sun and its brilliance during the day." That is "certainly" so!

Yet truly, what a strange education. And how are we to interpret it? Everything is once more *topsy-turvy*, at least in the order of appearances and appearings. As might have been expected, you may say? Yes, given the function of mimicry in this (so-called) progression. The place the man had once inhabited must be mimicked by turning it inside out and back to front and by gradually raising it up. By gradually verticalizing and erecting it. This erection will (theoretically) complement the horizontal operation of translation that we have already noted. That already provides the basis for Plato's cave. Since the men are unable to return, to turn back toward the mother, they will act "as if" it were possible to turn the scene of the womb or at least *its representation* back/over. As one might turn a purse, or a pocket, or a string bag, or even a wallet inside out. This is an effective way to prevent anything from remaining concealed, buried, shrouded, to stop it hiding, lurking, staying under wraps, in reserve. Let us get everything out into broad daylight.

But this turn-over is complicated. It supposes a new axis or plane regulating the symmetrical relationship—from down to up—which should now be taken into consideration. Or it may require one extra photo-graphic, photo-logical operation. *And how does one reverse, invert, the inchoate, while still respecting proportion?* True, the inchoate has already been transmuted by projection(s). From backward to opposite most pertinently. True, the inchoate has already been elaborated by/for representations. But some of its properties still resist change. It has to be credited with ductility, extensibility, and suppleness if the models constructed for it—plans, images, formulas, words—are not always already to be obsolete. Forms are moving in a (perhaps female) indefinite beyond and constantly risk being overwhelmed by a surplus, a *remainder* which (theoretically) has not been taken into account and which would go beyond all calculation, all operation on/with already defined symbols.

But how does one reproduce, *analogically,* what is not represented or representable? Certainly, there is already the cave. But. . . . And even in the cave there is no mirror. The cave itself is speculum, den of reflection. Even if you transfer it into the sun, the show still goes on *inside.* Otherwise, there is nothing to be seen. There is no show at all. In any case, it seems difficult to reproject the images reflected in and picked up by a speculum symmetrically, from bottom to top, without any kind of curvature. However . . . let us imagine something that might be like it. The vault of the sky would correspond to the covering, enveloping ceiling of the cave. The night would double for—or be doubled by—the dim light in the grotto, with no stars. The sun would be the fire as the fire had been called the image of the sun. The prisoners would be the prisoners, in an enclosure obviously much more spacious, infinitely, indefinitely more vast. The "bodies" of men would therefore be the bodies of men, but which? The shadows would correspond to the shadows. And effort will be made to convince you of this. What about the images in the water? They correspond to *nothing* figuring in the grotto since all mirrors are banned there. There are no more magicians, or at least none under that name. No more instruments used to effect the magicians' enchantments, no more fetish-statues with fascinating reflections. No more paraphragm, or at least none represented as such. No *path* even, merely a process, a progress of methodically forming the gaze. No more *materialized* transition between the outside and the inside or noticeable separation between the entrance and the "back" of the cave. Between the place where *the projection is screened* and the place *from which the projection comes.* Between the place from which *the deception was (or might be) plotted* and the one where *it wields its powerful spell.*

So the reversal of the scene is not simple. Once he has left his underground home, the man will not see on the outside—outside and up top—what used to happen in—inside and underneath—the cave. He will see both more and less. In a way other than he had from "inside" that confined space. And it is not fair to say that the scene has simply been raised up out of the "nether"/regions to the "upper" regions, which are also the regions of the soul. Out of the senses into the intellect, out of the passions into the harmonious love of truth, out of *doxa* into *epistēmē*. The precautions taken to prevent the neophyte from returning to his former place and to ensure that he only goes back down once he has been sufficiently confirmed in his *belief* in the new knowledge to convert others in turn, is enough evidence that something is lost in this accounting. That this "ascent" gives rise to some reticence, doubt, suspicion. Nostalgia.

Were It Not, Right Now, for a Sophistry Played with Doubles

So, once he has become slightly adapted to this new light, the first thing he can look at are shadows. No doubt the pedagogic strategy at the outset is to make him go back over what he was used to seeing: shadows. And the recurrence of the signifier *shadows*—*skias*—may give support to the mimetic intention. *Are they resorting to sophistry* now? In fact sophistry has long been surreptitiously at work in the demonstration. Thus *skias* = *skias*. And it is a fact that shadow, even by day, is easier to look at, more like what he used to look at, for a man accustomed to gazing at the half-light of the grotto and the underground projections. Therefore shadow = shadow, a visual and not acoustic signifier this time. The practice remains the same. Whether phonetic or not, it plays on the signifier, but does not refer to the same signified, the same referent. The formation in truth is perverted. It uses in a general manner and within a more general economy sophistical procedures which are not overt, not admitted as such but which will operate implacably, almost "unconsciously" as soon as Truth has taken root. Mining its foundation and the space-time of its sovereignty.

The shadows are not the "same" shadows. They can only be submitted to analogy, to displacement, to transfer, can only be "sublated" by resorting to the *signifier*. And the way the signifier intervenes here abuses desire in particular, or even the senses; in place of the cunning sympathetic magic of the magicians—which depends upon the effigied instruments of their prestige, emblems placed between the fire and the back of the cave, erected over the top of the wall curtain and seen by retrovision on the farthest wall of the cave, which acts as screen and basis for the projections—we are given the shadow of a "present body," of a (present) "being" which, presently, intercepts the light of the sun. All this—shadow and body (re)presented *simultaneously*—occurs *face to face*, in full daylight, in the wink of an eye. And it can be checked by *scientific* measurements. To replace the nether shadows by the upper shadows is the first part of the treatment followed in order to effect the proposed change in vision. It's a real operation. And it will easily be admitted that the man undergoing the operation will hesitate to fix his eyes immediately upon the "things" corresponding to the "shadows," and so also to the fantasies. He is trying to win himself one—more—detour, some—more—time. To win the benefit, if not the shadow, of a doubt.

The prisoner has never seen, at the same time, the shadow and the "body" that shadow would double for. A half-turn separates their appearance together, even if the teacher had recourse to the comparison. Moreover, what used to cast the shadow in the cave—and one will always have to go back there—was the "objects" that depended upon the desire of the magicians and were a result of tricks whose forms had been determined by "human" motives. They were fetish-statues for which the model, and the motive, remained nonetheless hidden, unprovable. There was no "ultimate" referent that could be seen, or even demonstrated. Copy of a copy of which one will never see, never know the original. Sign of what? Of whom? Coming from where? Signifiers in what sense? Becoming manifest in what time scheme? Those nether shadows in any case demand a complexity of time and tenses for their production: if they are to work, an attempt must be made to identify projection, propagation, multiplication by reflection on a screen, retrovision, with a (proto)type. But in the sun, in the presence and the present of the sun, such complex operations will be dodged, reduced to the instantaneous and synchronic duplication of a (natural) body and its shadow.

The exposure of the "body" and the shadow would not need to be deferred in the light of day. *The present is doubly adhered to.* The diurnal shadows take over from the underground shadows by *forgetfulness, loss of memory.* Not only is the time/tense of (re)production of the past forgotten but also the future perfect tense, the preterit. And certain effects of retroaction. But these will leave a few traces behind. A hint of a gap, of a separation cracking open the fiction of the present. A few dizzying vestiges of dehiscence. A reminder, in its permanence, of a stitch sutured between front and back, behind and before. Or else again, between a man and his shadow. His other? A few lips remain that may open, like a cave, revealing a slit that has been covered up with an art that will be attributed to nature.

For the man has evaded, at an early point, a confrontation with his own shadow. The black shade spreading out over the earth at his feet. Coming out toward the east, the shadow is in some way hidden. Still behind. It is under the cover of the shadows of others—men or things— that the man moves out into the sun.

Is this to say that the entry into philosophy would not require man to inquire about his own doubling, in appearances? But to question that of other "beings" instead? Different beings? In any case, this differing and deferring will soon be supplemented by *passage through the mirror* (of water). Images in the water will play their part, luminous, clear, clean, before the shadows and the "bodies" they duplicate are admitted simultaneously. The time it takes for specular reflection, or even perhaps for speculation, will, despite it all, introduce *a gap, one gap more*, between the wise man and the shadows. His shadows? His shadow? His other, that is not lit by the sun. His solar night. The nocturnal double will (theoretically) be seen, recognized, intelligible in its doubleness only if it undergoes the redoubling of the diurnal double. Sealing and concealing the problem of inversion that it thus raises: *the inversion of the reflection*. A specular and speculative reassurance occurs and, necessarily, no one will notice what it masks of the past, what it conceals behind it. What has thereby been scarred over from time past to future, from the anteriority that has always already been subverted in/by posteriority. What gash has been bandaged up between men and shadows—not only the nether shadows but also, for as long as any remain (and some will always remain), the upper shadows. An almost inexistent time of reflection will have been enough to inscribe a new pivoting in the solar scene: its reversion, its reversal, *within* the (eye of the) speculative soul. So as to support the illusion that exterior and interior, inside and outside can be reversed. As well as same and other. Product and producer. The future and the past tense of its nonfulfillment, of its half-opening. Indefinitely. The time of specula(riza)tion is almost nonexistent, but it opens (or reopens) in the present, in the scene of presence, in the sun even, the whole question of the guarantee and therefore of the credit allotted to its reproduction in the inverse direction, to the inversion of its (re)production. Basis for a mirror that assists the eternal identity with self of the Sun (of) the Idea.

Reproducing itself instantly and in(de)finitely, in self-likeness, in a process that closes up/off the past time of or time passed for its production and its effects of retroaction. These will be glimpsed only much later, so difficult is it to conceive of projection on this plane of the "unlimited."

A Frozen Nature

The mirror images will also have disturbed the implacable journey of the sun from east to west, making the shadow pivot round from west to east. *The course has been inverted.* Except at noon, it is impossible to turn toward the sun and toward one's shadow at the same time and, disregarding men and objects in the way, to master both *together* with the same look. Solar lighting is challenged by that section of night that the specular, the speculative, will try to conjure up with its almost immediate re-presentation. The daytime double will have to be passed off as the nighttime double. Shadows = images in a mirror = copies. Difference and deferral are gradually banished in this way. Certainly they still remain but within a *reduplication* that is more and more instantaneous, instantly masterable and mastered. More and more clear, luminous, evident. Or at least that's the idea. Particularly since by acting "like" a mirror, water freezes access to the bottomless depths of the sea, to its night. Water serves as a reflecting screen and not as a reminder of the depths of the mother; it sends back the image of the sun, of men, of things, even of the prisoner-child. These *appearances* veil the risk of falling back, returning into the darkness of those chasms.

Frozen soil separates "up" from "down." A surface, *a protective layer of ice,* ensures the autarchy of the solar scene—that is henceforward, perforce, reversed. One more time. The mother is covered over by some new paraphragm that creates hosts of symmetrical effects: from top to bottom, from outside to inside, from forward to backward. And vice versa. The transposition—or transpositions—at work in the project of the cave are repeated and redoubled, both like and other. Are these attempts at reducing the aperture? Access to the den is closed up and recessed in/by the establishment of proportions, harmonies, correspondences. Expertly calculated analogies are more or less good, more or less adequate to the model. In any case, assessment of that model depends upon axes, planes, screens, that are now considered, "as it were," natural. The hand-crafted contrivances of men on the underground scene have, supposedly, been suppressed.

Here, then, nature is shut off in order to direct men to the spectacle above. The sunlight comes to be reflected on/at the surface of the water that has been frozen into ice and glass. That serves as screen-basis for solar reflections. And this time the reflections are guaranteed not by the cunning, the magic practices, the spells of the magicians—since these can result only in "opinions"—but by nature.

Strange process, strange progress. Time is cut up, over and over again, and lost in all kinds of caesuras and scansions that will be forced to toe the party line by deceptive plays of relationships. Are fancy, fantasy, and belief creeping furtively back in here? Now with the support of the *episteme*. Calculations of proportions have difficulty in controlling a desire to reduce the (mother) earth to a flat surface that can be measured by solar projections. But the sun does not easily penetrate the depths of crypts, for these are formless, impatient of measurement and rationalization, and must thus be forced into comparisons, assessments, enumerations that they—in truth—exceed.

So shadows (below) = shadows (above). *Reflection obliterates enchantment.* The game of "as if," anticipating, projecting, and repeating the time spent on their production, are frozen and framed in a specular duplication. Presentation of the copy and of what it theoretically copies is (*almost*) *simultaneous.* The copy—symmetrical, synchronic, and motionless—is thus reproduced as being *less* beautiful, *less* true than its model, and from now on it will index the time of its reproduction-production as only an instant. The instant in which an inversion, a cross-over, a turn-over and an overturning would simply occur once, or so they say,—in the time it takes to raise them to the sky—between the paired opposites of down/up, backward/forward, left/right, east/west. The one passes *virtually* into the other in the sun's light.

Starting with shadows (above) and going on to reflections (in water), the master-teacher will finally come to men and to other things that are doubled in those shadows and images. But he does not dwell on them, and, without comment, passes over the new relation established here between "being" and "copies." He skims over the analogic subterfuge, the rhetorical boldness whereby in this demonstration men are substituted for fetish-statues, shadows for shadows, a "natural" mirror for a projection screen.

This new step into metaphor and negation is resolutely withheld from interpretation. Just as the relation between the prisoner and "his" shadow is never raised here. This is not the time for auto-reflection, much less for calculating its incidence upon the scene of representation. The difference between one man and another, one man and his other, is still not made clear by specular information. By reflection (on) the auto-copy. There is still no autonomy, even for the gaze. Relations between—points of view, men, and all "beings"—are regulated by the light of the *alētheia*. Brilliance of silver-backing in suspension. Spotlight on an unreflected gaze illumined by truth, which in turn is suspended within the Idea, arbiter of the equivalency of all relations between. Syntax dominated by the desire for Truth which makes the decisions of agreements "between" without ever having recourse to distinguishing, defining, recognizing those who gaze and speak. The "subjects." Who henceforth become *mirrors, specula,* for reflections, images, fantasies, of Truth.

Because it is not represented, because it is forbidden to appear in the show, auto-reproduction is able to inform and mobilize its economy: *the search for more and more copies of the same,* of the *autos* whose term is eclipsed by the domination of the Idea. Nothing, including man, therefore, can rejoice in its own image since "own-ness" is dictated, commanded, monopolized by Truth. And Truth will in fact repeat, reproduce, represent only itself, in the shape of more or less good ideas, more or less faithful copies. *Autogamous offspring of Truth.* Thus man is a more or less good copy of the (more or less good) idea of man. The soul is more or less capable of reflecting the Idea of ideas which, in turn, is more or less closely affiliated to the idea (of) Truth.

The mirror, the appropriation of the specular, are both stolen from the auto-reflection (of man), of the (self) representer, but they are operative, covertly of course, in the Idea that dictates the scene of representation. *The Idea (of) Truth*—like, and unlike, the cave—*is the room/womb* (*of/for*) *the speculum.* Like and unlike the *soul,* a place of pivoting, and reversal—turning inside out and back to front—where representations are collated and bilocated: place of meeting and mingling. Like, but unlike, the *eye,* whose properties are separated out, pulled apart, dislocated, dismembered. Point of view—limited, closed, turned over and inward—rhapsodizes in the luster of the Idea, that shining focus of light which, always already, informs all reflection. *Selfhood is yielded up to the Idea.* Inexhaustible store of visions and specula(riza)tions.

The Auto . . . Taken in by the A-lētheia

Now, in the process of representation, man is *introduced, inter-posed* within the cave, that reflecting speculum. And the ambiguous quality of these nether shadows results, one may think, from the fact that they are not pure auto-reflections (of man), even though they are possible thanks to the light of a fire. The matrix is already lit by an image of the sun, but in which man *appropriates to himself* certain functions of the mirror, certain qualities of the light. For example, he may make statues of men's bodies, or reproduce his morphology or mechanize the projection of bodies in images that entrance the prisoners who are fascinated—no doubt? or among other things?—by the uncertainty of the relationship of these shadows to origin, to nature, and by the possibility that these might be one's/someone's *own*. These captives do not know exactly to whom or to what they should attribute the reflections and projections. Might they be attributed to the captives themselves, who have a part to play between the fire and the reflection screen?

This mimetic system is thus not referable to *one* model, *one* paradigm, to the presence of *one* reproduced thing. These "images," cut off from the genealogy of "own-ness" dominated by the Truth, are reinforced, nonetheless, and moreover, by an echo, by voices—or a voice—which allow phantoms and fantasies to speak and thus authenticate their reality. Sound, *phōnē*, is also the slave to artifice, and rather at a loss in its relationship with *alētheia*. Discourse wanders, fails to designate a singular being, cannot be referred to an enunciator whose degree of *paideia* would be the measure of truth for the language. Shadows, then, cannot be equated with the *logos,* though they are not totally foreign to its functioning either. They belong and do not belong. They are *impure* because man has been added to and mixed up with the operation of reflection; through his manipulation of specular powers; through his auto-reflexive projects which change the shadows, the copies that are the representations of Ideas. Therefore man will have to be expelled from this speculum, from this still specular cave, so that no possibility of a self-portrait may remain. No two ways about it, a form, even if it be a shadow, must be sired by, standardized against *one* face, *one* presence, *one* measure: that of Truth. The *alētheia* suffers no confusion, no confrontation of figure(s)—no overdetermination of any kind, one could say. *Alētheia* alone will appear, more or less disguised or unveiled. *Jealous of its singularity.* And those who would lay claim to some contemplation of themselves—to some representation of a narcissistic jouissance, perhaps?—would thereby lose wisdom and reason. They would lie asleep, a prey to dreams, paralyzed-chained by a spectacle that delights their eyes. In this way they would neither achieve knowledge nor rise to govern the city in justice, but would languish unwanted in underground prisons.

Now, in the *apaideusia* of the cave this misunderstanding about identifying shadows, reflections, and even copies is still possible. It is even probable. The virtualities of verisimilitude have yet to be banished. Particularly since the "things" projected remain behind the men and are reflected *as* a man would reflect "himself," by inverting the usual visual coordinates of "bodies" and of all natural beings; note that the light leaving the right eye meets the left side of the "object" under inspection. If we add, or repeat that the "things" being reflected are the effigies of men's bodies. . . .

Bastard or Legitimate Offspring?

So the philosophy candidate will be brought out of the cave so that he can be introduced to views that are fairer, loftier, and more precise. To the *orthotis*. He is dragged away from error, indistinctness, indifferentiation, indecision. Away from the cave in which it was still not radically impossible to reflect (upon) and reproduce the self and thereby constitute oneself within (an) origin and (as) an original. Such an economy of reproduction-production of like (to the self) cannot be reconciled with that dictated by the pre-existence of Truth. Therefore man will be taken out of the cave and referred to an *other* origin—the origin of sameness— an *other* life, which both predate everything and are still to come, to come back, still to be recollected. *The Idea is an infinitely receding matrix,* and man will not enter or turn back to it, any more than he was already able to get out of it. For the infinite is not to the measure of man, is not on the scale of *his* history, *his* self. Or at least it is *reasonable* to think so. He will only be able to move close to the infinite or away from it in asymptotic fashion, by more or less good, true, enlightened visions, by more or less harmonious numerical relationships, by more or less appropriate language.

But the genealogical conception has been broken. The child—at least this seems to the intention of the *paideia,* of the *formation* or education— will be cut off from any remaining empirical relation with the womb. From everything that might remind him, bring him back toward, turn him in the direction of *his* beginning, an origin that is still inscribed within and also inscribes a *proper* individual history of one's own—one that re-marks itself in its projects, its projections, detours, returns, as well as in their metaphors. One that determines and overdetermines sight, hearing, language, tropism, and thus renders them improper in the sight of Truth. Degenerate shadows of Truth, fakes, fantasies occur once man meddles in the process of reproduction and representation. *The offspring of Truth become bastards.* No one knows what origin, what originating being to attribute them to. Orphans of a simple, pure—and Ideal—origin. At best, hybrids. Engendered in a matrix that is still empirical, by the relation of man to a beginning that remains diachronic, and by the "fire" that in that cave is a figure for a more legitimate ancestry.

So the man held captive by this excessively "natural" conception and birth will be uprooted and referred to a more distant, lofty, and noble origin. To an arche-type, a Principle, an Author, and he would have to re-cognize himself through his relation to it. Since no neat line can be drawn around the representation of the womb/matrix, which never offers itself as a "presence"; since the relation of that place to its "copies" cannot be entered as evidence; since there is no possibility of making "being" and reproduction of "beings" out of that original *topos*, that *khōra* whose formlessness and amorphous extension exceeds all "beings"; since there is no way to get round or behind that formless origin by seeing it/her, naming, representing, standardizing it/her; and since there is also no way of simply ignoring it/her, *then she/it will be extrapolated into the infinity of the Idea.* Not that the Idea is visible or representable either, but *it conjures up a blindness over origin.* It is the source that informs any recognition man might have that his own creation is outside perception, his suit beyond appeal, his journey (back) to the daylight impracticable. The Idea is both root and branch of a genealogical tree according to which the establishment of a chain of relationships can be set up, the calculation of degrees of kinship are henceforward all regulated by "mimesis."

The Father's Vision: Engendering with No History of Problems

A Hymen of Glass/Ice

But this source is already a mirror. The enlightenment of the Idea makes flames just like a mirror that has concentrated the light. Of the Sun, of the Good. And, in a different way, of the eye, of the soul, of the eye (of the) soul. Since these are also specula. This speculogamy blinds all the more effectively because it amounts to a *specular auto-gamy.* The same, (specifically) mirror, brings its reflections together and spawns a genealogy. It has to be the same if the hierarchy of ideas, their progression as well as their infinite regression, is to arise out of a certain order. A single one will reproduce itself differently in each, according to how clean, shining, polished each may be, how apt it is for reflection. Descendence and ascendence are degrees of perfection in the realization of the reproduction of the Idea. Which is already, also, a speculum.

The Unbegotten Begetter

And the dazzling brilliance that a certain Sunrise will light in those *hymen-marriages of mirrors* makes it necessary to avert the sensitive eyes a little longer from that blinding, fiery light. The membrane of the eye, at the very least, must be preserved for future generations. The fire of the eye is not yet sufficiently akin to the Sun or related to its solar ancestry to join the Sun without experiencing a real bolt from the blue. Disaster strikes any unmatched match, any relation between different genres, any marriage other than a contemplation of one's likeness in the joining of gazes by father and son. Which is produced in the light, ultimately of the Good. Master and Father, God of all good intelligence. *Without origins, or course.* Or at least no beginning will be known for him and he knows no beginning. Father and son take pleasure in the Good, whose interests they represent, though no estimate is possible of the capital at risk. These are the dues that Socrates will not pay to the apprentice philosopher, that he in turn will pass on in his theoretical chain without any possibility of their being evaluated or made good. This is the balance that cannot be traced to any account. For the only marks of identification are to be found in certain attributes of the (so-called) creditor. In that, for example, he procreates everything without being himself engendered and *thus puts an end to what has been staked in the game of generation.* Permanence, ad infinitum, of him who dies away with the time of (his) gestation and projects (himself) into specula that are more or less appropriate in truth, into the immortal semen of light. Origin unknown. And this in order to harvest necessarily speculative fruits, to gather them together and add to a capital in the name of which you will be required to keep accounts. Not, as you might have imagined, so that you regain your goods that way, all that you had (re)produced in the accumulation of such wealth, or that had been stolen from you, taken by eminent domain. No. Rather so that you acknowledge a debt in order to profit from at least *a mirage of so much gold.* And the indebtedness continues. Rightfully. The son will defer paying off a debt that gives him benefits. Even if he suffers from being in debt, if he pays to prolong this mystification. He will go so far as to give up his life to keep up this overbid on eternity. The eternity of the Father's Good. Since he has been promised a share in it, provided it is made over in his image. All this, of course, requires that he turn his back on any beginning that is still empirical, still too material and matrical, and that he receive being only from the one who wills himself as origin without beginning.

He who has never dwelled within the mother will always already have seen the light of day. The oblivion of incarceration in the shadow and the water of the mother's cave, room, womb, that immemorial home, the blindness shrouding the memory, blocking reminiscence, that inoperable leucoma covering the eye (of the soul)—all this the Father vows to do away with by dazzling you with an endless day. It is too early, however, to put such an *alētheia* into operation. *Forgetting you have forgotten* requires a long and methodical initiation. Some time must elapse, some distance must be covered, some turns managed, mimes enacted. There must be a continuing and overlapping of operations which repeat and seek to transpose traces that are effective particularly perhaps because they resist appearing. Scenographies which precede and prepare the possible re-inscription of ideal forms. Within the soul.

Exorcism of the Dark Night

So, there, it is proper to look at *the shadows*. Necessary to go back to nocturnal gazing and back through the darkness of the night. It is "easier." "Without any doubt." It is, above all, essential. A deliberate repetition can first revive and then extinguish the pregnancy of impressions that elude all demonstration. A skillful graphic treatment can betray the meaning of the associative tracks, may invert them, for example. Shadow, that stolen backdrop that makes night, will thus be re-presented in front. Directly opposite and, if anything, high up. The originary blindness that resists the perception of what had occurred, earlier, underground, of that left-over merchandise that follows the progress of the *paideia,* haunts its prospective development, affects its aim, is made into an "easier" sight to see. This backside becomes less ghostly once it has been set out front in the field of vision, even if it isn't very shiny. The important thing is to ensure that no re-apparition, no phantom, rises out of the bowels of the earth. All nostalgia for going back toward the mystery of the earth's womb must be banished. The shadowy, the impenetrable, the secret, the night, are henceforward set down right on the horizon, in front of the gaze. Once a new role for them has been worked out in this way, it will undermine their premises, their ante-cedence vis-à-vis the present. At least this is the notion, and one that can be tried out by *topographic* manipulations. All the more effective for being silent, at present. No speech can accompany the permutations at work. In the present of its word, the logos is powerless to put the back in front, the forward backward. Even though that is its whole project and labor. Even if it will benefit, in doing so, from writing tricks whose duplicative effects entail more than one twist. Language always proceeds from a beginning to an end, from a past to a future, but as it necessarily has recourse to writing, this progression is always liable to turn around on itself. It is an artifact that must in this case be covered over lest it under-

mine the *teleological credit rating*. And initiation into the irrefutableness of
the final end, the first cause, enforces silence. Fracture(s) in the unfolding
of discourse that mask(s) the part played by the power of him who
redoubles, setting everything upside down and back to front. And vice
versa of course. And even if night is still a place to be in, even if man still
finds himself "in the middle of" the night, night is no longer at the
source: at best it is an enclosure, and all that is irreducible in this mid-
night seems set to become the object of a mere optical transaction.
Among men. The darkness must exist for the light to appear. In the
shadow, one can more easily start to re-habituate the gaze to the power
of the Sun. "It is easier." The shadows will thus serve as relief for the
Sun's brilliance.

Astrology as Thaumaturgy: A Semblance (of a) Sun

In fact "the heavenly bodies and the heavens themselves" are what the
initiate now turns toward. And what he will contemplate in the night is
the light of the stars and the moon. Methodically getting closer to the
sun's light. Reflections precede and prepare for recollection of the original one. One grasps what the original is capable of re-producing, what it
causes, before arriving at recognition of the cause itself. Which the eye of
the body cannot perceive.

The foundation continues to hide from mortal gaze. It is in fact always
buried beneath, always *behind:* the earth, the mother, birth, the surface of
every body. Always *inside:* the womb, the cave, the soul, the Idea. The
inscription of the foundation is overlaid by all its offspring that people this
life, this earth, this gaze. Its attraction must be resisted if an ideal source is
to be imposed upon them. They will therefore be represented as *less* good,
less true, *less* right. Less resplendent. Pale echoes of a more dazzling reality,
replicas of a more valuable model. Now, all the things that currently
figure as copies are reminiscent of the fakes in the cave, give or take a few
twists and turns: shadows/lights, facing backward/across from, fetish-
statues/cosmic process, limited space of the grotto/world. . . . The specular objective is displaced, but without a word. They pretend to reduce it
and in fact make it disappear.

Obviously there are no more magicians. The higher level of fakery
forbids their being called back. The recourse to astrology at this point
functions as thaumaturgy, all covered up by the "natural." Is nature
herself becoming a mirror? Reflect on (or in) that! There's no wizardry in
it, or so they say. Providing that the object of reflection is directed by the
Father's Good. Or by the Sun here. The double will then be "authentic."
Appropriate. *The fact that semblance has passed into the definition of the proper
will have gone unnoticed.* It wasn't seen. And yet it is there. That little,

pedagogic, detour through astrology—"it is easier"!—determines the fate of the story that follows.

And since the power of fantasy is now circumvented in/by the star, "last of all" man "will be able to look at the sun itself." One might add: this is what he will wish to do. This will be his only desire, even. The sun has a monopoly on attraction. And if the sight of its "reflections in water or any other medium" could hold the attention of one unaware of the waste involved in such reduplication and procreation; if it was necessary to retrace the links in the chain of "copies" in order to sustain proof of the model they are based on; if the struggle with childhood, with the blindness correlated with birth (in another body) was unavoidable and demanded to be methodically pursued in order to purge the sight of its fascination with the charms of the senses—perhaps with all this behind it, the preliminary education, the formation, has arrived at its goal now. At its first goal. The Sun. Quit of the "mediums" that permitted his reproduction in images of more or less good, truth, and beauty, freed from the matrical and material support he had needed in order to spawn so many more or less bastard offspring whom the apprentice philosophy had put up with in the childhood of philosophy, now the Sun at last will be envisioned in his omnipotence. His sovereignty. His autonomy. Himself, "in his own proper place, and contemplating him as he is."

A Question of Property

The Idea of Ideas, alone, is itself in itself. Confusing signified, signifier, referent, *Idea holds nothing outside itself.* It neither indicates nor indexes anything *other* than itself, however akin. And needs no heterogeneous *vehicle,* no foreign *receptacle,* in order to signify and represent itself. The idea goes beyond such mere methodological, generative procedures. It is the end of every road, even the road of dialectic. Closing it off and/or opening it up to the One (of the) All. This steep rocky ascent along which an obstetrician and then a philosophy teacher have dragged the child, the adolescent, the young man, ends at last in the crowning glory of the Idea. Of the Idea (of the) All. End of all. Which holds the project of all genealogy, though it is never made flesh for all that. Greedy of its substance whose economy sustains its reality. An ideal that will not submit to being determined by the diversity of any matter, but confers and conserves its own indefinitely identical identity. Like unto self, unaided by any re-presentation or figuration. Certainty of self-identity, unassisted by any mirror. Is this true? In that case, how do the ideal organization of the All and absolute intelligence relate to one another?

But when notions like this are raised so early on, the philosophy candidate is being forced to make discoveries that are too important. There is a risk of turning his soul inside out, sending it hither and thither, disturbing the harmony of its makeup. Perhaps for a good while. For, at the point he now is, he still risks confusing "sensible" and "intelligible," what can be seen and what, invisibly, informs the whole view. Thus he will perhaps imagine that the cause of all that is (*aitios*), the maker and father of the world, could easily appear before him. In a *parousia* that would stop him cold, dead in his tracks, sear his vision. *To see the father face to face . . . is as much as to say—die!* And our young man is not ready to choose that kind of life. No doubt he will surreptitiously be brought round to it. But he must be reassured, told stories that veil the truth, as children are. How about the story of the sun?—that's always been a great favorite. Or the one about the poor larva, prisoner in a dark cave who metamorphoses into a Prince of the City when he discovers his solar origin? Why not? So here he is introduced to his illustrious ancestor. Not to some degraded image of the latter's prestige, but to himself, "as he is." But will man be able to bear the sight? "Certainly."

Certainty is necessary if the fable is to have full effect. The myth here is in the service of the demonstration. And just as the solar shadows are "natural" and thus have imperceptibly introduced the fake into the economy of property, so gazing upon the sun will have served to subordinate the gaze, which is still mortal, to the intelligible order. The fiction at work in the tale has achieved this piece of dialectical sleight of hand. Charmed, sleepwalking under the spell of fairy tales, encouraged to daydream by his teacher, permitted to dream again to a *certain extent,* according to a *certain calculation,* the child has apparently given up his fantasies, without being able to come to terms with them. He has left the place, still based in the senses, where the traces of his desires were inscribed. No doubt he will not be thrown out violently, once and for all. The wound suffered by being thus torn away might leave scars in the memory. Reminders, rejoinders. Passages, and hemorrhages, between sensible and intelligible. Resulting in sensation-ideas, ideal sensations. Any self-respecting philosopher avoids confusion like that. The rise toward essence must be ensured by a regression away from the senses.

Naturally. The "natural" excludes, little by little, any impression with a hint of the senses, any epigraph with a touch of the body.

But within that progression, some *switches-over have taken place,* without anyone noticing. Instead of the objects in the cave, the fetish-statues which afford the shadows underground their phantasmal quality, cosmic elements are substituted that cannot be suspected of human manipulation. It is God-the-Father who created the heaven, and the stars, and these convert you to his idea. To his image. This world is "true" only insofar as it is engendered by Him alone, and related to Him alone. This is fairly evidently the case for everything that dominates and stands above the earth, treading her under foot, under its erection. As far as what happens *beneath and within* is concerned, caution is in order. Trickery is always possible, escapes attention. Of course the father is the final cause of that too, as will be demonstrated to you. But things can occur beneath and within which go beyond the father's previsions, projects, projections. One may challenge his power by making oneself a demiurge. By giving birth to children *also.* And that raises the question of appropriation, of property. Doing as the father does is right only insofar as it serves his unique prestige, the supremacy of his Good. Sharing out the credits makes "men" ungovernable. Therefore anything made under the earth, within that almost-mother, has arguable, and certainly secondary, value, and tends to distract the attention from concerns worthy of consideration. In fact, any reference made to such things serves only to turn man away from them, *seeing* how "unnatural" their products are. Real "nature" is unveiled on the path up to the heavens, not on the track back into the earth. The mother. That place connected still with artful conception, haunted by magicians who would have you believe that (re)production can be executed by skillful imitators, working from the divine plans. The cave gives birth only to phantoms, fakes or, at best, images. One must leave its circle in order to realize the factitious character of such a birth. Engendering the real is the father's task, engendering the fictive is the task of the mother—that "receptacle" for turning out more or less good copies of reality. Property, ownership, and self-definition are the attributes of the father's production. They define the work of the father "as such." To be. To own. To be one's own. Properties. Semblance exists, it seems, only because of the scene of reproduction that remains *material, matrical.* Here the cave is the "lowest" representative of that place.

300

Thus the mother-matter gives birth only to images, Father-Good only to the real, insofar as he can make himself known in the eyes of mortals without recourse to the senses. In a chiasmus of family benefits, the father is given all rights and powers over "his children." Provided that they are not bastards and have sloughed off the hybrid character of their mortal birth, these children resemble only their sire. *An optical chiasmus operates too.* The father denies the conditions of specula(riza)tion. He is unaware, it would seem, of the physical, mathematical and even dialectical coordinates of representation "in a mirror." In any case he insists on remaining ignorant of the irreducible inversion that occurs in the identification with the other, as other. After all, he refuses to be at all unless he be, if not identical with himself, at least like himself, though nothing must shape this as an act of faith or a tenet of law. This is an exorbited, exorbitant empire the father has, requiring the mother to be a mere receptacle for his germinating seed, the matter needed to give birth to his deeds of credit, charged with the maieutics of making them appear "as such." Unveiling them, digging them out of the mother lode that is still too close to the body, to the earth.

That the figure given to the father's potency might have been *inverted by being inscribed* will not be considered. That the mother might be capable of *reversing the self-identity* of the potency that manifests itself thereby, will not be evaluated in such terms. The crisis whereby power might possibly be overturned, the risk of some change which might sap the continuation of the same power, is at the heart of the (de)negation that underlies and threatens the coherence of the Socratic line of argument, and of the Platonic discourse. Their foundation is always already set in a bottomless pit in order to uphold overall the authority of the paternal logos. The seeds of life, truth, goodness, and beauty depend upon the excision of the specular base.

Yet, *the disavowal of the mirror,* that hard currency of speculation whose value will go unnoticed, willfully unnoticed, in the rectitude and purity of the *orthotis,* the gaze, *will burn the eyes* of anyone who dares to look upon its splendid causality. Let us not even speak of the father. He need only delegate his representative in order to blind us. *The Sun, brilliance of silver-backing in suspension.* Convergence upon one place, which would have no other place but its own, of the light reflected in every looking glass, every speculum. Focus of incandescence, in that it has captured all the flames. In that it deprives the reflection of the cause of its luster.

Deprives the "earth" of the charm of her mirages, the fiery play of her hollow, concave mirrors. Earth's burning, incendiary chambers are stripped of their function as cause, of their native and future wealth, for fear they may produce change; now they are mere dark holes in which lucid reason risks drowning. Old mines, fallen into neglect, where no precious metal gleams anymore. *Hysteras from which the philosopher's stone has already been taken away.* If any fire remain, it is lit by the hand of man. An artful blaze. Mother-matter, surface obedient to imprint, docile to embrace, nourishing stock for sending out the new shoots of the patriarch, can, theoretically, only send back a dulled echo of the brilliance of the being that warms, lights, and fecundates her. As he wills. Sometimes distantly, turning her to ice in which he mirrors himself, without coupling. Such frigidity is required for an exact self-knowledge, for the maintenance of self-identity. She is just chilled enough to prevent his being deformed in her waters, lost in her ever receding depths, but not so chilled that she might shine with tenfold radiance, multiplying the light's power. A mild, mat frost. A cold whiteness that will send back the light. But not concentrate or absorb it, in truth.

Occasionally the son/sun gives a new silver-backing to the mother-mirror. This is seen, every day. All the same, he too scorns the place of generation. Takes a turn around the ground, but at a distance. With a certain hauteur. Unwilling to owe fire to anything but himself. For all time. Consuming his no doubt celestial body in disdain for any entry into matter. As for the immortality of combustion, that is assured by the father's desire. His will is that the sun should "order" the universe in conformity with his divine ideas.[5] Invested with power, the sun/son will rule the world in his absence, according to his law, including the "earth." Taking for himself most of her attributes. On a vaster, universal scale. Making "all things we see visible," causing "generation, growth and nourishment," source of "their existence and reality."[6] Birth that will no longer be limited by death but will beat to the rhythm of eternity. Enumeration of mornings and evenings, sunrises and sunsets, seasons, years. Over and over again. Like and unlike. Harmoniously ordering the process of living beings, but under the constant threat of materialist anarchy. Teaching them to count—*moving image of a time without memo-*

[5]*Laws*, XII, 966e, 967a.
[6]*Republic* VI, 509b.

ry—but also to measure and survey the surface of the earth. Such geometry would be unthinkable without the power of solar projections. Only
earth's crust will be given consideration, as if she were dead; for all the
flames have been pressed back into the core, at a depth beyond the
boundary of proof. Almost unknown to this whole world dominated by
light. For the most important function of this scion is to make the whole of
"being" clearly visible. As the torch of absolute intelligence, the sun/son
initiates the eye in the distinction between false and true, between the
shadow and the body it doubles, the copy and its model, the reflection and
the original. Appropriating certain privileges and maternal rights, this son
takes after his father, imitating him in all things, to their mutual self-
interest.

Sun, ex-stasy of the copula. Cause of all that is. Focus of a jouissance
which now is reduced to merely dazzling the eye. Luminescent receptacle. Matrix for reproducing images. *Lucid* intercourse will give rise only
to appearances now, will limit itself to bringing more or less adequate
representations (back) into the world. And the basis for them will remain
external, will no longer go *inside.* Matter is always subject to decomposi-
tion, and the membrane of the eye will not suffer the introduction of
dead flesh.

A Form That Is Always the Same

The Passage Confusing Big and Little, and Vice Versa
Pleasure becomes more lofty and subtle. Multiplies almost on the
instant. It takes place in the twinkling of an eye. Coming together in
swift complicity with the Sun in order to recognize *forms.* Earthly forms
still, admittedly. Yet ga(u)ges of the relationship of all things to the
Father's good. Immediate assurance that they participate in the immutability of his power. Which, of course, knows no modification of its
attributes, no change in morphology, no detumescence ever. Always
identical to itself, no ups and downs.

Such constancy, in truth, moves beyond the viewpoint of mere mortals. What one sees everyday is more variable. It is transformed according to the distance at which it is perceived: sometimes smaller, sometimes bigger. In point of fact, it appears as smaller or bigger, bigger or
smaller, without proximity and distance having anything to do with it.[7]
Such perceptions "lead to contradiction" and "call for further exercise of

---

[7]*Republic,* VII, 523.

thought." What troubles the mind is that sight should tolerate the fact that big and small are not, necessarily, distinct, separate terms, that the one may become the other. Similarly the mind finds it inadmissible, should the need arise to consult another sense, that "the same thing is felt to be both hard and soft."[8] What precious experiences these are which "puzzle the mind and need investigation," "strike our senses simultaneously with opposite impressions."[9] Thus the eye that is disturbed by the contradictions set before it will gradually learn to train its gaze upon ideas. Fixed ideas. In order to gain a more rigorous appreciation of "big" and "small," the eye will be trained to approach them only when armed with mathematical instruments. Knowing how to estimate real size is *a job for science*. It is a matter of estimating the relation of the thing in question to another or several other things of the same type. And if you have no skill in the matter, you are advised to consult an expert.

The Standard Itself/Himself

But for ideal measurement and ideal value, reference will have to be made to the *standard*. Unfortunately, this is not about to display itself, which is in fact for the general good. Its size outstrips anything nature can envisage. It is not that it refuses to materialize but that its activity knows no intrinsic limits. In the first place, it has no need or desire to be made manifest and come into existence. Its being and perfection are self-sufficient. If it does appear, this is through pure benevolence. Restrained goodness because it can never fully exercise its potency. For that is incommensurable with the extension of the universe. No receptacle can satisfy it or is capable of holding it entirely. Thus it remains each person's duty to imitate the standard according to his "intuition" and "the measure of his ability," "because it is the property of the most unchanged and the same, and body is not included in this class. That which we term heaven or the universe . . . partakes of a bodily nature, and therefore cannot be entirely free of perturbation."[10]

Better to Revolve upon Oneself—But This Is Possible Only for God-the-Father

The forms set before the sight—and indeed any of the senses—are thus submitted to modifications. Alterations which indicate that they are still mortal. These phenomena of growth and decline, of failure to reach higher, of falling back at last into another body, threaten every living

[8]*Republic*, VII, 524a.
[9]*Republic*, VII, 524d–e.
[10]*Statesman*, 269c–d.

man, and the man, according to his ability, begins to keep them at bay by avoiding any overly rectilinear tension, and overly linear tropism: from a beginning to an end, from a birth to a death, and reciprocally.[11] By preferring to submit to a motion "single and in the same place, and of the same kind, and therefore . . . only subject to a reversal, which is the least alteration possible."[12] Imitating in some measure the movement that the demiurge has imprinted upon the world. Cartwheeling, catherine-wheeling. Turning indefinitely on one's axis, around one's center, without moving in any other way. But "the leader of all moving things is alone able to revolve perpetually on himself."[13] Only God turns eternally round upon himself. To that part of mortality that resembles him most—the universe, the sun, and the soul of men—he to some extent grants this privilege.

In fact during the propedeutic the student is taught a number of pirouettes and flip-flops. Taught the, disguised, *circularity* of its process. As for the rest, man makes constant moves backward and forward so as not to fall into the chaos of a nature that has yet to know divine intervention.[14] The souls of men, then, would begin to escape the avatars that are the fate of being in this universe. On condition, however, that they turn their "gaze" only upon ideal forms.

We are not at that stage yet. Even if the time to get there is running out. For the sight of the sun "in his own place" runs a strong risk of putting out bodily eyes from their sockets. Ravishing them ecstatically, consuming them utterly, leaving gaping holes. Unless of course the sight of the sun has closed the eyes forever in a defensive occlusion of the diaphragm before such brightness. In any case there is a loss of the opening that might serve to regulate adaptation to the quantity of light, to its quality, to the distance from its source as well as to the size of the forms to be reproduced. Such sun-burns can destroy anything that has not yet become frozen by the "like" or "as if" of metaphorization. Heliogamy is disastrous for the still organic membrane of the eye: living tissue, unfit to receive the glare of such a fiery star.

The sun, no doubt, figures at this point in order to remind us that any hierogamy demands the sacrifice of this present life, this present earth

[11]*Phaedo,* 72b.
[12]*Statesman,* 269e.
[13]Ibid.
[14]Cf. the myth of the *Statesman.*

and gaze. All animate matter must be reorganized if Being is to be imposed in its truth. Only the dead see God. Men's gaze will, at that time, be opened onto the eternity of the invisible even as their eyes, finally glazed over, are closed by those still living. They gaze at something that cannot appear to them, of course. They cannot perceive what it is. This is true for the sun: the gaze will gain no understanding of its "*ti estin*" and only a little of its "*oion estin.*" What manner it may be. Exclamation that stops the breath. Halts, abruptly, the unfolding of your address, the thread of your induction or deduction. What *ellipsis of being* is this that cannot be represented as it is. The copula *blinds* any "subject," especially in regard to its demonstration. In this blind state, this *slit* in vision, being shines forth. And its brilliance is covered by the "subject's" claim to ownership of its attributes. The copula, ultimately, rules out any statement of attributes for they can never be fully adequate. Even if they were enumerated ad infinitum, their summation would be inexhaustible. Even if one were to repeat, indefinitely, the operation of the proof, the sum total of the working would not add up to the motivation that brings them about. (The) being interrupts the simplicity of the relationship with the self, alters presence. (The) being splits the "subject" off from all his representations, from every predicate. Projects him upon the screen of its mirages—Plato's *hystera* which has been turned inside out and back to front—or refers him back to something that might be behind him, existing before his constitution as an entity, as a proper noun/name. Only God who refuses all determination and has nothing behind him, nothing that goes back earlier than he does, is. Extrapolation of the copula of all existence, of all that is, effectively. Has been, one day, conceived.

The lapse in time between the moment of conception and consciousness can never be caught up with. And it cannot be evaded either, as it returns to the memory, even in its visions: dazzling intuitions of seeing, unreflectedly, without target or measurement. The lapse is also expressed in the arrogance of a logos that remains unaware of the process of its gestation, an in-fant when it comes to the mystery of its (re)production. Yet that mystery will *encircle,* imprison the "subject" just like the amnios, the uterus, the mother, which he refused to take account of. Claiming to be self-sufficient. Or to be succoured by the father alone, to be indebted only to the father's law.[15] The receptacle upon which the father inscribes his will, and casts the seed of his truth, is not designated *as such* in the present of speech. No explicit reference to it can be made at each stage in the progression of discourse. Nothing denominates it in any

[15]This is true of Socrates, who wishes to be child of the laws alone.

statement that is made, and yet it under-lies the formation and transformation of all statements. No proper sense, proper noun, proper signifier
expresses the *matrix* of any discourse, or any text, even the legal text. The
necessity of its (re)production is absent from what it lays out. Eclipse of
the mother, of the place (of) becoming, whose non-representation or
even disavowal upholds the absolute being attributed to the father. He no
longer has any foundation, he is beyond all beginnings. Between these
two abysses—nothing/being—language makes its way, morphology
takes shape, once the mother has been emptied out. Enumerating all the
"beings" formed in her, and their properties, in order to relate them to
the father. In conformity with his desire and his law.

The Mother, Happily, Does Not Remember

Or so the theory goes. She is always a clean slate ready for the father's
impressions, which she forgets as they are made. Unstable, inconsistent,
fickle, unfaithful, she seems ready to receive all beings into herself. Keeping no trace of them. Without memory. She herself is without figure or
face or proper form, for otherwise "(she) would take the impression
badly because (she) would intrude (her) own shape."[16] Thus she is nothing, but shares in everything: "Wherefore, the mother and receptacle of
all created and visible and in any way sensible things, is not to be termed
earth, or air, or fire, or water, or any of their compounds, or any of the
elements from which these are derived, but is an invisible and formless
being which receives all things and in some mysterious way partakes of
the intelligible, and is most incomprehensible."[17] Properly speaking, one
can't say that she mimics anything for that would suppose a certain
intention, a project, a minimum of consciousness. She (is) pure mimicry.
Which is always the case for inferior species, of course. Needed to define
essences, her function requires that she herself have no definition. Neither will she have any distinct appearance. Invisible, therefore. As the
father is invisible? And the origin of the visible escapes representation.
She is in excess of any identification of presence. The "beyond" of the
mother, however, cannot be measured alongside that of the father. The
two must be separated to avoid conflicts of pre-existence and a crisis of
authority. The power of the father must supplant that of the mother if
order is to be maintained. But there will be little discussion about the
respective economies of these two excesses that exceed "presence." It
seems that the decision has already been taken and must not be ques-

16 *Timaeus,* 50e.
17 *Timaeus,* 51a–b.

tioned here. It is already settled elsewhere, once and for all. On "another" scene that informs this one, knowingly or nor.[18]

A Source-Mirror of All That Is

Similarly, it seems to have been resolved that *the mother's relation to the specular* is an issue that cannot be raised. Yet it is certainly the mirror which, memoryless, forgetful of all traces and imprints, re-presents the image of things set before it. And as far as the intelligible goes, has the mirror any other function than to define things by withdrawing itself from specific characterization. No doubt it may be designated as "sensible being" or even "intelligible being," but not insofar as it produces the veri-similitude of every "being" (étant).

The father does not accept—for himself or his word—that everything has already been started by resemblance, for he wills himself eternally self-identical. He prefers to be (his) absolute mirror, reflect (himself) in(de)finitely. *As-if-the-standard for everything that is.* Is this for fear of an alteration in some mirage that is always on the verge of being deformed, or transformed? But of which he still claims to be the source. *Is Being a mirror? Or a source?* Speculative aporia. The "subject"—being (être)—has already *become* the re-source of specularizations. Failing anomalies, the predicate, the attributes—mirror, source—already testify that they belong in some relationship to the "subject." The copula—is—reenacts the specular game. If the "subject" of discourse is the father, he is the resource of all specula(riza)tions. The crucial thing is not to know that, one day, the subject *came into being.* That is relied upon a *copulative conjunction* in order to (begin to) be. As a result, you will never see the Father appear, come into life, into existence. The father is, always has been, pure speculation. That which escapes the eyes of a body that is, of course, still mortal. Harmony, hidden from the gaze of simple citizens, reigns over the ministry of public funds. If people saw it, they might demand some accountability or, even, take back some part of the father's goods, of his Good. Dismember value, capital. Divide it up between two genders, at least, *two kinds* of resources and specularizations. The logos would no longer simply be, for itself, the means of translating his will alone; of establishing, defining, and collecting his properties into one Whole. Truth would lose its *univocal* and universal character. It could be *doubled,* for example. At the very least it would have a *reverse* and an *inverse* to shore up its constitution as such. In any case, another, still

---

[18]Cf. all the statements on the function of woman in the City, and on the need for her to give up the specificity of her gender if she is to take part in public life. For example, in *Republic* v.

hidden, aspect. Or another focus? another mirror? There would be no way of knowing which way to look anymore, which way to direct the eyes (of the soul) in order to see properly. People would go crazy. So it is far better—he says in his wisdom—for light to be his exclusive preserve. He will dispense it bountifully. Lighting the earth, the gaze, the soul. Warming and making them fertile as he will, with benevolence. But leaving them partially in darkness. Yielding them up the night, dreams, fantasies, fakes.

Thus the sun, in his own proper place, is without shadow. It is the earthly "beings" that, by resisting the light, give rise to shadows. Someone who is still fearful or unwary will recognize the "presence" of the sun there by blinding himself, for he cannot look at it directly. And perhaps the solar illumination deters people from looking at it and turns them in the direction of *darker doubles,* less closely akin to the source of light. Essentially, however, light is their origin all the same. Just as it is the cause of its reflection in/by the moon, and of its reproductions at the surface of the earth, of the sea, for nature is less brilliant than the star that dominates her. Cause, then, of shadows, reflections, images. Impotence of "beings" and of the gaze before the omni-potence.

And since nothing must escape light's principle, it is also the cause of the fakes. The father's offspring fall back into the cave. Down again into that almost-mother where it is forbidden to go lest one forget the measure (of the law of the father, alone), lest the imprints on memory fade and confusion set in as to what is true and false, good and ill, fair and foul. As to life, birth. As to Being (être). From then on opinions lose assurance, get confused and variable. Moving, vague, evasive shadows: fantasies. Truth seduced and adulterated, spawning ever more bastard representations. Obviously, the staging has already trans-formed the original place. And the "son" gets in there only under cover of trickery. The place's power has already been manipulated, its emblems made into fetishes. Man only reenters the mother forewarned and forearmed, masked, furtive, behind a curtain. And all he exposes to her infinite depths is an erection that has been turned to effigy, statue, mummy. Otherwise he may be imprisoned once more. In which case, paralyzed, chained, bewitched, he gazes at the shadow, cast on the back of the cave, of figurines made by magicians in their/his own image. Skillful imitations of the demiurge. Projections that fascinate because they have been *pulled out of true,* away from their relationships to the cause, from the engendering process of the Cause. Because they are per-verted, that is. And because they therefore allow us—if only we could turn around—to interpret the per-version that is inscribed in representation.

The Analysis of That Projection Will Never Take
(or Have Taken) Place

But who is aware that perversion has always already taken place? That the *hystera* has already been turned around, for example. And even though Socrates uses it as a kind of subterfuge—by some "mythical" chance, as it were—for pedagogic ends, this does not prevent him from being caught in his own game. In this game. *Analysis of the projection seems never to have taken place.* No proper value will be put upon the *specular inversion* that projection erases by magic. Being, Truth, Good, the power of the Father, are in no way amenable to being turned around. They go on and are eternally made manifest in their *rectitude.* With no back side or flip side. And the receptacle, the place of becoming, remembers nothing. Otherwise it would—perhaps—bear witness to the irreducible inversion that occurs in specula(riza)tion and in the re-production of any imprint, any trace, any form, even ideal ones. If the process of the Idea's inscription is to be lost to consciousness, if the mirror that has always already reflected it is to be covered over, then it is obligatory to forget that the Idea once came into being. It must, absolutely must, not be known how much the procreation of the "son," of the logos, by the father, owes to inversion. Nor that the mother is the place where that inversion occurs. That she is the one that makes it possible, practicable, that sustains it with/in her "unconsciousness." The mother, happily, seems to have no memory. She submits in all (new) projects, blind to all (new) projections. Screen-base, helping them to multiply.

But the father's empire forbids the "son" to find any shared pleasure, or even any auto-satisfaction in her. If he began to take pleasures like that—to seek his good in ways other than the search to match the image of him who alone conceived him from all eternity—he would sink into "madness." Condemned to a life sentence in the pit of irrationality. Unable to see clearly, to move around, walk, or even stand up there. As for the man or men (let's not even mention the woman as she is there only as the setting necessary for the drama) who might have lured the son into such pursuits, abusing morphology in order to lead him off the path that leads to the recollection of Ideas, they would be banished from the City. Condemned publicly for their contempt, or misunderstanding, of the workings of the law. For there can be no question—as you will have realized—of the tutor neglecting the "body" of the child. It is essential that relations of man and body should be in the service of the Beautiful and the Good. That their aim—*telos*—should be to rise up toward the Father. And that precludes them from keeping company in a place that in any way revives the maternal realm, since the dream of a mortal birth has not yet been totally banished. The urge to regress into a "nurse," a matrix, that is too material and inchoate to reproduce ideal types without smudges, spots, mess—blind spots on the eye (of the soul). *Hystera* in which conception is not even *im-maculate*. All this arouses many a fantasy bewitching to a gaze, to a soul that is still sensible, but the philosophy tutor—who is a pederast in fact—will rid the child of such things. He delivers him from the repulsive naturalness of that womb, to the point when he spurns it underfoot, under his erection. Moreover, he blocks out all nostalgia, any longing to go back to something that might have existed beforehand, apparently by occupying his rear. The order of progression must be rigorously observed at present, or there is a risk of straying down other paths. Now this is a critical moment in the coming of reason.

Completion of the *Paideia*

The Failings of an Organ That Is Still Too Sensible

The time indeed has come at last, after all this painful process, when man may *gather together*—relate in logical fashion: *sullogizoito*—his thoughts on the subject of the sun," and "proceed to argue that it is he that gives the seasons and the years, and is the guardian of all that is in the *visible* world,—to say nothing of the 'world' discovered by 'natural light'—and in a certain way the *cause of all things* which he and his fellows have been accustomed to behold." Of all that delighted them, held them captive with its spell. And so, obviously, he will *come to his decision*—with or without "evidence" (*dēlon*) after he has, theoretically, left all mere shadows and reflection behind him.

After all dreams, all fantasies, all fakes have been condemned by him as childish nonsense. After he has dealt with them once and for all. It is also best if neither "shadows" nor "reflections" have any further right to his consideration, enjoy any further credibility with him. If he has paid off the mortgage on their existence, that is, interpreted as one moment in the conversion to the *noēsis*. Henceforth he is able clearsightedly to cut through the issues of truth. His gaze has progressively become adapted to the contemplation of truth's (only) Principle. Such light is unbearable to the organic membrane of the eye, and bodily vision is, moreover, always limited by a cavelike socket. It also takes place in a camera obscura. And is at the mercy of a play of panes of glass that turn the sun's rays aside, breaking, bending their reflected and inverted trajectories, also upon a projection screen. The bursts of light are limited, de-fined when they have to squeeze through a hole that varies in size. Sometimes even their forcible entry will be blocked by the intervention of the para-phragm (of the) eyelid. And what is more, some of them will have to be spent in vain: what sterility in a blind spot unfitted to reproduce the eternal seed of the Father! What humiliating adjustments for the Father to make, he whose omnipotence suffers no shaping authority foreign to its essence.

Thus the sensible—any organ that remains rooted in the senses—is too individual to suit heliogamy. For the soul, or at least its more lofty part, things are different, it seems. The soul alone would be fitted by nature to ensure the hiero-grammatic or ideo-grammatic function. Working alongside reminiscence that would restore the soul to its true essence. Free of any memory of a past except that one which predates and is more finished and perfect than anything a mortal can conceive within time. The soul is led back to the proof of what once had been, before it suffered its fall back into the body: Being. And Being is never made flesh as such. It is thus, in the strict meaning of the word, without shadows, reflec-tions, images, of self. Leaving these (its) doubles to anything or anybody that persists in assuming a material form. Being, store of non-birth. Completeness of what has not been engendered in an empirical matrix. *Unity, totality, entity of one who or that abstains from any conjunction what-ever.* That claims *to take the place* of all conjunctions, but has (had), for its own part, nothing in common with any relationship(s) that can be enu-merated. Im-matriculated. Perfection in a copula that defies modes, times, ways of intercourse. Of conceptions. Reversing the relation of the "subject" to his "attributes," and by means of this inversion, retrover-sion, tying up the loose ends of the script. The phallic scenography.

A Seminar in Good Working Order

The philosopher is now invited to this erasure of the beginning. At least if he wants to get to the highest point of his climb. But this erection, even though it is entrusted to the higher part of man's soul, is not achieved without risk, notably the risk of falling back down. New shocks to the senses. Recurrence of the attraction for certain bodies, of a liking for fakes and fetishes. Relapse into dreams and fantasies that cast a veil once more over the purity of intelligence, sending man off in different directions. Unsure of what is true and false, good and evil, . . . of what really is and what just appears, like-unto-truth. Doubting everything to the point of returning, skeptically, to the existence of materially perceptible impressions alone. Imprints of pleasure but also of pain which, for one who set out on the journey to a greater light, always make themselves vividly felt. Excess of rapture. Patho-logical ecstasy. The soul's balance is upset by the attraction it feels for "beings" that are out of proportion to what, now, dominates its organization: the Father's word.

So a man can no longer, simply, turn back toward what he has already left behind him. Even if he never knew exactly what was at stake there. And burning. Even if he has been prematurely detached and torn away from it by the convictions of a master. Has been seduced, without realizing it, by the authority of a philosophy teacher who sometimes abuses his power a little. Who takes back from the child—and childhood—what he needs to ensure the pro-ject of his course, to go on lighting up the paths of reason with geometric optics. Who makes use of his pupil's receptive "soul," a matrix that remains intact, to sow the seeds of truth which are guaranteed to grow and sprout because of the vigor of that still virgin soil, increasing the fertility of his seminar tenfold. Sending him back, moreover, an echo that is embellished and idealized by the credence of youth. Reciprocal fascination, love—but there is a need to question the status of this "shared" activity, to calculate what is lost and won by each "subject's" participation in the "attributes" of the other, in the inversion assumed by this operation—which grows and glorifies itself ceaselessly. Inspiring the older man to push the younger one's "body" further and further on in front of him toward an unreflected glory of light, in a one-way transport. He takes part in this, but contemplates and observes it, thus fulfilling his own needs. The pleasure and profit he gains in this way are of course devoted to his teaching, and willingly so since they make it possible for him to go further into the exposition of the father's rights and properties. He will not speak of these but will, thoughtlessly, by his acts, his steps into action—which escape a rational cause, if only by a flicker of a suspicion—let slip the fact that the father's rights have to turn things upside down if they are to be (re)produced.

Thus, "the father's image" will be rediscovered in the soul of the son, which has come out of self. It will be most clearly apparent in the eternal and continuing *childish unconscious* of the "son." Otherwise the son, also, would know how much that image owes and denies to specular projection and inversion. He would already have recognized that the "father" is that which is reproduced in him in order (not) to be mirrored in his absence (of self). The cover over a *blind spot* in consciousness which he fails to recognize but/and which dictates, indefinitely, the repetition of the same process. Desire to come (back) to the place where what draws one out of the self has shone forth from the beginning of time. Dream of (self) reappropriation that will pass through identification—which is, strictly speaking, impossible—on to the mirage of the ancestor.

All of this makes it imperative that there be no going back. No going back down toward the earth, or into the earth, before this journey upward has been completed, *brought to a close, at least once.* One must walk, without stopping, toward the "sun," taking no notice of the shadow that it still projects, *behind.* That double (of the self) must be neglected if one is to persevere with the climb. Leaving it to the still *material* extension of the path that one is following and ascending, in the *inverse direction.* Perhaps abandoning it also to the profit of the tutor who is helping with this progression. Who more or less keeps up with the race, perhaps slowing down from time to time. Who keeps an eye on the repercussions of this method, of the steps taken, in order to report his findings elsewhere, but urging the "candidate" to give up any autonomous observation, evocation, figuration, in his approach. For this is the indispensable condition for arriving at the only purity of conception recognized in philosophy. Thus he goes on with his "ordeal," the success of which is gauged by his blindness to everything around him. His eyes, starting from their sockets, gaze only upon what has and will have no definite representation: the father's desire. For that never appears as such, but abstains from all adequate, exhaustive in-formation. It is the store of being, the excess of all (self) re-production. Certainly, the father names his delegate and scion, the Sun. And if one is to try to win the game, one has to bet on the sun's brilliance. Which prevents one from seeing and brings on theoretical impotence. All the same, the sun must shine, it must not be night. And in fact the sun's illumination never constitutes more than one stage in the demonstration. One cannot remain at that stage, and end with impressions that are also sensible, with beliefs that

314

are also visible, also "apparent." But, if this be so, how does one go on rising? Reach a new milestone along the road upward?

What the child does not see, because it never offers itself to proof, is that he is being required to become, to be the "son," which is equivalent to saying that he is required to send the "father" back an image of himself. But who (is) the father? Where (is) the father? The Father is. Pure specula(riza)tion. That which is never simply represented. And if someone—the tutor, for example—takes over, usurps his function, this will happen only insofar as he wishes to set himself up as reference, guarantee for the son's entry into the "world" of philosophy. He is, himself, only standing surety for the shared birth into knowledge. Yet "the father" defies *any particularization of the form* of his mandate. Whatever his relationship to the economy of representation(s), to all that makes it possible and perpetuates it. To all that founds it, in fact, over an abyss whose opening it will be no simple matter to catch sight of. Infinite projection—(the) Idea (of) Being (of the) Father—of the mystery of conception and of the hystery where it is (re)produced. Blindness with regard to the original one who must be banished by fixing the eyes on pure light, to the point of not seeing (nothing) anymore—*the show, the hole of nothing is back again*—to the point at which the power of a mere bodily membrane is exceeded, and the gaze of the soul is rediscovered. *A-lētheia.* Reminiscence of the ideal ex-stasy, intuition of essence(s) that draws the "son" (back) out of himself, into the name(s) of the Father. Before any empirical beginning to his story. Jouissance of the truer being who re-illumines, at last, the screen-base for ideological projections: the soul, which has been darkened by the materiality of a birth still all too rooted in nature.

An Immaculate Conception

But what becomes of the mother from now on? The mother (is the) becoming of (re)production which is progressively "sublated," raised, refined. She is idealized, but only by being reversed: conception becomes not only eternal but that in/by which death itself would engender life.

A monopoly on family benefits. An optical monopoly too. Henceforward harboring the bio-logical germ falls to the father alone, and he feeds his children with his word until their definitive re-birth. As for the place in which he now inscribes his will, the soul (of the son): that, in its more elevated part, is merely the matrix for the father's image, the assurance that his self-identity will endure. Obviously, he needs this remnant of incarnation in order to subsist, at least during a life that is still earthly, sensible. But turning the Other over, or turning back toward the Other, which transforms everything into mirrors, guarantees an absolute transparency for his Being. Beatitude in which his children will contemplate him/themselves in(de)finitely. Specula(riza)tion, at last, without images, without determinate representations, without the shadow of a reflection that might still suggest a role played by some body. Irradiation freed, also, from point of view, from defensive delimitation, restriction on principle demanded by organs that are still too natural. The whole field of vision, *including depth,* will be equally flooded by a light dispensed, equally, in its omnipotence. Without deformation, transformation, or loss, and equally without blindness or blurring of any kind. *Extreme confusion of sight and gaze—of the father and of the son—in an ex-quisite, ex-schizoid immortality.*

As for those who may have neglected to re-remember the source of the only good, they would be left to "the world," abandoned to the earth, a prey to metamorphoses, destiny of shadows. Buried, perhaps, in some dark hole where they are attracted and held captive, again, by their dreams and fantasies.

We are not quite at that stage yet. Even if the "time" is running short in which we are to make a choice. To decide. About true and false, good and evil. About the meaning of life. This one? The other one? About the origin of conception. But which one? We must, a while longer, trust the orders of the tutor. He follows the increasingly dangerous course of the child, preventing him from turning back and thus seeing that *the shadow he leaves on the ground gets longer with each step he takes toward the sun,* that the blind spot that the screen of his body projects upon the path grows even as his gaze is illumined. The darkness, behind, is abandoned to the calculations of a master who, under that form, still takes into account the part played by the material opacity of the "being" (étant) in his epistemological appraisals. Those still geometrical hypotheses which he makes in order to reach, by demonstration, the infinite order of Being. And this, in the last analysis, resists any estimate proportional to its essence. It is a harmony, in the strictest sense, without predicate. Exceeding all discursiveness, which will henceforward be left up to the philosophy class.

The Deferred Action of an Ideal Jouissance

But there, in that solar *paideia,* that preliminary education that remains cosmo-logical or even "physical," the tutor says little. His behest, though urgent, does not so much offer a line of reasoning as it pushes the adolescent forward into a dazzling ecstasy. Jouissance is still part of the system here, but it is in the process of being curbed and enslaved to the imperatives of Truth. Which does not compromise about the figures of its domination. And if scenography is tolerated or even required here as a substitute for a discourse incapable of expressing Being, this is so that the inscription of ideal forms can be re-produced in the soul. Repercussions of a jouissance that has exhausted the gaze—that remains mortal—re-marking within the *psyche* the limits of its field. Circles, in black, that rim the intuition of essence(s). Light encircled in a decisive fashion because it has been, for every "being" (étant), extremely saturating and weakening to the potency of the eye: *eidos*. "Natural" vision pierces through, crosses through, and overturns itself, at its highest point. The spindle will no longer inform the gaze, the memory, or the point of view a mortal can have on his elevation, calling up, calling back other observations, other "sensible" experiences of its attributes. Both like and unlike, sometimes contradictory. But the violent pregnancy of an all-powerful erection, tearing the ocular diaphragm that regulates the opening in response to the quantity of light, inscribes on the projection screen of the soul the inexhaustible framing of its *ideal* morphology behind and on the reverse side of every view. In the view of this deceitful *phallic* stamping, a spindle's only function will be to make manifest the paradigm it relates to. This is the case for "the spindle" and any other "being" (étant) that still relies on the senses. They are only more or less adequate copies of a prototype ortho-graphed in the memory.

As far as "intelligibles" are concerned, even though their (re)inscription derives more directly from the striking force of the paternal logos, it yet has to undergo that blinding which results from the eye-wearying excess of the production of *light*. Brilliance of the Sun, mediation by the Father's scion which brings about the loss *of sight*. Dazzling rays, images of the projections of divine seeds of Truth, annihilate the still empirical gaze of the child, inscribing, *behind,* the shadow of the *extent* of its field. And this is necessarily limited, given that he is the "son," and mortal to boot. Which is as much as to say that he still retains something of the/his mother, of the "place of becoming." Universe that cannot contain all the potential, all the germinative virtualities of the demiurge. The recollection of "intelligibles" thus takes one back before the material, matrical conception. It is a matter to be settled "man to man." Really man to man? Where, in that case, is the mother? The mother is at the point *where* all this is produced, reproduced. In the ocular *membrane-screen* that is *consumed*—in particular because it also emits light, mimetically—by optical overactivation. In the ravished gaze of the "son," open wide as it is set on fire and devoured by the flaming torches of the (Sun of the) Father.

Within this *circle,* this *ring* that will *limit* the power of diffusion of the bursts of light, of each one introduced, inserted in the point of view. It will also limit their infinite multiplicity, their indefinitely prolific regeneration that revulses and overwhelms the space and spacing of the visual field to the point of blindness. To say nothing of what may take place also, on the *reverse side* of that ecstasy, for that is withheld from evidence for the moment.

The mother is in this *death therefore,* crossed and re-marked by the impression that is still rooted in the senses. Receptacle(s) which the father's monopoly on daylight, size, and potency ruins by his excessive power; all that is left of it is a fringe of shadow that will envelop the clarity of the father's Ideas, in order to define them. But it will also revive them, once they have been turned backward for immortal specula(riza)-tions.

The End of Childhood

So the mother's child is engaged in stripping away the membranes, the inheritances that he finds too material, too physical. Subject to fading and death. And if this enlightened gaze was already rising above baser and darker attractions, it must also be purified of overly terrestrial sights, and equally he must give up his trust in so finite an organ as the eyes. He must make the passage to that region beyond the one which the sun's dazzling light has made possible. *Forcing* its way *through* anything that regulates the entry and profusion of light, *burning* the place where it produces itself. In this rape, when view and sight are consumed, extinguished, the soul and the gaze of the soul are recalled. Place for recollecting eternal ideas, where the immediate vision of essences is rediscovered. Place, therefore, illumined and illuminated, ocellated with ideal forms of immutable contour. Points of view that are, it seems, determined once and for all in the perfection of their rectitude, of/upon Being that assigns self-identity to each thing and fixes its nature, freed from the metamorphoses of existence. Soul, *specular screen,* mirroring an infinite number of eyes: God. Pupils deprived of their natural foundation, whose "good" will henceforward be decided by the authority of the Father alone. Who would, in the last analysis, regulate the opening-diaphragm of the "spot"—simple eye (of the) ocellus—mimicking all Ideas on the projection screen of the *psychē,* but would ensure, furthermore, the harmony of their relationships—multi-faceted sphere (of the) soul. Beginning to turn on itself, like the demiurge, in order to reflect the plurality of perfection of (self) knowledge. Conjugating in this way the fragmented sparks of light into one ultimate blaze. Love of the Father's Good: *noēsis.*

But where is the Father now? Love has no parents "for he is the eldest of the gods,"[19] and yet he is the "youngest of the gods."[20] Does the "son" therefore resorb (his) genesis into himself in loving contemplation? This is what they say. For "her," love would probably be the child of the one who knows all, particularly the cunning moves of seduction, and who yet knows nothing: Poverty. Child of the lovable and the loving, conceived as a function of her desire, not his.[21] But "she" is not invited to undergo the preliminary education. Yet, if you look for her carefully, perhaps you will uncover something about her exclusion, about how necessary she is in *outlining the circle* and providing the *diameter* of that ideal form, in the/those *mirrors* reflecting the divine potency, in that *speculum* that is the soul. Place(s) where Love and noetic knowledge come into being. Ex-stasy of a copula that has at last been saved from the degradation of entry into matter, and, more radically, alien to all alterity, pure of any alteration. For, at this final point, the Father would theoretically not affect, or no longer continue to affect the son's becoming. The recollection that his Ideas, his logos, are inscribed within him completes the *paideia*. He is henceforth im-mortal. No doubt he has, in appearances, begun to be (again), and this is only possible—it is stated— because he had already been (being), before he was conceived in the mother. The Father, for his part, is eternal, because he has always refused to be born. His being, as a result, continues throughout time identical to himself. Such is his Good, his Truth, his Beauty. His logos. In(de)finitely defined and finite. Immutable, unchangeable.

Life in Philosophy

Always the Same (He)

Sharing in such attributes thus marks a stage in the progression. Transport into (the vision of) the other world, in which walking, *making one's way*, ceases. Even the *method*, which took the place of the crossing that had still to be made, fades away at its height. No more *passage*—neck, pass, shaft, climb—between the inside and the outside, the outside and the inside. The down and the up. The *arkhē* and the *telos*. Eidetic intuition

---

[19]*Symposium*, 178b.
[20]*Symposium*, 195b.
[21]*Symposium*, 203b–c. (Diotima, a wise woman, tells Socrates in the *Symposium* that the beggarwoman Penia, or Poverty, took advantage of the drunken stupor of Plenty to conceive a child by him. The child, Love, takes after both parents, "never in want and never in wealth . . . a mean between ignorance and knowledge."—Tr.)

does away with the interposition, the intervention, the mediation of any kind of path or trail, the need for the opening of any *diaphragm,* disavows any division by a *paraphragm.* Eidetic intuition is produced, whole and entire, in the immediacy of the *noēsis.* No delays, no tinkering, no "organ" to defer and measure the economy of the jouissance, for that sustains itself, it seems, in its all-powerful illumination. What rapture there is in the mirage of the specular intro-jection. What giddy joy in turning round imperceptibly in the universal orb of the Father's field of vision, constellated with points of view that are always absolutely the same. The ideal morphology of the Father's vision excludes all change, all alteration or modification—optical, directional, or semantic. And thus it authorizes the perfect equivalence to his logos, the appropriation to/of his word.

If only it were possible, right now, to detach oneself from existence, to submit oneself to the achievement of absolute wisdom. Which confuses all individuality in the extrapolated operation of the specular. Refusing all knowledge, henceforth, of the specificity of the reflections, or indeed of the specularizing setup, the speculative machinery, all of which are thus saved from determinations or conflicts and run no risk of *historical* manipulations or recasting, "for example." Conforming to the Father's "discourse" is thus equivalent to the "son's" renouncing "his" image, "his" reflection, "his" bio-graphy. To his being assimilated into the mirrors whose effectiveness has always already been calculated by the Demiurge; not only each, fixed, archetype of the Idea, but also their architectonic—the ascending hierarchy toward the (Father's) Good. The terms and syntax of ideology would, thus, be defined once and for all in their rectitude, providing that the soul, that the gaze of the soul, has been turned in the right direction. This requires, of course, a conversion of the whole "body," its determinative and unreserved submission to the divine visions. *Telos,* finally, inscribed in the *psyche.* Which, in one last reversal, will re-envelop "matter," upsetting the oppositions of exterior/interior all over again. The *"interior"* now circles back around the *"exterior"* of an invisible but impenetrable paraphragm. Plato's *hystera,* closure-envelope of metaphysics. Ever moving in circles in the direction of the same. The ecliptic of "the other," which would theoretically turn in *the opposite way,* serves to recall differences or differings.[22] Such "shadows" are needed for the rhythmic beating of the universe's pho-

[22]*Timaeus,* 36c.

tological economy, for marking "time," but they always threaten to disturb its harmonious circumvolutions. Happily, and in conformity with infallible divine foresight, the movements of that "other" would take place only *inside* the sphere of sameness, hemmed in by its orbit.[23] Impacts occur only in an *oblique fashion*, incidentally, and serve (only) to show and confirm the encirclement of/by self-identity of Sameness. Being. Which will not easily allow itself to be thrown off its axis, especially not in the faithful circle of philosophical optics.

An Autistic Completeness

Indeed, in order to preserve the integrity of the Father's image, philosophical optics deprives the being that most closely resembles the Father of the use of all its senses; for these might generate alteration. Gives that being, of course, a *spherical* shape—for the sphere is of all figures the most perfect and like unto itself—and polishes the outside curve to a perfect finish.[24] Also makes it a mirror, but one turned inside out and thus unable to lose anything or receive anything from the outside, both because there is nothing outside it and because everything that it brings about happens inside it. That is to say that He who is from all eternity— God the Father—grants autarchy to him who aspires to have "intercourse with himself and needing no other, but is in every part harmonious and self-contained and truly blessed."[25] *Blind* except for the contemplation of his Ideas. *Deaf* except to the sounds of his soul revolving in harmony, and the soul speaks only to itself without the aid or assistance of any voice.[26] Thought now capable of doing without "discourse" or "dialogue." *Auto-logical muteness,* for "thinking is the conversing of the mind with herself, which is carried on in question and answer."[27] Moreover, "his own waste providing his own food, and all that he did or suffered taking place in himself."[28] *Without hands or feet,* organs unfitted to the movements of intelligence and reflection, which rather require turning around upon oneself, staying in place and passing indefinitely back over the same points.[29] *Taking care not to touch* any "strange things," also, and *deprived of legs* so that there can be no walking off toward something attractive outside the self. Completeness of one who is self-sufficient: this is the destiny to which the souls are called who have donned the nature of the living being most able to honor the Gods.

[23] *Timaeus*, 44b–c.
[24] *Timaeus*, 33b–d.
[25] *Timaeus*, 34a–b.
[26] *Sophist*, 263e.
[27] *Thaeatetus*, 190a.
[28] *Timaeus*, 33c.
[29] *Timaeus*, 34a.

Love Turned Away from Inferior Species and
Genera/Gender

This superior condition is the lot of the sex which, subsequently, will be called masculine.[30] It still remains for him to disengage himself from his human double, his female understudy, launching himself into the sky in a philosophical flight, raising his head toward what alone has a real existence. Ideas. Careless of things here below, of earthly realities, since an appetite for sensations leads to irrationality and injustice, and risks making him fall back down *to another sex,* which is much further from the divine love. There is also the threat of finding oneself in a woman's body after rebirth, or even in the body of an animal. The female creature who is most drawn to the earth and dives deepest into the sea suffers, as punishment for ignorance and "beastliness," the most despicable fate. Forced to live out life in the "uttermost parts of the world."[31] To fall back into the lower depths of darkness and degradation—this is the fate of the soul of the man who loses his wing feathers.[32] Because he is attracted by Wisdom or philosophical education, of course. For only the philosopher's thought is truly winged, though this earns him with the crowd the reputation of being "mad." Whereas, although he is indeed beside himself, delirious and out of his own control, he is rather "inspired," possessed by a God.

This "God" will, often, take for himself the face of a *young boy,* closest equivalent in this life to absolute beauty. As that has been defined in philosophy, of course. Where one never gets away from the search for sameness. Thus love will strive to chain himself to the one most like him. He will become attached to what is closest to the wise man, or what he would like to be closest: his younger, fairer, more desirable, other self. His "son," in some manner? The goal of this inclination will be to make the loved one as like as possible to the lover, so that the lovers "do their utmost to create (in the loved one) the greatest likeness of themselves and

---

[30]*Timaeus,* 41e, 42a.

[31]*Timaeus,* 90e, 91, 92.

[32]*Phaedrus,* 246c–d. ("And therefore the mind of the philosopher alone has wings; and this is just, for he is always, according to his abilities, clinging in recollection to those things in which God abides, and in beholding which He is ever what He is. And he who employs aright these memories is ever being initiated into perfect mysteries and alone becomes truly perfect. But, as he forgets earthly interests and is rapt in the divine, the vulgar deem him mad; they do not see that he is inspired."—Tr.)

of the god whom they honour."[33] Love, indeed, will be insensibly aroused in the loved one because his eyes have been enchanted, without their realizing it, without their suspecting that "the lover is his mirror in whom he is beholding himself."[34] Thus he is in love. But with what? With his image? That would be a comedown for love, truly. The wondering contemplation of self-reproduction is not the privilege of living humans, even if they are men. If it is granted to them, it is always through the mediation of the Good, the Father. And what makes the beloved young man fall in love is the *gaze of the older man* in which his image is formed, that *enlightened point of view of a father* whom he lacks and who, out of love for himself and an equal sense of lack, claims to constitute him as an equal.

Vertigo reigns in the consciousness in regard to its own constitution: self-identity. Where even a God seems to need to create a universe—one impelled into circular motion, admittedly—in order to uphold his own (self) knowledge. Being also goes out of itself when, in its generosity, it reproduces equivalent offspring in order to gaze upon itself in them. And they are well finished, well polished, carefully turned (and turned out), but they have no eyes. *Seeing remains the special prerogative of the Father.* It is in his gaze that everything comes into being. This is so for the "son" and for his love. And even if the high point of desire occurs when the "father" and the "son," the "wise man" and his "beloved boy," love each other equally, that is to say, offer each other the *target point* at which their (self) knowledge fails, they will be sent off into another world for that rapture. Transported on their newly feathered wings beyond the celestial vault in order to contemplate together the *Ideas*, whose essence—which really is "colourless, formless, intangible"[35]—demands that the glance, source of all illuminations, be torn from its socket. The ideal, even if it be a loving one, escapes mortals. For if each lover could in truth see himself in the other, the eternal essence of Ideas would thereby risk being reduced too obviously to the quest for appearance, for the appropriation of appearing. And the Father cannot intend this, as he might thereby lose the necessity for his ex-sistence. The emergence of a living being from the environment in which he continues to become,

---

[33]*Phaedrus*, 253c.
[34]*Phaedrus*, 255d.
[35]*Phaedrus*, 247c.

even if the environment be one of love, can only be achieved through ecstasy. In God. Each one progressively achieves the purity of his being only by coming out of the self, and above all out of "that living tomb which we carry about, now that we are imprisoned in the body, like an oyster in his shell."[36]

Thus the beloved will be loved only insofar as he reflects the divine light, of which *a man is a more faithful mirror than a woman or any other animal.* These latter, in relation to the Immortals, correspond to much later generations, and even, strictly speaking, no longer have any bond of kinship: woman and beast are born, after a second and third life, from men who by ignorance and lack of virtue have deserved such a disgrace. As such, they are thus foreign to the design of the Demiurge who, in his goodness, cannot be suspected of having decided upon the existence of living beings who are disgraced by their difference from him. These are mortal procreations and their desire, as a result of and in accordance with their "nature," will above all be to couple in order to give birth. The only way for them to rise in the hierarchy of "beings" will be to transform, as far as it lies in their power, their stupidity and the disordered impetuosity of their sensations into intelligence and reason, hoping in this way to become again what they had once been in their first state: men.

The Privilege of the Immortals

It is thus neither good nor fair for a living male to leave off the loving pursuit of his self-image, though all the while he must remember that his prototype is (in) the Father. And from inferior species and genders he will move away and above all avert his gaze, that most precious gift accorded to him, the organ most like that of the soul, once one has turned it toward the inside. He will place himself as high as possible in his "body" since the top of the body is the place inhabited by that daimon which God granted to each man at the time of his first birth. "In as much as we are a plant not of an earthly but of a heavenly growth . . . the divine power suspends the head and root of us from that place where the generation of the soul first began, and thus makes the whole body upright."[37] The body will suffer all kinds of upsets, will fall over its feet, for example, if it fails to obey the

---

[36]*Phaedrus,* 250c.
[37]*Timaeus,* 90a.

movement of that lofty erection. Yet, this earthly type of locomotion must be left to women and beasts, who are supplied with two or four legs according to their degree of imbecility. These props take the place of nobler means of transport:[38] *vertical* ascent and *circular* revolution. The latter will give support to the progression of the former with the reminiscence of what took place when the very vault of the sky was *pierced through*, when that envelope, which had remained material and matrical to some degree, had been *violated*. Sublime destiny of the Immortals who come and go through that ultimate dividing wall without any fatigue or suffering. Going into the limitless Plain of Truth to seek nourishment for that wing plumage which gives their "soul" such perfect lightness.[39]

The Science of Desire

As for other living things—this is true at least for the males—seized by an ardent desire to gain the heights, they try to push their "heads" beyond the celestial divider, raising them and then lowering them again. But the violent agitation which urges them on, the chaos in which they pierce the barrier, means that they get only a glimpse of some of the realities that can be reached there. Powerless, as yet, to climb serenely upward, they are carried along pell-mell. Overwhelmed. Jostling, crushing each other underfoot, each trying to get ahead. And this all results in an enormous confusion, and perspiration, and extremity of effort. And also in the fact that some return from the breach lamed, that many another loses or at least damages some feathers, and that all, overcome with weariness, come down again without having been initiated into the contemplation of the real.[40] In discouragement, many will henceforth be content with fakes and fantasies, but not the best, who will once more engage in the "hour of agony" and "supremest conflict"[41] after having perfected *their knowledge*. Thus they will no longer exercise it in relation to individual and sensible things, for then their science is slave to becoming and all that they know is dependent upon the change of object. And they risk, moreover, confusing what for a time one calls "being" (être) with the essence proper to all copies of that kind.[42] Yet it is this essence, alone and immutable, that is worthy of holding the attention consistently, since it allows man to progress upward without falling back into the anarchic movements of the sensations. Such as those of the animals with x feet which keep waving around uncontrollably. This

---

[38] *Timaeus*, 91d–92a.
[39] *Phaedrus*, 248b–c.
[40] *Phaedrus*, 248a–b.
[41] *Phaedrus*, 247b.
[42] *Phaedrus*, 247d–e.

leaves them constantly riveted to the surface of the earth, even makes them move down into its depths or into the depths of the sea. Like a foundation losing contact with the soil, they lose their limbs in fact. Wandering here and there without any firm seating or assured means of being able to return to the same point. Assuming that they have not forgotten the last geometric landmarks which enabled them to find their way, and to stop roaming indefinitely.

Sad is the lot of the man who has neglected the task of recollecting Ideas, yet this threat always hangs over every mortal because of the diversity of his soul and the equally impure character of the living things surrounding him. Thus it is indispensable to his happiness that, as far as the soul is concerned, he strive to keep within his *highest* part: the immortal part whose seat is in the head, separated from the irascible and passionate part by the isthmus-border of the neck. In this way the divine principle may remain unsullied, unadulterated by anything not of its essence. Moreover, since his mortal condition requires that he also partake in the mortal species of the soul if he is to be complete, for the soul's sake he must at all costs keep to the *upper* half also: that above the diaphragm, isolated from the more bestial half situated in the lower abdomen by a *partition* similar to the one that divides the men's apartments from the women's.[43]

The soul must operate in the middle in this way because it has been charged with bringing the good into being, as well as the bad. It is a composite place between good and ill, in a "being" that is created and thus unable to conform to the model of absolute intelligibility. Nonetheless, the soul must try to get closer to the model if it is not to fall into the nether regions. And, specifically, the "intermediary" soul's store of fire and ardor must be devoted to the quest for divine light. Without those flames, no *daimon* can do anything, especially none can reach what it desires: to know Forms and imitate them. Obviously, Forms will have to be transformed into visions, illuminations, which enlighten without burning. And to achieve this, and in order to put the "vehicle" of the body to some use,[44] it is fitting at the outset to cast one's eyes upon *fair*

[43] *Timaeus*, 69d–e, 70a.
[44] *Phaedo*, 99b.

boys who, here below, best reflect Beauty. But soon it is their intelligence alone that the wise man will seek out, and he will even come to neglect their/his external envelope, this "mere shadow or image" that is but a wretched imitation of its model.[45] It is true that the image may achieve a kind of perfection, "and is not the fairest sight of all . . . for him who has eyes to see it, the combination in the same person of good character and good looks to match them, each bearing the same stamp?"[46] Love of this kind involves no risk of straying and can be given free rein. It inspires the contemplation of the ideal. Of the same. But this combination is rare. In order to guard against any disenchantment, any disillusion, it is better to become directly attached to that which, better than anything else, guarantees right knowledge: the awareness of self (as) same, the search for identity with the self.

A Korē Dilated to the Whole Field of the Gaze and Mirroring Herself

The only men who love each other are, in truth, those who are impatient to find the same over and over again. And, in order to do this, they must not turn or direct their quest toward some other part of man or any object whatsoever, but only toward that very thing in which they see themselves: that *mirror of vision* in which they can look at themselves in the very gaze of the other, perceiving, in one and the same glance, their view and themselves.[47] But this image (of oneself) in a pupil is always dependent upon a *korē*. That is to say upon a *young girl*, a young *virgin*, or even on a *doll*. A reduced image, then, which cannot satisfy someone who wishes to have knowledge of the All. But he must not linger too long over the double of man that the *korē* represents (for him). The specula(riza)tion is too limited, involving only one organ which, though

[45]*Laws*, XII, 959b.

[46]*Republic*, III, 402d. (Whereas Jowett translates "in the same person," the French translation is "chez un homme": in a man.—Tr.)

[47]*Alcibiades*, 132d–e, 133a. ("*Socrates*. Can we think of any objects, in looking at which we see not only them but ourselves at the same time? *Alcibiades*. Clearly, Socrates, mirrors and the like. *Soc*. Very true. Now is there not something of a mirror in the eye with which we see? *Alcib*. Certainly. *Soc*. Did you ever observe that the face of a person looking into the eye of another is reflected as in a mirror; and in the visual organ which is over against him, and which is called the pupil [*korē*] there is a sort of image of the person looking? *Alcib*. That is quite true. *Soc*. Then the eye, looking at another eye, and at that eye which is most perfect and which is the instrument of vision, will there see itself? But looking at anything else either in man or in the world except at what this resembles, it will not see itself. *Alcib*. Very true. *Soc*. Then if the eye is to see itself, it must look into the eye, and at that part of the eye where sight which is the virtue of the eye resides? . . . May we say, then, that as mirrors are truer and clearer and brighter than the mirror within the eye, so also is God by His nature a clearer and brighter mirror than the most excellent part of our own soul?")—Tr.)

exemplary, nonetheless remains too matrical when envisaged in this
way. The reflection (of self) that would rely entirely on a support like
this would risk forgetting the most important thing: the gaze of the soul.
Veiled in/by this mirage, upon which one must learn to close one's eyes,
so as not to succumb to the exclusive attraction of appearances. Even if
the gaze is that of a young boy. Abusing what attracts one most in his
eyes sometimes leads to drowning clear reason in mirrors that are not
faithful enough, not *frozen* enough. It is rather the soul which has been
educated and strengthened in good sense—the philosopher's soul, for
example—that one should ask for the guarantee of self-knowledge.
More specifically one must turn to that point in the soul which is the seat
of the thought of Sameness itself and of the most satisfactory knowledge.
In a like manner, is the pupil that point in the gaze by which one regulates oneself in order to catch sight of sameness, and to see oneself? Going
beyond this discernment, which remains rooted in the senses, one seeks
what one needs in that part of the soul that is most identical to the self,
the part that reflects best—the most divine part. For this self-identity is
most certainly to be found by conforming to the divine principle, sharing
in the attributes of him who, from all eternity, in(de)finitely knows
himself, in a total self-transparence. A mirror clearer, purer, more resplendent with light than all those which, already, have been made in his
image.[48] A mirror untouched by any reflection, *like a pupil—a korē—*
dilated to encompass the whole field of vision, and *mirroring itself.* Reflecting nothing (but) its own void, that *hole* through which one looks.
Which, of course, is not one (hole) anymore, as then it would risk being
sometimes bigger and sometimes smaller. This could never happen to
the gaze of God which, ever on high, sees everything at one and the same
time, looming over the whole universe from his high place. From that
perspective one cannot glimpse, calculate, or even imagine what the
vanishing point might be. A summit infinitely receding from the convergence of all verticals. Supreme erection that exceeds every horizon;
even the sharpest, the most piercing gaze will be incapable of calculating
its angles of incidence, for the eye remains captive in the world of the
visible and does not embrace the totality of viewpoints and their harmonious organization.

Only the divine vision is without liabilities, encompassing the All, with no
trace of opaqueness left. Light that nothing resists, going through *any
paraphragm,* reaching everywhere, without deviation of any sort. Ever

[48]*Alcibiades,* 133b–c.

identical to itself in its rectitude. Not allowing itself to be bent by any mirror since it knows itself throughout time (as) the one who has the most power of all. Gazing upon itself (as) that which in reality is brightest.[49] Good, alien to all shadow, outshining the Sun itself: its clear-sightedness will never be dazzled by any stars, for it overflows the sphere of their orbit, encircling the All which turns around in the space of its field. Gaze that no bodily organ, nor even any essence, can limit. Without any blind spot, even one that might represent something forgotten. For God is *in the instant* all that (he) has been and will be. Such tenses of becoming are inadequate to analyze his present, which has neither before nor after, earlier nor later. Being has nothing that predates it, nor anything ahead that it should aim for. Everything is already (in) Him. *Arkhē* and *telos*. And if he sows forth seeds of light and truth, it is from excess of goodness. He has no need to pour forth in this way. Or else the need is only to supplement Good and is born of a desire for everything to be like Him. Flooding the universe with the seeds he scatters everywhere. Ever equal to himself. Lofty and all-powerful. Absolute model of sovereignty who must be imitated if one is not to fall back into lower states.

Thus, every "being" (étant) in his "being" (être) can only try to mimic God, copy him more or less well, for there is no other perfection to rely on. The whole Universe, in its essence, conforms to his divine projections. There is nothing outside, or even behind, that is not subject to his designs. *Everything is enclosed in a super-celestial gaze,* moving in a circle, after confused with before, future with past, earlier with later, in harmonious circumvolutions. And the autarchy of this motion is always the sign that some divine principle is involved. Auto-nomous, auto-mobile tropism, index of omnipotence that would resorb *into the en soi of its circle* anything that might still be withholding itself on the other side, any remaining cause, outside the self, capable of disrupting the sovereign economy. Gravitating endlessly around its axis, describing a circle while the things on the other side, whether future or past, are always constituted *from the inside* of the circle. As for the something that had not been envisaged, represented, or representable, it is *expelled outside* this sphere. It constitutes *the back of the set,* available to the divine rays only, penetrating man, the paraphragm-envelope (of the) All, in some way rectally. And man himself is no more aware of his own back than he is able to bear the vision of the Good face to face.

[49]*Republic,* VII, 518c.

Divine Knowledge

The Back Reserved for God

The mime becomes loftier and more sublime, but remains necessarily within the scenography of sameness. Thus the magicians, the tutors and philosophers, the Demiurge, or God-the-Father always have a fall-back position. They alone have some point of view on the backside of things. But this is denied *in the facts* which they claim are their exclusive interest. Facts projected upon the back side of the cave, of the picture, of the soul, all screens of representation that must never, under any circumstances, be turned around. The retroversion is forbidden to public scrutiny, masked in the circularity of the process which gives the impression of turning the inside out and *thereby showing it right side up.* A kaleidoscopic optical illusion out of which, eternally invisible, steals God. Hidden *behind* what each being can look at during his life. God is the foundation hidden from sight but offering himself to intuition, placed infinitely far away, above and in front, in his teleological Beauty and Goodness. How desperately hard it is for mortals to understand and, more especially, to demonstrate God's reality and truth; yet these have the force of law. They regulate the orderliness of the universe that has been formed in God's image. All that *really* exists is like Him. Anything divergent will be abandoned—at least for a while—to the depths of the earth, or of the sea. Thus he finds himself in the presence of his Ideas alone, though this is not to say that he recognizes himself equally in each, male and female. The fact that each is in some measure his reflection still allows for a hierarchy in the degrees of self-realization, the degrees of affiliation, of ancestry. A complex network of relationships is set up in which the generations interweave in order to define the exact form of each, male and female. To ensure a good game, each piece on the backgammon board is placed by the "King" in the proper position, determined once and for all, since God will never leave the place from which He watches.[50] Eminence that nothing can move ever again, and that embraces the All of all eternity.

The Divine Mystery

But isn't it still necessary to affirm that because these reproductions of Him are always in the same place—at least during life—they are also turned *right side out* in the *plan/e* of the universe? Otherwise there would be a risk that what He creates, in his image, might seem to have another face. A back perhaps? But that has to be God's secret. And He, as far as

[50]*Laws,* X, 903d–e.

one can tell, only (re)produces himself, only projects himself frontward and, moreover, in his prudence, demands that his "reflections" be unable to turn inside out. What extreme confusion would result if God were to perceive himself backward and the wrong way up, thus losing an immutable awareness of the position of right and left. If He had lost his grasp on those geometric landmarks that are indispensable in keeping the world moving along properly, in distinguishing and subordinating Same and Other, "for example." There is no point in repeating that Same always moves in one identical and therefore correct direction, whereas Other flouts that rigor, making its shadow. Now, these "good" or "bad" directions are derived from the right and the left of the Demiurge (in particular).[51] And if they were to get confused or even inverted. . . .

But who knows that this has not in fact happened? What if God is unaware of all that specula(riza)tion owes to inversion? What if he doesn't know about the projective mechanisms of his representations? What if he is imprisoned in the field of his own vision, quite incapable of analyzing his perspective which, though aerial and isometric, nonetheless suffers *planification* effects that are not resolved by the *spherical* nature of the surfaces in question? And if he paints himself upon those surfaces again and again, they are bound to reflect Him, and somewhere a mirror in which his image has formed is bound to be involved. And God does not want this. For fear his power will be overturned perhaps? That He will be altered in/by another gaze? That, once caught in the becoming of a looking-glass game, his Being will suffer innumerable, unpredictable transformations?

In order to maintain self-identity, he may still have recourse to a *double mirror;* the second rectifies the image sent back by the first, in a substitution for the information from the eye of the other that has thereby been appropriated. Could it be that divine representation passes through a *double specularization, a duplication of speculation?* The copy's copy would be wrapped up in/by God's permanence in its unity and its simplicity. Its self-sufficiency. Ex-schizoid, ex-quisite. To which no controversy will ever be able to give the lie, since the—*ideal*—optics of the other has already functioned in defining the Same. God would, theoretically, simulate himself (as same) twice in order to ensure the immutability of his reflection. Could his reality be the faking of a fake? With the first re-

---

[51] *Timaeus,* 36c, 43e, 44a.

production "being" already "in a mirror." But, unlike the painter or poet who takes pleasure and glory in this per-verting game, the divine order wills that things should be put back right side out, through a *repetition* of the mirage, a renewal of the operation that inverts the image. Thus increasing the specular base, at least in the Absolute. Keeping, for himself alone, the key to this mystery: his frozen hysteria, in which he engenders himself, truly identical to himself, by reproducing himself twice over. At least. Ex-stasy of a primal scene in which two reflections of sameness come together and then give birth to Being itself. An ideal copula at last, freed from the avatars of becoming, yet in(de)finitely multiple. For, once the angle of incidence of the two foci, the points of convergence at which the rays of light fuse, has been found, once this *specular hymen* has been achieved in which, now the same, now the other, he assembles and unites the two faces of his being, then he can reiterate indefinitely the procreation of HimSelf. Conceiving himself under all his aspects without any one of them being able to dissociate itself from the whole. They are merely different sighting points upon the Same, which, in order to know itself completely, including all its attributes, suffers no change and must in no way move its position. All that is needed, it seems, is to twist this cunningly calculated setup around Him, while He remains self-identical in the center of the sphere that he projects in this way: his looking-glass enclosure.

The realization of this speculum, which can thus be analyzed into the properties of the Father, is problematic only for a "being" that is still material, one that occupies a place and lives in a *khōra,* unlike God who is everywhere and in-heres nowhere. Ubiquity of the divine light which, where a *shadow* might have been expected, reflects itself in a *second mirror* that reflects back the first. And so on indefinitely. Describing a globe where the rays proliferate and gather together without loss and also without generating useless heat, since they do not become concentrated upon a single focus except when numbered within the divine gaze. This economy of clearsightedness never yields itself up to a single reflection and, by multiplying the points of view, it elaborates them into the whole of its omniscience. No viewpoint is so clearly outlined as to obscure the balanced harmony of the whole.

Thus God gives no privileged status to any of his visions for fear of becoming embodied (in) an appearance. By refusing to choose one vision over another, to give priority to one part, one fraction, one ex-sistence, he is, through all time and at this very moment, the unity of all co-possibles. And no alteration is imaginable given that the principle of the Other is here included in the definition of self-identity and submits to the cause of Sameness alone. The result is that, where we might expect the *shadow* (of a double)—or equally the semblance, the fantasy, the opinion, indeed the uncertainty as to what, really, is—we find instead *a second specularization* that corrects and raises the angle of reflection. Thus the only representation we shall have are its analogues, but these can be envisaged from every angle and can be related to their totality by a rigorous estimate of proportions. The progression is, in fact, geometric and rapidly tends to infinity. Eye of God, model of intelligibility, of the exhaustive knowledge of self which no mortal can attain in that perfection of (self) awareness.

Some—relatively sensible—hints are, however, offered to the mortal seeking to interpret the relationships at work in this divine science.[52] Thus, for example, the Demiurge creates the Universe only by looking toward "the Living Absolute" and is therefore attentive to a *duplication* of mirrors. Or again, in this *turning* sphere of the world, *two circles,* the one forming an acute angle to the second, describe the orbit of the same and the other. And this will apply equally to the higher soul of man that is installed inside his (round) head. The duplicity is necessary as an instrument of measurement, and takes its paradigm (or at least its created paradigm) in time, beaten out to the rhythmic alternation of light and "shade." Similarly, it is said that anything that essentially is, partakes in the image of God, and these more or less adequate "copies" are organized by the Father into a harmonious whole: that is to say, one obedient to the proportional laws of geometry, the enumeration of which exhausts the sum and the relationships of everything that exists. Thus the Universe *envelopes* all living things without exception, and moves *on itself,* pivoting upon an axis that passes through its *unmoving* center. For this "sensible" image of the "intelligible" model, the eye is the most precious organ of comprehension. Of course, the eye must be turned straight in the right direction so that finally it changes into the gaze of the soul which mirrors *from all points on its circular surface.* A privileged optical structure, which figures throughout the progress of the discourse, at each stage in the argument.

[52]In the *Timaeus* for example.

This Power Cannot Be Imitated by Mortals

All the degrees of generation, of ancestry, would thus serve to re-mark the working of the divine understanding. It would fall to mortals' lot to mimic this in order to ascend the hierarchy of beings (êtres) and reach, if not eternity, at least happy immortality. The problem seems to be that their material birth makes them *opaque* to light rays, unsuited to total transparence, translucence. Mortals always cast a *shadow* over the scene, if only because their silhouette is an *obstacle*. Furthermore, their fall back into a *khōra* forces them, at least in this life, to remain always in some place, in some "body." They cannot be reduced to a *central point* in an ideal specular system. Thus, this "matter" of theirs would produce a distortion in a perfect circumvolution of the image of self. Conception is not yet immaculate.

That is not all. The very soul of man, it seems, forgets the teaching it has received from its Father, the workman. As a result of an *alliance*—between mortal and immortal—it has also lost the ability to discern what can bring it back to unity. It is uncertain about true and false, real and seeming, which is to say, same and other. This makes it turn first in one direction and then in another, ignorant of whom it should devote its being (être) to or derive it from. It is the gap and link between (the) two, an intermediary, *metaxe,* in which the positive and the negative face each other, joined edge to edge or sometimes mingling, taking it in turns or else acting in concert so as to mobilize, for the needs of the cause, a copula that has fallen from the self-evidence of its olympian objectivity. The Being that has finally been freed from predication cannot, simply, be shared with those who still exist, the "sons of the earth," of the mother. These latter must submit to growth, which modifies their attributes so greatly that they never know exactly where they are. Subject to/by becoming. Though they are already affiliated with the (logos of the) Father, they are yet a mixture, and live "as a community," which implies a few impurities. There is no prototype for their pluralism in the perfect divine autarchy.

How, Then, Can They Evaluate Their Potency?

It must also be admitted that this mirror—God—which alone they must take as standard if the theorists are right, is extrapolated to infinity for them, and this makes reflection difficult. Without the support of any hypothesis, they can only guess at its demands. They can never be sure that the final appearance in court will confirm that their rectitude has worked. Yet rectitude would guarantee that they can go on rising upward. That they can continue to move forward, even though they are never quite able to catch up to the phallic measure of omnipotent sameness. They strive to catch up with, if not join, a gaze that recedes and embraces all dimensions, and their excesses. *Pupil of the Other into whose fathomless depths sinks a pro-tension that is still unreflected.* How then is the soul to be duplicated? Measured, and mastered, "in reality"? Since it is never determined once and for all. Since it falters in the definition of its ideal form. Is comparing it to the *others of the same* (aux autres des mêmes) the only thing to be done? But whom are we to call upon to arbitrate that specula(riza)tion except the "father" once again? Thus reproducing, at best, the relationship of bigger to smaller, of older to younger, of the wise man to his darling pupil. But proportion, henceforth, is still envisaged in its variations.

As for the relationship to *the others of the others* (aux autres des autres), *to the other of the other,* anyone who ventures near it will be threatened with loss of self (as same), for it does not exclude the possiblity of there being a reversal. When all is said and done, the other is *the reverse, the negative* of the properties of sameness; it *overflows* the unit of self–identity, endangering both the latter's boundaries and what it leaves outside the field of its affirmation. The outside, backside, other side cannot be ringed in once and for all for he "himself" has not, it seems, achieved a perfect conception of Himself as Same. Thus, a store of in(de)finite alterity, a multiplicity of not-yet-beings, would exist, and there he will draw the nourishment he needs to erect his sublime form. A dark reserve, still impenetrable to an intelligent eye. Matter that cannot be made to fit any proper sense, which one can continue to speculate on provided one calculates the proportions involved according to an *other same,* or the *same model.* Otherwise there is a risk of becoming in(de)finitely big or small. Misshapen, formless. Measureless. For *that other is lacking in principle* and moves without any foundation. It is inconstant and indeed inconsistent by nature. And though it is possible to subject it to a few laws, to make it adhere to a few propositions, it is quite essential not to ask it to fix its own rules or hope it can be resolved into movements, sizes, speeds, numbers, . . . that have been established definitively. It has no memory for/and it has no words. It is incapable of the slightest reasoning. Illogical, as you know. Noisy, perhaps, but with no concerted articulation, no coherent links between sounds, no consistancy in its emissions (no point in this case of talking of "ideas" or even "opinions," really). Thus it only reproduces auditory "sensations" that, at best, are tied to rhythm and harmony: it is musical in fact, but has of course no meaning. Even its consonancy will occur only if it has earlier yielded to the arithmetic of sameness. And this condition is realized only in that image of God we call the universe. The rest is mere lallation, prattling, an unbearable cacophany in which man will find little profit.

Except over Someone Like Themselves?

Thus man has to find knowledge of himself as he is between the mirror that is so infinitely far that it escapes the gaze—God—and the abyss (of) the other, which is limitless in a different way. Incomparable disjunction, dislocation, except that the *targets are blind* and nothing is known or at least understood about their angles of incidence, their convergences and common foci, the decisive reason for their ex-sistence. And all this leaves man in grave difficulty. Searching for his being (être) right and left, high and low, in front and . . . ? Anxious about the reality of what he sees and what he sees in himself, he seeks everywhere for that mirage that is defaulting upon its completeness and, as a result of his wanderings, he ends by retreating back into his soul *in order to speculate (upon) his like.* Henceforward the other figures only as a shadow cast upon that loving appropriation of self, periodically eclipsing the changelessness of its discrete form. Acting to seduce and distract, still an-archic and in need of being educated, now and forever, in truth. It is essential that the reiteration of sameness should subjugate these "fluxes" which work the wrong way and thus occasion all sorts of transformations, displacements, and transfers. Soon you don't know where you are anymore. Whereas what is needed is, simply, to stick with the repetition of the same, for that repetition finds its representative basis in the image of the like and its speculative model in God—who, throughout all eternity, has not, and will not, suffer the slightest alteration.

If man is to climb back up to the Ideas, his plan of action would therefore be to stick to sameness, whether it takes shape in the *like* or whether it be counted out, unrepresentably, in the recurrence of the *circle of the identical.* These two movements are indissolubly intertwined in God in whom turning around his still center would be indistinguishable from the exhaustive production of self (as) same—the matrix of all representations. For anyone who has fallen back down into a body, however, the two movements are different, it seems, and even divergent. Thus, when a man looks into the mirror of another man's eye, he knows nothing of the back of that eye: the point of view of the *same's other* (l'autre du même) is hidden from view just like, and unlike, its backside. And if that self-image may distract or even confront or overturn the double of himself that man knows in his soul, this is because God's other is always a more or less good copy, whereas the forms inscribed in the *psyché* are, on a little reflection, pure divine truth. *The reversal of the double* represented by the soul is thus dictated by the *straight/right* vision of the

Father. And, moreover, this reduplication can achieve self-identity only
if it submits to the Father's word. The repetitional automatism at work
in language stops there and thus ensures the permanence of a (good)
mimicry, which otherwise might move about indefinitely as a function
of perceptions that are too rooted in the senses. A mimicry of that kind
might almost be imagined occurring—even within the intelligible—
sometimes on the front and sometimes on the reverse side, according to
the different plays of retroaction in discourse. But no: from all eternity
God has known and contained *the outcome of every enunciation,* of which he
has also been the source. He is *telos* and/or *arkhē* who makes every
speaker "in truth" a "subject" of his logos alone.

The Father Knows the Front Side and Back Side of Everything, at Least in Theory

Thus the "Father" monopolizes and indeed mobilizes the *reverse side* of
the self-image accessible to a mortal, and that other side therefore becomes for Him his finally real face. *Man is unaware of the way that (his)
representation twists back (upon the self).* As can be seen in his statements
that it is not up to him to make decisions about his own Good, that the
guiding object of Good remains invisible and impenetrable to him. And
even though the preliminary education has initiated him into several
twists and turns, it has not succeeded in getting him to see both the front
and the back of things *in conjunction.* At best man has been assured that
what he was now turned toward was "more" true, had more "being"
than what he had been used to looking at, and that he had a "greater"
rectitude of vision—*orthoteron.* But the joint appearance of front and back
had never taken place. It was channeled into the arguments, or even the
peremptory assertion, of a master, for the "child" always constitutes an
obstacle. *An opaque but pivoting paraphragm,* his body is placed in the way
of recto-verso vision. Dislocation, disjunction, disarticulation, open up
between *the more sensible and the more intelligible,* which are never presented to the sight together. The field of optics would have to be overturned
and at the same time maintained if the interplay (in game and flame) was
to be measured simultaneously. But that would be possible only for
someone who in-hered in a man's body. The "others" don't even have
eyes, the theory says. Dark night of matter. As for divine clearsightedness, it is alien to all shadow, to all screens but that of (its) reflection.
But, being intelligible in every dimension, it would have only an ideal,
or even speculative, relationship to sensibility. Manifest in the enlighten-
ing intuition of the Good, and more rigorously no doubt in the consideration of the harmonious proportions that regulate the Universe, divine
clearsightedness is revealed only in that which best reflects it, being most
like it, that is, the gaze of the higher soul. Even there, it is "ill" served

and subjected to deviations, since the higher soul still risks being disturbed by various sensations, opinions, fantasies, which affect the permanence of the divine mirage.

How, then, does God know the *sensible* face of things, given that his relationship with them must be wholly theoretical? Only in Principle does he have correspondance with existence, for his word sustains the logical and geometrical order of the life of this Universe without his ever participating in it. (The) All resembles him, but there is no reciprocity. *Everything mimics him, but he imitates nothing,* or so the story goes. Pure Truth, defined once and for all in its fixed Ideas that nothing and nobody will ever succeed in moving, or even modifying or swaying. In the Immutability of his reflection, God would have resolved in advance all the ob-jections placed in his way, and would never need to ask anything of anyone. He is, for all eternity, right about everything. And this cannot be shared, or even duplicated (except in Himself) for fear of no longer knowing infallibly where science is, or fiction, or ignorance.[53] Or wisdom, or craziness, or stupidity. And a decision has to be made. The Father alone, therefore, would know absolutely everything. But this knowing would result from the fact that everything is made in his image. Ultimately he only recognizes himself; that is to say, once again, *the organization of his field of projection.* And the "others" would have to internalize the "proper" characters and identify themselves therein so that the "world" can go on turning in the right direction. This makes them the same, by cutting them off from themselves, or at least from the irascible and passionate parts of their "souls" that must bend little by little before (good) mimicry. They do not abreact mimicry, bring it into consciousness, since it is still correlated to their material, matrical, and thus hysterical heritage, but they bend and twist so as to offer their newly polished surfaces to the Father's desire. In order to assimilate and incorporate it. Guarantee of immortality. Forgetful (of self) in order to remember what had been before they were conceived. And that, of course, never falls simply under the senses. Absence of "representation"/presence of being (être). A *blindness* bars the way that would lead from the beginning to the end. Faint, that line would begin to curve back upon itself; the before, the after, would begin to be confused with the behind, the anterior, as if nothing had ever happened apart from the insistence of these/its circumvolutions—and not the detour, but also the

---

[53]*Parmenides,* 133 and following.

experience of being thrown out of true, of ecstasy in the point of view of God. Center projected in unnoticeable ways, inserted into the soul and around which one must now turn. But the places where these two trajectories might possibly intersect are the object of a radical blindness. Even the hypothesis is lacking here.

The Meaning of Death for a Philosopher

Thus the father's "face" is never made known to the son, the excellence of his Good can never be fully demonstrated. He is not in fact in any *spot,* or at least any that can be represented, nor on any *plane* that can be conceived by man. Man always remains *beneath* the project God has for him. At least in this lower life, separated from the "other" by that *impenetrable paraphragm,* death. Obviously, no mortal will gaze upon death as he experiences it at the very moment of dying. He will still not know whether or not "the entrance to another existence" corresponds to the desire to appropriate the "other side" of representation which constitutes his "interiority" but remains outside the field of his perspective. Break-through into what *remains* God's secret; which ensures the repetition of the same (history). No upheavals, no revolutions in which what had always *been* would appear as the *flip side* of what might be, the *shadow,* masked as such, of what would be, or else a possible perspective on things, a potential interpretation of reality which, because withheld from evidence and always positioned *behind,* defies all comparison. By excluding the gaze of the other, or others, this extrapolated point of view organizes and projects the world into a paralyzed empire. Formalizations of laws laid down in perpetuity, logos of the Father. And He never questions that (Id) which causes (him) but lays univocal claim to all that is, in his absolute science. Which would give account of everything without any change, for all eternity. Embracing from the outset all enumerations of "beings," their proportions and relationships, all the abstract operations that can occur betwen them and the very development of those relationships. Which are essentially copulative. Their causes, ends, and results. And perhaps their modes as well?

An Unarticulated/Inarticulate Go-between: The Split between Sensible and Intelligible

A Failure of Relations between the Father and Mother

Such thoughts on divine truth are available to man only when he has left *behind* everything that still linked him to this sensible world that the earth, the mother, represents. Are these thoughts also to be understood

339

from behind? This backside duplicity is resolved only in God, it would seem, who sees all and is thus also at the beginning of all. As for the mother, let there be no mistake about it, *she has no eyes,* or so they say, she has no gaze, no soul. No consciousness, no memory. No language. And if one were to turn back toward her, in order to re-enter, one would not have to be concerned about her point of view. The danger would rather be of losing one's bearings (or perhaps finding them?). Of falling into a dark hole where lucidity may founder. Resurgence of the *other's other* (l'autre de l'autre) which, in its blindness, would upset the repetition of sameness. And overwhelm self-identity. Which, by dint of denying that which it "fantasizes" as the beginning of its being—that behind (of) the mother—is re-born, in truth, in the Father's gaze. Redoubled, being (être) is conceived (in the) intelligible—without the distortion that results from this insistent presence of a first term that remains all too amorphous.

Some *fault of articulation in language* recalls, however, the copulative aporias between the eye of God and that behind (what theory claims is) the mother: *an unchallengeable split forever divides intelligible and sensible.* They are always on different sides. Of representation. Prior existence is attributed to the "face" that would theoretically see the other without being seen; without having to be recognized by the other. Perfection of divine (self) knowledge that had never shared in, never mixed with those material, matrical beginnings that are the blind spots on the souls of mortals. Truly never? Not even by a backward look? How, if this were so, could even the truest logos find a vehicle in configurations which try to make a metaphor of/for it?—though it may not realize this as it strives to take back the "essential" in ideal forms and relationships, freed from the improper character of their appearance and projected, of course, infinitely far ahead. Thus the "mother" is found again in the *circles, rings, spheres, envelopes, enclosures* in which being has (been) kept since its conception. Ideas, but also Universe, but equally All, and One. And their images, therefore the soul. Dwellings, in the form of cave, or womb, in which the living being would sometimes rest, at other times move around in the farthest, most backward, and hidden place. Going back into the most secret and impenetrable place of birth. Behind the last membrane: a paraphragm that resists all incursion, even by the eye, and that would open of its own accord only for an "other" life. *Links* in which the Father claims to lock up his germs of truth. Greedy of his substance, jealous of his mirages. *Rings* to bind the Idea which, though virgin, is yet pregnant with the seeds of the divine light. Immaculate conception, inaccessible in this world, at least "in reality." Privilege of the Father's logos.

A One-way Passage

Yet a *path* would seek to bring you there: the philosophical *paideia*. A steep and arduous path, full of difficulties, which the child will not follow without pain and which he would not risk taking if someone—some master, of the male sex—did not draw him along, constantly pushing him forward to the "day," toward the "natural light." Despite his resistance, his nostalgia, his longing to go back to his former home. His pain, his blindness, his dizziness. This journey culminates in the solar glare and the ex-stasy in God. But a *cut* separates these two "visions of the world," These two modes of representation. A transition is lacking—or lost?—between inside and outside, but also between outside and inside. Access, and egress, from one to the other, from the other with relation to the one, is, in essence, relegated to a different life. Progress flags at the limit of this existence, it ends on the border of death, in the expectation of entering or exiting on the other side. Where there will be no more walking—*khōrein*. The distance to be covered is limited to this universe. But, to get past it, to go beyond it, there remains a *leap* that one will not simply make in one's lifetime and that one cannot make in reverse—or at any rate not the same as one is—after death. And if they promise you the sublimation of that threshold, in the form of immortality, it is on the condition of trans-forming your "body" into "soul." And if you sublimate a body it is nothing but airs and phantoms. Fantasies? Ideas? From now on nothing stops it. At least no division, separation, or even opposition. Things like that are rather what makes it a body. So, without the "other," would the soul have to constitute itself as the place where the like is duplicated, the same is remembered? Without the other, does man need this retreat of/into the "interior" of the *psyche*? Does God need a soul? But if in the soul the purest, most divine and intelligible principle is to be distinguished from the impure, the earthly, the sensible, then it is essential that both be represented, isolated as far as possible by "isthmuses" and "partitions." Just as the "parts" attributed to men are isolated from the "chambers" reserved for women by corridors, walls, and so on.[54]

But *the passage* that, hypothetically, links the one to the other *is not one-way, not univocal.* If, in order to preserve his integrity, man does not go into the gynaeceum, into those "lower regions of the abdomen," it is

[54] *Timaeus*, 69e, 70a.

nonetheless crucial for the coherence of (his) theory for him to know its layout, intuiting with the gaze (of the soul) the forms that are, or are not, invoked there. Thus he "re-enters" only in order to confirm his knowledge, his self-identity, and to try possibly to put some order into the seductive impropriety, the moving anarchy of what is (re)produced there. As for women, unless raised to the dignity of the male essence, they would have no access to the sublimer circles of sameness, to the heights of the intelligible. It is true that in their highest moments—*when they are most like the male sex, naturally*—women aspire to that sublimity. They rarely, however, rise above the level of exchanged sensations, of communal daydreams; at best they express opinions on events in the city, or merely pass on the opinions that are making the rounds. Therefore women are incapable of realizing whether some idea—Idea—in fact corresponds to themselves, or whether it is only a more or less passable imitation of men's ideas. Unaware of the value of the names given them by the logos—assuming that some really specific names exist—women would, it seems, not know their definition, their representation, or the relationships with others, and with the All, that are maintained in this way. Women would thus be *without measure,* as a result of being without limits, without proportions that have been established once and for all and that can be referred back to the whole. *They have no proper form.* Given that this is so, how could they devote themselves to loving those like them in soul, the guarantee in another way of the permanence of their relationship to the origin? This process, this progress, toward representing the identical and the eternal return of sameness would not be woman's lot. Unless, let it be noted again, women renounce their inferior condition and choose to be men in order to have a better life—which may take ten thousand years.

Thus, that the soul may be intermediary between one and other, between same and different, . . . does not mean that it participates in both in the same way. It is not even certain that a *path* between the two is practicable, though the soul aims to be the place of that articulation. For the sensible will never rise to the perfection of the "type," to the ideal character of its morphology, even if it tries to mimic it more or less effectively. And as for the model of sameness itself, it will never go backward into those lower regions, the seat of passions and fakes, unless reason or the governance of the City demands it. But, should that happen, its return to the other side would be in submission to an *order* (from the Father) and thus redeemed from the transgression of that stealthy journey down.

Compulsory Participation in the Attributes of the Type

The climb up from the sensible to the intelligible—that is to say, from the "lower abdomen" to the "head," you recall—aims at participation in the attributes of the "type," which is also defined as model. Ideal mirror which one must strive to conform to, now and forever, the only mirror in which one may look, in order to escape the *infirmity* that always threatens the other in its unstable diversity. And the most perfect image would be the one that imitated the type most exactly, that is, the one in which the type recognizes itself best: reflection of a form that is immutably discrete, cut free from matter. Its gaze, illumined by Reason, would be the place in which the decision is made as to the degree of perfection of the other's mime, its ability to correspond to the norms of the intelligible, or its decline into hysterical convulsions and contortions. Thus the sensible must yield and measure up to the specula(riza)tion of the form of sameness in order to enter into knowledge. This is the only way. Though the way is progressive and set out in stages, the approach to it is exclusive. That is to say that the diversity of representations, of fantasies, of sensations, can be traced back to the type alone, which re-produces them as effects as soon as its form is imprinted in the receptacle (of) the other. Properly speaking, to recapitulate, only the type speculates the multiplicity of all that happens in the *khōra* when it in-heres there. Everything is thus to be attributed to the type as in-formation, trans-formation, de-formation, . . . of what it causes. The type is the source of all these specula(riza)tions. Origin—?— of the specular. As for the place in which it is (re)produced, that can attain a measure of beauty, goodness, intelligence only by obeying the imprints to which it owes submission: by duplicating them, *poorly,* thus always *below* the self-realization of the type. And in fact the place would achieve some kind of figure, appearance, only if it is passively reappropriated by that "ideal" morphology.

A Misprized Incest and an Unrealizable Incest

As for *the rest*—limitless indeterminacy. One may always try to save it from the indefinite extension of becoming, from the amorphous extent of the "mother," by turning *toward a superior type.* However, clarity of conception demands that only *one* type be cathected at a time. This does not rule out that they all stand in hierarchical order in relation to the Father, or that, in the search for an absolute model, one need retrace the paths that lead to all its descendants. But the higher one climbs up the branches of the family tree at this divine level, the more difficult relationships become to establish. They operate at a distance and need intermediaries. Mediation of "souls." For the offspring closest to the Good do not descend from their height back into a world where they risk being bastardized. They tend rather to congregate together according to their similarities, their genealogical rank, their proximity in the chain. They contract logical unions, or even copulative, harmonious ones, and speculative engenderings with no problems. Based upon the paradigm of the Father and the son, of the Father as self-same: the son. A form of union and generation which should be imitated, particularly since it is apparently the only model possible for what may occur in the order of discourse. *Incestuously paternal by/for essence(s)*. And what will be called the "sensible," or matter, or mother, or even "other," will have to yield if she wishes to have some face in this "universe." For she can only be known and recognized under disguises that denature her; she borrows forms that are never her own and that she must yet mimic if she is to enter even a little way into knowledge. And when she does this, she will no doubt be stigmatized, after the fact, for owing her power of seduction to *deceptive* appearances. She will be blamed for claiming to compete in this way with the real attributes of the types in her modes of being, and in the relationships she has with other beings. Whereas the logos, in order to preserve the purity of its conception, so veils her in the truth of his word that it is no longer clear what she is hiding in her store, and all the desires and delirium of potency denied by measured Reason can be projected onto her. Thus is she manifest and exalted, even as she is masked and lost, in discursive parades that set her outside herself; ideally offered to the oratorical disputes between men. *As for the rest,* it lies buried under the earth, deep down in dark caves where all is shadow and oblivion. And to which we will need to return one day. But by what path?

Obliteration of the passage between outside and inside, up and down, intelligible and sensible, . . . the "father" and the "mother." Whatever intermediaries have been produced to make up for this lack of relationships, they are always already slaves to (the) one, to the same. To the principle that is said to have caused them from all eternity. Father's word(s). And if Father's sovereignty over this "world" is such that no living thing escapes his domination or indeed yearns for any fate other than fullest participation in his Good—all of which implies a single way, a single method to rise up to truth: a "good" mimicry—what approach can hereafter be used to get back to what was left behind? The way back to the mother is barred. *Incest, here, is forbidden,* do what you will, and is quite rigorously *impossible,* say what you like. For "she" is always already transformed for/by the projected representation of the father. A matrix for reproducing images of him. Which are always a bit hybrid, it's true. The only traces of an other gender/genre that must be reduced to the clear light of the Idea. Thus effaced into pure, simple, indivisible . . . Form. *As for the rest,* blind and mute opacity of matter. How, then, is one to descend to it again? Even if one wanted to give it a more suitable status, a fairer situation, in the City also, how is one to go about it? What is to be made of matter? No memory of any practical way of getting together remains in the perfection of reminiscence. *Forgetting that we have forgotten* is sealed over at the dawning of the photological metaphor-system of the West.

She herself knows nothing (of herself). And remembers nothing. Providing the basis for the wise man's auto-logical speculations, she lives in darkness. At/as back of the scene of representation which she props up by not/without knowing it. She makes no show or display. For if she were to shine, then the light would no longer, simply, belong to sameness. The whole of the current economic system would have to be recalculated. And if she is granted the life of appearance, it will be a darkling affair. Underground shadow theater, lunar reflection of the star that makes everything light and fertile. A lack-luster double of the self-duplication that man carries within him, his "soul," when "she" doesn't stand in the way with her "body." With that still amorphous extension. Virginity that continues to resist the philosopher's speculative solicitations, and that is indeed mandatory for the purity of conception. Polished surface that will not be scratched or pierced, lest the reflection be *exaggerated* or *blurred.*

Thus, ideal command forbids the "path" between outside and inside. That path is doubtless doubled in different ways on each side, but it no longer provides a transition between the two. How, then, can one return into the cave, the den, the earth? Rediscover the darkness of all that has been left behind? Remember the forgotten mother?

Return to the Name of the Father

The Impossible Regression toward the Mother

"And when he remembered his old habitation, and the wisdom of the cave and his fellow prisoners, do you not suppose that he would felicitate himself on the change, and pity them?"[55] What would you say to this? Do you think he can remember his "old habitation" and "the wisdom of the cave?" Does the logos set up a space in which fantasies, phantoms, hallucinations, can re-emerge? Where even the babbling and stuttering of childhood can revive? Or does the coherence of the logos demand that these be named, or even connoted—as poor copies, for example—thus eliminating any value they may have as truth? Such clear-cut distinctions conjure away realities that are a little too expansive, set them in frames of definition, and thus prevent their antecedents from overflowing. From now on, relationships with those antecedents can only be reconstructed, raised in a dialectic that is always already a descendant. The place (of) dream is occupied by representations of its topos, which is thus irrevocably meta-merized. The fact that the place has been covered over for all useful purposes by the language of reason is only now beginning to be interpreted, in the shape of a dream that is *also* truth. Of *another kind or gender,* no doubt. But inscribed upon the divagations of becoming, upon that still material matrix, truth continues to wander a little, if only within the divine possession. The dream space remains, but it is projected infinitely far ahead. Excess of logos, which one no longer reaches by returning into the mother, but by trusting in the ex-sistence of the Father. Fantasies would be chased away from "the mother's body" and sent into an infinitely external world. Other, beyond. Ex-stasy of the dream in God, in the Highest. How could one not believe, as a result, that anyone who had intuited the smallest hint of that meaning would "pity" the others? Those still unaware of the exalting rapture of *teleo-logical projection.* Going beyond representations themselves, in the end, though this is not to imply that project does not assume closure. Thus the orbit of the cave organized into cinematography everything that had been left outside its enclosure: the *hystera protera.* Other excess to language. But these two "terms" to the logic of discourse cannot/can no longer be related. A whole system of kinship—that is, in this case, of analogy—makes contact between them impracticable. *The economy of metaphor that is in control keeps them apart.* And these surpluses added on the resemblance of the "mother" and the "father" can no longer copulate because they have

[55](*Republic,* VII, 516c.—Tr.)

already yielded to a genealogy of sameness which makes them substitutable, and thus exclusive, even in their excesses.

Not in the same way, of course. At the bottom and at the top of the "chain." Extreme *difference of degree* that submits to the standardization of sameness. But as far as form is concerned, the supreme model has needed to save his Goodness from fading away into the formlessness of the other, if it is to rise to its omnipotent height. Therefore it is not possible to return to the other as a den for reflection since *that concavity is still auto-specularizing, and thus constitutes the property of Being,* of the Father. Who copulates himself indefinitely without any alteration. And anyone who in wisdom has acceded to participation in such a Good can but "felicitate himself on the change." And rejoice alone, on his own, in his new power. His possession of new knowledge—or a new self?—which would unchain him from his "first habitation" and set him apart from his fellows who are held prisoner there and whom he now looks down upon with "pity." The commiserating look the philosopher casts on those still prey to subterranean passions, prisoner of fantasies that, for his part, he has raised in the solitary contemplation of the divine. He is impassive in the certainty of enlightenment, quit of all nostalgia for regressing back. That return will henceforth take place only in the name of Truth.

A Competition the Philosopher Will Decline to Enter

"And if they were in the habit of conferring honours among themselves on those who were quickest to observe the passing shadows and to remark which of them went before and which followed after and which were together, and who were best able from these observations to divine the future, do you think that he would be eager for such honours and glories, or envy those who attained honour and sovereignty among those men? Would he not say with Homer, 'Better to be a serf, labouring for a landless master', and to endure anything, rather than think as they do and live after their manner?"

In the cave where he remained prisoner so long, under the spell of shadows which distracted him from the evidence of natural light, certain honors of praises were apparently bestowed upon the man who could best make out the things that went by, who could best discern the particular features of each projection, careful not to confuse it with any

347

other and thus to reduce to unity the procession of things that he sees produced in front of him every day. The man who, moreover, as a result, could remember the things that always happen first, those that only happen afterward, those that may occur simultaneously, and who is able to predict what is most likely to appear. Honor, then, is paid to the man who is most gifted in the analysis of what is set out before him, who has the clearest vision of the "things" and even of their differences, and who would remember them most faithfully.

But what "things" and what "memory" are being referred to here? That, without doubt, will be the objection raised by the philosopher, anxious not to be compromised in this business, not to enter this kind of competition, for which, perhaps, he has little talent. For, as far as "things" go, you know that he claims to know their essence once and for all, and to have, at best, a pedagogic concern for their existence—which is, more or less, a faithful copy of their truth. As for the memory which is being thus extolled, it risks getting in the way of reminiscence, which is all the philosopher cares about. In fact, what happens every day, or comes with the night, doesn't count much with him. It is still derived from darkness, instead of being eternally luminous. The brightness is of the earth and is thus mortal also. The philosopher pays no attention to it, concentrating instead upon the strong beams that suffer no eclipse and thus ensure him an unfaltering projection. Sublime interests, free of mere material contingencies. Thus he disdains the realities that come into being each day, not bothering even to look at them. And if you ask him what happened (to him) this morning, this noon, or this night, he is unable to reply since he doesn't care but attends to "things" that are placed far beyond this mundane life where you are begging for an answer from him, and which no longer affects him. You are questioning him about "shadows." And if in a season of darkness these may serve as indexes of greater truth, he will still not take the time to analyze them. Such complaisance would be a useless occupation for his *psychē*. And anyway, identifying fakes is no easy matter? Or at least telling them apart. You have to be a "child" or a "madman" to try that or believe that you can manage it and, what's more, intend to master the cinematography of the thing. Crazy demiurges in a world without models where order can come only from chaos or drift. Except in the phantasmagorias of naive folk that no longer have any hold over the wise man.

In more ways than one, in fact. For, when it comes down to it, *contact between "things" is of very little importance to the wise man.* If such and such a thing should follow upon such another thing, or happen to be in its vicinity, or even right up against it, he may be moved to crack a joke, if it stares him right in the face, but proximity of that kind is not what he's looking for. He would prefer to get rid of it in order to concentrate upon the "types," and their chain of organization. And it will be necessary to go through genealogy—ultimately the Father's genealogy—for him to appreciate such a meeting or not. For him, the value of any relationship is estimated at that price alone. The rest is such short-lived fancy that it would be ridiculous to give it any meaning whatsoever. And the philosopher takes little pleasure in insignificance, or what he judges to be such. And though he loves to use irony, he is beyond laughter at his own expense. Thus, before establishing a link, he will give lengthy reflection to the congruence of its forms, to the appropriateness of their characters, to whether they suit, in short. All of which is far from a light-hearted embrace. From touchings that might give too great a hold over him to luck. Or dream? Or fantasies? Or a charm that is always slightly magical, occult? Cheap tricks that still have a place in the space-time of the cave? Or the womb? The orbit is still maternal even if it is always already inverted to allow images to proliferate. Is this moving picture that starts up every day worthy of serious attention? If one succeeded in observing and rigorously cutting its sequences, as well as remembering their order and predicting them, would one thereby be delivered from their recurrence? Wouldn't the same old scenes be reproduced the next day? Memory in fact relies on them returning, yet we are supposed to surpass memory here. And all this leads to the failure of reminiscence.

Two Modes of Repetition: Property and Proximity

Two modes of repetition are arguing over "time." Recommencement/infinity: return/eternity. Their divorce draws attention away from the transgression of *the same history*. History is extended when it is based on financing of this kind, it can continue to pay its way as a result of such dichotomies, deferring the effects of their articulation(s) for the time being, as well as the aftermath of their conjunction(s). Earthly chronometry that would have to fade into the eternal elsewhere of the Father. The mid-night of the mother would be covered indefinitely by the mid-day of the Father. But in this instance the sun is a star that runs too great a risk of falling back, once again, into the sea, to be trusted alone to guard that abyss of light. Another torch is needed to ensure illumination without eclipses. The Father's potency must be free from the uncertainty of dusk, from the rhythmic succession of nights, from the flare of fire. And even if it be remembered that the sun is there in the morning, at noon, and again in the evening, this does not prevent night from coming on.

349

Even though the sun is one way in spring, another in summer, and yet another in autumn, the fact remains that winter returns. An icy deadness dreaded by the philosopher who still has cold in his eyes. Therefore he hates the shadow that recalls his weak sight, and his need to take refuge in a "soul" or screen, upon which the blazing spectacles are turned over/overturned. Thus everybody—or so they say—yearns for what he lacks. And the wise man's greedy urge to look things straight in the face is proof of his inability to do so. His eternal midday is testimony to his blind reliance upon the Father's clearsightedness for the Father's ubiquity solves every shadow, even the shadow of a doubt. The universe is lighted from end to end by the eye of that Other.

One has still to be in the universe. Which is scarcely true for the man who dwells forever underground, chained in a bare closed space that light can barely creep into. A dark room where projections—of shadows, of course—are fed by an almost magic lantern. A place the soul will (may) occupy but which will only duplicate its lower, and darkest part. Foci of bewitching but shifting sensations which cast a spell that yet cannot be held onto, unless it be transformed, deformed. Dubious opinions that will be transmitted here and there without ever attaining the rigor of the Idea.

Anyone who devotes himself to describing and memorizing such a show is certainly not without merit, and he deserves his reward. But on what grounds? And what risk would the City run if all the people got caught up in that game? Stayed, endlessly, in that *psyche* analysis that distracts them from more useful duties. Attended to phantoms, fakes, fantasies, that turn them away from more objective realities. Not even realizing that they are under the spell of thaumaturges, because they are unable to turn round and take measures against the "shadows" that bewitch them. Which, in any case, they perceive as being in front of them, opposite.

What's behind is always withheld from view. Even if one took a tour halfway round it, it would retreat, yet further, into the background. Evasive, invisible. How bitter it is to be incarcerated in an enclosure when nothing is known of what lies behind it—outside: other—sustaining a longing to return there but with no knowledge of the road to take. The passage between is forgotten. Every misconception is thus made possible, every misconstruction. Pleasure and pain multiply. But how is one to find the "right one"? Go back through whatever constitutes the closure of that screen where images are now parading? Where something (the id) is (re)projected forward, leaving a way (or ways) behind without any representation. Where man would never pass (again) if someone—a male someone—did not lure him on. This is as much as to say that he returns only as the slave to a discourse of *another genre/gender,* dominated by *another transfer,* whose metaphors make the road practicable but only by avoiding it. *Contact is lost in the analogy* that wraps it in its re-presentation, holding it paralyzed on a one-way journey. And the sensible world always evokes contact as well as rupture, birth as well as death; yet here it suspends the alternation between its phases into one genealogy of images, of "copies" whose closeness to the model moves outside the time of generation, instead regulating itself according to the propriety of form (and) of name. These resemblance relationships of the true origin of conception would, the theory goes, be less fallible guarantees. They hold the promise of an immortal memory because they have already ringed "life" within a repetition—a re-naissance—which speculates/specularizes it. Life is thus frozen, for all eternity.

In other words, man does not get out of the "maternal waters" here but, by freezing the path that would lead back to her, he gazes at himself, re-producing himself in that paraphragm. That hymen that will divide his soul with its mirroring surfaces just as it divides up the Universe. The search to perpetuate self-identity stops all contact dead, paralyzes all penetration for fear one may not find oneself always and eternally the same inside. Hence their metaphorizations in terms that roll them up, wrap them up, taking them further and further away from what or who "causes" them, into associations that are nothing but analogies. The "passage" would, in the end, be (or have become) the identity of reason to itself, and return would merely be the recurrence of sameness. For enumeration is the guarantee of the immutability of anything that is counted out in valid forms. One never need pay off the debt, either in the past or in the future, if one can only attain the ideal of sameness, which of course defies deterioration of any kind. Alone at last. Fully equivalent to its being, based on none other, repeating being, close to himself alone. But on what space-time is this sovereign self-appropriation raised? Re-production (of self) without matter, or mother. Mirage in the *gold* of the Father's speculation, which would do away with the "death" that at the outset is credited to him. Quite given over to resembling something never perceived. *Therefore* to resembling himself? What the logos testifies about him (as) same? The relationship whereby utterance conforms to the one that causes (it) must be continued at all costs.

Better to Work the Earth on the Father's Account Than to Return to It: Metaphor/Metonymy

So it is greatly preferable "to be a serf, labouring for a landless master" than to think as do the men in the cave and "live after their manner." Tilling the earth with no certainty of gain would be better than losing the prerogatives of reason. To break up and turn over the "earth," even if the master of the house gives no payment for the work, is far more worthwhile than being enslaved to the phantasmagorias that haunt the men chained up by these mysteries. The exploitation of what is called the maternal on behalf of a father whose authority is one of form alone cannot be compared in prestige with the incarceration of the son in the closed space—be it an imaginary one—of his birth in the womb. Still captive of childish dreams that ever call him back into that den whence he could no longer stray, being wholly absorbed in the immediacy of the sensations he finds there. Skillful, no doubt, in the art of distinguishing between them, of portraying them in a thousand and one ways, but for this very reason "insensible" to the dictates of reason. A fate unenvied by the philosopher, who takes no pleasure in competing with it. Truly? All the same, he does choose *"working the land"* as a mode of existence more deserving of envy. How odd! Turning the earth over rather than turning back to it? Doubling the impasse already constituted by the cave? Breaking up and closing and overturning, all in the same motion? In a transfer of funds to the father's account? For if the father lacks resources, he will at least have "sons" to prove his potency; guarantees of his authority, signs of the wealth of his house, until the time comes when he can exploit the space he has appropriated enough to bring in some extra capital. And no shame is attached to being an employee of the head of the family, or even his slave, for "working the land" is already to do *as* he does. At another point on the scale (of values), at a different level of the analogy. But nonetheless *miming* the father's attributes is achieved here and now. And is the triumph of his logos alone. Which, as far as work goes, even, may still give payment in metaphors. *A bonus for resembling the master,* which would make up for the "horror" of being close to the "earth." Balance the cost of that relationship. This would no doubt be the argument put forward by the wise man to justify his continuing to plow his mother. He raises the prohibition progressively by clearing land that still produces its own fertile growth, that is still virgin of (his) proper names. Breaking up and seeding matrices that are still dumb to reasonable words. Receptacles in which some new idea might yet germinate, if he were to come down and water them with his knowledge.

But we are almost forgetting that the whole Universe is already under the Father's monopoly. And that in these meetings it is at best the inscription of his eternal truths that he revives by repeating (them). Thus, man is swindled of the price of his own work. For he is now and always nothing but the more or less effective doubling of an omnipotent Phallus. Nonetheless, he submits to this fate and is even ready to die in order to perpetuate such an empire. The important thing is that history go on. In other words, the same discourse, which gives him status, if only a secondary one, as substitute or successor to forms that alone are valid. The "other" doesn't count at all, of course; only provides the materials. Which are more and more abstract, in fact.

The Threat of Castration

But this phantom, this shadow that is necessarily represented also by the doubling up of the father in the son—and the opposite—will once again be left to the earth. They fall and are buried in her entrails, hidden, unseen. *Mother-matter who furthermore seals up the waste products of specula(riza)tion.* Agony of fantasies barred and masked by a screen offered for projection, a polished surface caving in, gaping open, arousing nothing henceforth but dread and disgust. A crazy journey through the looking glass in which representation is formed. Auto-copies, "faithful" provided that they take a detour through the credit accorded to the father's law, which defines the speculative plane/e and claims thus to banish death. Understand—clearly for this once—*the threat of castration!* The anguish, the horror of castration will henceforth be reserved for the mother's womb. Which there is no going back to. Except in the father's name.

"Woman's" *Jouissance*

A Dead Cave Which Puts Representation Back into Play

Two modes of representation are tearing time apart. The one is inscribed— whether or not it realizes this—in the reiteration of the event, a "prison" that it never leaves. The project of its ever invisible surge forms a backdrop for the proliferation of "fakes" that march over/in *that blind spot of conception.* A shadow theater where only the shakiest of certainties are produced—phantom presences, dim memories, expectations of something unforeseen—which disappear as fast as they appear and reappear. An ever-moving flux, sent this way and that according to the shift of the projection source, the deformation of the horizon-limit, the attractions put in its way. The current is hard to delineate but it is not infinite; its framework can be regulated almost magically by artificial reduplication of its process: scene of the cave, whose measure cannot be taken, whose space-time cannot be evaluated by man for he is their prisoner. Man is limited in/by the cave-vault, awed by spectacles that make time pass for him not in neatly measurable units but in repetitive rhythms that are hard to pin down. And anyone who succeeds, nonetheless, in distinguishing its different phases, in remembering their interactions and in predicting when they will return, certainly deserves to be congratulated on his performance. But what time has he analyzed? And how could that analysis be possible, except as a simple mechanical repetition, since man knows only one time? The time that flies (here, now) without any stratification that would allow some kind of perspective. No doubt in the cave the thaumaturges and their arts are set back and placed between the fire and the back of the den, thus setting up a "depth" of field. But what if they were not there? Would the flow stop at any point? Would any decision be possible as to what is, is not, now? Was, was not, yesterday? Etc. Assuming that the identical position of the men chained up is already a stratagem, a highly sophisticated device of the stage director, who pretends to be able to solve the problem by thus leaving it in suspense. And this is inevitably so because of the necessity for defining an other time. For in that representation, the son's soul is not reflected by or reflective of the father's words, the basis of inscription is still elsewhere and all that is marked in it is only painted reduplications of objects already manufactured by men. But it is the goal of death that will lead to the passage to something beyond.

Death really? But how does death come into this in(de)terminable procession? And, were it not for the tutor's orders, who would bother about death? It is not even sure that these "children" have a word to designate it by, any more than a dream system to figure it in. And everything that happens/passes for them proclaims not an ending but the promise of a return, the next day. Were it not for the words of the philosophy teacher who talks to you about immortality, who would be preoccupied with such an issue, wholly absorbed in his dream that begins over and over again? Messenger of death, then. But which death? That of the beginning? Of "matter"? Of the mother? Only recognizing life in (its) representation? In (its) specula(riza)tion? Its repetition, with terms that can be enumerated? All of which is, of course, impossible in relation to the indefiniteness of what had been before? Conception, "for example," which would find its "proper" meaning only in the re-birth into truth. And truth, in order to escape any hint of verisimilitude, will be situated in a time that predates birth. An eternity beyond appearances, that closes (over) the in-herence of re-production. Which demands *its double repetition* in the Being that is, always, in one way or another, *a trinity*. The One is the One only when mirrored *at least twice*. But this two obviously doesn't simply amount to a sum. Each specula(riza)tion modifies the properties of representation to the point at which it makes a complete *ring around* its attributes that thus become, inseparably, the constituents of the subject itself (as same). And the subject is claimed to have always existed in that perfection of self-identity from before birth.

A precedence battle is set up as to what comes next, after. Whatever came after is sent back earlier so as to mask its relationship to projection and the repercussions of the way it was determined, the re-mark of the definition of beginning. Origin thus suspends all of time in the feigned immutability of its genesis: its presence. No scission. No death. The two deaths and their two betweens and their den (of) death sink endlessly into the blindness of a certain divine speculation in which the question of the auto-copy of being is withheld. This is not the case for the tricks of the magicians, those demiurges who bastardize the divine projects by making them obvious, making them apparent in their very conception.

Theater of the cave, in which man's attributes figure only insofar as they have been made into statutes, immortalized in deathly copies. Any reference that might be made to it—if one could only turn around—is from the outset a *formal* one. The potency of the enchanter has always already been captured, *made into a corpse by morphology*. As a result, it can be raised, without risk of falling, "above" a first screen that is used for representation, a screen that will allow only an effigied copy of the "living being" to project over the top of its impregnable barrier. The "living being" remains behind in a position of retirement, invisible in relation to that *sign-object* whose deathliness goes beyond the wall curtain which prevents any penetration into the back of the cave, in relation to the fetish that would represent him in truth, were it possible to catch sight of it. In truth—that is to say without leaving any trace of specula(riza)tion, since its reduction to the size of a statuette is the price paid for veiling the inversion that sustains the work. This first time, which operates by seduction, will thus not be seen. This unfaltering rebirth of the magician's power escapes evaluation. He in fact forbids himself to look at it. Paraphragm that is also an eyelid. The eye does not see to what sepulchral mummification it owes its enchantment. And were it not for the assistance of a projection screen—a dead cave—which provides some goal for representation, no doubt representation would fall short. It is the

355

cave's part, then, to supply a charm that all too quickly fades, paralyzed in the elaboration of its prestige. Projection gives some movement, some sensible mobility, some semblance of becoming. Phantoms swarm about something that has become embalmed in an excessively faithful image. Offspring of that speculum (of) death.

That Marvelously Solitary Pleasure of God

Two modes of fiction are tearing apart the time of presence. But it/they always come(s) down to the same thing in the end. And the aim of this rending apart—which is in fact only mimed in this case—is to tear away the mother's, the earth's function as space-time of (re)production. To push the projection of the cave back into infinity. Into the eternal elsewhere. *Aion* of the Father that, ceaseless, shadowless, would perpetuate representation. The screen, which recalls the inscription and the reversibility within the inversion of sameness, is hidden away, and the deathly cost and coup are borne by the ideally inexhaustible Good of the Father. What does it matter if the cave, if the other, behind the son is closed off, buried in its crypt, all access to it frozen over, provided that some (male) One has taken on omnipotence as one of his attributes, provided that the child can "fantasize" himself identical to Him—to an ideal ego—without recalling the *double* that in this operation relates, also, to sameness.

Brilliance of silvered-backing in suspension. God gazes on nothing (but) the same. Pure being (of the) mirror. In which reflection has no reflection, no obvious replicating effect, no shadow of a doubt as to self-identity, no trace of something having taken place. No foundation to attest that the being itself once had a beginning. No material matrix that would remember the death in that specula(riza)tion, conjuring up again in the disturbed night of the cave the phantom remnants of something or someone that might at any moment rise up into the (so-called) intact presence of his glass. A cave explored, or even exploited, and for their loss, by painters and poets who can accept the figuration of repetition—and *hysterical mimesis*—but not by good citizens. Certainly not by a man who has taken on the task of teaching them truth: the philosopher, who cares only about Ideas. Speculations that have absorbed into themselves any hint of a past of reflection. Specular dens that no one will open up again to take a look inside. For in Ideas, any possible image of the spectacle has already been dammed up as it came to be formed. That formation implies, at its highest point, a new silver backing. And loss of vision, reversed within that mirroring orbit. Only the Father would still be engaged in this, in the form of complementary or supplementary light. For his eye sees the All instantly and for all eternity. And the brilliance typical of a stamping that has been perfectly fixed in its outline in no way threatens to overwhelm his eyes, to dazzle or inflame them, to break or destroy the membrane-the ideal essence. At the utmost, he would feel disappointed, unsatisfied—if God can still have such feelings—at finding there only a partial illustration of Himself (as Same). He should, thus, mirror them all at once. But as all are already in Him, He has no need of anyone in particular in His absolute autarchy. Turning indefinitely in/upon his circle, tracing a ring over and again, he would thereby achieve a hymen of ice and fire, without violating his mystery. The conception of the hysteric is still *paternal,* set on fire only by its fantasies of copulating with Him who is recognized as the sole source of Sameness. Inflamed with an indefinite number of ocellae, all of which are brought back into the unity of a divine mirage that lacks the altering separation afforded by an eye, a sex, a speculum, a "soul"—for if these were to intervene, or interpose themselves, they would spoil that marvelously solitary pleasure. God-the-Father, the Self-Same He, to the exclusion of any (female?) "other," would have knowledge from all time of what lies beneath hysterical jouissance. His seeds of truth would be produced to supplement that incomparable sensuality that He reserves for himself. The logos is immutable because it is secretly nourished by the most extreme of pleasures: mimicking oneself before any other has begun to be. Scion that will doubtless represent his progenitor-father in his form. But the price they pay is that the Self of that re-production suffers a fall and thus reopens the question of how they come to be alike. Through the woman-mother? Receptacle for the spawning of images, where they can measure the faithfulness of their resemblance to the model of sameness. Tear away at its propriety again and at that veil of conception. In order to cut through the issue in the interest of all, that of the orderliness of the City. The Father will seal over the mystery, draping it in the authority of his incontestable law. Such assertion of power should not be brought to account. And it only repeats the same thing over and over again: the absolute identity to self, without any possibility of contradiction for/in that sovereignty.

A Diagonal Helps to Temper the Excessiveness of the One
The method, the path, the shaft, the neck, the split even, will certainly have proved useful in ensuring the Father's authority. But how are they to be found, these holes in an imperious unity? In the squaring of the circle of its glory? A potency whose squareness would have swallowed

up the potency of the *hystera*. Playing with the *passage* by/to the *immeasurability* of his greatness. Since no estimate in whole numbers is possible, the *diagonal* will supply the excessiveness of a *diaphragm's* non-integrality. A paraphragm on the slant, dividing and thus duplicating and determining the primitive dyad of big and small. A matrix that remains material and whose diagonal, or diameter, will halt, or cut, the infinite progression or regression, and oppose it with the definition of a second side. Symmetry that will artificially have organized, by a *reversing projection,* the first as such: half of one same whole square. The geometric construction will have eliminated the reliance on a *root* to which no value can be assigned—in its extraction or its power—because it lacks a common measure with the finite. The operation of duplication will use the, possibly, fictive tracing of a line through the middle to achieve the possible reduction to a *relationship of equality*. But, as soon as the figure has been traced, the *inverted* shadow produced by that fraction will appear, or at least *its mirror image:* Plato's *hystera*. And, *by mimicking them on the inside:* space of magicians, space of prisoners, the di-lemmas of Plato's *hystera* will, hey presto, have concealed the fact that there is no common measure with the unrepresentable *hystera protera*, the path that might lead back to it and the diaphragm that controls the cavity opening. The plan(e)s that establish the similarity of numbers must therefore be raised up in the thinking and not allowed to be too much controlled by designs upon the earth. The mother.

The confused and changing multiplicity of the other thus begins to resolve itself into a system of intelligible relationships. And the philosopher's arithmetic, unlike that of the ordinary man, will distinguish between big and small by establishing, from the outset, the *homogeneity of each unit involved*. The calculus needed for both private and public life demands that one lead the spirit, by a real conversion, to rise above the sphere of becoming—bigger or smaller—, to consider relationships only in terms intrinsic to the numbers themselves. But at the point we find ourselves, geometric progression or geometric regression can only be *ordered hierarchically,* in a nonreciprocal manner, and the ascent toward the Ideas, principles of the analysis, does not imply that equal truth inheres in the still visible and sensible things that led to the recollection of those Ideas. The foundation here implies that hypotheses be determined in order to establish the foundation. The ancestor and the descendant do not enjoy equal privileges. The son is second, deducted in some sort, even if it is he who leads us to climb back to the father, as to the one that causes him. "For example." But father and son, at least on the level of purity of the intelligible, should yet be related to the *form of the unit*. This is not the case, however, for the "sensible"—the maternal, the feminine—for their diversity, discontinuity, and process cannot be boiled down to a single model. They have fallen from the world of the *noēsis* and its uninterrupted chain of Ideas. The *vacuum* that has been in place between them becomes the essential principle of ideal figures. This is so for intervals between the points on the "line" that by calculation of proportions has been brought down to a progression of the *paideia* methodically and continuously conducted, except for the *final, a-hypothetical leap* into the transcendental. Philosophy's auto-nomy has found its scientific assurance in that useful intermediary, the still *geometric representation* of the unmeasurable. The irrational. Yet that theory, in its technical accomplishment and its exorbited ideal, has left unexplored, at the "center" of its construction, a sensible hole.

But, because its size varies, because it moves around constantly, that hole ought to be limited; some term must be placed on the contradictions it entails; it should submit to the (re)mark of the *one* and hence to a determinate number that at least gives it a meaning within a set of objectives. The *one* will therefore be empowered to fix the dual movement of progression and regression that expresses the nature of the dyad. *Stopping* it continually at a *stasis*, a station, in the present. Thus the balance *point* between two, getting bigger, and four—or 2^2—getting smaller, is obtained by the stabilizing operation of the One, which thereby engenders the first triad. But the One owes its effectiveness to the fact that it has already set out in evens, in twos—prototype of the first *determinate* dyad—anything that threatened to go beyond measurement and move toward the infinitely small or big: evil.

The double, thus, is *ambivalent* in the function attributed to it. Certainly its lack of determinancy makes it a duplicator and thus a matrix for engendering the series of numbers, but nonetheless it cannot ensure the immutable permanence of the first numbers. In some way, these are always odd since they need a one if they are to be defined in their evenness to themselves. The double reproduces indefinitely, and can only do so in disorder unless the one—or the One—imposes the effectiveness of its term at each stage. The One produces the even by subsuming under it the less and the more, and the gaps between them, which are

359

operative in the dyad, and in this way the One swells to infinity. But as *sameness:* the One (of) the Idea. An extension that has resorbed all progression, regression, and empty intervals in between, into its indefectible greatness. What is to be said, then, of him who, now and forever, through all eternity, contains all these essences, these powers, while going beyond them in a pre-existence that engenders them as such and regulates the connections between them? The Good (of) God-the-Father.

In the most rigorous terms, then, to what is the value of the ideal to be assigned? To the *one?* Or to the *tetrad?* To the square of two? Difficult question? Or merely naive? The square is defined only by means of the diagonal that determines that its two halves, or isoceles triangles, *are equal.* That they can be folded over upon each other, into each other— indefinitely—by a shift around an *axis of symmetry.* This axis may vary in length, but the crucial thing is that it not be divisible at any *point,* that no *hole* can be made *in the unity* it represents. For this would allow the *passage* of something, of greater or larger number, power, or extent, in one of the two (sides). Line, surface, volume, these must submit to the rule of engendering by halves at least on the level of paradigms for all forms. The imperceptible "void" that geometry was unable or unwilling to take into account will thus be taken from all "bodies." And, by being raised into intelligibility, it will have brought the spirit into its own ideal conception.

That which separates, divides, splits, must be taken away from the other, from the "feminine," for otherwise mathematics and dialectics no longer know what they're about. Lost in differences that cannot be analyzed by dint of their non-relationship with Sameness. The opening up of a heterogeneous space—a space-time—must now and always maintain silence about anything uneven that it might allow to appear in the functioning of the logos itself. For even in its categorically clear-cut distinctions—into less and more, for example—the measure of the logos has left outside its defined forms and their associations something (of) that nothing (of) emptiness in which they are assured of their (re)production. Virginal and mute surface, memory which would no longer remember where it (the id) passes. And which would only repeat and reflect the same, now and always, without making another hole in the screen where it takes its origin as such.

A *paraphragm*—a diagonal, a diameter, or even a *diaphragm* manufactured for specula(riza)tions—bars and forbids the access (to) the excessiveness of an "other" side. God-the-Father, no doubt, thereby gains a bonus of power, for his omniscience is well informed about ideal numbers. But not the mother, the woman, who are silenced and banned because their pleasure is blind. Immersed in the shadow of that infinitely calculating star. Whose potency is amenable to the incommensurable and has dazzled with his knowledge that blind spot in which man might still have been able to ask the question of his difficult relation to the other.

The Infinite of an Ideal Which Covers the Slit (of a) Void
Two kinds of blindness are competing for the mystery of the infinite of the immeasurable. And the surplus of it that remains in conception. But the blindness that can argue that its relation to truth, and therefore to property/propriety, is well founded, will carry the day. Better to be fascinated by an omnipotence that can make you become its *equal* than to cast an eye on something that changes its form as soon as you penetrate it. That ceaselessly transforms you into another in its ice, consumes you in its fires, drowns you in its flowing waters, without any capital being assured anywhere. The fact that the first is placed *so high* that it can no longer be seen, that its accumulation is so great that, logically, it must be covered with a *veil* in order to see it or oneself in it, that its appropriation is so *twisted* that a glance fading into the vanishing point of an oblique ray can scarcely attempt an approximate calculation of the elevation of its power—all this counts less than the terrible peril of its instant squandering in/by the other. Which must be closed off, therefore, in its crypt. And since everything, here, becomes by means of participation, perhaps God might always have mimicked that diaphragm—"mimicking" for his part nothing: the void—which opened out on these/his excesses. But, in order for this imitation to be truth-like, He would have changed it into a paraphragm. Mystery surrounding him on all sides, diagonals or diameters of his circle that cannot be calculated, forms-ideas that keep his seeds of truth within their ideal closure . . . which is not to say that He doesn't retain something—something infinite, immeasurable, invisible—of an Other that will not easily be reached in the depthless separation of its jouissance. Except, so rarely and so unpredictably, in ex-stasy. Or else—they tell us—in an "other" life. An "other" world.

But how is one to get there? Or get back there? Turn back? Since that blind spot which in the gaze (of the soul) might still have reopened the question of an *other path* is covered over, or dazzled, by the Father's knowledge. And since, coming out of its fascination with that Sun, the eye cannot help but be offended by shadows. Since man has become blind by dint of projecting (himself) into the brilliance of that Good, into the purity of that Being, into that mirage of the Absolute. Since, therefore, if he were to "come down . . . and be replaced in his old seat" in the cave of his past, he would see nothing. And if "he had to compete in measuring the shadows . . . would he not make himself ridiculous? Men would say of him that he had returned from the place above with his eyes ruined; and that it was better not even to think of ascending."[56]

Losing Sight of "the Other"

Two kinds of blindness are arguing over the monopoly on conception. For the optics of Truth in its credibility no doubt, its unconditional certainty, its passion for Reason, has veiled or else destroyed the gaze that remained mortal. With the result that it can no longer see anything of what had been before its conversion to the Father's law. That everything foreign, other, outside its present certainties no longer appears to the gaze. It can perceive nothing more of them. Except—perhaps? sometimes?—the pain of being blinded in this way, of being no longer able to make out, imagine, feel, what is going on *behind* the screen of those/his ideal projections, divine knowledge. Which cut him off from his relations with the earth, the mother, and any other (female), by that ascent toward an all-powerful intelligibility. Alone, then, in the closed circle of his "soul," that theater for the re-presentation of likeness, that vertigo of a god that recognizes nothing but himself now. And who, *if it were suggested he identify a (female) other,* would no doubt come up with the confession that he can't see it very well—anymore? That he needs time to evaluate, to take the measure of, what and whom he's dealing with. Time to accustom his eyes to what is in front of him? Or to bring this "object" into his own perspective?

And what if what he was asked to judge were only a "shadow"? How could he do it? The duplication figured by the shadow is now supported by all that *mimics* him, by those specularizations of him that fill, to the incommensurable limit, his horizon. His "Universe" indeed: his double full of doubles. All more or less close to the reproduction of Sameness. More or less appropriate. Specular reflections exposed in full daylight? Except that their paradigm is never visible. The concentration of light

---

[56](*Republic,* VII, 516e., 517a.—Tr.)

informs the gaze by a *shadow hole* that makes a screen across the sight of the other side. The ideal always holds itself *behind* the circle that limits the field of prospection. Behind the mirror? Concealing the inversion?

But the inversion has always already taken place. Now it is night—at least for a mortal—that provides illumination, whereas in the half-light of the cave a torch had to be there to assist in the projection of the shadows. Has everything been set upside down and back to front? But, in that case, where's the front? And the back? The only thing that remains constant is the retreat of what is behind. But it is at present sent infinitely far in front. And up. Beyond the sky. Thus, when he takes a detour back toward his childhood, goes back down into the den where he had once dwelt, the philosopher is confused as to how to envisage things. And he will need a "very considerable time" to move back through the—reversed, inverted, retroverted—sphere of his gaze. What should be placed in front from now on? Up? Back? Down? How is the *hysteron* or the *hystera* to be turned over and rediscovered, replumbed? Scene of representation that will always already have made you twist your head, even walk on your hands, as soon as you set foot in it. Making you spin in all directions around axes—on one axis?—of symmetry. And no one breathes a word about that artifact necessary to your entry into that echo-nomy. A mime in which not a word can be said in truth. Forgotten, for lack of a representation, which will give the philosopher a good laugh for he is so enthralled by his divine possession that he has caused the seed of his—still mortal—gaze to abort: *diephtharmenos hēkei ta ommata.* He is detached from human passions that hold others captive still, but lost in contemplations that wall him in on every side, separating him from everything by projection screens; and he can no longer even perceive that they are playing a part.

And if, protected by a hierarchical order, by the privilege of the progenitor, the father, he is still able to lay down the law in the city, even in an academic context, it is not sure that his "descent" into a prison full of children freed from their chains will be met with equal success. For imagine what would happen "if anyone tried to loose [others] and lead [them] to the light," that is, take the measure of their former captivity, of the rules that prevented them from moving, that forced them always to remain in the same place, held them motionless, spellbound by the formal skills of masters who have a touch of the mountebank in their practices, held them polarized by the front side of a tableau on which the pro-jected images of those masters or the effigy that they already represent file past. That way, every day, since childhood. Paralyzed by the confusion between this theater and the still maternal stronghold they have not yet left, have never come to any decisions about, being children still. Dumb because they do not know what to say and take everything they see to be truths, and this to the exclusion of everything else. Especially since the demonstration will be supported by the echo of a seductive voice.

The Vengeance of Children Freed from Their Chains

Imagine then that someone, not for pedagogic reasons this time, but moved rather by other political goals, or by a perverse desire for entertainment, rouses these prisoners who have been freed of their chains at the very moment that the philosopher, still a·little lost in his idealities, has sat down among them, in his old place. Don't you think that if they "catch the offender, they would put him to death?

No question, he said."[57]

All that remains to be known is whether what they caught was not already dead: the poor present of an effigied copula. And whether in this fight they did anything but tear themselves apart. Making blood flow from their wounds, blood that still recalls a very ancient relationship with the mother. Repeating a murder that has probably already taken place. Mimicking once again in that gesture what Plato was already writing, Socrates already telling. "No question, they would put him to death." It had long been inscribed—surely in the conditional tense of a myth—in their memories.

[57](*Republic*, VII, 517a.—Tr.)

Precise references in the form of notes or punctuation indicating quotation have often been omitted. Because in relation to the working of theory, the/a woman fulfills a twofold function—as the mute outside that sustains all systematicity; as a maternal and still silent ground that nourishes all foundations—she does not have to conform to the codes theory has set up for itself. In this way, she confounds, once again, the imaginary of the "subject"—in its masculine connotations—and something that will or might be the imaginary of the female. Let all, then, male or female, dead or alive, recognize themselves as same according to their desire or their pleasure, even in the parody of capital letters. But if, in the resistance set up against that male imaginary, distortion gave rise to discomfort, then, perhaps?, something of the difference of the sexes would have taken place in language also.

Library of Congress Cataloging in Publication Data

Irigaray, Luce.
  Speculum of the other woman.

  Translation of: Speculum de l'autre femme.
    1. Feminism.   2. Women—Psychology.   3. Women
and psychoanalysis.   4. Femininity (Philosophy)
5. Sex (Psychology)   I. Title.
HQ1154.I74   1985   155.3'33   84-45151
ISBN 0-8014-1663-9